C0-CDD-588

Peabody of Groton

By Frank D. Ashburn

FIFTY YEARS ON

PRIMER FOR PARENTS

PEABODY OF GROTON

PARENTS' GUIDE TO INDEPENDENT SCHOOLS

WITH P. M. ASHBURN

THE RANKS OF DEATH

The Rector in 1935. Oil painting by Ellen Emmet Rand

PEABODY
OF
GROTON

A Portrait

Frank D. Ashburn

The Riverside Press, Inc. *Cambridge*

1967

Copyright © 1967 by Frank D. Ashburn
Copyright 1944 by Frank D. Ashburn
All rights reserved. This book, or parts thereof, must
not be reproduced in any form without permission.
PRINTED IN THE UNITED STATES OF AMERICA

For P. B. A.

Who Also Helped Found a School

Only—but this is rare—
When a beloved hand is laid in ours, . . .

When our world-deafen'd ear
Is by the tones of a loved voice caress'd,
A bolt is shot back somewhere in our breast
And a lost pulse of feeling stirs again:
The eye sinks inward, and the heart lies plain,
And what we mean, we say, and what we would, we know.
A man becomes aware of his life's flow
And hears its winding murmur, and he sees
The meadows where it glides, the sun, the breeze. . . .

And then he thinks he knows
The Hills where his life rose,
And the Sea where it goes.

MATTHEW ARNOLD: *The Buried Life.*

CONTENTS

A Portrait Gallery Follows Page 446

AUTHOR'S NOTE
1944

The story which follows is a combination of two kinds of treatment; one a topical arrangement, the other a general chronological pattern. The two overlap; occasionally, to illustrate the former, letters out of an exact chronology are used. Similarly, since certain topics are as applicable to one period of life as another, no attempt has been made to limit the treatment of any topic to a single chapter.

Inclusion or omission of names and dates has been entirely arbitrary. Where a name is of evident interest in itself and its use neither hurts nor betrays the original author, it is included. Where either names or dates would cause pain or embarrassment without adding to the story, or in a few cases where dates might confuse, they are omitted.

A more detailed account of the book's origin, sources, and usages is given in the Author's Postscript and Acknowledgments at the end of the volume. The matter of punctuation is dealt with there. It should be emphasized that this is a portrait, not an attempt at a definitive biography.

NOTE TO THE SECOND EDITION
1967

Mrs. Peabody's first name was spelled both Fanny and Fannie by friends. The y ending appeared to be more common and was accepted by her and the Rector when used in the first edition. Too late to permit change in this edition, it was pointed out that she herself used Fannie and that she is so identified in her will and on the memorial tablet in the Groton Chapel.

At the suggestion of several who had been close to Endicott Peabody (the original edition having been out of print for some time), it was decided to republish the book. Few changes have been made from the original version. Chief of these are the omission of some letters and descriptive material; a final short chapter telling of the Rector's death; an enlargement of the chapter listing the achievements of Grotonians in "life;" and the deletion of some material in the original appendices. In the main the book stands as originally written. The author wishes to express his deep gratitude to R. Minturn Sedgwick, members of the Peabody family, Henry H. Richards, and Mrs. Nathaniel Bowditch for help given in many ways. No attempt to bring details in regard to Groton School, in which many changes have taken place since 1944, up to the present, has been made, nor has there been any intention of dealing with Grotonians or others who were connected with the school after Peabody's time.

F.D.A.

ORIGINAL PREFACE

To be writing the life of a schoolmaster at a time when one's ears and mind were filled with the noise of flaming thunder, with the pathetic cries of anguish and despair from all over the earth, has frequently seemed a strange occupation. It was all the stranger when one reflected that the subject of the book was neither a statesman, a soldier, a philosopher, a scientist, nor an artist.

Yet there was never at any time any question but that the thing had to be done. There was a compulsion about it, as though the very fact of a world at war made it necessary to tell of things that are the denial of war, yet survive in spite of war, and, indeed, are the only things that make war bearable or justifiable in any sense.

Endicott Peabody was a man who avoided publicity; who defied the spirit of his age by setting quality ahead of quantity. There is perhaps a lesson for Americans here. We forget in our daily encounter with bulk, in our inevitable preoccupation with size and inexhaustible richness, how many of the supremely important things have been small and simple in their beginnings. Bethlehem was a little town in an obscure corner of an empire. Drake circumnavigated the world in the *Golden Hind*. The *Mayflower* was not to be compared with the *Normandie* or the *Tirpitz*. Emerson wrote in Concord, a small place, though larger than Monticello, or even than Jamestown. Bunker Hill is not as lofty as Chimborazo, but they have built a monument there.

Endicott Peabody lived in an age which steadily tended toward the exaltation of the average; the unlimited extension of credit; the recognition of happiness as a goal in itself; in the faith that man can be legislated into goodness and endeavor. All his life, by the manner of it, Peabody denied these things. Profoundly sympathetic with the average man and desirous to help him, Peabody denied that the average can ever be as good as what is better than the average. When all mankind (it seemed) rushed into installment buying, Peabody held it was better to do one's duty than to gather possessions. He held that happiness can never be obtained in itself; it must be a by-product, the fruit of discipline, humility, and duty done. He had no confidence in man's ability to know the truth of himself. Only when man appreciated himself as the child of God did he put on greatness.

Then the human being became the transfigured Person, and with God working through his life he became the instrument of the great purposes of God. Life became simplified because its devotion was simple. It became enormously interesting and absorbing because it was devoted. All this was, of course, no new doctrine. Jesus and St. Benedict, for instance, knew it long ago, but it was uncommon in modern America. To Henry Adams the dynamo became the symbol of unity, power, and beauty no less than Chartres itself; but where Adams, who for all his knowledge lacked faith, and for all his intellect lacked joy, saw in his modern world only sadness and degeneracy and reiterated "nay" gloomily again and again, Peabody remembered that God works by creation and that He has always chosen persons as his instruments, and that the dynamo itself—power, light, and strength—is lifeless and meaningless except in the hands of men. Wherefore he said "yea" and used the dynamo.

One may take issue with Peabody. One may use words like "aristocratic," "old-fashioned," "Victorian." He believed in old-fashioned things; quality, smallness, personal integrity, the family, the League of Nations, goodness resting on strength. One may belittle the diamond, saying, quite rightly, that it is hard and expensive (the rare and precious stone, tougher than steel, of enduring and deep-seated beauty), but diamonds have a way of lasting and they are still rare and desirable, even in wartime, when they are put to uses requiring the characteristics that diamonds have.

Over the portal of Constitution Hall in Washington are engraved these words of the first President of the United States. "Let us raise a standard to which the wise and honest may repair. The event is in the hands of God." It was such a standard that Endicott Peabody raised. Having done that, he was well content to await the event.

Peabody of Groton

I

JOHN ENDICOTT AND
JOSEPH PEABODY

THERE are at least two factors, the scientist and our common sense tell us, which affect every human being. One is heredity and the other is environment. Before telling of Endicott Peabody himself, therefore, let us examine his ancestry and background.

A brief genealogical table † shows that Endicott Peabody and Fanny Peabody were first cousins. They are, like nearly all of the name in America, descended from Francis Peabody who landed at Ipswich in 1636 and settled in Boxford, Mass. It is an interesting thing that in the lives of two ancestors, one named Endicott, and the other Peabody, one can find many characteristics of their descendant Endicott Peabody, who bore their combined names.

In 1623 a group of English merchants formed an association called the Dorchester Adventurers to maintain a fishery off the Massachusetts coast with a base at Cape Ann.* The fishermen were first neglected, then deserted by the gentlemen at home, and the little colony, led by Roger Conant, moved to a new location at Naumkeag. At home one merchant, John White, conceived a plan for sending out to the settlement a group of worthy and industrious colonists instead "of a multitude of rude, ungovernable persons, the very scum of the land." White found as a leader one Master John Endicott (or Endecott), "a man well-known to divers persons of good note, who manifested much willingness to accept of the offer as soon as it was tended." He

† See chapter 3.

* For material in this chapter acknowledgments are due to Fiske's *Settlement of New England*; *The Story of Essex County*, edited by Claude Fuess; Samuel E. Morison's *Maritime History of Massachusetts*, and C. E. Trow's *Old Shipmasters of Salem*.

sailed bearing a grant giving him authority over all of a strip of land lying between three miles north of the Merrimac and three miles south of the Charles in one direction and between the Atlantic and Pacific oceans in another!

Endicott landed at Naumkeag in 1628 at the head of newcomers whose advent might have led to trouble with the original settlers had it not been for Conant's forbearance and determination for good will. The two groups joined with Endicott as the recognized leader. The name Naumkeag was changed to Salem or Peace. It was the largest of the New England settlements at this time, considerably larger than Plymouth.

It would be a mistake to think of these early settlers as being merely a rough sort. John White had carried out his plan to send "worthy and industrious people." Fiske writes in his *Settlement of New England*: "the settlers of New England were homogeneous to a remarkable degree . . . in all history there has been no other instance of colonization so exclusively effected by picked and chosen men. The colonists knew this and were proud of it." It would be a still greater mistake if we attempted to judge the colonists' conception of civil and religious liberty by our own measurements. True, they had crossed dark, stormy waters to be free; but again Fiske says, "If we mean by the phrase religious liberty a state of things in which opposite and contradictory opinions on questions of religion shall exist side by side in the same community . . . nothing could have been farther from their thoughts . . . there is nothing they would have regarded with more genuine abhorrence."

John Endicott, like his contemporary Americans fresh from England, succeeded in combining a preoccupation with religion with the practical matter of building in a wilderness. Some said later he was "as arrant a fanatic as ever drew breath," but for thirteen out of fifteen critical years he was governor of the growing Massachusetts Bay Colony, facing alike domestic grief, fever, want, and restlessness. He was quite capable of independent action as when, in a period while he was not governor, he figured in the episode of the Red Cross Knight. The official banner of the militia bore the red cross of St. George. John Endicott considered this popery, publicly cut the cross from the flag, and was promptly haled to court and punished by being forbidden to hold office for one year. If he regarded defiance of popery as a personal civic duty, he was not troubled by soft qualms in dealing with those who rebelled against his authority. There are descriptions of his towering rage at offenders. When Obadiah Holmes, a courageous and convinced Baptist minister, appeared before him charged with offenses against the principle of infant baptism, Endicott sentenced him angrily to thirty lashes, the same penalty as applied by Massachusetts law to rape, adultery, and counterfeiting.

This religious conviction is perhaps best seen in Endicott's dealings with the Quakers. By basic tenet the Friends walked in scorn of earthly magistrates and often showed great dignity in upholding their belief. This was not always so, however, and when Quakers hooted at the Governor as he went up the street or rushed noisily into church on the Sabbath to interrupt a sermon, they were unlikely to rouse sentiments of tolerance and sympathy in a breast as heavily laden as that of John Endicott with belief in the importance of authority and decent conduct. When, therefore, he returned from an absence to find that Bellingham, the deputy governor, had, after due warning, locked up two Quaker women behind boarded windows, burned their books, half-starved them for five weeks, and then shipped them home, Governor Endicott was disposed to grumble at Bellingham's conduct as too gentle. He would, he said, 'have had the hussies flogged." It is interesting that one Quaker lady, Mary Fisher, having gallantly attempted the more difficult task of converting Endicott first, then went to Adrianople and tried to convert the Grand Turk. She did not convert Mahomet III, but at least he treated her "with a grave courtesy." *

About 1658 the Quakers began to be really troublesome. A law was issued saying that any Quaker returning once was to be flogged and imprisoned at hard labor; returning twice, his ears were to be cut off; returning thrice, his tongue was to be bored with a hot iron. If he came again he was to be put to death, and this law, fathered by Endicott, added one more to the list of capital crimes of the colonists.

* The Quakers were distinctly unpopular, and Endicott's opposition to them had general approval. Only one strong voice was raised in their defense and that voice had itself, although it claimed Endicott as friend, been driven to Rhode Island. Roger Williams addressed a touching appeal to Cromwell for "freedom of different consciences." It is almost startling that Williams, the courageous, brilliant, and difficult rebel so far ahead of his time, should have been, while minister of a church in Salem, an intimate of the stern and relentless Endicott, receiving from him encouragement and support.

3

This severe law roused a fierce quarrel in Massachusetts. It had ardent supporters and equally ardent opponents. Endicott himself begged the Quakers to stay away, but in 1659 two defiant and brave men, William Robinson and Marmaduke Stevenson, and the equally defiant and brave Mrs. Dyer returned. Endicott saw his duty clear and aided by the unpleasant Rev. John Wilson, had the three arrested, tried, and sentenced to be hanged on Boston Common. Mrs. Dyer was temporarily saved by her son, but later returned again and was hanged. The two men were denied Christian burial. "I thank God," said Endicott, upbraiding judges who were inclined to be lax, "I am not afraid to give judgment."

Endicott does not seem to have been much loved, but he was respected, and all admitted he did what he thought was right. In the quarrel with the Quakers, the martyrs' cause has of course been victorious. Endicott appears to have perceived the depth of the quarrel, which was between freedom of conscience and the theocratic state. He was not a scholar himself, but a man of duty; not a scholar, but he founded schools, being one of the first trustees of Harvard College. He did not believe in freedom of conscience, except his own, but he was one of the real founders of New England and the United States.

One is tempted to wander far afield and describe in detail the daily life of those early Puritans, how guests were treated and seated at table according to social standing; how children were expected either to eat separately or in silence; how they were brought up to address their parents as "Honored Sir" or "Esteemed Parent." It may be comforting, when one feels youthfully oppressed, to read the following instructions to young Puritans in an old book of etiquette: "Never sit down at table till asked, and after the blessing. Ask for nothing; tarry till it be offered thee. Speak not . . . look not earnestly at any other that is eating. When moderately satisfied leave the table. Sing not, hum not, wriggle not. Spit nowhere in the room but in the corner. . . . When any speak to thee, stand up. Say not I have heard it before. . . . Snigger not; never question the truth of it." * Or to quote at length from the chronicler Weeden as to dress: "the function of dress to their minds was not only to cover and dress people, but to classify and arrange them. . . .

* Quoted by Miner W. Merrick in *The Story of Essex County*, Vol. 1, p. 96.

Social prestige, rank, estate, and breeding, were to be formulated in the garments of the wearer. It was not only that the precious capital of the community was wasted by expensive dressing, but the well-ordered ranks of society were jostled and disturbed by the glitter of silver lace, the sheen of silken hoods, the tramp of long boots." † Or to tell at length how, if religion was stern, it was also demanding of human effort; how if every man and every household prayed God to bless all endeavors, each individual furnished those endeavors and, if he trusted God to bless, did not lay on Him the burden of provision; how a strong sense of community responsibility and interdependence developed and an awareness of obligation to that community. But to tell all these things would take too long, falling as they did generations before our bearer of the name of Endicott was born.

A very different type of man in many ways was Joseph Peabody, merchant of Salem. He was born at Middleton, Mass., in 1757 and marched (too late) with the Boxford Minute Men to Lexington, many miles away. During the Revolution he served first on two privateers, the *Bunker Hill* and the *Pilgrim*. Later, while on the *Fish-hawk*, he was taken prisoner and sent to St. John's, Newfoundland, from where he was exchanged. He became second officer of the Letter-of-Marque *Ranger*. One night when the ship was attacked by Loyalists who outnumbered the crew three to one, Peabody in his nightshirt led such a spirited defense that the attackers were beaten off, although he was severely wounded. After the war he became captain of a Salem merchantman and soon after purchased a schooner of his own. In this ship, the *Three Friends*, he traded with the West Indies and Europe. Prospering, he bought more ships and began to build them. He founded a huge business, trading with the Baltic, Mediterranean, West Indies, India, and China. In the days when Salem was at its greatest Joseph Peabody was the greatest merchant in Salem. He is said to have employed nearly seven thousand men and was noted for being a generous employer.

Perhaps he was a good employer because he had been so long a sailor himself. At any rate thirty-five who entered his service as boys rose to be masters of ships. Forty-five captains trained on the *George* alone. She was a famous vessel; not a big ship; most of his vessels weren't, he never went in much for size. She was a hundred and ten feet long and 228 tons. She usually went

† Op. cit. p. 97.

5

out with specie and came home with indigo, silks, and cotton fabrics. Her first voyage gives an insight into Salem and the Peabodys. She sailed in May, 1815, and reached Salem again in June, 1818. Hardly a man of her crew was twenty-one years old. It was said that "every man of her crew could read and write but the cook and they were the best blood of New England. . . . Her drill and appointments were worthy of any navy in the world, and when her uniformed crews manned the captain's gig for the interchange of courtesies between her officers and their visitors in foreign ports, the appearance they made elicited no little praise." Endicott Peabody's father had a set of silk flags and signals presented by the merchants of Calcutta. The *George* was small, but she was splendid. They called her the "Salem frigate," and "even famous clipper ships with a record of over three hundred miles a day could not outsail her"; a beautiful thing, low and dainty in her hull, tall and gracious in her spars.

Joseph Peabody was loyal to Salem. He built his ships and unloaded his cargoes there, true to Essex County. It is interesting to read Samuel E. Morison's description of the type of ship he owned: "seldom over five hundred tons burthen, and usually smaller . . . they were not sharp ships or clipper ships, or one quarter the size of the famous clippers, but they were the fastest and most economical carriers of their generation. With their burly bows, lofty rigs, flush deck, and bright waist or painted ports, these old Boston East Indiamen have a certain charm the clippers lack. Happy they born in a time to have seen such a ship rolling down from St. Helena, lee and weather studding sails set alow and aloft, and bearded sailors on her decks." One of these ships entering Calcutta found four sisters there belonging to Mr. Peabody. Like all owners of the time he picked up considerable income in the opium trade between India and China.

He became immensely wealthy; it was said that he paid annual taxes of $200,000, an enormous sum when we consider that he died in 1844. His reputation was such that his credit was held equal to the government's; he was so fair in his dealings that he was never beset by litigation. In 1812 he helped frame Salem's petition against "Mr. Madison's War," but when war came, unlike many of his friends, he supported the government.

Of course, it would be easy to make too much of individual

FAMILY OF ENDICOTT PEABODY

Children

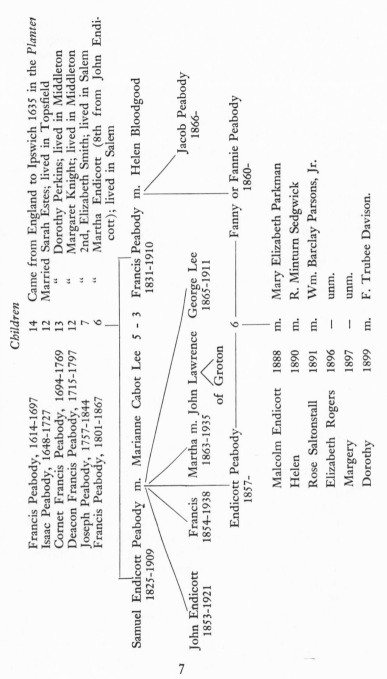

Francis Peabody, 1614-1697 — 14 — Came from England to Ipswich 1635 in the *Planter*
Isaac Peabody, 1648-1727 — 12 — Married Sarah Estes; lived in Topsfield
Cornet Francis Peabody, 1694-1769 — 13 — " Dorothy Perkins; lived in Middleton
Deacon Francis Peabody, 1715-1797 — 12 — " Margaret Knight; lived in Middleton
Joseph Peabody, 1757-1844 — 7 — " Elizabeth Smith; lived in Salem
Francis Peabody, 1801-1867 — 6 — " Martha Endicott (8th from John Endicott); lived in Salem

Samuel Endicott Peabody m. Marianne Cabot Lee 5 - 3 Francis Peabody m. Helen Bloodgood
1825-1909   1831-1910

Jacob Peabody
1866-

John Endicott
1853-1921

Francis
1854-1938

Endicott Peabody
1857-

Martha m. John Lawrence
1863-1935   of Groton

George Lee
1865-1911

Fanny or Fannie Peabody
1860-

Malcolm Endicott   1888   m.   Mary Elizabeth Parkman
Helen   1890   m.   R. Minturn Sedgwick
Rose Saltonstall   1891   m.   Wm. Barclay Parsons, Jr.
Elizabeth Rogers   1896   —   unm.
Margery   1897   —   unm.
Dorothy   1899   m.   F. Trubee Davison.

7

ancestors. John Endicott and Joseph Peabody were but two of many. When we reflect that each of us in ten generations has had more than two thousand ancestors and in twenty generations (which might be five hundred years) over two million, one hesitates to emphasize individuals too much. As a matter of fact there was probably more Putnam in Endicott Peabody than either Peabody or Endicott. In the Endicott line the name of Putnam appears eight times in three generations. And one is tempted to investigate the Rev. Henry Whitefield, the great preacher who was also an ancestor of the subject of this book.

However that may be, there was a John Endicott and a Joseph Peabody and there were all the rest. They lived, wrought, died; and in all their fears and hopes, knowledge and thought of the individual personality we know as Endicott Peabody entered not at all. They were necessary that he should be; he was, we may suppose, a little of what each of them was. Of that we can know nothing and perhaps, even if we knew all, the entire matter would still be obscure.

2

SALEM

SALEM, Massachusetts, lies a few miles north of Boston, in the shelter of Marblehead, watching the sea which it defied and mastered. It was the greatest seaport of Essex County. Possibly no other county in the United States has played a larger part per capita in early American history than Essex, and no spot in Essex County had as large a share as Salem. Neither Essex County nor Salem is large, but in New England it seems that from the beginning quantity has never been held a particularly desirable attribute in itself.

Everyone knows the Massachusetts of the witchcraft trials and the Puritans, of Bunker Hill and Lexington and Daniel Webster. We know the Salem of Hawthorne, of *The Scarlet Letter* and *The House of the Seven Gables;* the Concord of Emerson and Thoreau and *Little Women;* the Cambridge and Boston of Longfellow, Lowell, and Holmes. These are all true New England, but they are only part of it. There was another New England that was not so well known, but in its own way just as great.

It would be hard to find a better example of this other New England than Salem. When Hawthorne wrote the *Scarlet Letter* to pass the time in a deserted customhouse, the glory had in a sense departed and it was natural to dwell upon days past. But it was only from the water front that the glory had fled. Just a few blocks away, on Chestnut Street, the glory had settled down and established itself. It was primarily these things, this glory: an unusual combination of energy, faith, and love of new worlds to conquer.

A Salem boy of good family in Joseph Peabody's time had probably packed experience into his first twenty-five years. Consider the cruise of the *Benjamin* in 1792-94 under Captain, later Senator Silsbee. Silsbee, a veteran of five years at sea, was nineteen when he took command. His mate, Charles Derby, was twenty, and Richard Cleveland, the clerk, was eighteen. Silsbee put his second mate, who was twenty-four, ashore for insubordination. The *Benjamin's* cargo was Madeira, glass, mahogany, and tobacco. She sailed to the Cape of Good Hope and Ile de France, places and names strange or unknown to modern Americans until after Pearl Harbor. At Cape Town she slipped her cables in a gale of wind in the dark to escape a British frigate; "got away from a French warship by drifting out of Bourbon with the ebb tide," and stopped to go fishing at Ascension Island. "The voyage of the *Benjamin* and its youthful officers and crew took nineteen months and brought a profit of nearly five hundred per cent on the investment."

The homes in which these boys lived were fine houses. They were not ostentatious, because Salemites cared little for show, wanting the fact. Essex County and Salem in particular were dominated, as they had been since well before the Revolution, by a group of merchants, business men. These men and their families also dominated Salem society. Salem's population when she rose to power was only about 8000, and even in the middle of the nineteenth century was less than 30,000, but the fine houses on Chestnut Street were gentlemen's homes and their owners were recognized as gentlemen, by themselves and the other inhabitants. They lived in a grand style. They or their fathers had left the plow and taken to deep waters; they had defied the elements and all the traders of the world. They knew their strength. They also knew an old tradition, for Salem was the oldest going society on the continent. There was good food on the tables and plenty of excellent wine in the cellars. Ships from India, Ceylon, the East Indies, Manila, China, the islands of the south, the coasts of Africa, the Baltic, the Mediterranean, the Caribbean, and Europe came home to Salem not only with predictable cargoes of silk, sugar, hemp, indigo, tea, and spice, but with many more exotic things. Many a house dined on priceless china, used furniture carved from rare woods, and looked familiarly on rare possessions that any king would have envied, but few kings could have possessed.

In addition to wealth and belongings each house possessed several consciences which were perhaps even more durable and priceless than the products of the East. This accumulation of consciences expressed itself forcibly in religion, business, and politics. By and large the owners of the consciences were Unitarians and Federalists. The Essex Junto was one of the most startling examples of their corporate conscientiousness.

Federalism and Salem seafaring alike began to dwindle; but while the former was utterly transmogrified, the latter simply altered gradually, after the embargo of 1807-1809, to several other forms of activity. The war of 1812 hastened the slow but steady decline of Essex County shipping, even though there were famous Essex ships in the war and famous Essex ships long after. Shipping disappeared except for a few great fleets such as that of Joseph Peabody, and by the middle forties he had died and even his ships no longer pushed in past Peach's Point.

3

CHILDHOOD

A S SALEM changed from using the ocean to living beside it, changes took place in the life of its citizens. Young men were brought up at home or went to Harvard College instead of shipping before the mast. Money which had gone into hulls and rigging went into mills and land transportation, into investments in the great new territories opening up west of the Mississippi. Life in Salem became stable and serene; the ladies kept their spacious houses, the men went to Boston for business. The great city of ships became a residential town, remembering vicariously its Puritan past and the blue ocean.

Joseph Peabody had a son Francis,* who was a studious, quiet landsman. He was not a gatherer of wealth; on the contrary the family tradition is that "he spent no end of money," mostly on inventors and inventions which speedily became lost causes. One difficulty was that the inventions which interested him did not interest other people for another generation or so. He invented the pianola himself and a new way of manufacturing gunny cloth. Anything having to do with science and its applications appealed to him. He bought a large place called Kernwood, on the Beverly side of Salem, and spent most of his time in the study there. Endicott Peabody remembers him as "rather a strange person, very quiet, gentle, and sweet, but undemonstrative. If he had lived in a succeeding generation he might have done rather remarkable things. He also had a large brick house in Essex Street. After dinner he would go into his study, where he had a drop light with a green chimney and nobody could talk because he was reading. Grandma [Martha Endicott] outlived him, a very charming and intelligent person, fine looking. Grandfather was artistic as well as scientific. The family always had Thanksgiving dinners with them and would

* For pungent and partial comments on Joseph Peabody's family and friends (together with most of their New England contemporaries of any degree of prominence) see *Rich Men of Massachusetts* by Abner Forbes and J. W. Greene, published in Boston in 1851.

then go to George Peabody's [Joseph's other son] for high jinks."

Francis and Martha Endicott Peabody had a son Samuel Endicott Peabody, who was born in 1825. He went to school in Salem, to Harvard for a year and then, since his father still owned Joseph Peabody's ships, he finished his education by going round the world as supercargo in one of them. Then he came back, went into business, and married Marianne Cabot Lee, the daughter of John C. Lee of Salem, the founder of Lee, Higginson and Co. Miss Lee was a lady quite able to hold her own even in Salem. Her mother had been Harriet Rose, daughter of John Rose, a Scotch merchant of Antigua. Samuel Endicott Peabody was known as Tot, and he and his wife lived in a house on Warren Street, Salem, where all the children were born. There were four sons and a daughter: John, Francis, Endicott, George, and Martha. The first two and the last all married Lawrences.

Samuel Endicott Peabody's brother Francis married Helen Bloodgood of Providence, who brought the returns from Perry's Pain Killer into the family and who moved with his wife to the Lindens, a lovely place in Danvers. One of this Francis Peabody's children was Fanny Peabody, born in 1860.

Endicott Peabody was born on either May 30 or 31, 1857. He was never quite sure which date was exact, being indefinite, for almost the only time in his life, about the exact hour of his arrival. His first recollection is that on hearing of Lincoln's assassination he went about spreading the news gleefully, delighted with the excitement of telling. He spent the first twelve years of his life in Salem or thereabouts. He remembered distinctly going up to the Lindens and playing with his cousin Fanny, who had a pony. It gave him pleasure to drive the pony to the dump. His most intimate early playmates were girls, especially Fanny Pickman, Catherine Silsbee, and Mary Tuckerman. He was on intimate terms with all the people round, promiscuous in acquaintance. He went first to a dame school, where he was a cut-up and frequently kept in. After a year he shifted to Hacker School. Again he had the reputation of being rather mischievous. He was feruled twice, once for eating an apple. What the other heinous offense was, history does not record.

The Warren Street house was destroyed in the Great Salem fire, and the family spent more time at Kernwood. In the summers they moved to Beverly. Endicott Peabody had grateful recollections of those summers. He learned to sail a catboat which had to be kept "absolutely perfect." He made friends with a good sailorman named Tucker who taught him seamanship and racing small boats. Tucker had a large yacht and often took the boy along as crew in races. He loved the beautiful sail from Beverly Harbor to Marblehead. The Peabody family had several horses. Endicott learned then the love for horses he kept all his life. He had ridden since he was six years old.

It was a happy, healthy, restricted childhood. There was plenty of good food to eat, good books to read, good conversation at home, and a family love full of mutual affection, high standards, and high-minded living. Samuel Endicott Peabody was a good Unitarian, devoted to his church and interested in religious matters and all phases of Christian life.

When Endicott, or Cotty, as he was always called by his intimates, was thirteen years old there came a great change in family affairs. The first American banking house in London had been established by George Peabody of Baltimore, a distant relative. George Peabody was a silent sort of man, a recluse, but he was a most successful banker and a remarkable philanthropist who did much for both England and America. He was a great favorite of Queen Victoria, who wished to knight him, but he would not give up his American citizenship. At his death, to show her appreciation, the Queen sent his body back on a British man-of-war, and he was mourned in two countries. His partner was Junius S. Morgan, whom he had brought over from Hartford. George Peabody had neither wife nor child, and by his request after his death the Peabody name was dropped from the firm, which became J. S. Morgan Company.* Mr. Morgan invited Samuel Endicott Peabody, who had won his spurs as a business man, and Jacob Rogers, Peabody's brother-in-law, to go over to London and join him as partners in the business. They accepted and Peabody stayed in England seven years, so that to a large degree all his family, including Endicott, were brought up in England.

They all sailed from East Boston on the *Aleppo*. The start was not promising. Driving in to board the ship Endicott Pea-

* And later Morgan and Company. When the New York house became the chief office, still later, the title of the London branch became Morgan, Grenfell and Co.

13

body heard a terrific crash. He looked back and saw that the horses of the carriage behind had been cut down by a freight car. The horses were killed, but almost miraculously the family were uninjured. The *Aleppo* was barely past Minot's Light when she smashed into a brig. Joseph Peabody must have disapproved.

4

CHELTENHAM

E. P. *aet.* 14-19

OF COURSE the boys had to be put in school. Before they left the States a Scotchman had come to visit Fanny Peabody's relatives in Providence. He was very attractive and very enthusiastic about Cheltenham, a recently founded school, recommending it warmly. On the strength of his enthusiasm, when S. E. Peabody reached London he went to Cheltenham and interviewed the headmaster, "who was so simple that father thought it must be a very good school and put Francis and me there." A little later the parents went to see Winchester, but Mrs. Peabody thought Winchester was very damp and that American boys would take cold there. So Cheltenham it was.

Endicott Peabody entered Cheltenham in the spring of 1871 and stayed five years. His brother was there three years. In Cotty's second year a boy named Parker came, with a trunk which contained a case of dueling pistols. A shooting match was suggested. The boys put up a mark on a tree and shot at it. Cotty turned to say to his friend Cowan, "You are ahead," when there was a bang. Cotty looked at his hand and observed a large red hole. After brooding a minute, he remarked, "I have shot my hand," turned, jumped over the palings and ran a mile to a surgeon's house * and told him the bullet was in the hand. The surgeon probed a bit, suggested a poultice, and told the boy to

---

* He ever after regretted that he was not timed, being convinced he had set a record for the distance.

14

go back to school. On leaving him, Peabody observed the size of the bump on his hand and returned to the surgeon, insisting the bullet was still there. The obliging leech cut another gash and again dismissed him. The boy returned to Mother Fay, the matron, who put him to bed, where he remained for five weeks with a badly swollen hand and a fear of lockjaw. The first news his family had was from the housemaster, who eventually wrote and said the boy was getting on as well as could be expected, but failed to mention which boy or what sort of expectation would have been reasonable. The hand had been in a splint and was perfectly stiff. A great London surgeon did what he could with it, but the injury meant no rowing for a long time and Cotty Peabody took to cricket.

At Cheltenham he developed his lifelong love of athletics and exercise. He played on the cricket eleven, rowed when his hand allowed it, played fives and racquets, winning a brown wooden cup with a silver top which long stood in his study. Later at college he also played court tennis. Cricket and rowing he loved. He later said, "Cricket is a grand game. It really does teach you to play the game." Even as a boy Peabody kept himself always in superb physical condition. Billings, years after, said he always made a sacrament of exercise. He was tall, strong as a horse, graceful.

He made three special school friends. One was Walter Roper Lawrence, later Sir Walter, secretary to Lord Curzon when the latter was viceroy of India. Many said he ran India, because when Curzon and Kitchener were at swords' points the only way they could reach one another was through Lawrence. Another friend was Cowan of the shooting match; "He was a most audacious fellow." The friendship with Lawrence, which will last as long as the two men live, was a quiet one. Lawrence was a scholar, with a great love for Dickens, but Peabody and Cowan would run over to Circencester. One time they missed the five o'clock train and turned up at eight o'clock. "We were received coldly by the Headmaster," who gave them each five hundred lines to write out, though there was a cricket match the next day. The lines got done. The third friend was Charlie, known as Cochin, Griffith, a delicate boy and a hard worker with a spiritual turn of mind.

The relationship between masters and boys was mechanical. Peabody thought the English boys were rougher than American

15

boys but not noisier. On the whole the masters made singularly little impression on him. The two heads who were at Cheltenham in his time do not seem to have been very strong men. Peabody enjoyed his Cheltenham days, although he sometimes said that the main things he learned from his English school were things to be avoided and not to do.

Of course the phrase "public school" in England means something very different from the same phrase in America. With us a public school is one freely open to all and tax-supported; a day school as contrasted with an independent school owned and run by an individual or a corporation and depending for funds on its income from tuition.

In England the public school idea is very ancient, as old as the Christian church there at least. Some of the schools there today seem to us of unbelievable antiquity, but before these old schools were born there were other much older schools, older then than Winchester is now; great schools which flourished long and were forgotten. Such was the King's School in Canterbury, founded by St. Augustine himself, such were Dunwich, Rochester, St. Paul's, York, and an earlier Winchester by far than that of William of Wykeham. Education was the province of the church, and the teaching was done by churchmen, occasionally monks, but usually secular clergy. Generally a school was connected with a cathedral or a collegiate church. These schools continued serenely through the Norman Conquest.

The first of the modern public schools was the present Winchester, founded in 1382 by William of Wykeham, a most interesting person with a real concern for education. His motto was "Manners Maketh Man," and when he founded New College (it is still called New College) at Oxford he also established a grammar school next door to Winchester Cathedral to feed his college with scholars. At Winchester he provided for a warden, seventy scholars, ten fellows, three chaplains, three lay clerks, a schoolmaster, and an usher. In 1440 Henry VI followed Wykeham's example at Cambridge University, by founding King's College and Eton to supply it. Eton, like Winchester, had three parts in its early days. It was "a college of secular priests, a school for boys, and an almshouse for poor men." The last func-

* For this article by Peabody on English and American schools see Appendix A.

16

tion was of brief duration; the first endured about four hundred years; the second is Eton College today. Winchester and Eton were followed by Harrow, Charterhouse, Rugby, Shrewsbury, Sherborne, Westminster, St. Paul's, and Merchant Taylors. There were periods of leanness, periods of prosperity. At the beginning of the nineteenth century most of the schools had fallen on evil days, but in the middle of the century there was a sudden spate of new and successful foundations: Marlborough, Cheltenham, Radley, Uppingham, Lansing, Rossall, Wellington, Bradfield, Clifton, and Malvern. Still later came Oundle, and as late as after the First World War, Stowe.* Some of these are large, some small. Eton has about eleven hundred scholars; some of the schools less than two hundred. Most of them are boarding schools, but some, such as Clifton, have a high percentage of day boys.

What caused the sudden swing to favor of the public school? It may have been Thomas Arnold (which of course means to a great extent the other two Toms, Tom Hughes, and Tom Brown), who has passed into English literature by way of *Tom Brown's School Days*. Certainly to an American mind accounts of the schools early in the last century indicate a need for an Arnold. Real scholarship, decent morality, and common kindness seem to have been lacking. It is amusing today to think of Keate's exhortation to his boys at Eton, "Boys, be pure in heart, for I'll flog you if you're not," but it might not have been so amusing at the time. The descriptions of the viciousness of the old fagging system are distasteful to us, and our anger at the brutality obscures our judgment of the virtues of the system. For there were virtues, as can be demonstrated by a visit to the Provost's house at Eton. There on the walls are portraits of old Etonians who have served England and the Empire. It is like a spreading out of British history. Prime ministers, cabinet members, viceroys, generals and admirals, great writers and thinkers, scientists and priests, they are all there. It is probable that at least

* Paton's *List of Schools and Tutors* for 1938 gives the names of more than 200 public schools "represented at the Headmasters' Conference," including, among those better known on this side of the Atlantic: Bradfield, Charterhouse, Clifton, Eton, Fettes, Haileybury, Harrow, Loretto, Malvern, Marlborough, Merchant Taylors, Oundle, Radley, Repton, Rugby, Sherborne, Shrewsbury, Stowe, St. Paul's, Uppingham, Wellington, Westminster, Winchester.

17

half of the great names of Britain for four hundred years are on the rolls of Eton, Harrow, Rugby, Westminster, and Winchester. These men all passed through the fagging system and were all flogged or birched in their time. Perhaps there is a case for corporal punishment which Americans cannot see; perhaps it is good for a boy to be obliged to do menial tasks and be at an older person's beck and call. Perhaps it was particularly good for the boys at the English public schools, for they came from the upper class and at home they were born into the habit of command and the assumption of authority. The public schools were class institutions, no doubt about it. They didn't quite go to the extreme of the noble lord who so heartily approved the Order of the Garter "because there is no damned nonsense about merit," but they expected one to belong to a social group, and if he did not they branded him as an outsider and made him understand they did so.

The result was twofold. Almost all the sons of the wellborn went to a handful of public schools, and, since the class system applied to government as well as to the schools, an extraordinary proportion of the positions of government were held by those who had been to the public schools. Wherever the British Empire went, they went, bearing with them rule and power. It was a great achievement and they were aware of it and of their responsibility. The response of public school boys to England's danger has always been magnificent. Possibly the thing which struck Peabody most forcibly of all in his English school experience was this sense of duty and responsibility to the state.*

The following letter written to Mrs. Peabody in 1935 seems so pertinent that there is no need to explain its inclusion in this chapter.

Cottie and I were born in the same year, were at the same English School, and lived in the same boarding house. We were chums, and here is a definition of this word: "A chum is one who knows all about you and still likes you." I have liked Cottie for over 63 years. Schoolboy fashion we were brutally frank, and personal, in our talks, but Cottie's outbursts left no sting. The sunlight in his face and the sunshine in his heart soon dispelled any lingering clouds of resentment.

Since those schooldays, merry-and-long-ago, oceans have divided

* For instance, four prime ministers went to Harrow under Dr. Drury: Lord Goderich, Sir Robert Peel, Lord Aberdeen, and Lord Palmerston.

us, but we have kept our friendship in repair by correspondence, but it never needed repair, for it has never been broken. And of all the gifts I value in my long and happy life, Cottie Peabody's friendship has the highest value for me.

I first knew his elder brother Frank. He was in the same form but he was a few years older and so joined the Seniors. Cottie and I were Juniors. Frank was charming, but in some ways he was more American than Cottie. He used to impress me with the glories of a city, which he called BORSTON. I foolishly, for it is foolish to argue with a Senior, insisted that he meant BOSTON, and for a few hours there was an estrangement. That afternoon as we sat at our desks in the form room under the vigilant eye of an excellent master, who was also our House-Master, I passed to Frank a small paper bag which contained Pear Drops, my favorite sweet. Hiding his head under the flap of his desk, Frank munched with his strong, and very white teeth the sticky confection, and said with emotion, "these are bully candies." I was puzzled and asked him what "candies" meant. But after this when Frank gave me sweets, I accepted them as candies, and left it at that.

I think that at first, to most of the School the brothers Peabody, as foreigners, were a distinct disappointment, for they were so adaptable, and fitted into our narrow and rather exclusive life, as though they had always been English. The old British tradition— "he's a stranger, heave half a brick at him" seemed for once to lack point, and from the start these delightful brothers were free of the School. Here I must make a confession. Although my school reports always stated that I was above the average, my only knowledge of America was derived from Fennimore Cooper's fascinating, and, veracious novels; and I could have wished that the first American I had ever met, had some greater resemblance to the "Last of the Mohicans."

I have no wish to criticise our system of education but looking back I think that the teaching of geography was in fault. I knew that Barcelona was in Spain and famous for its nuts, and that Riga connoted tallow and hemp, but America was not on our map. In History we read about the Tudors, and Stuarts, we read up to the Revolution, and then silence. I had never heard of Washington and Abraham Lincoln. But later thanks to Cottie's kind father I was the owner of a fine edition of Oliver Wendell Holmes and I devoured American literature. I became, and still am a lover of America and this is due entirely to the influence of Cottie and his family and friends. A wise native wishing to establish friendly relations with England should send boys of the Peabody type to all the schools of Great Britain.

But I set out to write about my friend Cottie. He soon made his mark in the School. He was fairly industrious, and excelled in games. But what we boys noticed, was his resolute character. It is perhaps fortunate that boys at school never think about the careers and the future of their comrades. If I had known that this bright, joyous and fine looking Cottie would become a Priest, Missionary, and great Schoolmaster, our relations might have been less free and unrestrained. But looking back I can see that Cottie was unconsciously directing his life to the great cause, for which he has worked so nobly and so successfully.

Right and wrong were always in his young mind. He was very outspoken and emphatic. If he thought a thing was wrong, he would fight against it, and would never give up. But he was never an uncomfortable companion, never a prig. Always laughing, always sunny, yet, always vigilant. We rose together in the house and in the school, and I know that our house was the best in the school, best at games and best in tone, and this was due to the influence of Cottie. He never talked of principles, but he acted on them. From the first he had fallen into line with the life and the rules of the School, and he won the friendship of the boys, and the esteem of the masters, but on three occasions he had broken through convention, and had argued,—I shiver now as I recall this—had argued with a Master. There was a Master, scholarly, but prone to sarcasm. We were in form, and after some satirical remarks on an English poem, which I had sent in for the prize, he turned on Cottie and said something about his nationality and up rose Cottie. We were reading Cicero, and Cottie's fierce denunciation of our form Master seemed to me more pungent and direct than Cicero's attack on Catiline. Next this brave young boy of principles grappled with our beloved House Master, most able and most excellent. He had given an order which Cottie thought unjust. The House Master was astounded but listened and we all listened, for such a thing had never happened before. Cottie's argument was weak but his sincerity and his real earnestness prevailed and the order was held in abeyance.

Worse still Cottie argued with the Head Master. He was a very great person, and it is as dangerous to argue with a Headmaster, as it would be to argue with a Dictator in Europe today. I was not present at this awful debate but again Cottie's downright sincerity won the day. I remember how impressed I was when I was told of this interview. I had an uneasy feeling that this chum of mine was out of the common and that I had been entertaining an angel unaware. But there was nothing of the angel or saint in this strong, happy, healthy boy; just a love of justice and right, and an innate hatred of wrong.

He was full of sympathy, liked to hear about my home and family, and in turn told me much about his own belongings. Just as

Frank had praised Boston, so Cottie praised Salem, and even now Salem is to me the centre of American life and culture. There was no such place in the whole world as Salem. The men were strong and brave, the women beautiful and good, the boys chivalrous to the girls, the girls the equal of the boys. Such ships, houses, and horses! Alas I have never seen Salem and shall never make my Salaams to that incomparable city by the sea. I rather think that our School knew of Cottie's partiality for Salem, for in Chapel when we sang the 76th Psalm, ("At Salem is his tabernacle"), six hundred heads and twelve hundred eyes would turn pointedly to Cottie's pew, and the fair face would flush crimson.

He went to Cambridge, & America, I went to Oxford and India, He entered a business house and after about a year wrote to me that business was at the best uncertain, that he had decided to give American boys the same chances he had enjoyed in England. And so sprung Groton School. A bold venture for so young a man, but Cottie always had pluck and determination. I have twice visited Groton School and Groton boys have come to me in England. Two came to me in India, where they impressed good judges by their mental equipment and their perfect manners. It is a fine School, and I can see the hand and the mind of Cottie throughout. He deliberately kept the School small so that he might know each boy from the beginning to the end. His courage, common sense, and humanity have borne good fruit and it was a happy day for man when he turned from golden business to the brighter gleam of Groton. I cannot help the thought that if sixteen years ago someone infected with the Groton spirit had been directing the policies of the U.S.A., the unhappy folk of Europe would not still be wandering in the wilderness, loitering too long by the waters of strife.

Cottie was the finest boy, physically and mentally, I have ever known. He is still a boy to me, and others can speak with greater knowledge of him as a man. But I have seen him at frequent intervals. I notice a change, an improvement, and I venture to assert that much of the success of the Rector of Groton School is due to his happy and most fortunate marriage. It is by the wish of the adorable Fannie that I write this halting, most unworthy appreciation of my old friend.

WALTER LAWRENCE, Bunce's Cottage, 19 August 1935.

5

ARNOLD AND THRING

HERE is one more English visit we should make and that is with two English headmasters, because by their example, at least indirectly, they contributed to Endicott Peabody's life.* As long as he was headmaster, the American remembered and quoted Thomas Arnold and Edward Thring.†

* Material in this chapter is taken from Bernard Darwin's *The English Public Schools;* Butler's *Life of Samuel Butler;* Parkin's *Life of Edward Thring;* Stanley's *Life of Thomas Arnold;* and Arnold Whitridge's *Arnold of Rugby.*

† It is quite possible we do not know about some of the very greatest headmasters simply because no one wrote a good book about them. We know of Dr. Samuel Butler because his grandson, also a Samuel Butler, the author of the *Notebooks, The Way of All Flesh,* and *Erewhon,* a trifle unwillingly, it seems, discovered his grandfather's worth and wrote his life. In Arnold's case, his pupil and devoted admirer Dean Stanley wrote a good biography; but for one person who has read Stanley's *Life* a hundred have read *Tom Brown.* It helps a man's fame to be known about.

Dr. Samuel Butler of Shrewsbury became headmaster there in 1798, when the school was in a very bad way as to boys and money. He applied later for Rugby, but was passed over, and he remained at Shrewsbury until 1836. He was a remarkable teacher, and his greatest contribution to public school education was that he raised abruptly and permanently the quality of scholarship. He did it through the classics and succeeded, wrote one of his boys, "in making us believe that Latin and Greek were the only things worth living for." He believed in competition and used marks and examinations for all, if not more than, they were worth. No boy who could not produce good marks or pass good tests was safe in the school.

Yet with all this Butler was an appealing character in whom an at times playful temperament combined with a vigorous and formidable temper. It is said that for thirty-six years he and his second master did not speak, but held their communication through courteous and tolerant correspondence. He dabbled in the occult and the mysterious. He brought back water from four European rivers, the Rhine, Rhone, Po, and Danube to make a punch *aux quatres fleuves,* smoked a pipe while listening to boys' speeches, counted comedians among his friends, and preached a "scathing sermon against Puritans at Cambridge." In his youth he had been gay and (*horrible dictu*) idle, according to his friend Nimrod, who wrote of him in connection with another famous Shropshireman, Jack Mytton. But Butler set high standards for

It was Thomas Arnold of Rugby of whom Dr. Hawkins of Oriel said that he would change the face of education in the public schools of England. He was born in 1762 and lived much of the time near Portsmouth. A student of his has suggested that his familiarity with the military and naval life of the place affected his ideas later. "In his way of looking at things there was a strong bent towards strictness of discipline. He turned the Sixth Form into a corps of young commissioned officers for a campaign against offences in school. Hodson, afterwards the leader of Hodson's Horse in the Indian Mutiny, was the boy he chose to put down disorder in a boarding house."

Arnold went to Winchester, and it is gratifying to find that he was sometimes, in a schoolboy fashion, a rather bad little boy, playing penny loo for shilling points. His own attitude toward the masters appears to have been that of East at Rugby. "What one has always felt about the masters is that it's a fair trial of skill and last between us and them. We're natural enemies, that's a fact. If one can slip the collar without being caught, that one's to us. All's fair in war, but lying." It may have been Arnold's recollection of his own sinful youth which caused him so much concern over the souls of boys. Certainly at Rugby his fore-knowledge of what they were up to often startled them, and equally certainly he had dark forebodings of their innate iniquity. He flogged the younger boys at Rugby because he felt it a punishment "fitly answering to and marking the inferior state of boyhood" and approved its use for "moral offenses, such as lying, drinking, and habitual idleness."

From Winchester, Arnold went to Oriel College in Oxford, where in 1818 he was ordained. He settled down at Laleham, a village eighteen miles up the Thames from London, where he prepared a few boys at a time for the universities. For eight

---

his school and thus for all England, and he made his boys rise to his standards. If he had an easy youth, "he worked hard afterwards, and made his boys work too [but] retained a soft spot in his heart for the less industrious and beat them with a relenting smile." It may have been his youthful memories, too, that brought a faint foreshadowing of the idea that a headmaster can be more than a pedagogue and a pastor in his relationships with his boys; that he can be a friend. This is not pronounced in Butler, it is not entirely apparent, but nevertheless clings to him as a subtle, characteristic aroma of which one is vaguely aware without realizing it. His influence on Peabody was certainly less direct than that of either Arnold or Thring, but was probably of large indirect importance.

years he attracted no attention except among his friends, one of whom protested that at Laleham he was "cutting blocks with a razor." But Arnold was growing while biding his time and thoroughly enjoying himself and his family, one of whom was his son Matthew Arnold. In 1827 he applied for the vacant headmastership of Rugby and was elected, taking over in 1828. He was head for only fourteen years, but in that time he did indeed change the face of education in England and spread an influence in education that still endures.

At first he was by no means popular. The older masters were suspicious, the parents dubious, and many of the boys downright indignant at the man who interfered with their privileges and old liberties while insisting on strange new practices of his own. He introduced some interesting curricular changes, but nothing he did in that respect would have brought him the fame he acquired.

"Above all," said Stanley,

it was necessary for a right understanding not only of his religious opinion, but of his whole character, to enter into the peculiar feeling of love and adoration which he entertained towards our Lord Jesus Christ—peculiar in the distinctness and intensity which, as it characterized almost all his common impressions, so in this case, gave additional strength and meaning to those feelings with which he regarded not only His work of Redemption, but Himself as a living Friend and Master.

Arnold's religious feeling was "ever bursting forth; he seemed to be battling with the wicked one." He drove himself and he drove his boys to Christian duty. Even in vacations he cautioned himself against giving way too much to enjoyment lest he neglect dutifulness. To his mind and in his practice education without religion was a meaningless word. Sometimes his earnestness was overpowering, sometimes his intensity so great that it involved lack of judgment, as when he ascribed childish sin in boys to "the great number of exciting books of amusement like *Pickwick* and *Nickleby*." His prepossession with moral goodness gave even his antics, which unbending he believed his pupils always liked, a ponderous quality and one which "cast a gentle melancholy" upon his own soul. If all Rugby was his empire, the Chapel was the place in which he was most full of power and splendor. The effect of his sermons (which read well, but not greatly) on the boys was prodigious. He felt that the opportunity to preach is a headmaster's most precious privilege. Listen to Tom Brown:

It was not the cold, clear voice of one giving advice and warning from serene heights, to those who were sinning and struggling below, but the warm living voice of one who was fighting for us and by our sides, and calling on us to help him and ourselves and one another. And so wearily and little by little, but surely and steadily on the whole, was brought home to the young boy, for the first time, the meaning of his life; that it was no fool's or sluggard's paradise into which he had wandered by chance, but a battlefield ordained from of old, where there are no spectators, but the youngest must take his side, and the starters are life and death.

Next to this intense religious drive should come Arnold's determination to make the boys themselves vicars of righteousness. It was not enough for a boy to be a scholar, he had to be a personal force for good in the society of which he was a part. Incredibly, it seemed to his contemporaries, for all his misgivings as to boys, Arnold used them, worked with and through them, trusted and uplifted them. And as time went by they worshiped him and made his school what he wanted it to be. To understand what he and his chapel meant in those days one must read Matthew Arnold's poem *Rugby Chapel* and the end of *Tom Brown*.

It was all the more incredible because he scared them to death and was very shy with them himself. He had a habit of thrusting out his lip and tossing his head that was enervating to his pupils in the extreme. When his sense of justice was involved he was relentless, but he possessed under his sternness a real humility. When one of his pupils at Laleham whom he had to rebuke expostulated, "Why do you speak angrily, sir? indeed I am doing the best I can," Arnold took it to heart and told his children afterwards "he had never felt so ashamed in his life."

He ran the school through his sixth form and praepostors, and in the holidays his boys came to visit him. But his faculty were devoted to him, too, and his demands on them are given in the following letter quoted by Stanley:

What I want is a man who is a Christian and a gentleman—an active man, and one who has common sense and understands boys. I do not care about scholarship but, yet on second thought I do care about it very much; and besides I think that even the elements

25

are best taught by a man who has a thorough knowledge of the matter. However, if one must give way, I prefer activity of mind and an interest in his work to high scholarship.

Another thing Arnold did was to establish the independence of the headmaster of the trustees. And still another was that at the very center of Rugby he lived in a gracious home with a lovely woman as his wife who shared deeply in all the life of the school.

There was another side to it, of course. A. G. Butler, a headmaster himself and a staunch admirer of Arnold, wrote:

No one can have read Arnold's life without being struck by his deep, perhaps excessive feeling of the evil incident to school life, and by the part praepostors were called on to play in the moral government of the school . . . this reacted in many cases injuriously on the character of these boy masters, making them self-important and unnatural.

And Arthur Hugh Clough, a most interesting Rugbean, star pupil of Arnold, intimate friend of Matthew Arnold, and close friend of all the family, wrote (in a dialogue weighing the good and bad of the system):

It's all Arnold's doing: he spoilt the public schools . . . not that I mean the old schools were perfect . . . but whatever else they were or did, they certainly were in harmony with the world. . . . [Arnold's young men] are full of the notion of the world being so wicked and of their taking a higher line, as they call it. I only fear they'll take no line at all. [Arnold] used to attack offenses, not as offenses—the right view—against discipline, but as sin, heinous guilt, I don't know what beside! Why didn't he flog them and hold his tongue? Flog them he did, but why preach?

And Lewis Carroll, who was at Rugby four years after Arnold died, "did not look back on his life there with any sensation of pleasure or feel that any earthly considerations would induce him to go through his three years again."

But when we have said all these things, there still remains the inexplicable thing that made Arnold Arnold. Call it character or personality, whatever it was, it was there, powerful, dynamic, and thrilling. His American descendant Arnold Whitridge says,

He was not a philosopher and he was not always capable of understanding a nature weaker than his own, but he caught the imagination of the average schoolboy, the young barbarian as well as the

26

scholar, and he led the public schools out of the wilderness of ignorance and brutality where they had so long been wandering.

His was perhaps the greatest triumph of personality in the wonderful story of Anglo-Saxon education. And his boys carried on the impulse long after Arnold was gone.

Archbishop Temple wrote:

More than fifty years ago whenever I saw Arnold . . . I thought him far above most men I had seen. And now as time has elapsed and I find the image of Arnold rising before me, I perceive that the greatness which was then not so plainly distinguished becomes plainer, not to me alone, but to the world. When we look back on Arnold we recognize the mark which always distinguishes the truly great men—his greatness is more and more appreciated as we move further away.

Jowett, Church, and Newman, all of whom knew him, agreed that Arnold's greatness was that of personality.

The second man who influenced Peabody was Edward Thring of Uppingham. When he went there in 1853 it was a tiny local grammar school with twenty-five boys and a single Elizabethan schoolhouse. It was overshadowed by near-by Rugby and Arnold's fresh fame. But Thring knew what he wanted to do (self-confidence was not a deficiency in the Thring family, he told a friend), and in thirty-four years he did it. He did most of it astonishingly quickly, battling his trustees most of the way and risking all his own small funds. He built from nothing a school which was as great in its way under him as Rugby had been under Arnold.

Like Arnold he began with an intense religious conviction. It was said of him that "he was the most Christian man of his generation." Thring was less fervid, more full of worldly wisdom. "Like Arnold," one wrote of him, "he wanted boys to be Christians and gentlemen, but in the case of boys who 'ragged' at prayers, one gains the impression that he would have laid stress on such behavior as being ungentlemanlike rather than Satanic." Arnold had no humor; Thring had a good deal. Arnold repeatedly expelled boys, not for breaking rules, but because they were in his judgment "getting no good from the school and doing harm to other people." "Till a man learns that the first, second, and third duty of a schoolmaster is to get rid of unpromising subjects," he said, "a great public school will never be what it might be or what it ought to be." Arnold sent Thomas Hughes's brother, a praepostor, away for not backing him up in some school affair and then, very characteristically, asked him to spend the next holidays at Fox Howe. Thring, on the other hand, hated the idea of solving the difficulty of unpromising material by expulsion and thought it a cowardly procedure. "I fear I have mismanaged the boy and it humbles me," he wrote; "the central principle on which all my work has gone on here is the wickedness of turning boys out of a school on any opinion of masters, head or other, and the duty of training each boy and teaching him, however intractable he may be. It is the one thing I live for."

It was a difference of temperament. When Arnold saw a knot of boys of whom he did not approve gathered around a fire, he said, "It makes me think I see the devil in the midst of them." But Thring said, "If W. breaks a law he must answer for it. But even then how much can be done in seeing the right thing at the right time and not seeing too much." In his biography is the story of a rebellious boy who continued to rebel in spite of floggings. A master demanded he should be crushed. "A. shan't be crushed," said Thring, "he is a very good boy, but just at present he is standing at bay, like a rat in a corner. Punish him slightly for this, and for the next month shut your eyes resolutely to everything you are not obliged to see."

Another thing about which Thring was very emphatic was what he called "the almighty wall." By this he meant that to have a good school a man had to have good buildings, suited to his purpose. "I take my stand on detail," he insisted. As to corporal punishment he said, "I conceive it to be the proper retribution for breaking main discipline rules. . . . Contrary to most opinions I do not inflict floggings for lies or sins against God unless they violate school order too."

He was a pioneer and actually introduced into his public school a carpenter's shop and music for everyone. He was a classicist, but he was a large-hearted and open-minded man and a great schoolmaster.

Thring made five great contributions to education. First, he insisted on the importance of the individual boy and the responsibility of the school for him. Second, he insisted that the training in the classics was the best training for anything a man did in life. Third, he insisted that other subjects, such as art and music, filled out the aesthetic side of education and that this was important. Fourthly he insisted that games and other nonscholastic activities should be used to good educational effect. And lastly he insisted that a school's primary job was developing character, a whole boy, not just a boy's mind.

Thring and Arnold agreed that they wanted their boys to be Christians, gentlemen, and educated, probably in that order. They made boys love them and love their schools. To catch the flavor of their lives and works one should read two passages which close this ramble through England. The first is a poem by Henry Newbolt, a loyal son of Clifton; but the poem might have been written about any English public school:

> This is the Chapel: here my son,
> Your father thought the thoughts of youth,
> And heard the words that one by one
> The touch of life has turned to truth.
> Here in a day that is not far,
> You, too, may speak with noble ghosts
> Of manhood and the vows of war
> You made before the Lord of Hosts.
>
> To set the cause above renown,
> To love the game beyond the prize,
> To honor as you strike him down,
> The foe that comes with fearless eyes;
> To count the life of battle good,
> And dear the land that gave you birth,
> And dearer yet the brotherhood
> That binds the brave of all the earth.
>
> My son, the oath is yours: the end
> Is His, who built the world of strife,
> Who gave His children Pain for friend
> And death for surest hope of life.
> To-day and here the fight's begun,
> Of the great fellowship you're free;
> Henceforth the School and you are one,
> And what you are the race shall be.
>
> God send you fortune; yet be sure
> Among the lights that gleam and pass,
> You'll live to follow none more pure
> Than that which gleams on yonder brass.

"Qui procul hinc" the legend's writ—
The frontier grave is far away—
"Qui ante diem periit:
Sed miles, sed pro patria."

And Mr. Brown's advice to Tom when he left for Rugby:

I won't tell him to read his Bible and love and serve God; if he don't do that for his Mother's sake and teaching, he won't for mine. Shall I go into the sort of temptation he'll meet with? No, I can't do that. Never do for an old fellow to go into such things with a boy. He won't understand me. Do him more harm than good, ten to one. Shall I tell him to mind his work, and say he's sent to school to make himself a good scholar? Well, but he isn't sent to school for that—at any rate, not for that mainly. I don't care a fig for Greek particles, or the digamma, no more does his Mother. What is he sent to school for? Well, partly because he wanted so to go. If he'll only turn out a brave, helpful, truth-telling Englishman, and a gentleman, and a Christian, that's all I want.

Endicott Peabody found that not far from the truth.

6

TRINITY COLLEGE, CAMBRIDGE

E. P. *aet.* 19-21

PEABODY was at Cheltenham five years. "The English boys were quite at a loss to see Americans at first," but both the Peabody boys won respect and affection. Francis Peabody was captain of the crew and Cotty Peabody was a prefect and an outstanding athlete.

In 1876, having finished Cheltenham and being nineteen years old, Endicott Peabody returned for a summer at Salem. He attracted a great deal of attention, including that of his "little cousin" Fanny, who found him "rather different from the usual young man, with his school ribbon round his hat and his white suits, so that people were charmed by him." A study of a contemporary portrait indicates it wasn't just the ribbon and suits. He was a fine-looking young man, alert, lively, and with a face already showing strong character and confidence. "People were charmed by him."

He was charmed by them, too, and plunged willingly into a round of visits, seventeen in all! "I had the time of my life," he said. He always loved social life, people, activity, and he had his fill of it that summer until he returned to England in September. He was one of a group known as "the Quarteete," consisting of young William Endicott, Minna Hall, Fanny Peabody, and himself. They rode and drove much together.

When he returned to England he entered Trinity College, Cambridge. Most of his friends of Cheltenham went to Oxford; Walter Lawrence, for instance, to Balliol; but Cochin Griffith was also at Trinity and he made new friends there: Pellew Arthur, his tutor; Caroe; Jones; and Ryle. When Peabody made a friend, he kept him. He kept all these, corresponded with them regularly and at length, and several of them have said that his purse was repeatedly opened for them without their asking. In some respects these English friends were the closest he ever had.

Cambridge he found perfectly delightful for the three and a half years he was there. He had a short-tailed collie, he rowed and played cricket. He lived in the Great Court. "I bagged the Tower and used to go up there, friends were too apt to come and shout at me." For all his enjoyment of Cambridge life he intended to work hard because he wanted a good degree in law. He went in for the lower tripos and got a first class. He has always had the ability both to work and play hard.

"A man named Thompson," he remembered afterwards,

was Master of Trinity when I got there. He was a dreadful fellow, so aloof. He used to have what were called "stand-ups" where you went and stood around and wondered when you could get off. A man named Taylor was my tutor. If you were going in for Tripos you had a coach and paid him extra. Dear old Arthur was my first coach. When I go back I always go to see him. He will say, "Hello Peabody, have a cup of tea?" I will say, "Hello Arthur." "You will have some tea Peabody, O! hello Peabody" even if I haven't seen him for three years.

I used to get up early in the morning to work and the bed-maker would come in and cook me some porridge. I would work for an hour, then breakfast would be sent up. I'd work through the morning, have lectures, then lunch either by myself or with a friend. The bed-maker would look after your lunch. Then you would go down to the boats if you were a rowing man; perhaps stop at the

31

Pitt Club. You could post a letter there without putting a stamp on it. In rowing, you would always have a coach with you who would ride along the tow path. In the Bumping Races, the undergraduates would run along the bank with fog horns, bells, everything imaginable and when they got near a bump it was the most complete presentation of a row.

In addition to Trinity there were the vacations. During one of them he took a walking tour through Normandy with Cowan and Stumpy James. Another time he went with his father and mother to Italy. Art and architecture made about as much impression on him as they do on most young men, but he remembers his great pleasure when Mr. Silsbee got up in the night to light a candle and put his finger in the inkwell. "Mr. Silsbee, by the way, was a great heeler for Shelley." In other vacations Peabody often stayed with his Uncle Jake and Aunt Lizzie Rogers near London. He made one more trip to America before returning home for good.

He does not appear to have done a great deal of general reading, but did acquire the contemporary love for Dickens and Thackeray, especially the former. In poetry he venerated Tennyson, especially *In Memoriam* and the *Idylls of the King*. For him, as for a whole long generation, Tennyson spoke their hearts' beliefs and ideals. Ever since, Peabody has done almost all his quoting of poetry either from Tennyson or Matthew Arnold. It is not altogether easy to understand his regard for the latter, as he has never shown any of Arnold's groping, doubting, or struggling. Perhaps it is because Arnold wrote *Rugby Chapel*, which the Rector quoted more often than any other poem. But his love for Tennyson is easy to follow. Such passages as

> Strong Son of God, immortal Love,
> Whom we, that have not seen thy face,
> By faith, and faith alone, embrace,
> Believing where we cannot prove;
>
> .   .   .   .
>
> Thou seemest human and divine,
> The highest, holiest manhood, thou:
> Our wills are ours we know not how;
> Our wills are ours, to make them thine.

Or from *Oenone* such lines as these, which he often quoted:

32

> Self-reverence, self-knowledge, self-control,
> These three alone lead on to sovereign power.

But aside from formal education, England and English life inevitably left their effects upon him. There is a striking similarity between the Rector's humor and that of *Punch* in the days when he was in Britain. They have the same touch, the same sense of the humorous, the same nuances. At Groton he often read aloud to the boys from two books which were his favorite examples of this kind of humor, *Three Men in a Boat* by Jerome and *Happy Thoughts* by Burnand. They are very funny books and it is a very good, very genteel humor, very different from, shall we say, such American funniness as that of Mark Twain or Artemus Ward or Mr. Dooley.

And there is one other influence that touched him profoundly in England. He studied law and he was gay and he was athletic, but his most intimate friends were deeply religious men and they were all Anglicans. Cochin Griffith was studying for the ministry; Pellew Arthur was ordained; Lawrence and the others were devout churchmen. At home, he had gone to church regularly and the Unitarian church in America in the period of his boyhood was a powerful force, an astonishingly productive intellectual force which produced perhaps the most vigorous thinking and philosophizing that America has known. But it was an intellectual force in which reason dominated emotion, and there was a certain Stoic coldness about it, a certain absence of warmth and color even in such men as Emerson. And with Peabody feeling had always been more potent than thought. In the Church of England he found that warmth, color, and form which his soul needed, and there can be no doubt that his English friends exerted a profound influence on his religious life, as will appear in following chapters.

33

7

DECISION

L IKE many other young men leaving undergraduate existence he was undecided as to what he wished to do with
his life. Except for one thing. He wished to be useful.
That was clear. Although he had studied law, the law had no
real appeal. He had considered the ministry. The whole family
was going home, as his father, having made a fortune with
Morgan and Co., had retired and wished to live in the United
States. Peabody finally decided to follow his father's example;
enter business and make enough money so that he could retire
and devote his life to worthwhile endeavors. Here is a description of him at that time written by a cousin of his, Miss Clara
Endicott Sears:

He came to his native land a wonderful specimen of stalwart
youth, tall, broad shouldered, fair-haired, blue-eyed, with an irresistible capacity for laughter, based largely upon the fact of his
abounding health, his love of life, and an ingenuous belief in everybody. Of course a young man like that landing in the midst of
Boston society played havoc with the fair sex. They fell before him
like ninepins. There wasn't a young man far or near as good looking
as he was, but he seemed quite unconscious of the effect he was
producing, and that added to his charm. And very soon a change
began to come over him. In the midst of a happy, laughing mood a
sudden seriousness would sweep over his face. No one dared ask
him the reason for this, because in spite of his genial spontaneity
with those he met, even with members of his family, he held himself
a little aloof when he was questioned too closely. But those who
knew him best wondered about it. Something seemed to hold him
in its grip and absorb him—and then his mood would change and he
was his old self again. One did not have to know him very well to
be aware of the fact that all the adulation he was getting ran from
him like water off a duck's back.

When he reached America he entered Lee, Higginson, and
Co., which was really a family firm. He was assistant to James
Jackson, and under him Peabody learned "to compute interest

and run errands." The plan of the firm seems to have been to train Peabody to succeed Jackson in charge of collateral. By all accounts Peabody showed promise in business matters and was regarded as a person with a future in the Street.

But he was neither happy nor satisfied in his work. His restlessness increased, and the pull to the ministry became overwhelming at the time his brother Francis got married. Cotty Peabody felt business was not what he wanted and determined to go consult Phillips Brooks. Though staunch Unitarians, his family had been long enough in England to be appreciative of the Episcopal service. Furthermore, their oldest son, Jack, had seriously considered taking orders and had given up the idea only because of the opposition of his father, who considered the ministry "too emotional." Jack had obeyed his father's wishes and turned to art and architecture, but never showed real zest for either, and Samuel Endicott Peabody was not too sure his dissuasion had been wise.

So Cotty went to see Phillips Brooks, who was then at the height of his powers at Trinity Church. Brooks was a big man in every way. He was enormous physically, powerful mentally, and superb spiritually. He was certainly the greatest preacher of his time and very possibly the greatest that America has produced. Standing huge in his pulpit, he seemed to fill the church. The words came in a torrent, tumbling over one another in a passion to escape, and blowing the hearts of the congregation before them as in a mighty wind. Few men ever spoke so fast so understandably. There was little rhetoric, few flourishes, but it was the Word and all who heard him realized it.*

Brooks, too, was the son of strong Unitarians, and his decision to enter the Episcopal ministry had caused heart-searchings at home. He, too, had had to feel for his proper calling. He had

* The official life of the great minister by A. V. G. Allen gives a large detailed account of his thought and growth, but somehow it does not live and Phillips Brooks was vibrantly alive. The book leaves out his humor, his prejudices, and his high temper, his appealing temperament. "I will not have any good in him," he said to a friend of a mutual acquaintance whom the friend was defending, "I will not have any good in him"; and then, when the man had died, Brooks paced in his study in remorse exclaiming, "To think how I never understood him." Even his friends were big; Richardson the architect, and MacVickar the clergyman. Even beside Endicott Peabody, that large young man, Brooks still looked big, and Sunday after Sunday he poured out his eloquent spirituality upon the crowded pews of Trinity Church.

failed as a schoolmaster. But he was a man to admire and follow, and Peabody, who had long admired and hearkened to him, was right in going to him for counsel.

When Peabody arrived at the Rectory, Mr. Brooks was not in, and Peabody walked up and down in front of his house until he came. Then the following dialogue ensued:

"Mr. Brooks, I am Endicott Peabody. My brother is going to be married by you."

"Oh, yes, come in."

"What do you think of brokerage?"

"It doesn't lead to anything and has little in it except a fortune, if that."

"What about the ministry?"

Ah! That was a different matter, and Mr. Brooks and his new young friend talked earnestly. The most difficult question was why, why should one enter the ministry? Mr. Brooks put it very simply. "If, he said, "it appeals to you as the most interesting and desirable thing in the world to tell people about Christ, you had better come in. Does it appeal to you?"

"Well," the Rector has said, remembering, "that was pretty satisfactory. It was perfectly simple and true, so much better than arousing your feelings. My whole heart leapt up."

Brooks told him to take a week to think it over and come back to see him. Again Miss Clara Sears remembered:

One day when all the good things of this material world seemed easily within his reach he announced to his family that he had decided to take orders and become a clergyman! It was at first an overwhelming blow. He could easily have started at the top of things. His Mother was an ardent Unitarian and she was all upset by the Episcopal Church (although he had already been confirmed in England). She could not understand it and she made it very hard for him. But if she was firm in her protests, he was equally firm. They could not turn him from the career he had chosen and he stood his ground unwaveringly and entered this new life with enthusiasm. He used to make me think of the Knights Templars of old. He was such a wonderful specimen of a young Christian, so big and strong and so well able to fight the battles of the Lord.

His father finally agreed and all the family felt it was, after all, a fine thing a person should have personal conviction. So Peabody went back to Brooks, who asked him what training he had had. Peabody replied that he had studied law and been in busi-

36

ness. Brooks was enthusiastic over this as a preparation for orders. Peabody, thinking of the English custom, suggested he should read under Brooks. "Why, no," said Brooks; "here you must go to a theological school, and we have a good one in Cambridge."

Peabody took himself to the Episcopal Theological School and found Dean Gray, a kindhearted but outwardly austere man, walking a path between buildings. He informed the Dean of his decision and the Dean, too, asked what his preparation had been. Hearing of it, with the expression of a man whose saddest fears have been confirmed he conveyed his opinion that the preparation could scarcely have been worse, but nevertheless agreed to take the postulant on.

8

THEOLOGICAL SCHOOL

E. P. *aet.* 23-25

PEABODY wrote, six decades on, of the days in the theological school and of the causes which led him to take the decisive step of entering the ministry. It was a decisive step, one which changed his whole subsequent life. In the ministry he found peace and power and central unity. Even the further tremendous step of deciding to be a schoolmaster was in a sense no more than a logical development of the initial commitment to the service of God. Once in that service, the question naturally arose as to where (given his character, his abilities, his background, and his inclinations) he could be of most use. In the event, Groton School became his permanent parish, and he never forgot, in all his long years there, that if he was headmaster, he was also and first of all a priest. This basic premise colored all his acts and all his aims as a teacher; it was an impelling, driving force in all he was and did.

It should be remembered that he was committed to the priesthood before he was committed to the school. There is no doubt as to the order of commitment. But it is also probably true that very soon after the original decision an inclination to teach began to make itself felt. The unconscious leaning became insistent after his return from Tombstone and emerged into full consciousness at the time of his brief experience in St. Mark's, which is told of in subsequent pages.

The Episcopal Theological School at that time was a very small place. A class frequently consisted of half a dozen men. Through or at the school Peabody made several lifelong friends. One was Julius Walter Atwood, who came to be one of the most intimate. Atwood was a class ahead of him. Here, too, was Sherrard Billings, slightly younger, and here were William Lawrence, a young clergyman obviously destined for a high place in the church; and Henry Nash. Nash, whom Peabody loved and reverenced as he did few men, had a small mission church near Cambridge and taught at the school. He took all knowledge for his province; learned Italian to read Dante; went through Homer and Kant's *Critique of Pure Reason* once a year. Someone asked about Henry Nash once, "Who is that medieval saint eating ice cream in the corner?" Peabody always regarded him as a true saint and read one of his books, *The Atoning Life*, year after year.

But let us turn to his own recollections of those days: *

The ministry was suggested, I think, especially by the *Life of Charles Kingsley* which I had read early in my college career. His biographer set forth his subject's enthusiasm in connection with social problems, which were new at that time, and introduced me to a man of vigorous, virile, enthusiastic character; a gentle, sympathetic, and unafraid example of muscular Christianity, a "very gentil Knight." Late in life he said to an American audience that there was one thing it was always becoming to say under any circumstances to any gathering, educated or uneducated, which should be the lodestar of their theology and of their lives—"He hath showed thee, O man, what is good, and what doth the Lord require of thee, but to do justly and to love mercy, and to walk humbly with thy God." This was the foundation of Kingsley's own life and I wished to make it mine.

On my return from England, following the line of least resistance, I accepted the opportunity to enter upon a life of business in a brokerage firm which had been established by a grandfather many years before. It was not difficult for one with my inheritance to understand, but gradually I discovered that it did not promise to

* Written in 1944.

bring into my life the interest and satisfaction I hoped would be there and the thought of entering the ministry which had passed through my mind in earlier years became more vivid.

At school and college in England I was in close touch with one [Cochin Griffith] who became my intimate friend and companion through years of youth and early manhood, who embodied the simplicity and unselfishness and spiritual quality of a personality *naturaliter Christianus*, who influenced those who loved him not by exhortation or argument, but just by being the kind of person he was.

There came also aid for my problem from one [Pellew Arthur] who was my Cambridge tutor and life-long friend from my entrance to college to the end of his days, who believed in one and by his faith and sympathy helped one to hope for the best for one's life work. There were others, too, in England who helped to open up what seemed to me the finer possibilities of life, a good many others, for the English have a genius for friendship, the deepest and truest friendship, as I learned from experience, and from *In Memoriam*, one of the greatest of English poems. The joy and hopefulness that they brought me continued through my college life and are with me still.

Above all, there had been re-established since my coming home a companionship and resulting inspiration of one with whom I had been in touch since her first years and who from a very early stage of our renewed friendship became the outstanding power for good in my life, who seemed to believe me justified in listening to what appeared to be a call to the ministry.

The call became increasingly persistent and the hope brightened, yet there were uncertainties and possible hindrances, so I turned to Phillips Brooks as many a young man had done before in his attempt to find out what God intended for his life. He decided me to give up business and enlist for the work to which I believed I had been called.

The Theological School was young in those days. Being situated in Cambridge and near to Harvard it was regarded by some people for a while, by a few for a long time, with suspicion as to the soundness of its teaching.

At the School emphasis was placed upon what has been counted by some the centre of Christian theology—Justification by Faith. That was made clear by one of its teachers. "God's belief in us," he said, "is like our friend's belief in us: it makes us humble and it makes us strong. We accept God's belief in us, God's estimate of us, just as we accept our mother's, our friend's—on faith. We know ourselves to be unworthy of it, but our acceptance of it is a source of strength, enabling us in some small measure to live up to it. Thus

39

when we believe that God believes in us, there comes a new power into our lives making for righteousness; we are justified, made righteous, by faith—by our faith in God's faith in us."

"This is what the School stands for," one had said and the account made a strong appeal: "Candid, advanced, unpartisan, manly preparation for the ministry of Christ in this comprehensive Church. Nothing else is feasible, in the presence of a great university, where men have learned to think for themselves."

Some years after he had directed me toward the School, Phillips Brooks commended it in his Convention address:

"We may well be specially and profoundly thankful that we have in our great seminary at Cambridge a home and nursery of faith and learning, . . . which no School of our Church has ever surpassed. Full of deep sympathy with present thought; quick with the spirit of inquiry; eager to train its men to think and reason; equipped with teaching power of the highest order; believing in the ever-increasing manifestation of the truth of God; anxious to blend the most earnest piety with the most active intelligence, and so to cultivate a deep, enthusiastic, reasonable faith, the Cambridge School stands very high among the powers which bid us hope great things." That is a description of the School as I found it.

Its outstanding characteristic was manifested in the sympathy of its teachers, men of deep learning, understanding the movements of the times, encouraging the students to feel free to express their thoughts however mistaken they might seem, eager to lead them to that which had been revealed to them as truth.

As one looks back it is naturally the teachers who engage our attention—to whom we look with especial gratitude. Our first Dean was George Zabriskie Gray. He had served churches in various dioceses of a more conservative character than that of Massachusetts. As he began his work as teacher he used the methods of the early days of almost all educational institutions. His teaching consisted in hearing recitations on Van Oosterzee's Dogmatics and on Pearson on the Creed, assigning to the class the learning by heart of the thirty-nine Articles in Latin. When the class rebelled he compromised on having them memorised in English.

The Dean was, always unconsciously to himself, affected by his surroundings and is described at the time of his death as having "united in a singular degree conservative devotion to consecrated Christian truth with an open eye and receptive mind for new thought and the best methods of theological teaching." Superficially, he appeared pompous and somewhat aggressive but he was one of the kindest of men and his house was always open to the students. He was an able administrator, and by his keen management he established the School on a sound business basis and greatly contributed to the increase of its roll of pupils from many quarters of the country.

The reputation of the School and its consequent growth during the first forty years depended in large measure upon the teaching of its two devoted and outstanding teachers, Dr. Steenstra and Dr. Allen.

Dr. Steenstra was born in Holland in 1833. In 1867 he was called to the Theological School as Professor of Old Testament and there he instructed and energized the students who came under his care for forty years. At the beginning, influenced greatly by the conservative spirit of the Church of his youth, he gradually became one of the first Biblical teachers of this country to realize the significance of the critical and historical study of the Bible. He was influenced, he has told us, by Wellhausen's book on the Pentateuch. He was never carried away by radical writers, yet he was not "nervously orthodox," i.e., he never feared that "something would happen to the truth." He was no more distressed as to the effect of the critics on the Bible than as to the effect of the astronomers on the stars. One who was first a student and his assistant has told us "that he has been impressed all these years by the union in Steenstra's mind of clearness, candor, and restraint. The real students have felt in him an intelligence so much larger than any opinion or set of opinions that Truth in her cleansing and creative power has become for them a real presence."

The other teacher who impressed upon us from the beginning that "History is not merely a collection of facts to be learned by heart but a revelation of the working of God through the ages" was Professor A. V. G. Allen. Said Allen of himself, "I am always moving underground, beneath institutions and customs and formulas of thought, and trying to get at some deeper meaning. To study history is to bring one near to the process of God, that is, the study of it upon a large scale, which takes in great reaches of events. The undevout astronomer is mad. The same might be said of the undevout historian." Said C. L. Slattery, '94, "the result of his teaching was to make men feel how tight a hold God has upon human affairs." This was the purpose which prompted him to write "Continuity of Christian Thought." It was a book which had wide circulation abroad as well as in this country. At the time of his visit to Boston, the Archbishop of Canterbury, to whom Dr. Allen was pointed out, remarked "Is that Continuity Allen? Certainly I want to meet him."

Describing his method of teaching, "I use a text book," said Allen "which contains a condensed summary of the principal events. In the classroom I examine the students on the portion assigned. I then lecture or comment upon the events in order to bring out their connection, to discover the causes which underlie them. I seek to induce the student to go beneath the surface and inquire for the real significance of a movement."

Henry S. Nash became professor of the New Testament a short time before our class graduated. He was with us, however, long enough for us to appreciate the rare quality of his nature and the brilliance and cogency of his mind. At the Theological School's fortieth anniversary Dr. Allen said, "There has never been another student in the school as brilliant as Nash." He graduated in 1878 with the reputation of having taken more books out of the college library than any man who had ever attended Harvard. He read rapidly. His phenomenal memory enabled him to retain what he read. As one met him in casual intercourse he gave one the impression of a man of singularly plain features, but there were times when "the face of Henry Nash was a transfigured face. When we fastened our eyes on him in prayer, in preaching, in meditation, in sacred fellowship, we saw his face illumined. The homely features were transfigured in the light of the eternal. Like Moses he had seen God on the height and his face shone." He was most sympathetic with all students and lifted the least sensitive into a higher realm of thought and being by his personality.

Nash was physically delicate and he overworked. After a long illness in 1907 he was found to have a severe sickness from which he never recovered. Shortly after, his second son was attacked by an incurable disease. "Under this double sentence of death" one has written, "the words of one of his great prayers take on a new meaning."

> O God, author of the world's joy, bearer of the world's pain, make us glad that we have inherited the world's burden; deliver us from the luxury of cheap melancholy; and at the heart of all our trouble and sorrow, let unconquerable gladness dwell.*

He wrote four books. By many readers his style has been counted obscure. With me the small volume of "Prayers and Meditations" has been a constant companion and an unfailing source of inspiration.† "He impressed upon us" one of his pupils has said, "as no man we ever met the sanctity of reason and the majesty of prayer."

For active service in the Church I was fortunate in being allowed

* This was a favorite prayer of Peabody's, used repeatedly in after years.

† Dr. Norman Nash, headmaster of St. Paul's School, wrote in 1944: "The Rector and my father (Henry Nash) were intimate friends. . . . Their admiration was mutual, and I well remember my father's saying, after a last visit from 'Cotty' a fortnight before his death, that of all his friends in the ministry this one had come to mean most of all to him."

to assist Dr. Leighton Parks at Emmanuel and to listen to his vigorous preaching week by week. From that church a fellow student and I were encouraged to start a mission at the South End of Boston which has become the Church of the Ascension.

Peabody, as at Trinity, worked hard. The curriculum was still essentially a classical one, with Hebrew in addition to Greek and Latin. One can find no evidence that his studies at this period produced a very profound effect on his mind. He was by nature a believer rather than an inquirer. Theological perplexities and subtleties simply did not affect him. He believed in Christ, therefore in God and the Holy Ghost. His approach is illustrated by his conversation in regard to the proof of immortality. Peabody was sure of immortality and when asked why said simply, and with a degree of surprise:

"Why, the Bible states clearly that Christ assured us of life immortal."

"Where?"

"Why, when he turned to the penitent thief on the other cross and said 'Today thou shalt be with me in Paradise.'"

That was all there was to it. He was just not interested in details of the Higher Criticism or lower skepticism.

On the side he taught Sunday school and helped out with the Boston mission. He looked forward to a usual course through the school and then parish work, when an unforeseen interlude occurred. A man named Grafton Abbott had gone to Tombstone, Arizona, in charge of a mine. When Peabody had been at the theological school three or four months, Abbott wrote Francis Peabody that the vestry in the local church had quarreled with the then rector, who had left. Abbott wanted to know if Cotty Peabody would come out and take charge of the church.

Descriptions of Tombstone available in Boston agreed that "it was the rottenest place you ever saw." Atwood thought that was what decided Peabody in favor of going.

But it was a difficult decision to make. First, because it meant interrupting work at the seminary; second, because going to Tombstone, Arizona, was very different from going to Trinity College, Cambridge; and third, he had become very much interested in the person to whom he referred as "his dear little cousin," Miss Fanny Peabody of the Lindens, Danvers. It was a problem. To begin with he didn't want to leave her anyway. He was by no means sure that she cared for him except as, perhaps,

43

a very dear brother, a state of affection unsatisfactory at the present and likely to grow worse if in his absence some one should come along for whom she should care more than that, and again, lastly, he was by no means sure that it would be proper for him to marry his first cousin anyway, and Arizona was a faraway place in which to know two minds.

At last he said he would go for a short while, and in January, 1882, he set out on his long journey.

At this time began his correspondence with Julius Atwood, which continued unbroken for more than sixty years. Atwood (later Bishop Atwood of Arizona) kept every line the Rector ever wrote him, year by year, neatly tied up with pieces of string. The significant thing is, of course, that these were letters written, not to Peabody, but by him to an intimate friend to whom he opened up his heart with no possible thought that the letters would ever be read by or of any interest to anyone but Atwood.

Julius W. Atwood was as short as the Rector was tall. He was as nearsighted as he was bald. Lack of hair on the top of his head was compensated for by a luxuriant growth on his chin. He was a great reader, a voluminous reader; a great visitor and a lengthy correspondent. The best testimony as to the quality of his letters is that people read them in spite of the atrocious hand in which they were written. Ability to read them improved with practice, but never became absolute. He was a great friend of Whittier and an indefatigable student of art and literature here and abroad. He called his friendship with Peabody an instinctive friendship. It was remarkably loyal on both sides. The Rector and Mrs. Peabody loved him, but were a little wary of his reminiscences as being sometimes scampish.

9
TOMBSTONE

E. P. *aet.* 25

ALMOST sixty years after he left Tombstone, Peabody gave the following account of his early experiences there:

I came to Tombstone because some one in the community had heard that I was studying for the ministry and urged me to begin in his bailiwick. I therefore wrote him that I should be glad to answer the call with a view to beginning a short ministry in Tombstone. A telegram promptly urged me to come and so I pushed off from the Atlantic seaboard.

The name of the town struck eastern folks as somewhat grim. They discovered later that the place was not as menacing as it sounded. Some of you doubtless know its origin. Ed Schieffelin, a prospector tarrying in Tucson, expressed his intention of visiting the Dragoon mountains with a view to discovering stone (stone being the surface indication of mineral hidden in the earth). As it was a region infested with Indians, Ed's friends assured him that the only stone he would discover would be his tombstone. He persisted in his purpose, however, and returning after some time reported that he had found his tombstone and had located several mining claims there. The name appealed to the people and it was adopted.

Reaching Tombstone shortly after midnight, I was shown to a room in the hotel which was over-ventilated for midwinter owing to both the windows and the transom being broken. As I began to unpack my suitcase, there came a loud knock at the door, and in marched three men. Standing in line, the chairman bade me welcome to Tombstone, apologizing for the late arrival of his committee owing to the fact that they had become interested in a game of cards and had failed to notice the clock. These three gentlemen were as genial as any committee could be, and with them I began a friendship which lasted long beyond my stay in Tombstone.

The life in the place was not without its crude, or even cruel features. Shortly before my arrival, there had been a fierce battle between the Earps, brothers who were guardians of the town, and, I may say, in my opinion were trustworthy officers, and a band of cowboys who were toting pistols in the town, a practice contrary to law.

45

Later, the son of a lawyer who was an intimate friend of mine, was murdered as he came to answer a knock on the door of his assay office.

Another incident came within my personal knowledge, for one of the police, a fine, upstanding fellow who had done his duty in the face of great difficulties, was answering at night a call to Fort Huachuca when he discovered that he was being pursued by a band of ruffians whose enmity he had incurred. He pulled onto the mesa just in time to avoid them as they rode by, picked his way over the cactus plain, and in the morning reported for duty.

There were some dangerous spots in the middle of the town, although generally petty thievery was not common, the brigands operating on a larger scale. The bank, however, was a place which called for special precautions. When one entered it, one came to the receiving teller with a pistol near to his hand. The paying teller was still more fortified, while, at the back, on the manager's desk, lay a pistol; at his side was a gun, and in a box at the other side of the barrier at which a customer of his would be standing was another pistol which, unbeknownst to him, would be pointed directly at his diaphragm.

The manager, himself, was a man of calm temperament. As he was going out of the bank one day, he discovered lying on the floor near the entrance an easterner who had been doing business with him. Asked for his reason for the attitude, the visitor replied that they were shooting outside. "Oh," said my friend, "that was five minutes ago."

This friend of mine occupied a somewhat precarious position. Once, owing to much disorder in the town, there had been called together a vigilance committee, and he suggested the lynching of the leading gunmen. The committee was large and the motion failed. The gunmen were duly informed of my friend's suggestion, and were described by detectives as "laying for him."

My association with the manager constituted almost my only danger of a personal nature. As we walked home from the restaurant where we dined each evening, there was a chance of my friend being attacked before he could use his own weapon that was in his hand within his pocket.

As one approaches Tombstone today, one's attention is called to the graveyard at the entrance to the town known as "Boot Hill Cemetery," the name suggesting the rougher conditions of the earlier days. And there I buried a good many of the miners who, in some cases, needed the assistance of their fellow workers. Their companions were always ready to subscribe with a view to giving them worthy burial.

In the case of the death of a prominent citizen, it was usual for the band to turn out and to march ahead of the long procession, following the hearse to this now historic enclosure.

Outside of the town there were sometimes stirring incidents in connection with the highway robberies; the story being that one of the highest officials, on being informed of the event of a holdup, would mount a posse of men on horses from his own corral, duly charging expenses to the town, and dividing the proceeds of the robbery with the perpetrators of whose rendezvous he had information. There were also occasional alarms from the Indians breaking out from the Cochise Stronghold where Geronimo held sway in those days.

My activities were not concerned immediately with these people. I was in touch with the more peaceful citizens of the town and vicinity and their children.

We organized a baseball nine which created a great deal of interest and brought me in touch with the younger people. Our services were held at first in the court house and were well attended, some people doubtless being drawn thither by curiosity. At an early stage we set to work to build the church. There was a goodly group of men and women, stalwart persons who were not influenced, as persons sometimes are, in more civilized communities, by public opinion, but aimed at doing right because it was right, and because they had the highest interests of the people at heart. They worked in the church, they brought their children to Sunday school, they gave generously for our new building, gathering funds from the people of the town and from friends in both the east and the west. So energetically did they throw themselves into our project that the church, a comparatively small, but attractive building, was constructed in a very short time.

One found an almost unexpected number of fellow workers, men and women who were joined together by a spiritual bond and who exercised a definite influence for good in the community. Among these I was especially bound, as were many others, to George Parsons. His business was that of a prospector, but he was interested even more in the welfare of his fellow citizens. At all times he was ready to lend a hand. So unselfish was he that he laid up for himself very little in the way of a fortune. Like his Master, he "went about doing good." In addition to his cooperation with the church he established for travelers in the desert signposts which pointed the way to water holes, without the knowledge of which many prospectors had lost their lives.

Occasionally he would visit the school in the East where I lived and would delight the masters with stories of Tombstone, drawing, it may be somewhat upon his imagination, at any rate he knew of many incidents, stirring ones, of which I was ignorant. On the mas-

47

ters' leaving us, George Parsons would turn to me and say, "Come on, Peabody, let us talk about the good old Tombstone days."

They could almost fairly be so described, for they helped one to discover the ideals and the generosity which are latent in our people.

The need is for men of such courage and determination as in the early days transformed our frontier towns into civilized communities to so build today that men and women and children may find security, and opportunity for service to our country and to a world as chaotic as we ever knew in the days of our country's youth.

So much for "emotion recollected in tranquillity." There was more emotion and less tranquillity in '82. The Rectory was a shack and the services were held in the courthouse. That first night and the welcome of the three citizens meant much to the boy far from home, far from the shaven lawns of Trinity, far from the Lindens. This friendliness seems to have impressed Peabody as much as anything in the west. On the trip out he had to borrow money twice; once from a naval officer and once from a drummer. Neither had ever seen him before; both lent him what he needed at once and without any suggestion of security. "It taught me," he said, "that in America we are all just 'folks.' "

Several decades later he received a communication from another gentleman who claimed that Peabody borrowed twenty dollars from him, but more than won it back playing poker the same evening, so promptly reimbursed him, all of which produced a favorable impression of the church in the correspondent's mind. Peabody said it wasn't true. As a matter of fact, he was a little touchy about what his friends call the "Tombstone legend," saying it was nearly all apochryphal. One cannot be sure. The people who knew him and Tombstone in those days agree that if the stories weren't true in fact they certainly were in character and were quite possible.

The Rector himself tells, "At the services in the Court House I occupied the judge's seat. At Easter I had a curious experience. Just behind where I was standing there was a door. I felt something was going on behind me and looking down, saw a rascal whose name was Dibble coming in on all fours. I took him by the back and sat him down, but don't believe I converted him." Another time he was taking a bath and with New England diffidence had pulled a curtain over the window. A passing miner pulled the blanket aside, explaining, "I want to see what you're so damned private about."

48

The local paper, still flourishing under the name of the *Tombstone Epitaph*, often indulged in encomiums on the new preacher. Possibly the happiest of them was the earliest: "Well, we've got a parson who doesn't flirt with the girls, who doesn't drink beer behind the door, and when it comes to baseball, he's a daisy."

He met everybody, of course, magnates, marshals, miners, and barkeepers. His first aim was to build a church. There is a story, once removed, that he once interrupted a two-table poker game to announce he wanted funds to build a church. The leading Episcopalian present subscribed $150, and other players followed suit. A performance of *Pinafore* netted $250 more. However it was accomplished, the first Episcopal church in Arizona was built and has been out of debt ever since.

Sometimes the services were marked by events not in the rubric. There is a story that Mr. Smith won twenty dollars at seven-up from Mr. Stebbins. When Stebbins passed the plate next morning he stood by Smith shaking the plate until the twenty dollars was forthcoming. And Grafton Abbott never came to church at all.

Meanwhile, back of all this, what was Endicott Peabody thinking and feeling? By good fortune we are able to get a large glimpse of his mind and heart from the following letters to Atwood written between his departure from the east and his return there in June, 1882. It will be seen that inside he was a very different young man than the legends indicate.

January 23, 1882

You would have hardly thought me an amiable person had you been with me this morning when I was told that the next train for St. Louis leaves at 3:20 P.M. The idea of remaining six hours in this hole of a place [Columbus, Ohio, where "dear Julius" was later Rector of Trinity Church for many years] on a cold blustering day was far from agreeable and if there had been any one near on whom I could have vented my displeasure it would have been vented. However, now I have had a good breakfast and after sitting before a warm fire discussing the morning's news I begin to feel a bit better and the world and things in it look a little less blue. After leaving you on Saturday I sat smoking and thinking for some time. . . . The ride to Philadelphia was a somewhat disturbed one and being unused to night travelling my slumbers were not as deep as they are wont to be.

49

I repeat now what I have so often told you, that I feel sure that you have formed far too high an estimate of my character.

I will tell you a little about my experiences of the last few days but only a little for to do it satisfactorily I ought to be in that arm chair in person and you before me as we used to be and how cozy and pleasant it would be! I shall skip the last day or two of my journey for nothing of note occurred beyond making acquaintance of a very few congenial persons and speeding rapidly through valleys and over mountains wh. were all interesting and for the most part beautiful, but my poor pen is incapable of a decent description. At the Santa Fe junction the Bishop met me and we had a ½ hour's talk. He is an Irishman and treated me very kindly merely making a few suggestions without giving me many and complicated orders as he of Vermont would have done. On Saturday afternoon we arrived at Benson the station for Tombstone. The village of B. is about as wretched a place as you can imagine. A line of wooden shanties and adobes (mud huts) nearly all mud holes and inhabited by roughs and Chinese who are in great force in this part of the country and a very unclean element they are. The stage was awaiting us —a dilapidated old affair covered with dust and drawn by 4 decrepit looking horses driven by Sandy Bob as the coachman was named. I climbed to the top intending to see the country and though requested to descend was firm in my decision, as you know I sometimes am, and remained. The first part of the journey was through a flat sandy country covered with brown grass interspersed with many cacti and a stubly undergrowth—not particularly picturesque — But in the distance were rugged hills and up these our way lay— The passengers outside were Seth Cook—a Calif. millionaire, a Major on his way to the frontier fort, and a Jew aged peddler who was most entertaining. The driver after recovering from sulkiness caused by so heavy a load became very chatty and gave us a graphic description of his experience 3 weeks before when he was 'Stood up' (as they call robbing here) by 2 highway robbers. The stage ahead of us which carried the express had two armed messengers and I expected certainly an adventure but, as is usually the case, it did not come. After a six hours' drive through very bold country we arrived at Tombstone. On the outskirts were tents and the usual adobe huts and shanties but as we came into the middle of the town I found it more of a place than I expected. The main street is long and has several two storied buildings in it and most of the others tho' small are well built—altho' they are for the most part "gin mills" as they call saloons here. I made my way to the Grand Hotel wh. owes its name to its being a house of 2 stories or perhaps even 2½ but is otherwise unpretentious and was shown to a pretty wretched little room. Just as I was going to bed feeling tired and rather blue, three gentlemen connected with the church came up to see me. One of them—Mr. Clapp invited me to his house and you may be sure I was glad enough to accept the offer. He has a small adobe house with 7 rooms all on 1 floor but comfortable enough and I was much happier when I retired. On Sunday I found it snowing hard when I awoke. They had received news of my coming too late to arrange for service and I was not sorry for I was pretty well fagged after 7 nights in the train.

We breakfasted comfortably at a little restaurant and I saw Tombstone in a more cheerful frame of mind. It has 3 long streets parallel to one another—all of them broad and with fair houses, while small streets run across numbered in New York fashion. The streets were thronged with loafers chiefly miners and gamblers but all were quiet and there was a total absence of rowdyism wh. I had fully expected. The majority of the men are well behaved but the cowboys are a troublesome element and there is unhappily a feud between them and the marshal's party. The misfortune is that the cowboys are countenanced by the sheriff for political reasons and the marshal's party on the other hand is not quite above suspicion. 3 months ago they had a fight in the street when 3 cowboys were killed and 2 wounded—and they retaliated only a short time since by attempting to assassinate the marshal. This feud of course keeps the town wh. would otherwise be quiet, in a state of uneasiness for there is a constant anticipation of an outbreak wh. is sure to come sooner or later. The ordinary citizen is unmolested and the only danger is from a stray shot from these or some incensed gambler— but in my circumstances one is safe enough, so there is little cause for anxiety and I feel, perhaps more because of my errand, that it is best to leave it all with Him for whom I am trying to work. We are up on a table land entirely surrounded by mountains which are beautiful in their outline altho' rather brown and barren. The air is pure and delicious and I expect to be very well here. The people have received me most kindly. I am surprised to find so many well educated and refined persons. There is a ladies society of 30 females —fancy that when I had expected to get alone among the men— however, I daresay it will be just as well. At present very little has been done among the miners and they are, I am told, for the most part an extremely poor lot. But as soon as I get at all settled—wh. will I hope be to-morrow, I am going in among them and shall stick to them for 6 months and perhaps I can do something for them.

51

I feel sure that you will make allowances knowing that I have much to do if I want to accomplish much in this place in the short time I have allowed. By the bye, it seems a jolly long time when I think how far away I am and how much I should like to have a chat with you, and a ride with my dear little cousin who is now disporting herself at Washington, and I fear but hope not, winning somebody's heart. But the thing for me to do is to work away and indeed I feel much inclined to do so having received already great encouragement. On Sunday we had perhaps 110 or more at the morning service and we collected $25—a larger sum than was ever taken up before in the church here even when the Bishop was visiting the place.

I started a Sunday School in the afternoon. My predecessor, an awful outsider, by the by, who only stayed here 2 months, having thought it better to organize a school when we got our church building had let the other churches Method. Presbyt. or Cath. get all the children. Enough however turned up to start 2 good classes and we had beginnings for 2 more. For my Bible Class I had 8 or 9 men and 2 females—far more than I had expected in my most sanguine moments. So you see here I am started already with a fairly large Church—when I expected to begin with 10 or 12 miners and 1 or 2 respectable persons. It is much more than I looked for, and i confess it seems almost too much for me. I have written two sermons—1 on Religion and 1 on St. Pauls's 2nd Epis. to Timothy—wh. several people told me they liked. The miners are more in the back ground than I should like—for most of my congreg. so far are well educated and well to do mining superintendents, lawyers, doctors, etc. but I shall stick to them feeling sure that by so doing I can get to know some well and perhaps induce them to take an interest in the Church or, still better, in the object of their own lives. The feeling comes now and then that people are more interested in oneself than in the Gospel and it is a terrible responsibility lest one should be too much set up and cease to work for the Master—but I pray that it may not be so—indeed perhaps I care less for the personal regard of these people among whom I shall be so short a time, than I should if among people of my own class and my old friends. Don't think I don't care for these—I do very much and have already some very good friends among them. I only speak comparatively.

Good night, old Chap.

Tombstone, February 24, 1882

I am feeling somewhat blue and depressed to-night and am going to vent it upon you. To tell you the truth I am homesick—homesick for my people, homesick for my cousin, homesick for you and

for the East. There is partly the cause of depression. Then I have
just returned from a Lenten service (of wh. we have 1 on Wed. and
1 on Friday evgs) at wh. I feel that I did very poorly indeed. The
congregation numbered about 25 wh. is fair as an average. I tried to
lecture on St. Paul. I had intended to speak without my notes as
much as possible but I saw one or two of the people closing their
eyes evidently on slumber bent and I betook me to my MS and read
the whole boiling. I may be, in fact I think I am, over-sensitive in
such matters but little things—such as a person smiling or going off
for a snooze—put a complete damper on me for the time. I sh'd
despise myself if I allowed the disheartening effect to be permanent. On the contrary I trust that it just makes me determined to
try to do better, to make it more interesting next time and if I don't
succeed still I will go on as I announced even if I have only one man
or woman left to bore. But I suppose it is ungrateful of me to go on
in this strain for I have much to be very thankful for. I have not
done anything like what I would wish of course but still we are, I
think, growing larger gradually. The Bishop wrote me the other
day that he had heard from more than one source that I was succeeding admirably and that ought to brighten one up. Still I am not
succeeding admirably as I count success—for success with me means
getting in some of the miners and gamblers et id genus omne and
trying to induce them to aim higher than at present and until I do
that—and it seems at present far enough away.—I shall be unsatisfied.
Then another cause for low spirits is that wh. is the saddest of all
duties wh. a clergyman is called upon to perform—officiating at a
funeral. Already I have had two. The first day before yesterday.—of
a poor miner who was taken away very suddenly by pneumonia.
His name was John White at least that was his name here—but they
think he had gone by another elsewhere and that he was a man who
had met with misfortune at sometime. Little was known of him and
he said he had no relations. He wrote a good hand and was evidently
an educated man in his diary we found written this prayer, "O
Heavenly Father, I thank thee for thy mercy to me an undeserving
sinner. I pray thee to continue thy protecting care of me during the
ensuing years, that my life may redound to the benefit of my fellow
men and to thy honour and glory and my future happiness." Is it
not a beautiful prayer? And yet this poor fellow died all alone in
the world and not a tear was shed when he passed away. He was
buried out in the cheerless barren stony grave yard and "John
White, Aged 55" is the only thing to show that he ever lived. It
seems to me infinitely sad—and yet it is very encouraging at the
same time, for if this poor chap had high aspirations there must be
others like him among the miners—Ah! that one could find them.
Then this afternoon was the second burial. A little child of 3 who

53

had fought with death for 6 weeks and at last succumbed. His father, two little brothers and myself took him in his little white coffin out to the same dreary cemetery and with two friends read the last service over the little chap. It seems dismal enough to leave one whom one has loved in such a place and I pitied the poor father and mother very much indeed. It really does not matter where one's body rests when the spirit has left it—but I should like to be where there is something green—where nature is beautiful—or else in the deep—but to be left in a perfectly sterile soil with only rocks and lime over one seems to me incomparably dreary.

So, when you have read these several causes, you will not think it unnatural that I should be a bit down. I was very glad indeed to get your letter of Feb. 12. You don't know how much I depend on letters. At such a time one values one's friends and has a deeper satisfaction in them than when one is with them and perfectly happy, for then it seems simply natural and one is not half thankful enough for them.

Tombstone, April 13, 1882

I had a delightful ride the other day to Bisbee, a little town about 30 miles distant. I bought a little horse and with a broad brimmed white felt hat, a grey flannel shirt, riding breeches with yellow gaiters; and blankets strapped on behind and a gun hung on the pommel of the saddle you would have taken me for the worst kind of a western rough instead of a quiet man of peace. It was jolly to get away from the town and I felt quite the boy again. We struck an old Indian trail and followed that over mountain and valley, over rocks and sands for 30 miles. After riding about 12 miles we came in sight of trees—wh. are unknown in these parts and it was indeed a happy relief to rest one's eyes upon them once more. There is something very enjoyable in getting away into the country where there is absolutely nobody but one's friend within many miles and to experience the feeling of perfect freedom. The country is safe for travellers on horse back—but we take the precaution of always going armed and generally travel in company with at least one other if possible. I have undertaken one rather painful duty—that of visiting the Hospital. At present there is a poor fellow there dying of consumption and a cowboy who was shot through the lung in a fight with the police, and he too will probably die. It is hard to know just what to say to such men, and one comes away with a feeling that one has not done half what one might—much less what one might have said. I am so glad that the Ipswich parish is so satisfactory and so seemingly to your mind. Do you have many of the workmen in your church? How do you manage about sermons? I suppose you can hardly find time for writing a new one each week.

The East is the place for an Eastern man to live in—and don't you forget it! Have you ever read Livingstone's life? I finished it only a short time since and was much impressed with his entire devotion to the cause of Christ. I know of no man who has so endured suffering and hardship of every imaginable kind out of a pure love for the Master. I am convinced that the subtle questions of doctrine ought not to trouble a man—One ought to look at it in the large light and if one feels a love for Xt and for his fellow man, to believe that God will accept him as a worker in His Ministry. I am sure that yours will be a useful life in that grand calling.

[No date]

—You don't know how inspiring it is to have the majority of the congregation men. I delight in it and take almost more pleasure than if there was a far larger congreg. with a preponderance of women. For it always seems to me that it is the men here in America who need to take a more serious and higher view of life and to acquire that humility and that love for God which they can only have by learning about Xt and of Him.

I must say that I am more impressed than ever with the good nature of the people—for they tell me that they—at least some of them —are interested in my sermons. Of course I don't care for their interest if it is not going to do them any good—and I think perhaps that last sentence sounds somewhat flippant. What I mean is this —that my sermons are very far from what I should like them to be—I should like them to be strong and vigorous and sufficiently striking to make people pull up and think but I fear they are tame and ill expressed.—what I call thin in substance and expression. I trust that the two years that are in store for me at the School will supply me with more power of thought and a store of knowledge which I feel that I sadly lack at present. My days are very like one to another—to wit—I get up at 7:30—or as near that hour as I can manage, breakfast at a Restaurant in the Town and then pass the morning in my study. I read the Bible and generally a sermon of Robertson and then either write on my sermon or study with a view to sermon or Bible class, but I do not accomplish anything like as much as I ought. At 1:30 I feel blue and homesick generally and lunch. Then I proceed to Stebbins' office to see him. It was a letter from Stebbins that so encouraged me just before starting. He is an excellent fellow and ready to do anything for one. After a short chat I wander about making calls on my Parishoners who are more in number in their homes than in the congregation. However it is by visiting in great part that one can work up a flock—and tho' it is not always a congenial task I keep pegging away at it. Escaping from my rounds of calls I get a base ball and 'pass' with some fellow

55

or go for a short tramp in the hills and get a view of the sunset which is simply exquisite—most brilliant and painting the many ridged hills with every conceivable colour. It is then that one likes Arizona better than at any other time. At 5:30 I generally dine at a Restaurant with a Mr. Clapp.—a very pleasant man—cashier of one of the banks, who takes an interest in the Church and is now quite a chum of mine. The evenings are consumed in making calls or else, as I prefer, in reading in my own room and writing to my friends and relations. I don't believe I told you about the 'cowboys' and Indians—did I? They are about here, but not in very great numbers —and the former seldom molest a man of peace. The latter are perfect brutes—but we do not go in their direction if we can help it.

Tombstone, May 15, 1882

—Happily the little church is going up rapidly now and I hope that it will be finished by the middle of next month. What pleasure to preach for the first time in the first Episcopal Church in Arizona. I pray that I may be enabled to preach something wh. will do good to those who come to our first service. We shall organize soon and get the Bishop to come down to consecrate the Church and I hope also that we shall have several candidates for confirmation at the same time. It will be a happy termination to my six months if all these things turn out as I am hoping now. I have been reaping an immense deal of pleasure and, I trust, some benefit from reading the life of Norman McLeod.

Tombstone, May 25, 1882
May 26, 1882

I intended to finish this yesterday afternoon. Possibly you already know of the cause wh. prevented my doing so. A fire broke out at 3 P.M. and lasted nearly 3 hours burning up 3 squares in the very heart of the town. It was a terrible affair. The fire began at the back of a Saloon and immediately seized the Grand Hotel—the largest building in that part of town. A high wind blowing soon spread the flames and the dry wooden awnings and porticoes caught like tinder. The hand engine was well nigh powerless and the only thing that prevented the whole place from going was blowing up end houses with giant powder. Everybody turned in to lend a hand and I worked for about a half hour in a gun shop getting out cartridges and powder wh. w'd have produced a frightful explosion if they had been left. One poor man was burned. They do not yet know who he was—probably a drunken tramp, but it is very terrible to think of his sufferings. The excitement was intense. Large amounts of liquor were rolled out from different saloons and I should think ¼ of the men were drunk. A great many armed themselves and

56

stood guard over the saved goods for the thieves were very busy at such a time. All the wealthiest part of the place is gone and the demoralization is great. Probably they will rebuild at once—at least those who can afford to do so—but many must be ruined. I am thankful to say that our little church wh. has got its roof on was unharmed as were all the other churches. The fire was making directly for "the Parsonage" and was within a few hours of it. We rushed down and got everything out—but fortunately they dragged away some of the intervening shanties and we were saved.

The Courtroom where our services are held, had all its windows broken in and was a little damaged—but we shall have church there Sunday. It will be a great drawback, I fear, to the Mission for the next few months—for all will be too busy to attend to religion—but after the excitement has subsided I trust they will return. There was a little shooting last night but nobody hurt. I passed a man on the street who was waving about a 6 shooter with his finger apparently on the trigger. I can assure you I was pleased when I had got by him.

Tombstone [no date]

The need of two years' more study becomes ever more apparent —for my sphere of usefulness would be very contracted in my present condition of ignorance:

With High Churchmen or Ritualists I can have little sympathy in thought, altho' I may like them well as men—but I do not see things as they see them and never shall. Indeed I do not think that the church can grow in that direction. Certainly it could not out here —nor in the West generally. We are having beautiful weather now— days of unclouded shine—a little warm in the middle of the day but deliciously cool and refreshing in the morning and evening. A finer climate could not well be found—but there the advantages of S.E. Arizona stop. It is a barren place for 8 months of the year and the life is crude. It is interesting and I am glad that I came—but the ideas and the tone of Western people generally are greatly at variance with those of the Eastern folk. All the more need of a hard working clergyman and indeed by remaining here some time a man could undoubtedly do much good. I have a very good friend in the chum who has joined me in the "Parsonage." He is a man of about 50 from Chicago. Poor chap, he was very "handsomely off" in Chicago but failed in business, had to leave his wife and children—whom he loves dearly—at home and come out here in search of a new fortune wh. seems thus far a long way out of his grasp. He is a source of much encouragement to me in my work, and cheers me no end. He assures me that I shall get a call to St. James' Church in Chicago after 2 years, if the parish is vacant at that time. How I should rattle in

57

anything except a small parish—and yet, in common with all theo-logs, I should like much to have a fairly wide influence sometime in my life. I feel it more and more—what you used to say—What a hard thing it is to be a commonplace man. On Thursday I am going to ride down to Tucson to hold services there on Sunday. We take blankets and rifles and depend on feeding at ranches on the way. Sleep out under the great canopy of heaven. It is grand being all day and night in the open air. I should "bully rag" no end if you were with me—but these chaps would not know what to make of it.

June 13, 1882

But for all in the wide field of Xt's Church there is room and every man can use every talent and all the power he has in some way. The ministry is so comprehensive and whatever has to do with man—"Nihil humanum a me alienum puto"—that is a grand thought—and then amid all the troubles and discouragements, to feel that we are trying to work for Him makes it all seem right. It is a great blessing that we have not to do with the result—that God gives the increase. There is a greatest responsibility however with him who sows or waters—to take care that he scatters the seed honestly and thoroughly—and when I fail—as I constantly do—I feel that it is be-cause I have been disgustingly lazy. I go back to Cambridge with the prayerful hope that I may learn more of Xt both of Himself and of His ways in the world and that I may gradually grow into greater enthusiasm and energy.

Tombstone, July 7, 1882

It has been at times somewhat dreary out here and I confess to seasons of excessive home sickness—and yet I am very glad that I came for I think that the experience has already been of benefit and as time goes on I think I shall feel still more good from it. The church has been completed and our congregations are quite satis-factory. The people have been uniformly kind and cordial and I shall be very sorry to part from some. My sermons have been very far from what I would wish them and I shall be glad of more study to fill my mind with thoughts. Last night I received a great compli-ment wh. has encouraged and at the same time humbles me. Clapp—the manager of the leading Bank and a man of more than ordinary cultivation said that he had heard all kinds of men preach in New York, San Francisco etc. and had never been incited to change his life for the better except by Beecher and myself. Clapp is a friend of mine and so he naturally sympathizes with what I have to say.

. . . Isn't there very good shooting in the autumn in Ipswich Bay? Where the bay is exactly I don't know—but we will look it up in September—what do you say? Just off to lunch—& jolly hungry too.

I was too lazy to finish this letter yesterday so will write a few more lines to-day. We had a sad shooting affray the other day in wh. a worthy young deputy sheriff was murdered by a drunken Mexican. They tried to get up enough excitement among the populace to lynch the murderer—but there was no leader. I really think that an example of frontier justice with the next white murderer w'd be a good thing—for the place is full of desperadoes who hold the lives of others and themselves very cheap.

He was twenty-five years old.

I O

MY COUSIN

E. P. *aet.* 25-26

HE RETURNED to the theological school, the Lindens, and Kernwood, very glad to be home again. But he was disturbed about his cousin. She was still fancy free, apparently too entirely so, and he could find little evidence that she was gladder to see him than any cousin should be. Furthermore, he was genuinely concerned as to the cousin problem. He had heard it was inadvisable for first cousins to marry, and while he was desperately in love his whole instinct of honor made him feel that before he pressed his suit he must somehow make sure that he had a right to do so. He felt there was a little coldness in his reception at the Lindens. He consulted with his father about it, told him of his love for Fanny, and asked his advice. His father gently counseled him to abandon the idea. He decided to do so and for a period of gloomy days renounced, as it seemed to him, all future happiness.

But he found he could not give up hope without more definite reason than he had and at last he went to Boston and laid the problem before the best and wisest physician he knew. To his great joy the good doctor was not only sympathetic, but heartily approved, and with a light heart Peabody resumed his suit. It was a slow business. Fanny's scruples had to be overcome, and he was fearful that she would never learn to love him. The extracts from letters * which follow tell something of the long bridge he crossed in order that he might live happily ever after.

Kernwood, July 26, 1882

At home once more safe and sound and thankful to find all my family well. Many thanks for your post cards. I shall try to get to Ipswich to-morrow (Thursday) if possible. If not, I should have to put it off until the beginning of next week.—but I shall do my best to come to-morrow. Such a reception, and such kindness and such happiness! It all seems too much for any man. How to repay it all to one's own and one's friends and to God? But it can't be done. One must ever be a debtor.

Salem, August 22nd, 1882

Many thanks for your welcome letter, old chap. It has just come to hand—written this morning too—almost as good as telephone. Your talk with William Lawrence I quite envy you for tho' I have known him some time and like him much I do not feel that I know him really intimately or have yet a deep insight into his character— but I am quite ready to believe what you say of him and glad that you had so good a time with him. It is a grand gift—that of being able to bring people out and inspiring them with confidence in one's sympathy. I trust that it is a trait which develops as one goes on in one's work and gets to a knowledge or apprehension of the deeper things of God and man. It is all right and grand and glorious as Charles Kingsley said—if we could only take life in the right way with a full consciousness of the love of God and Xt—and an intense love for man—One sees it dimly—but one is so far from it all—at least so I feel at times.

Cambridge, November 17, 1882

What a horrible day it has been! It is in a great part subjective on my part however for instead of jumping at the sight of the pure soft snow my heart seems to sink each time that I look at it. It is only for a time, I suppose, but it makes a great difference in the way that we look at the world—whether we are ourselves happy or despondent.

I was interrupted at this point by Baker's coming for a chat and we had a nice talk which has cheered me up a bit. At times I confess to feeling somewhat dejected. It all seems so hopeless—so almost impossible . . .

* From the Atwood correspondence.

60

Whatever comes will be right and I pray that I shall be able to feel it so—but one cannot help feeling anxiety at times.

Here is a nice evening collect:—

"O Lord our God, refresh us with quiet sleep, when we are wearied with the day's labour that being assisted with the help wh. our weakness needs, we may be devoted to Thee both in body and mind; through Jesus Xt. our Lord."

Cambridge, December 11, 1882

It is past midnight and therefore bedtime—but I feel so nervous and unsettled—so almost happy and yet terribly fearful that the night seems all too long and a hard thing to be got through. For after all I believe you have been the true prophet and that my little cousin is going to love me—not in a year or two as was the dismal and almost hopeless prospect, but very soon indeed. Yesterday she was certainly very different and in both her mother, who knows of all this, and her father, whom I suspect to be a partaker of the secret, I saw an increased cordiality. And when I said goodbye, she said that she was going to send me a billet doux. Now what can a billet doux be—except to tell me that she really does love me? She w'd never be so cruel as to apply that name to a letter urging me to give up all hope forever. After that, you may be sure that I have watched eagerly for the postman at each mail but the glad tidings have not come to-day. You may be sure that I wish the night were gone and the morning's mail come for by that should come the much longed for note. If it does come and if it does contain her consent how grateful and how happy I shall be! * It is what I have prayed for during many days—especially of late has it been always in my heart and in my thoughts. While it would have made me wretched and forlorn if it did not come, yet the very thought of having her give her life to me brings a terrible responsibility. What if I did not love her enough? That is the question wh. comes up at times—and the only answer is I could not give her up now—or if I did life would be very deformed and incomplete. But with her I should look forward to great happiness. She is such a beautiful character that she c'd not fail to make one stronger and better and truer.

The thought of having her by my side working and sympathizing with and loving me is a very very happy one. I pray that I may be faithful and true to her and, if God shall give me the opportunity, I make her life bright and happy. Such a companionship and such true sympathy as Charles Kingsley and his wife had together w'd be my dream. O that we may accomplish it! I shall go to Danvers to-morrow if I hear from her—possibly even if I do not, for the suspense is almost too great.

* Author's note: It didn't come, so far as any record shows.

61

Pray for me, my dear fellow, that I may act rightly and as God would have me act and pray for us both that we may love one another completely. God bless you.

Kernwood, Xmas Eve, 1882

Before I go to bed I must send you a few lines to wish you every Christmas blessing.

The moon is shining brightly outside of my window and the night is as fair and beautiful as it could have been on that blessed night when the Shepherds were watching their flocks in the Judean fields and there was born into this world of ours a Saviour who was Christ the Lord. O that we might appreciate all that means and enter more completely into the life of Him who was born on this night! It is far far beyond me and I am far beneath it and yet I think I can say that I should not care to live if He had not lived, for how He has changed life and shows us its true meaning—that we are to live for others and not for ourselves—that "he who findeth his life shall lose it and he who loseth his life shall find it." With that end in view we can submit to anything that comes to us—although not perhaps without a murmur, at least at present. You will guess from the tenor of my note that I have been feeling a bit unhappy because of my unfortunate position with regard to my cousin. As I see her now she seems so nearly my ideal of a wife and is so very dear to me that I can hardly tear out of my heart the hope that it may be so some day. And then comes the thought that it would not be right—it might be disobeying God's wish which He tells to our conscience—and so I am helped by the thought that it is my duty and must be done and that it will after all be happier for her. It is only in the light of Eternity—in the blessed hope of our all being reunited hereafter and loving each other forever—that it is bearable—at least at times. It is good however that one's life sh'd not be altogether free from care—I am, I trust, grateful to God for all his goodness to me —"How many gifts" the best of parents, family, many and dear friends, and almost everything I could wish for—and an opportunity of entering His Service and trying to do some good in the world. Surely I have been blessed indeed. I hope that you are happy, old Chap. It is a happy time. We are all drawn closer together in the thought of a common Savior who lived and died for us all. May we live to Him all our lives. May the next year bring you many blessings.

Kernwood, May 10, 1883 *

. . . For myself, I have never known what sorrow was. A life of almost unclouded brightness had been mine until the past year.

* Written after the death of his sister-in-law.

Even now that shadows have come I cannot at times realize their presence. It can't be really so I think—and then at other times there seems to be an impenetrable cloud with no light behind it. It is good for one I suppose if one can only look at it in the right way. I fear I do not at times. Indifferent at other times, almost without faith, I seem to be as far away from an Xtian patience and true love for the Master as ever. How thankful we are that He was a Man of Sorrows. If He had not been I don't know how we could stand up and face our present troubles and the dreadful possibilities of the future. But I must not go on in this way. I must try, so far as in me lies, to brighten my poor brother's dark lot. It is an especially hard day for him—coming down to his country home which he never knew without his wife. Death is awful, as we look at it in our ordinary moods. I feel almost afraid of having a wife sometimes because of the dread of losing her. And yet without a wife life is very piecemeal and lonely. It seems as if mine might always be so—for I see no prospect of my dear little cousin ever coming to me and caring for me in any other way than she does now.

They have chosen Peck permanent headmaster of Southboro' having set aside the byelaw which required a Presbyter. Thereby they have made it a lay school and if it seems right for me to do so, I hope to start a church school.

Kernwood, Salem, June 6, 1883

. . . Yesterday I went up to Groton taking my brother's little ones up to their Uncle's. Mrs. Lawrence drove me to a spot which has been selected for "the School" and surely a fairer place one seldom sees. It is a large plateau overlooking a glorious valley with great hills and mountains beyond. It would do one good to live there and it would surely be a fine thing for boys to grow up amid such scenery. It is of course in Nubibus all this school business but perhaps it will some day come down to earth and why not there? The thought of going there alone and entering on such an undertaking by myself is an indescribably dreary one—but with God's help I will not allow it to interfere with my enthusiasm and usefulness. It is I who am far from God and therefore feel alone—otherwise there is no real loneliness.

S.S. *Germanic* July 8, 1883

Here we are once more off the coast of Ireland. What a joy it is to see land after one has been at sea for a week. How grateful one feels, not as much so as one ought of course, but truly grateful for preservation from all the perils of the mighty deep. I felt happier than I have done for a long time as I gazed over the rail at the bold rocky coast half shrouded in mist with a background of dark clouds and up overhead the beautiful new moon in her glory. Don't think from this that I have been very despondent during the voyage. Of course I have hardly been in the old spirits but I think that in some ways it was rather a relief to get away.

May 31, 1884

Yes, it is a solemn thing, this birthday of mine, for the most important events of my life lie just before me. I am looking forward to the life work with great interest and pleasure and at the same time with a little shrinking, for I appreciate how utterly unworthy I am of it all and how my capacities fall short of what is required for so great a work. And yet I will go on and trust that God will help me and forgive my weakness and errors. . . . In regard to my marriage, I always pray that it may come some time if God wills it so and indeed if it did, I feel that it would bring a great happiness into my life, for superficial as I know myself to be, this love has sunk deep down into my soul and taken possession of my whole being. . . . I am just off to the Lindens now, but I don't know if Fanny will be at home. What a glorious day it is!

Oct. 25, 1884

I am happy to say the wait is over and all has come as I have so longed for it to come and we are engaged. . . . You may imagine that I am very happy at the prospect of having such a dear little wife. What a help she will be to me in every way and how she will enable me, I trust, to make the school almost what I should like it to be. She is such a strong and beautiful character that I shall be more than twice the man I am with her by my side.

This is getting ahead of the story, for as appears from the dates on the letters, we have jumped from July, 1882, to October, 1884. It would be out of character with either of the Peabodys to dwell at length on their love affair. No event of his life was as important to Endicott Peabody as her acceptance of him, and one dares say that for her nothing has ever compared with his love for her. No man ever cared more for marriage than he, and few if any ever made a more fortunate match. If he was handsome and winning, she was beautiful and every bit as charming and gracious as he. She brought a devotion and character and faith to match his own. Somebody has said that Cotty Peabody could never understand divorce because his own home was so happy and his wife so perfect. She may have been hard to woo, but once won there never was a more loyal or staunch helpmeet.

From now on she is implicit in all the story, as she is an indefinable and essential part of all Groton. She was the second of the three great forces in his life, and it may be that in his subconscious mind she was the embodiment of his other two great loves for God and Groton School. It is not likely that he has ever been wholly unaware of her since he was a boy, and it is sure that Groton would never have been what it has been without her.

I I

VOCATION

E. P. *aet.* 26

AT THE theological school he helped out in various ways. One invitation was to go to St. Mark's School at Southborough for Holy Week and make an address each morning. Mr. Burnett, the founder of the school and chairman of the board of trustees, asked informally if Peabody would consider going to St. Mark's as headmaster. Since Peabody was not yet ordained and the St. Mark's charter required a clergyman, there was a difficulty. Peabody was definitely interested and consulted Bishop Paddock about early ordination. The Bishop was discouraging and doubted that he would be called anyway, which rather set Peabody back. The idea of combining his ministry with teaching now seized upon him.

He was also at this time assisting Dr. Leighton Parks at Emmanuel Church and was devoted to him. Parks said, "If you are not called to St. Mark's, why not start a school yourself?" Peabody took to the idea at once and talked it with Phillips Brooks and Atwood, who remembered him pacing the floor in Atwood's rectory at Ipswich and saying to himself "Ipswich School, Ipswich School." Brooks suggested teaching a year at St. Paul's for experience, but after considering the idea, Peabody gave it up. Meanwhile St. Paul's asked another man to fill the existing vacancy.

Peabody went to visit the James Lawrences at their place, the Homestead, in Groton. Mrs. Lawrence, a devout churchwoman, suggested that he start an Episcopal church in Groton, which had none. Peabody replied he was thinking of starting a school and there were four churches in Groton already. Mrs. Lawrence said that if he would start a school at Groton she was almost sure her husband and his brother-in-law, Prescott Lawrence, would buy a site for the purpose. The Lawrences and Peabody walked to a near-by farm which seemed a likely place. They got F. L. Olmsted, the famous landscape architect, to look it over, and he pronounced it good. The following week the Lawrence brothers wrote a letter offering Peabody a farm of ninety acres if he would start a school for boys. The gift was in memory of Gertrude Lawrence, sister of the two Lawrence brothers and wife of Endicott Peabody's oldest brother John.

Peabody spent a week with Arthur A. Carey, a friend in Cambridge, and talked to him about starting a school. Carey was greatly interested and said he would be glad to give $5000. Then Peabody went to see William Wells, whom he did not know, but who, he knew, had a lot of money and who was a friend of Carey. Wells asked what Carey had given and said he would match it. Peabody was so pleased he rushed down the steps and bumped into a man who proved to be his father and who was not unnaturally curious about his son's precipitate happiness. When he learned the cause he said he would give $5000.

At the seminary Peabody had found a very good new young friend in Sherrard Billings with whom he had talked schools at different times. Billings had been planning on parish work, but he was the first man to whom Peabody turned for his faculty. Peabody asked Billings, "Will you come teach at Groton?"

"I thought you were going to ask me," replied Billings. "I may not do well."

Peabody seemed to think it quite possible, but assured his fellow-worker-to-be that in that case he might resign. So Billings agreed to come. He next asked Joseph Gardner, but the latter was too nervous and suggested his brother William Amory Gardner, who was itching to come. It is interesting to think today that another man he asked was Theodore Roosevelt, who was appreciative, but went west instead.

The next problem was that of trustees. The Rector felt that he had "quite outstanding men." It seems an understatement. Phillips Brooks agreed to be president of the board; William Lawrence, then dean of the Episcopal Theological School, was secretary; Samuel Endicott Peabody was treasurer; and William C. Endicott; J. Pierpont Morgan, Sr.; James Lawrence; and Endicott Peabody were the other members. A short time later Dr. Leighton Parks was added. If ever a board seemed safe and confidence-inspiring, that one did. They held a meeting at 205 Commonwealth Avenue in Boston on February 23, 1884. The Rector remembered, "Somebody said we ought to appoint a headmaster. I was silent. So long a time elapsed I thought it was half jocose. Then they appointed me."

The new headmaster reported that the ninety acres in Groton had been promised, that $34,000 had been promised with an additional $5,000 if a guarantee fund of $40,000 be raised. It was voted to authorize Messrs. Peabody and Stearns, architects of Boston, to build a schoolhouse at Groton for an estimated cost of $37,000. The Trustees drew up the Preface to the Records as follows:

In the early part of 1883, Endicott Peabody, who had been five years at Cheltenham College, one of the newer schools of England, who had also graduated at Cambridge University, and at that time was a student in the Senior Class of the Episcopal Theological School, Cambridge, Massachusetts, wished to make an attempt to found a boys' school in this country somewhat after the manner of the Public Schools in England.

As these schools, under the influence of the Church of England, have developed a type of manly Christian character, he believed that a School, under the influence of the Protestant Episcopal Church, would do a similar work in this country.

He was assured by men experienced in such matters that, owing to changes in methods of education and the rapid growth of the large cities, there was a demand for such an Institution.

In the autumn of the same year he began the work of Foundation in earnest. A fine estate in Groton, Massachusetts, was promised, unexpected support in money was obtained and much interest in the scheme was expressed both in Boston and New York.

After bringing the plans to a certain point, a meeting of several gentlemen who had consented to assist him was called and the whole matter was placed in their hands as Trustees.

It was provided in the By Laws of the Declaration of Trust that "the Headmaster shall be a clergyman of the Protestant Episcopal Church"; these by-laws being unalterable save by a unanimous vote of the whole board, with thirty days' notice required before a vote.

This preface was augmented by an announcement for general distribution which read:

It is our purpose to open a School for Boys next autumn at Groton, Massachusetts.

Especial attention will be paid to preparing boys for college, but the object of the school will be not the less to provide a thorough education for those who are to enter at once upon the active work of life.

Every endeavor will be made to cultivate manly, Christian character, having regard to moral and physical as well as intellectual development.

The Headmaster of the School will be a clergyman of the Protestant Episcopal Church. Mr. Endicott Peabody has been appointed to this position.

A farm of ninety acres, in a healthy and attractive situation near the town of Groton, 34 miles from Boston and in direct communication with New York has been given to the school, and upon this estate will be erected during the coming season a building with classrooms and dormitory.

A limited number of scholars will be taken at the opening of the school in the autumn.

The charge for tuition and board will be $500 per annum, payable half yearly in advance.

Parents or guardians desiring further information are requested to communicate with Endicott Peabody, Episcopal Theological School, Cambridge, Massachusetts:

> PHILLIPS BROOKS
> WM. LAWRENCE
> WM. C. ENDICOTT
> JAMES LAWRENCE
> J. PIERPONT MORGAN
> S. E. PEABODY
> ENDICOTT PEABODY

Reference to the following gentlemen is permitted:—

> RT. REV. B. H. PADDOCK   CHARLES W. ELIOT
> RT. REV. H. C. POTTER   ROBERT C. WINTHROP
> SAMUEL ELIOT

One notices the phrase "manly, Christian character." It makes one think, as it undoubtedly made the first trustees think, of Charles Kingsley and his way of thought and speech. Mr. Peabody, Sr., also admired Kingsley and had been influenced by him.

68

The headmaster's salary was set at $1200 and that of Billings and Gardner at $800. The school advertised, for the first and only time in the Rector's regime, in the *Churchman and Nation.*

Now all the necessities for a school were provided for except boys; and quickly the boys came, too, twenty-seven of them, and plans were laid for a formal opening on October 15, 1884. It was such a close call getting the building ready in time that the actual ceremony took place on Saturday the 18th. Mr. Peabody, Phillips Brooks, the Rev. G. Z. Gray, and Professor Goodwin spoke. The visitors admired "the regular and compact arrangement of the house."

Groton School had begun.

I 2

THE THEORY OF A SCHOOL

IT IS interesting to speculate what moved parents to send boys to Groton in '84. It was certainly not the teaching experience of the masters; they had none! * Peabody was twenty-seven and Billings almost the same age. Gardner was turning twenty-one, but he looked a lot less, in spite of a feeble mustache. The two younger men were not merely unspotted from the world; they were unacquainted with it. It is doubtful that Peabody himself knew any more about the theories of pedagogy than the man in the moon. Furthermore, the whole idea of such a school as Groton was strange in those days. Phillips Andover and Phillips Exeter had been founded in 1778 and 1781 respectively † and there were numerous· other academies, but they in no way resembled the English public school; they were not "family affairs" nor church schools, and the boys they took

* Except that Billings had taught one year at a boarding school in northern New York.

† The Phillips family tradition of having a share in founding American schools went on. Phillips Brooks, so vital a factor in Groton's launching, lived in the old Phillips mansion in North Andover, and Brooks School, in that town, was later named for him.

were older. Probably the nearest thing to Groton, except for St. James' in Maryland, founded in 1842, St. Paul's, founded in 1855, and St. Mark's, founded in 1865, were Hill (1851) and Lawrenceville (1810), the latter of which used a modification of the English house system.

St. Paul's was flourishing under the first Dr. Coit, an austere, medieval-saint sort of a man, and an unusual schoolmaster. St. Mark's had been having its troubles with several shifts in the headmastership. St. James' was too far away to be much known from New York to Boston.

A good guess as to why fathers sent sons is that they had met Peabody, liked him, trusted him, and thought he had character. This opinion was strengthened by the presence of such potentates as "Jupiter" Morgan on the board of trustees. Morgan dealt on equal terms with the government of the United States and, parents figured, would not allow his name to be used on any board or in any connection of which he did not entirely approve. The other trustees were eminently safe and satisfactory. Some of the early fathers do not seem to have cared tuppence for religion, except as a thing to be generally encouraged and strengthened. If character was Christian, so much the more respectable, but it was essential that it be real character. For scholarship as such many parents never gave a hang. Some of the most successful of them had never gone to college themselves but had helped build one western railroad as day laborers; perhaps were largely owners of others, to say nothing of assorted related businesses. They liked and trusted men who did things, built things, and were something. They believed Peabody was their type of man. Whether he built a school or a railroad didn't seem to matter much. They wanted their sons to be under him, although they may have thought it was absurd that a man with Endicott Peabody's ability and opportunity waste his talents on a handful of boys and a job that any able hireling could do. They never questioned the Rector's integrity; it was just his judgment that seemed weak.

It is also probable that there was another factor at work with those early parents, even though few of them were aware of it. Few of them had ever been to English public schools but they had all heard about them, read about Dr. Arnold, and highly approved any system that went in so solidly for gentlemen. The possibility that Peabody, who was so evidently a gentleman and supported by gentlemen, might establish such a system in America appealed to them. They in all likelihood regarded this as they did all their investments, with a wise dash of altruism, but with a bulk of matter-of-factness. If the thing panned out, they wanted to be in on the ground floor.

And thirdly, early Groton parents, like many of their contemporaries, were privately disgusted with the bringing up of well-to-do American boys of that period. They thought them spoiled ladies' men tied to women's apron strings, and heartily welcomed the chance to send their sons to a place where the boys had to stand on their own feet and play rough-and-tumble games.

What were the Rector's own views about education? We are on solider ground here, because he has written down what *he* intended and wanted. In the first place, to understand Groton one must understand the importance of the family idea. Peabody never, in his own mind, was able to nor wished to dissociate the two concepts of family and religion. A good family *was* religious to his mind. Further, the importance of the family in the whole human scheme of things is paramount. Where family life was wholesome and happy he believed that all would be well with the church and state; where family life was false or untrue or cheap all human institutions failed. Therefore it was the most natural thing in the world for him to think of his school as being simply a large family. To him the words *in loco parentis* meant just that. At the center of the big school family his own family grew and the beautiful home and family life was presided over by Mrs. Peabody, the most gracious and beautiful of wives and mothers. He and she said good night to every boy in the school every night when they were there. If they were away the senior master did it. In addition to formal chapel services, every night there were family prayers in each house. The Peabodys knew all about every boy at school, his other family, his relations, and their doings. There was an intimacy at the heart of things that was peculiar to the genius of the place. One can never understand Endicott Peabody's school until he understands this.

A long time after the school was founded the Rector set down the ideas of the founders, and it is worth quoting these at some length here, because by and large those ideas and ideals never wavered as long as he was at the helm:

71

A reason for the founding of the School was partly owing to the need of at least another Church School; for there were but few of them in those days. Another reason, and the chief one, was the call which the masters had felt for the carrying out of purposes which had taken possession of them. Of the outstanding aims which they had in mind:

The first was that of a Church School, which to them meant a religious community where there should be opportunities for preaching to boys and instruction in what was called Sacred Studies; but where above all other features of the life there should be opportunities for worship, and that in accordance with the spirit and method of the Episcopal Church, where masters and boys should meet together as a fellowship and enter into services of reverence, thanksgiving, and consecration day by day. The result of this they hoped would be the creation of a spiritual atmosphere which would have a conscious or unconscious effect upon all who entered into the life of the School.

It was to be founded, this School, upon a rock and that rock was Christ, described in the motto of the School—*cui servire est regnare* —which freely translated means "whose service is perfect freedom."

As a family we keep in touch with one another and share the different experiences of our lives.

It was to be, this School, a place of sound learning. From the first, we rejected the idea of its being regarded as a preparatory school, which implies a scholastic standard simply adequate to preparation for college. The boys were to take these College examinations as a matter of course without definite preparation for the event; and the greater part of them were expected to be ready for advanced courses at the universities. There was to be aroused if possible in the boys an interest in the various subjects of the curriculum, but in the absence of interest there was determination that the work should be done as a matter of duty. Into the growing knowledge of the world, there should be an attempt to introduce the pupils. The curriculum should be extended, the teaching kept fresh, but there should be always an insistence upon the work being well done and the training of the mind aimed at should be such as was described by the graduate of a French lycée, who found himself able to take up successfully any subject owing to his early training. There should be maintained in the school interest in athletics, not primarily to defeat any opponent, but as an activity which should conduce to the health of the individual, should increase his physical vigor; that he should learn to merge himself in his team, and should above all other things play honestly and in the spirit of good sportsmanship. These should be component parts of the education of one who was preparing for *service* in the world.

There was to be an insistence on the outstanding principle of our Lord "He that findeth his life shall lose it, and he that loseth his life shall find it."

How far these purposes have been achieved cannot be determined. We recall the incident in Jesus' life when at any early age He realized that He "must be about His father's business," and we hold to the faith that with many a boy today there is a response to the call for service, a consciousness that he is in the world not to seek only his own pleasure and success, but to carry out the purpose of one who bestowed upon him the gift of life.

So the hope persists that there may be a growth on the part of many intrusted to our care into that which has been counted by a man of science as the best description of all-round manhood; it is written, you will remember, of Jesus in His youth that "He increased in wisdom and stature and in favor with God and man." The ideal for you and me early as well as late, late as well as early, sound judgment, power of mind and body, with the hope that we may in some measure deserve the commendation which came to Jesus at the beginning of His life-work—"This is my beloved Son in whom I am well pleased."

And to the Groton Historical Society he said:

The first idea of having to do with a Church School came to me from friends who spoke of my being elected headmaster of such a School already in existence. Others suggested that it would be well to establish a new School. My own experience in Cambridge seemed to confirm that. Undergraduates of the University struck one as intellectually immature and lacking in the scholarship which might be expected of young men of their age. The ideals, moral as well as intellectual, with which they arrived at college seemed hazy and uninspired. Comparing them with the same class of men in England where I had been educated, they seemed to one as distinctly immature in mind and general development. The students at the English university were, I knew, the product of the English Public Schools. While I was well aware of glaring defects in their system, I was impressed by the fact that they turned out a race of men who understood men of their own age and were many of them leaders, while not a few were students who had already attained a high degree of scholarship. A serious defect in our methods appeared to rise from the fact that our schools had accepted the title of "preparatory school." That meant that they were planned with a view to "getting" boys into college, and their highest attainment was securing a certain number of honors in the entrance examinations.

Our aim was to try to provide a secondary education which

73

should comprise much that was not called for by the colleges and would at the same time bring boys forward so that they would take the college examinations in their stride.

It is in line with this beginning that we have gone on through the years. The power of a School lies in its teachers. That sounds a platitude. It seems, however, to be forgotten sometimes when vast fortunes are expended in what is known as the physical plant and the salaries for teachers are kept on a plane below those of clerks in banks.

The master is the key to the situation. He must be a scholar. The ordinary class man is generally not up to best secondary school work. The test, however, cannot be merely scholarship, which is sometimes the mistake made in English schools. The man must have the qualities of a teacher, one who not only knows but can inspire his pupils. It is not methods, which are over-emphasized today, that count, but men who create interest through their vivacious and enthusiastic personality.

He must be, not only a scholar and a teacher, this man; he must be also a disciplinarian able to devote his whole mind to his work save one little corner in which he is aware of what is going on in his class as well. He must care for boys, really care for them; not in a sentimental way, but really care. A lecturer on preaching once told his students that the parish priest must be sure to love his people and be sure not to tell them so. That is good advice for a school-master.

The other day I received a letter from one of our graduates who had accepted a call to Groton. He is speaking of the life which seems to lie beyond him. "The more I think about and talk over the profession of school-teaching—and I've done considerable talking during the last few months—the more I am convinced that it is a career worthy of the best of men, and I am only afraid that my small qualifications and capabilities will not be equal to the task. I am being perfectly sincere when I say that sometimes the thought of the responsibilities which the position entails fairly appalls me. It becomes a very serious business when one realizes that one error in judgment may be responsible for the virtual spoiling of a boy's life. I suppose it is largely the amount and the nature of this responsibility which makes the position of school-master so fascinating."

A criticism is sometimes made of Church Schools that they have too many Services and require attendance at them. One who was making this complaint to a relation of mine was met by the unanswerable question "If you do not like your boy to have such Services, why the deuce do you send him to a Church School?" There can always be found critics of every activity in a School, and the religious education must naturally bear its share of it. True, we

74

should realize the desire of reasonable moderns that Services should be fairly short. But on the whole, there seems to be a ready acquiescence on the part of the boys when they find that it is as natural that the members of the community should worship together as that they should meet for study and should dine at a common table. There is certainly a tendency for the graduates of the School to look back with feeling upon the Services that they have found at the Chapel of their School.

Conduct in a School depends upon something more than the teaching of ethics. It depends in large measure upon the atmosphere of the place, and this in turn upon the spiritual ideas and ideals for which the Headmaster is perhaps chiefly responsible. If the religious life is sincere, then the thought and conversation and life of the boy is likely to be wholesome. As we were about to launch our ship in 1884 one of our clerical friends, the best of men but something of a pessimist, met me in the street in Boston. "I hear that you are thinking of starting a School", he said. "That is my intention", I replied. "Do you realize," he continued, "that schools are sinks, (or he may have said dens), of iniquity?" I said that I knew that such institutions existed but that I was hoping that we might avoid such a result of our efforts. It is true that the moral tone can sag very quickly unless it is kept up to a high point, and in sagging it may degenerate into serious evil.

In practical ways, discipline is a foundation stone. Obedience must be prompt and unquestioned at the moment. Later the reason for an order can be explained. With obedience in the background, we can live on terms of cooperation. This is indeed the modern substitute for mechanical discipline. We make an effort to impress upon the boys that we are all here together to live a common life on the basis of friendliness and friendship, and that the old notion of a boy counting himself a hero if he commits some mischievous act, or some serious offence with the hope of escaping scot-free, is old-fashioned. That epithet "old-fashioned", by the way, is, I think, a valuable weapon in a schoolmaster's repertoire today. Cooperation from the beginning, with increasing responsibility as the boy grows older. The so-called prefect system looks after both discipline and morals. The older and more positive leaders are given the responsibility and the authority of masters, and they generally play up to it satisfactorily. "If the Sixth Form", remarked Thomas Arnold of Rugby, "is in sympathy with the School and with me, there is no position in England that I would exchange for this." It was he who set the example of dealing with boys on the basis of confidence.

Frankness is perhaps a marked characteristic of our time, but it requires more than just frankness to tell the truth and to do honest work and to be clean in thought and word and deed. For offences against morality, we inflict no penalty. A boy is reported to the Headmaster who talks the whole matter over with him, and then with his parents, who generally come to the School to discuss the incident; and the boy begins life again with the understanding that his continuing in the School depends upon his making a radical change in conduct and purpose. At Confirmation, much stress is laid upon the importance of one's religious thought and feeling issuing in the right kind of life.

Closely connected with the moral comes the physical development of the boy, and athletics are an important factor in the life of a School. How the collegian spent his spare time before athletics became a part of life of youth is described in a volume of Rhodes' History of the United States where he treats of the universities in the middle of the last century. Not only are athletics useful in the development of the physical man. They minister also to the mind— that is a partial offset to the routine drill and super-organization of our sports which tends to take from them the element of recreation. A graduate meeting a freshmen from his old School said to the boy "While you are at college, I advise you to keep in training all the time." They also, these athletics, may be a school for sportsmanship. They sometimes provide training in deceit. At a school certainly, and if it were possible at college, the coaches in the various branches of athletics should be the teachers. That is another quality that we desire in our masters. They should be not only scholars and teachers of the intellect and spirit, but also instructors in physical activities. That keeps out the spirit of professionalism and helps to maintain a sense of balance in values. A boy learns, or the attempt is to teach him, that he does not come to school first of all to win games or to devote most of his thoughts to sports, with the further advantage that there is less loss of time than when the professional holds sway with the almost inevitable result of many matches at a distance and a corresponding increase of expense.

In the education of a boy, then, our plea has been for a Church School comparatively small if it is to retain the family aspect, where all the members, old and young, may know each other intimately, and where the boys remain for five or six years, the normal period of secondary education. A small group, to be sure, but large enough for intensive effort and made extensive by the continuation of the friendships during the lives of the graduates.

Then there is that which is generally summed up by Grotonians as "the Chapel". Precisely what that is I do not know, but there it is, standing for the finest ideals; for everything that is true, beautiful, and of good report; and giving that divine spark enabling us to try our best "to live to the glory of God and the good cheer of our fellow men."

There is just one other comment to be added. The Rector mentions in passing that the boys should remain at school five or six years. As a matter of fact this was a very important part of his theory and practice. From the very earliest years it was extremely difficult to get into Groton above the second form; and while most Americans think five or six years in one school is an awfully long time, it is an interesting thing that very few Grotonians think so and on the whole the evidence is that the majority of them, if they had to do it again, would choose six years rather than five.* From the Rector's point of view it established and made possible the principle of continuity. Education he thought, since it deals with an entire boy and not just his mind, is a gradual and slow process. It cannot be accomplished quickly, and its effectiveness increases, up to a certain point, in a geometric ratio with time. The fact that only four years are required by other schools to prepare a boy for college had nothing to do with it. He didn't care about preparing boys for college. He wanted to prepare them for life.

13

FIRST YEAR

E. P. *aet.* 27

THE school stood alone then in a broad, unfenced meadow, a long, low building, called Brooks House, facing a large apple orchard, with a meadow beyond. The land was a tilted plateau sloping toward the Nashua River, three quarters of a mile away. To the northeast lies the beautiful old New England town of Groton. To the north and west, across rolling country, rises first Wachusett to the left, "thirty miles away, then Watatick, and slightly farther to the northwest the blue New Hampshire hills" with Monadnock just visible on a clear day. A Groton boy gets to know those hills and watches for their first proof of snow in a sharp October day.

That autumn day New England October was at its height, which is something that those who know it can never forget. A

* This was true for many years: it may not be in the 1960s.

nervous time was had by all, boys, masters, and parents; especially by the masters. One boy was missing, Gilpatrick, and the masters were worried, as he was only thirteen years old and they had been eager to help him. "The door opened, an unmistakable whiff of tobacco floated in, and a youth at least X years of age stepped briskly forward and shook hands, asking in a deep bass voice where he should sit." *

The pupils were all from the eastern seaboard; from Orange, New Jersey, to Saco, Maine; except for George Rublee, who came from Milwaukee. Rublee was an able boy, well fitted to lead the school and head the long procession of graduates out of it. He was there only two years (one of the exceptions), but he was a scholar and an athlete and the first senior prefect.

The Rector (he was not called that just yet, but the custom began early in the year) struck them as perfectly enormous, very frightening, and yet somehow very gentle and human.

They were wakened in the morning, as ever since, by the "outside" ringing. The ringing was irregular, as it was supposed to be done by Mr. G. The latter was troubled by what he called "a curious form of insomnia known as inability to wake up," and when he was a few seconds late, as sometimes happened, the Rector would spring from his bath and pound on Mr. B.'s wall, whereupon both Billings and Gardner would rush for the bell rope and struggle for possession.

Mr. B. taught Latin and Greek; Mr. G. taught mathematics; and Mr. Peabody taught everything else except French, which was the province of one M. Morand. Mr. G. remembered M. Morand well.

Half the school at a time attended his recitation. When his class assembled, the boy who had prepared the first paragraph arose without invitation and recited it, then another boy, who had prepared the second, and so on. The ordinary procedure consisted of crying with a unanimous voice for "The Anecdote." M. Morand never failed to respond. Once the class joined hands and danced in a circle round him. He used to drive to Ayer in a little sleigh behind a horse

* This, and several other reminiscences in this chapter, are taken from William Amory Gardner's delightful little book *Groton Myths and Memories,* which he had privately printed in 1928. Mr. G. was so pleased with it that he gave serious consideration to a full length history of Groton. The Rector wanted a history, but emphatically did not want one by Mr. Gardner and was considerably exercised to prevent it tactfully. Authorities claim *Myths and Memories* contains inaccuracies, but it is a wholly charming volume.

named Nellie—an old horse when Adam was a boy, he explained. "Ne criez-pas, messieurs, do not cry," he would plead as the enthusiastic farewells of his pupils caused Nellie to break into a savage dogtrot.

M. Morand lasted two years.

There was also, briefly in the second year, Signor Papanti, a dancing master. Mr. G. remembered him too. "The lessons were voluntary and attendance waned as daylight waxed. At last Signor Papanti, finding no pupils at all, took a chair, and having waltzed therewith thrice around the circle, departed for Ayer and never came back."

In those days there were no organized athletics because there weren't enough boys to go round. Masters and boys played on the same teams. Scrub football, hare and hounds, pick-up hockey and baseball, coasting, skating, and turtle racing all flourished. George Rublee recollected:

Football was very primitive. The whole school was divided into two sides and the ball was placed in the middle of the field. Then someone kicked it towards the opposite goal and everybody except the full-back set off in a mad pursuit of it. When we lined up it was body to body and hip-to-hip, as close as we could press, with the ball in the hands of the center rush, who had to kick it back. The ball was almost always punted and not infrequently dribbled along the ground as in association football. Blocking off and the various fine points of the game were never dreamed of in the philosophy of early Grotonians. . . . It was very straight football, entirely without guile. When Mr. Peabody received the ball he would make a touchdown.

The buildings, besides Brooks House, included a strawberry red barn, which served as a gymnasium, and a white frame farmhouse. For Chapel they used the high school. In the mornings there was school, and in the evening there were study periods. The latter were frequently trying for the new masters, especially Mr. Gardner. June bugs were used to transmit messages. Undue slappings led to the requirement that a mosquito should be produced for each slap. A mosquito was, and corpses littered the desk while no work was done. There was a great deal of singing, a great deal of reading aloud. In the evenings there was sitting around and talking in the dormitories.

Gordon Knox Bell wrote:

79

We managed to make evening work a gay and festive occasion. Mr. Gardner had left the desk and was walking around the old schoolroom in Brooks House, apparently looking out of the windows. This, of course, was a signal for any sort of disturbance that we could make. On almost every occasion, however, the offender was apprehended and punished. What happened was that Mr. Gardner pretended to be watching for the return of the Rector and Mr. Billings, whereas he was really seeing a reflection in the window-pane of what was going on in the schoolroom, the night being dark outside. At the end of evening work he very generously removed all the black marks he had been giving because he did not think it was a fair way to discover the various culprits.

The frog incident occurred at evening prayer one Sunday. That service, the first year of the School, was always held in the schoolroom. Mr. Peabody and Mr. Billings would put on their surplices in the Rector's house and march down the long corridor which led towards the schoolroom. As soon as we would hear them coming we would get out our prayer books and be ready to begin. On this particular occasion, just as we had assembled, Robert Emmons concealed an enormous bull-frog in Howard Cushing's desk. Cushing was very particular about the neatness of his belongings and personal appearance, and when he opened the desk he was, to say the least, dismayed when this enormous amphibian leaped at him and continued to leap, it seemed to me, two or three feet at every jump. A roar of delight went up from the boys, and the Rector, who had not yet reached the schoolroom, came running in, took off his surplice, and joined in the hunt for the frog, which was apprehended and thrown out of the window. Mr. Peabody again put on his surplice and went on with the service.

The second year of the School opened on Tuesday, September 15, 1885. The original faculty was at that time enlarged by two new members, Major Edwin Hall Higley, who had been a Professor at Middlebury College, Vermont, and Mr. Abner Ernest Strong, a graduate of Harvard, Class of 1885. Mr. Higley did not reside at the School and was never there at all on Sundays as he was organist in some church at Worcester. He came twice a week, spending one night at the School, and taught Greek, Greek History and German. The house in which he afterwards lived for so many years did not then belong to the School, but was acquired later when Mr. Higley became a permanent resident and moved into it with his wife and an adopted daughter named Margaret. The Major, on account of his long yellow moustache, was nicknamed "The Walrus", "Tuskers" and "The Growler", the last was an entirely wrong epithet, as he was always kindly, though at first reserved. His accounts of adventures while in the army during the Civil War were thrilling and dramatic.

At Christmas came the first of the Homestead concerts which continued for many years. The Homestead, as has been said, was the home of Mr. and Mrs. James Lawrence. It is about a mile from the school, and on the night before the Christmas holidays the entire school, masters and boys, went over. The beautiful old house was gay with Christmas greens. There was room for all in the big room that first year; afterward the school overflowed into the hall and onto the stairs. There were songs and instrumental music by boys and masters. Mrs. Lawrence sang, "The Flag's Come Back to Tennessee" (which became an annual fixture) and the "Kerry Dances." Mr. Gardner excelled himself (that was the only concert for a long time at which he did not read a most amusing topical poem written by himself). There was a fine supper and more performances with nearly everyone taking part, and finally the evening closed with "*Adeste Fideles*," and, with the music of that still in their hearts, they went home next day for Christmas.

In the spring, shortly before school broke up for the summer, the Rector told of his engagement. The following Sunday Mrs. Peabody (Miss Peabody then) was at church and the Psalms were inadvertently omitted. They were married that summer, just after the close of school, and several of the boys stayed over to dance at the wedding.

It is hard for a Grotonian to imagine Groton without Mrs. Peabody. Masters and boys fell in love with her at once and have remained so ever since. Her touch was felt in all phases of school life and yet it was never obviously so in any way. That was one of the things that made it so good and sure. It·was always there, one was aware of it, yet somehow took it for granted, as one takes what he loves in his home. The early Groton generations always addressed her and spoke of her as "the Madam." When the children came, they seemed a natural part of Groton, too. It was a home, a family.

All were in and out of Mrs. Peabody's house as though it were their own. Often boys were asked to breakfast and more often to faculty supper, an evening affair with a chafing-dish product or some other kind of good food.

The second year was much like the first, except that there were a few more boys. The third year began to see changes.

That year came Guy Ayrault, who also stayed long, and William Greenough Thayer, who after seven years, six spent at Groton, went on to be a great headmaster at St. Mark's. It was he who scored the first touchdown in the first St. Mark's game, at Lancaster in 1886, playing for Groton. The Rector and Mr. B. also played on the team, and the latter was the first Groton football captain.

During the year the old gymnasium was finished, and thereafter the services were held there until the first chapel was built by Mr. Gardner, in 1887. That year the custom was begun of holding May services in the Groton Town Hall each Sunday evening during that month, at which visiting clergymen used to preach. Some boys remember the long walks down and back as among the pleasantest things of all their time at Groton.

But this is the story of Endicott Peabody, not primarily a history of Groton School. One wonders whether a school's history can ever be told. One of the early graduates has said:

For me no history can ever be written, for a history has to be a sequence of chronological events, and my six years consist of a lot of memories and events none of which is of any importance. Successes and failures, likes and dislikes, nice things that were done for me. . . . I was one of the few boys that liked the winter term. I liked the freedom of it; no organized athletics for a while. I liked the winter scenery, the storms, the snow-shoe walks over the hills, and the skating and coasting. I remember walking with the Rector over the hills beyond Groton; and another time coming home in the winter dusk with some other boy with whom I had been out and looking down on the lights of the village . . . another time coming back from coasting on Joy's Hill, I looked back and the whole top of Wachusett was a flame of gold; I can see it and the long line of boys walking home now. In my fifth form year, I had the study on the corridor that led to the Rector's study. . . . I used to study with the door shut in the evenings because it was quieter and one night everything seemed unusually still. I opened the window and leaned out and there was not a breath of air stirring and the air seemed heavy and bleak. A wind from the west was rising and I could hear it in the distance rustling the trees and whispering far off.

One can say this. There is no doubt that Groton is in many respects a much greater and finer school today than it was some sixty years ago. But one is doubtful whether the boys have as much fun as those first boys did, and one wonders whether, in

82

spite of all the splendid buildings and experienced teachers, they get any better education. Groton was small then and informal; there was an intimacy between boys and masters that has not disappeared, but has changed. There is still the family, and always will be, or Groton will be no longer Groton; but it is a big family now, and it was a small family then.

14

E. P.

WHAT of the man himself? How did this personality seem to those who knew him in daily life at this period?

To begin with, one should emphasize his bigness and his cleancutness. Actually, numerous men have been larger, either in height or bulk, but few of them ever seemed as big. And with the Rector it was all solid, no fat. In the library at Groton there is a cast of Lincoln's hand. One boy used to examine it with considerable care and recollects comparing it unfavorably with the Rector's. One had to be prepared, when he got to know you, to have that hand laid, gently—and jovially—as he thought, on one's shoulder in such fashion as to make one reel from the impact. One got used to it and learned to brace, but it was a shock to the inexperienced. His arms were big, his shoulders broad, his chest thick, his hair very blond, his eyes very blue, clear, and steady.

He had a wonderfully pleasing and impressive voice of unfailing dignity. When raised it boomed; carried far; penetrated, dominated other voices. In ordinary conversation it was melodious and satisfying. When he read one of the great services, as at a wedding or a funeral, his voice was musical and moving. His speech was extremely cultivated, without ever seeming to be consciously so. It was not British, but neither was it ordinary American; it was peculiar to him; full-throated, pleasant, impressive, delightful. When exploding in anger it had in it the feel of heavy artillery.

83

In aspect, he was frequently severe: some of those who knew him well said because he was fundamentally shy and distrustful of himself. When angry, he could be extremely formidable; when moved by pity or love, extremely tender and gentle. He had a large sense of humor, with little phrases and tricks of speech of his own. He was quick to see the ludicrous and incongruous. He has been known to rake a boy from stem to stern and then, when the victim had departed shattered, chuckle heartily over the peccadillo which had occasioned the lecture. Sometimes he had a playful touch. Once a boy traveling on a train from Boston took the hat of a friend of the Rector by mistake. The owner informed the Rector, who bided his time until the boy said good night.

"I want to speak to you, my boy."

His boy, innocent in heart, but oppressed, as the rest of the school filed past with amused or sympathetic glances, by heart searchings and panicky doubts, saw that as the Rector turned to him he had a set chin and grim lips.

"You took a gentleman's hat from the train today."

"Sir, I—"

"Yes, you did. You go look in your locker. It's a brown hat with a feather in it."

Dazed, but comforted by the absurdity of the charge, the boy went to his locker, where to his horror he found a brown hat with a feather in it, just as the Rector had said. Limply he fetched the incriminating thing. To be caught red-handed with a stolen article was dispiriting enough, but what mangled his whole nature was the shocking clairvoyance of this large man, whose powers, in spite of generous imaginative efforts on his part, he had so patently underestimated. The Rector, without a smile, cautioned him against taking property belonging to others, said he would return the brown hat and recover the boy's green one, and dismissed him. Since the boy's name was in his green hat and his seatmate on the train had recognized him for a Groton boy and he was the only Groton boy on the train that day, the whole matter was quite simple; but the Rector's reputation was considerably enhanced. None of the boys thought it was astonishing, really, it was just a new manifestation of his capacity. But such playfulness, wholly delightful to those not involved, often left the victim with the feelings of a terrified baby in the presence of a romping elephant. Yet one never heard

84

him tell a bawdy joke nor anyone attempt to tell him one. And he was frequently exceedingly funny.

The school always claimed his brother, General Francis Peabody, a lawyer and a sportsman from way back, could cause the Rector trouble. The General's vocabulary was picturesque, and he practiced with great pleasure and good health many of the things the Rector preached against. Actually the Rector was very fond of him and he of the Rector, and at times they told one another of their mutual respect and affection. Sometimes they had differing points of view:

February 11, 1905

DEAR ENDICOTT:

I understand that you are doing what you can to dissuade Groton boys from taking rooms in Claverly Hall at Cambridge; indeed I have before me a letter which says that you have advised your boys to go to Randolph rather than to Claverly.

Claverly Hall . . . is the property of a trust, of which I am managing trustee, and which [is] let by us as trustees to Charles Wetmore of New York. I have a very large amount of money invested in this trust, much of it as a trustee. It is undoubtedly within your power to seriously injure the value of these buildings. This I know you would not do unless you had some good reason for thinking it your duty and if there is any well grounded objection to any of these buildings, or the way in which they are run, I ought to know it at once, and correct it. Meanwhile to recommend Randolph rather than Claverly is simply to boom a property which the Coolidges own at the expense of one owned by your family and friends. Will you let me know when you are in town . . . and until we can have an interview why not direct your influence to backing up President Eliot's attitude on the foot-ball question, which I regard as being absolutely right, and worthy of all the support that a man like you can give it?

Your affectionate brother,
FRANCIS *

* Sometimes other relatives could be pert as well:

June 12, 1905

MY DEAR COTTY:

I was sorry to learn that Rose's dog to-gether with a dog belonging to my niece Ruth killed a cat I procured for John six years ago. He was very handsome, good tempered and an excellent ratter. I have never seen him a hundred yards from the house. I do not know which dog was the ringleader, but Ruth's is quite young and Rose herself told me last year that hers was given to this despicable habit. I am surprised, because in England dogs are far better

85

Both the Rector and Mrs. Peabody have always loved to ride and rode very well. No one could ever say how or why it was, but every Grotonian will swear, as a matter of personal observation, that every horse the Rector ever owned invariably came with a nice straight back, and, after the Rector had ridden him a few times, invariably sagged badly in the middle. He used a bicycle even oftener than a horse, and in later years used a motor car often. There is a story that he was driving along a dark road one night when a man stepped out of the bushes and tried to hold him up. The Rector stepped on the gas and aimed for the man, who just managed to get out of the way. The Rector drove on.

In his dress he was always immaculate. He ordinarily wore either a blue or a gray suit with a low, starched collar and a plain white bow tie with the ends tucked in. Sometimes he donned a tweed suit, knickerbockers, wool stockings, and a soft shirt, but he was always neatly groomed and good to look at.

He had a very characteristic walk. Although his back was as straight as a die and when he stood or preached he seemed remarkably erect and in balance, when he walked he appeared to lean a little forward and moved with a kind of heavy, springy lightness, with a little give in the knees. There was a peculiar solid quality to his footfall; once learned, one could recognize it anywhere. He never seemed to move rapidly; it was a more deliberate and majestic procedure, a very substantial affair with a destination.

A favorite saying of his, quoted from President Eliot, was that a headmaster, like a college president, needs to have the capacity to inflict pain. He also often said that a headmaster "has to be a bit of a bully."

And yet, counterbalancing this, he had a definite strain of mysticism in him. When he gave Communion, for instance, he was oblivious to all personalities. He was lost in his duty as a

trained, and more intelligently cared for than in our own country. Also, there, a cat is *legal property* just as much as a sheep.

I would suggest that this dog be muzzled, if not, kept in leash when taken on the road. If all else fails I think it your duty to have him chloroformed. I would be only too glad to do it for you at a day's notice, any time.

Very sincerely yours,
R. Ashton Lawrence

86

priest and as humble servant of those who came to the Lord's Table. When he heard of sad tidings or something evil or harmful, he shook his head and pursed his lips in deep-seated disapproval. Graduates have seen tears gather in his eyes at a play which touched him and have heard him speak comfort to one in grief in such a way that even grief seemed healed.

It always amazed his intimates how he got his work done. He was up by six o'clock, often earlier, and had done a considerable bit of work by the time the rest of the school rose. At seven o'clock there were family prayers in his study. Then breakfast, followed by a visit to the infirmary and to the Chapel by eight o'clock. Chapel came at 8:15; then to the Schoolhouse for opening of morning school. He worked in his office there, except for classes which he had to teach and except for joining the school in calisthenics at recess, until lunch time. Then a brief word with the senior prefect and, by way of the filled Hundred House schoolroom, where he might sit quietly while the senior prefect read his notices, on to the school dining room. If there was a roast, he carved. Generally he had to wait, a little impatiently, for Mrs. Peabody to finish. In fifty-six years she failed to speed up an iota, which, the school felt, irritated him and won his admiration. Finally he would ring the bell with a single punishing blow. After lunch there was faculty coffee in his study for the men; in the "boudoir" for the ladies. He made a point of taking a short rest after lunch, then exercise for at least an hour. After changing, he went to his study again and worked until supper, while Mrs. Peabody served tea in the boudoir or sitting room. Supper came at 6:05. Then, usually, prayers and back to the study again until 8:45 when the little boys went to bed. He might attend "Faculty Supper" with masters, visitors, or boys if it was being served, but he usually went up to bed by 9:30.

This schedule cannot be accurately judged on a time basis. A headmaster's day is seldom marked by monotony. There are masters and boys to consult, cajole, admonish, and direct. There is an infirmary list and there are marks. There are letters from parents which praise, complain, suggest, or seek for information. Boys have diseases, injuries; they break things and lose things. There are sermons to write, papers to correct, and the desirability of being aware of what is going on in the world.

The Rector had an unusual capacity for shifting rapidly from

87

one thing to another entirely different. Nature provided him with the gift of decision. He has said,

It used to bother me when I made mistakes and I wasted a lot of time fretting. Now I have learned that if one does the best he can in the light of all his available knowledge and judgment then that is all he can do or could have done and there is no use grieving about it. I do the best I can under the circumstances and go on to something else. One thing at a time, that is the great point.

His correspondence was prodigious, and he attended to it systematically. For at least the first twenty years of the school he did it all longhand. When it was necessary to make a copy, he made it. As a result, while the records contain all the letters to him in this period, there are very few from him. It wearies one just to think of the labor he has expended on letters. In such matters as in all things he believed in system and was uneasy when it was lacking.

But if he worked hard nine months a year, he played hard the rest of the time. His travels were many. After 1894 he went abroad, principally to England, on the average of every other year. In the summer, if he did not go abroad, he usually went to his summer place at North Haven, Maine. Three times, in 1894-95, 1904-05, and 1910-11, he took a whole year off and went abroad, leaving the school in charge of Mr. Billings. In the shorter vacations he often went south with Mrs. Peabody for a change.

He had little interest or use for the arts. Basically he distrusted artists as a genus. Something Puritan in him told him that, in spite of his love for them often as individuals, they were a folk who have unreliable relationships with the world, the flesh, and the devil, with a consequent weakening of moral fiber. At best, he felt, artists are interpreters, and while interpretation is well enough in its way, it is not on a plane with genuine accomplishment. It is better for a man, he felt, to be part of his time than to be a spectator of it.

Two things were said of Peabody which have truth in them. One, after Tennyson's description of Galahad: "His strength is as the strength of ten because his heart is pure." The other was the friendly dictum of Bishop Atwood that "Peabody is the last of the Puritans."

88

15

THE ALMIGHTY WALL

I T IS important to know how the Rector built "the almighty wall" and what Thring called "the machinery"; that is, how he turned an unknown new school into a widely known, magnificently equipped plant and what his methods were of running it.

He began in '84 with a single building designed for the purpose for which it was used. Thereafter, for the next twenty years, he devoted an enormous amount of time and energy to raising funds for more buildings and making them good ones. Peabody and Stearns were the architects for almost all construction except the Chapel, which was done by Henry Vaughan. Also except for the Chapel, an early commitment was made to a simple style in red brick with white trim. This has never been departed from on the campus except in the one case.

Peabody was aided and encouraged by Amory Gardner, who was a rich man with knowledge of art, architecture, and literature, who again and again put a hand deep into a capacious pocket for the sake of the school. It was he who gave, in memory of Joseph Peabody Gardner, both the first and second chapels; the first, a simple but attractive structure of rough plaster and timber finish. It is interesting that when the new chapel rose this old one, which meant so much to the early boys, was offered by the Rector, with the approval of the Trustees and Mr. Gardner, to the Roman Catholics in the village, who had no church. It was moved to the town of Groton and still stands there in good use.

The first companion to Brooks House was the original small gymnasium built in 1886. The building was given by Mr. Augustus Hemenway, who subsequently also gave tennis courts and the boathouse on the river. Next came the first fives courts, in 1890, then plans for the great expansion represented by Hundred House, so called because it was designed to accommodate one hundred boys, or more than twice as many as Brooks House.

89

It also included the Headmaster's House, the school dining room and kitchen, study halls, and infirmary. Most of the money for this large undertaking (for Hundred House is a very big building) was obtained by offering each donor of $5000 the privilege of nominating a boy for the school. While this fund-raising device was successful, it was the only method concerning which the Rector subsequently had regrets, since there was misunderstanding later with some contributors as to just what was meant by the nominating privilege. At any rate, the building was completed, a little late, in 1891, and all boys moved in there. Brooks House was temporarily used entirely for classes, with Mr. B. moving into the first Peabody quarters. Mr. G. had meanwhile built a large house for himself and a small one for the school secretary, Mr. Jefferson. When the latter burned down, not long after, the Trustees, as Mr. G. explained, "voted condolences to him and a check to Mr. Jefferson."

About ten years later, in 1900, came another great building period. Prior to that a memorial gift by Frank Thomson, a graduate, made possible the library with a large endowment fund for it; a laundry was also constructed. Then came real enlargement. First, land with a house on it near the Chapel site was bought. New stables and a heating plant were constructed and another master's house for Mr. Sturgis. The fives courts were enlarged. Finally, on Ascension Day, 1900, ground was broken for the wonderful new chapel which is one of the most beautiful ecclesiastical structures in America.

There was considerable dispute, of course, as to the style of architecture to be used. Strong opinion favored either brick or "the New England meeting house," but the final decision was for Gothic. It was a good decision, for although the Chapel differed from the other buildings, perhaps a chapel should differ, and this chapel dominates not only the entire school grounds but the whole countryside. It is the first thing a boy sees as he comes to the school; the last as he leaves. It reaches at heaven, but it is substantial, simple, and spacious on the earth. In the tower is a full set of bells, which chime the quarter hours, and on Sunday boys and masters ring old rounds such as have come from church bells since time immemorial. The bells also ring often when a graduate is married and toll when a Grotonian is laid to rest. Some of the glass, which is done by Tower and

Kemp * is unusually good. And already along the walls are growing long lines of simple and dignified memorial tablets.

The next building was another very large structure, the Schoolhouse, which was also completed in 1900. It contains a huge schoolroom with a desk for every boy in school; an office for the Rector and his clerical and financial assistants, a faculty room, and a recitation room for nearly every master. The remarkable set of autographs of famous men on the corridor walls should also be mentioned. The most unusual feature of this is a collection of letters from every President of the United States. Again, later on, a complete printing press on which almost all the school printing was done, much of it by the boys, and a manual training shop were installed in the basement.

In 1902 came the final additions to all this program with the erection of a large new Gymnasium and what the Rector called the Cottage Infirmary, but everyone else knew as the Pest House.†

* Except for a single window by Clayton and Bell. All the artists were English.

† Something should be said of Groton architecture in general, since it was one manifestation of Endicott Peabody. Brooks House, the original model, was good, in the Kentish manor house style. Hundred House departed somewhat toward elaboration, especially in the neoclassical porticos, but on the whole kept the pattern. Both buildings, however, were covered inside with "a frightful yellow varnish" (also known as "Harlem oak" or "kitchen style") for years, and the heating and ventilation were not beyond reproach. The fives courts kept the pattern again. The Schoolhouse was an improvement in the interior over previous buildings. President W. A. Neilson is reported to have remarked that it ought to be as completely hidden by trees as possible. The Gymnasium was a peculiar development, some said an atrocity. Level ground was mounded up and a cellar put largely above the mound. Critics felt it was too near the Chapel. It was a square block "like an old style high school in a city. How W. A. G. did dislike that building!" Later additions to the plant were in good taste and yellow interiors eventually gave way to less jaundiced tones.

It is worth noting in this connection that American architecture (at its worst in 1875) was only just beginning to improve in 1884, but that it had gone a long way by 1900. Yet the best exterior at Groton (except for the Chapel) was built in 1884. The fact is that the Groton authorities were not art-conscious until very recent times. It is interesting to compare Groton building done between 1885-1900 with the Bryn Mawr construction finished in the same period. (This paragraph and the preceding one are paraphrases of comments made by a former master. They represent a point of view. In contrast is the larger opinion that the Groton buildings are dignified, in good, if not noticeable, taste, and usable. It is certainly true that the buildings taken to-

Of course all this meant untold work on the Rector's part. Mr. Gardner gave the Chapel, but almost all the rest of the money was raised laboriously by Peabody, through many trips to and meetings in New York or Boston and long correspondence. In the first twenty years of the school he received gifts amounting to more than $700,000. It may be that the most welcome of all was an anonymous one of $90,000 which enabled Groton to pay off all its debts. Peabody was also helped several times at critical points by his father, who generously loaned money.

Inside, the arrangement of the buildings was almost Spartan.* The predominating color was a brown stain or a varnished finish which was durable but in no sense sybaritic. Since the school has always been small, classes (and therefore classrooms) were also small. When the school more than doubled in size there were just more divisions, not larger ones. Of one thing the Rector made sure, that in each building there was a room large enough to take comfortably all the boys who might use that building at once. The Hundred House schoolroom, while much smaller than that in the Schoolhouse, had benches as well as desks and could accommodate the whole school and faculty for evening prayers or any other gathering. The general scheme was that all boys below the fifth form studied in one of the main schoolrooms under supervision of a master, except in later years in Brooks House, where the fourth form boys were elected to act as proctors. Fifth- and sixth-formers had either double or single studies. A study varied from a narrow, but longish, affair just about large enough to take a desk, desk chair, and a window seat to a considerably larger one able to take two desks, two chairs, and a window seat. No banners or pennants were encouraged and no tacks could be driven into the wall. No large, comfortable chairs were allowed.

All boys, in whatever form, slept in cubicles except for the senior and at times the junior prefect. A cubicle was a narrow alcove, about six feet wide and nine or ten feet deep, opening on

gether have a "feel" which is peculiar to the place. It is distinct from any other the author knows and greatly superior to most school plants. One comment was that the buildings as a whole are remarkably "undated.")

* No discussion of Peabody's buildings would be valid which did not emphasize this. He built solidly and enduringly, but always simply and in a certain sense, functionally. There is not a single room in Groton School which could be called fancy or luxurious.

92

a broad corridor. The walls of each cubicle were about seven feet high, above which there was vacant space to a tall ceiling. There was no door to a cubicle, but a cloth curtain could be pulled entirely across the opening giving a considerable degree of privacy. In the cubicle was a bed, a bureau, a chair, and a small rug. Suits were hung on hooks on the cubicle wall. No pictures were allowed on the wall, but family photographs were welcomed on the bureaus. Usually there were from twenty to twenty-five boys in each dormitory, with a bachelor master in charge. The dormitory was a very important social unit, and a good dormitory master was of great value to the school and to individual boys. He was assisted by two or three dormitory prefects, sixth-formers who had complete authority in his absence and who helped him in dormitory administration. Some of the closest and best of friendships were formed between such prefects and masters. Every evening after the period the boys would go to the master's study, where he would read to them before putting them to bed or where all would sit around and talk, read, or listen to a phonograph.

Attached to each dormitory was a lavatory, with showers (a cold one was required of every boy every morning), black soapstone sinks, and tin basins for washing. For every three or four boys there was a single cold water tap which had to be held open if it was to function.

Mr. and Mrs. Peabody presided over Hundred House (you had only to push a door to enter their house from the sixth form corridor) and Mr. B. over Brooks House. But houses never mattered much. The dormitory was the unit. All first and second formers started in Hundred House in the "kid dorms." The upper four forms were distributed between Brooks and Hundred House, most boys spending at least two years in Brooks House.

Most of these habits developed slowly, because, although Hundred House much more than doubled the school's capacity, the Rector was very careful to increase his numbers slowly.*

*The following table from the Trustees' records of the number of boys enrolled shows how gradual the growth was:

1885	27	1893	102	1899	138
1886	46	1896	110	1900	150
1890	50	1897	115	1905	158
1891	60	1898	127	1910	160
1892	85				

Everyone ate in Hundred House after it was completed. The Rector and Mrs. Peabody presided over the raised Head Table seating twelve to fourteen, in company with the prefects and visitors. The rest of the school ate at long tables seating nine or ten on a side, with a master or prefect at each end. If the master was married, his wife sat beside him. The new boys always started at Mr. Billings' table. Table seating, like dormitory assignments, were for the most part on a form basis. After about 1902, once a week each boy moved one place, but he kept the same boys on each side of him. Only the face across the table changed.

In the halls of the houses were long rows of coat lockers in which all overcoats and heavy garments were kept. In the basement each boy had a wooden shoe locker in which he kept all footgear except athletic equipment, all of which went into another locker in the gymnasium. Evening shoes or pumps had to be worn every evening.

So much for the Almighty Wall. The machinery was also simple, but sometimes subtle. The Rector had a great eye for detail, he was relentless in demanding that it be well done, and he had a great faith in the importance of little things. He knew a boy's love of color and insignia. At first the school colors were those of Cheltenham, blue and white, but when at the first St. Mark's game it was realized that St. Mark's had long since been using those colors, Groton adopted the effective red, white, and black. These colors were used in different arrangements to denote particular things. For instance equal horizontal stripes of red, white, and black were the regular school colors on a hatband or necktie. On the other hand broad red, narrow white, broad black was football; broad red, narrow white and black was crew; broad red, narrow white, black, white and broad red again were baseball. He took great pains to get a satisfactory coat-of-arms. The one finally chosen (after a preliminary one had been discarded) was designed by Ralph Adams Cram and was extremely effective. The motto *Cui servire est regnare* was suggested in 1893 by a sermon of Bishop Hall. A striking football jersey of alternating broadish black and white stripes gave Groton teams a distinctive appearance on any field, and, incidentally, made the team look bigger. The Rector could never bear to see the school or a boy anything but shipshape.*

Things ran by bells; boys got up by bells, went to breakfast by bells, went to classes by bells, finished school by bells, lunched by them, came in from play by them, supped by them, and then answered their summons to study, prayers, and bed. The Schoolhouse bell is a great one with a marvelous deep clanging that somehow sounds like Groton to those who have known it.

One had to be on time. Chronic lateness meant seeing the Rector in person and it was simpler to be on time. On Sunday all had to wear blue suits all day long, and stiff collars. The latter were also required every evening for supper. There is an account of a Groton day written by Mr. Billings for the *Churchman* at the turn of the century.

Perhaps the most noticeable feature of the life at Groton is that it is very busy. One often hears a boy say that he can't seem to find time to do anything like all he wants to do, that there is so much going on that he can't get a chance to squeeze in the particular

* Excerpt from letter written in January, 1944, by Thomas Robins, Jr.:

"I think the Rector was always satisfied that the rules and traditions of the School were so clearly drawn that a violation was quite readily determinable. The only exception that I can recall related to my brother Davis and C. V. Whitney, both '17. I think it was during their fourth form year that they decided to build a four-wheel buckboard-like contrivance, with motive power, consisting of an airplane propellor driven by a small discarded outboard motor. As I recall it, the Rector knew of the construction of the machine, but was quite confident that it would not work.

"The strange device was finally brought up from the School House Cellar Workshop and, after considerable cranking, moved off at a surprisingly high rate of speed.

"In those days no one even thought of the automobile problem and there were therefore no rules prohibiting them. However, there were strict rules against anyone except sixth formers having bicycles. The question confronting the Rector was, was the Robins-Whitney machine a bicycle? The four wheels were, in fact, taken from bicycles, and moreover, from a disciplinary standpoint, it was far more mobile than any bicycle. In fact, it would do about thirty miles an hour. I was a sixth former at the time and a prefect, and I recall distinctly all of us felt sure the Rector would forbid the use of the contraption. I recall further that the entire school was very agreeably surprised when he ruled that it was not a bicycle, and allowed the owners to operate the machine until they grew tired of it. I believe his reasoning was eminently fair. The machine was not strictly a bicycle, and the ingenuity of the owners entitled them to the most favorable ruling possible under the circumstances."

thing he has set out to do. . . . The day follows a fairly hard and fast plan the year through—School begins at twenty-five minutes past eight—the work at morning school comprises four periods of fifty minutes each. There is for every recitation, unless it be at sight, a specified preparation in which the Form is to study the lesson. . . . At twelve o'clock school is over and the long recess begins. After dinner comes one of what might be called the quiet times of the day—but this does not last long, for in a little more than an half an hour the bell rings for afternoon school, which consists of two forty-five minute periods.* During the recess that follows, before supper, the whole school in two divisions do gymnastics [and other athletics].

Things had to be done just so. After a seven-thirty breakfast, except on Sunday, morning chapel came at 8:15. The daily service consisted of a hymn, a lesson or psalm or reading, and several prayers. The school went directly from the Chapel to the big room in the Schoolhouse. There, when everybody was seated, the Rector came in and read out the list of first classes from the desk. At the end of school, with all assembled, he read out notices and the Detention list and expressed animadversions or satisfactions on school or other matters. Lunch and supper began with Grace, everybody standing until the Rector had said it.† He had mannerisms of speech; never affectations, just mannerisms. For instance, if a boy got into Detention too often he was apt to find his name peculiarly emphasized each day it appeared, as W. W.—pronounced *Double-you, Double-you*, very slowly and clearly, to the edification of the school. Or in saying Grace there was a solid emphasis on the Amen (the Grace never varied) that discouraged any undue haste to be seated and have at food.

Every night the Rector and Mrs. Peabody said good night and shook hands with every boy in the school. If evening prayers came right after supper, boys went straight from the dining room into the Hundred House schoolroom, where the Rector read a short passage from the New Testament, then all knelt at their desks or benches for the Lord's Prayer and two or three collects, frequently the one which runs, "Lighten our darkness

* Not long after this the two afternoon periods were moved into the morning, but Detention came after lunch for scholastic delinquents and five times a week there was a forty-five-minute afternoon study period.

† Mr. Ayrault said grace at breakfast and was in charge.

96

we beseech thee O! Lord and by thy great mercy defend us from all perils and dangers of this night." Then the Brooks House boys would file by. After the evening period the Rector and Mrs. Peabody would emerge again and say good night to the boys in Hundred House. Now and again he would say to an apprehensive youth, "I want to speak to you for a moment, my boy." It might be a dirty collar that he wanted to speak about, or a message from home, or a warning that one's work was not what it should be, but it always tended to put the listener in a thoughtful frame of mind.

The frequent insistence of Bishop Atwood that the Rector was fundamentally humble and self-distrustful would have seemed to any Groton boy the wildest babbling, verging on flat untruthfulness.* If ever the Lord created a human being who always knew his own mind, relied on its findings, and was able to make them perfectly clear and explicit, his pupils were sure, it was Endicott Peabody.

The two basic "soaks" at Groton were the lateness and the blackmark. The latter was given (a euphemistic phrase) by either masters or prefects. The maximum, by unwritten law, which could be given at any one time was six. If a boy had six, either at one gulp or in installments, he automatically went to see the Rector "in my study." Lesser amounts, and latenesses, were worked off in divers ways. That was a deterrent and a nuisance, but nobody, however much he admired the Rector, ever wanted to hear him discourse on too many blackmarks. Even if one had not received them one's self, it was still unpleasant and very, very definite.

There was never any fagging. It was one thing in his English experience of which the Rector never approved and which he never tolerated. The sixth form were an exalted folk; in many respects they had, in dealing with the rest of the school, disciplinary powers equal to those of masters. It was customary to address them by their last names. Undue familiarity or "freshness" of any sort was speedily discouraged, but let a sixth-former attempt bullying or unreasonable familiarity with a younger boy and he would feel the full blast of the Rector's displeasure.

* Yet in 1944, writing to a friend of an article which had been published about himself, Peabody said: "I agree with practically everything the author has to say about my personal qualities. I have always counted myself a second class man—physically, intellectually, and spiritually."

The prefect system was a very important part of the Groton scheme. The prefects, somewhere from three to seven or eight of them, were chosen by the Rector during the summer or at the end of a year after the faculty, the outgoing, and the incoming sixth had voted. The highest honor and most responsible position in the school was that of senior prefect. He lived in state, with a huge study and bedroom adjoining. He saw the Rector daily and was the instrument through which many policies and desires were carried out. Scarcely less important was the junior, or Brooks House, prefect, who was vice for the senior prefect and Mr. B.'s right hand man in Brooks House.

There has been a good deal of criticism of the prefect system as being un-American and not in line with representative government. But this overlooks the fact that it is not an elective system nor a legislative one. Legislation is reserved for the faculty, whose responsibility it is to train boys and who presumably are better able to decide what is expedient and just than the boys themselves. The prefects are an administrative body, working with the headmaster, guided by him, and given the authority and responsibility to carry out his policies. They are appointed by him and are responsible to him. The same theory applies to the dormitory prefectships, in which the sixth-former is an administrative assistant, working with his dormitory master, taking responsibility, but not making rules or dealing with parents. It is an invaluable type of experience. The appointees are not necessarily the most popular boys, and their duties in office frequently require them to undergo considerable critical unpopularity.

In some respects, at least, Groton was a most democratic institution. The life was in some ways almost monastic. The only basis for reward of any sort was performance. Differences in dress, little distinctions of wealth and background were not encouraged or allowed. Once a person was accepted, he belonged, and questions of wealth or class did not arise because everyone was in exactly the same class, the brotherhood of the school. If he did not "belong," did not measure up to the unwritten standards of that brotherhood, he did not remain long at Groton. Yet it is extraordinary and true that the number of boys who were expelled, sent away in the middle of a year, is surprisingly small. Given a trial and failing, they might be asked not to come back

98

another year, but expulsion was almost as rare as in English schools.

The Rector's belief in smallness when it could be translated into quality has already been emphasized. He proceeded on the theory that a law of diminishing returns operates in schools as in other things. He brought this theory to bear in many ways. He wanted a six-year school, because in a small school with classes, or forms, more or less evenly distributed, a six-year distribution meant smaller units with which to deal scholastically and socially. A graduating class usually ran from twenty to thirty.

Here again Groton was criticized for being exclusive, with the connotation that its exclusiveness was pure snobbery. Much was made of the fact that a boy had to be entered practically at birth if he was to be sure of a place. The fact was so; for instance in 1908 the Rector wrote a parent who wanted to enter a boy for 1920 that there were already more than a hundred names down for the latter year and the chances of his having a place were small. However, the reason that it was so was that the school was small and from the very beginning it had been established policy to take names in order from the list, provided the applicants could satisfy the entrance requirements. A moment's thought will show that this was just the opposite of an undemocratic procedure in one sense. The reason for the exclusiveness was that there wasn't any more room. As time went on an increasing number of graduates' sons brought a danger that the school might be ingrowing. Further, the Rector and trustees were aware of the desirability of providing for able and promising boys who were entered so late that they would have no chance on the list.*

* In 1907 a committee of trustees, appointed the previous year to consider the whole question, presented a report recommending changes "in the method of admitting boys to the school in order to secure a higher average of scholarship and a more representative membership." The committee urged "that in 1908 eight places, and in 1909 and thereafter fourteen places, be reserved each year to be competed for by any boy with proper recommendations, if he be under fourteen years of age, whether already on the application list or not. Four of these places each year should be reserved for boys born or residing south of the Potomac River or in Chicago or farther west. The competition should depend partly upon written examination in suitable subjects, partly upon a physician's report . . . and partly upon a recommendation of character from the candidate's former teacher. The fourteen boys receiving the highest ratings should be admitted . . . the remaining places each year should be

· The Rector often considered the possibility of having the boys keep their rooms and wait on table, but they never did in his time. His feeling was that if it were necessary financially to enable the school to reduce its tuition, work by the boys would be justified. Otherwise the time taken must come from other things more valuable. Most Groton boys never would have to make beds, but if they did have to they could do it without six years' practice. As the Rector surveyed graduates of schools who had made beds and graduates of schools who had not made beds he could not see any advantage either way so far as character, ability to cope with the world, or intelligence were concerned, and therefore he was not much interested.

Athletics always formed a keystone in the school structure, but a keystone strictly subordinated to and welded into the whole. To begin with, as indicated, he was an unusually healthy and powerful man himself, always in splendid physical condition and respecting strength and vigor in others. He saw in games not only a means of developing a boy's whole being—*mens sana in corpore sano;* he also believed that boys occupied were less likely to get into trouble than boys unoccupied. He may have venerated cricket with its handsome code of gentlemanly sportsmanship, but his favorite game was always football. He crusaded against what he considered abuses in football; professional coaches, dirty play, and so on. But football he privately admired because it is a game that is rough and hard, requiring courage, endurance, and discipline. Instinctively he trusted a football player more than a non-football-player, just as the boys did. He liked to win and hated to lose, but he would not stand for poor

---

filled, as heretofore, from the application list in order of the receipt of applications, with the provision that until action to the contrary is taken sons of graduates entered on the list within one year of their birth should have preference over all others on the list. . . . In recommending the foregoing . . . the committee have been careful to follow the established policy of the trustees that there should be no arbitrary, personal selection of boys." These recommendations were immediately adopted.

At the same time the Trustees voted that the charge for tuition, board, and washing should be increased to $850 a year. A number of years later-this was increased again to $1200 and eventually, much later, to $1400, which was the fee at the time of the Rector's retirement.

A better than average performance was always thereafter expected of those boys who entered under the competitive scheme described above, whether or not they actually received scholarships.

sportsmanship during or after a game. If there was any sign of it by a Groton team, he went on a rampage. If he saw evidence of it in an opposing team he took up the matter promptly with the school involved. He expected Groton boys to play hard and fair, and it is no chance matter that football has always been the Groton game *par excellence*. Fortune favored him in giving him an extraordinary coach in Guy Ayrault, who years before Percy Haughton at Harvard or Knute Rockne at Notre Dame was plotting strategy and tactics which later became standardized. But the coach was always the servant of the players, and for many years the captains ran the Groton–St. Mark's games with no interference from the coaches.

Nor was the Rector's interest limited to football. Every boy in school had to take regular daily exercise. At one time in a single year three major sport captains at Harvard were Groton boys: Dibblee of football, Haughton of baseball, and Higginson of crew. Groton baseball, in spite of excellent individual players, was not as good as Groton football. This may have been partly because it always ran concurrently with crew. Groton has produced many great oars, and of this the Rector, who coached many years himself, heartily approved. In addition there has always been fives (a kind of squash, but played with a small first baseman's mitt on each hand, with a small leather-covered hard ball, in either a double or single hard-walled and hard-floored court). Boxing, wrestling, and fencing have always gone on, with intramural basketball and track. The way of the non-athlete at Groton was not so much hard as inconsequential.

He also encouraged such activities as the *Grotonian*, the school paper, and debating, which is required of every boy. The *Grotonian* after the early years was not only written but printed by the boys. There were two debating societies, the senior and junior, which were in turn divided into Ciceros and Demosthenes. No fraternities were ever allowed to exist publicly. For many years there was an annual play, and the choir always was an important institution.*

Boys were also exhorted to partake in spiritual and charitable activities. The Missionary Society, in addition to supporting worthy projects by cash contributions, sent older boys to conduct "missions" and Sunday school classes in near-by villages.

* Cf. George Rublee's recollection of the first choir: "the only instruction was to aim at the tune and sing out loud."

In 1893 Groton established the Groton School Camp on Squam Lake to provide two weeks' camping for poor boys from Boston and near-by parishes, several contingents coming each summer. The Rector took great interest in this venture, which has been continued ever since, and often spent part of his own vacation there. So far as the author knows this was, except for the Balch Camp, the first charity camp in America, and it has done great good, not only to the campers, but in the opinion of many, to the Groton boys who staff it.

Studies, of course, were central, subordinate only to Chapel. A boy had to pass examinations to enter the school and had to keep on passing them to stay in it. A really poor scholar was given a fair trial, but if he could not or would not make the grade, he simply did not stay at Groton.

The early curriculum was predominantly classical. Latin was taught in all forms and required (it still is) of every boy, and Greek in the upper four. French was taught clear through and German for four years as an optional course. Two years were devoted to Greek history, one to Roman, two to English, and one to American. English was taught in all forms, consisting mainly in grammar and composition. There were two years of arithmetic, two and a half of algebra, about one of plane geometry, and the sixth form course went through algebra, trigonometry, and solid geometry. The only sciences were two years of geography and an optional one of physics. In sacred studies the lower school studied the Collects, the Catechism, and the Old Testament; the upper school spent three years on the New Testament in Greek.*

The value of hard work and good performance was held absolute; that of particular courses, of educational trends, of child-motivation was relative. If a boy learned to work hard, think clearly, know fundamentals, and to be disciplined in body,

* By 1910 this had changed somewhat. English embraced much more reading. Latin remained the same. Greek was the same in quantity, but optional, and a boy might choose between it and advanced mathematics, physics, and chemistry. Greek history had been increased by half a year; Rome and England reduced to one year, but Western Europe given a year. The United States had to be contented with a half-year course. French was taught only through the fourth form, and German for the last two years. There was no geography, biology, physiology, drawing, manual training, or music, except for the choir. Sacred studies continued. But see later chapters for further curricular developments.

mind, and soul, he would presumably be an educated person and able to hold his place in the world.

One must not forget the Rector's emphasis on the little things; on manners, on minor morals, on appearance, on conformity, on using little things that were good and striking. The best instance of this is perhaps the School Hymn, acquisition of which is in a way typical of both the Rector's good luck and perspicacity. In 1887 Mrs. Peabody asked Phillips Brooks, who besides being a great preacher was, in a certain strain (*O! Little Town of Bethlehem*), a remarkable minor poet, to write a hymn for the school. The result was incomparably the finest of all school hymns. The words were sung to music written by George Peabody, a great-uncle of the Rector and Mrs. Peabody. This chapter cannot be ended better than by quoting the words which are, in a sense, the charter of Groton School:

Father of all, below, above
Whose name is light, whose name is love;
Here be Thy Truth and Goodness known
And make these fields and halls Thine own.

Thy temple gates stand open wide.
O! Christ we enter at Thy side,
With Thee to consecrate our powers
And make our Father's business ours.

For days of drought which yet shall be
On untrod land, on unsailed sea
We kneel and fill our cup of youth
At these fair fountains of Thy truth.

O! world all bright and brave and young
With deeds unwrought and songs unsung,
For all the strength Thy tasks will give
We greet Thee, we about to live.

Father, Thy children bless the care
Which sheds Thy sunlight everywhere,
Shine on our School and let us be
Teachers and scholars taught by Thee.

16

PERSONAL LETTERS, 1884-1896

E. P. *aet.* 26-38

PEABODY hurled himself into the founding and building up of Groton with such vigor, that caution is necessary lest in appreciating what he did we lose sight of what he was. He was bound up in his teaching-ministry, and to the outward eye this was his activity, untroubled by introspection or domestic fret. Yet it must be remembered that during these early Groton years he was a young man, with a young wife, with children enlarging the family circle, with all the emotions, enthusiasms, and doubts that young men commonly have, and numerous desires, yearnings, and modesties peculiar to himself.

It is in his personal, unofficial correspondence that these things are best seen; his keen satisfaction and relaxation in getting back to England again during the holidays; his joy and content in his children and family life; his constant care and thankfulness for Fanny; his discontent with his own ability to live up to his own spiritual standards; his quiet humility, as in declining a degree which he felt he had not yet merited. It will be well to turn to this inner life of his before proceeding further with his more official development.

February 19, 1884

You have doubtless heard of the sad event which called me to New York. Theodore Roosevelt, who married a cousin of mine, Miss Lee . . . on Tuesday was summoned from Albany to see his little baby just born. When he arrived in New York he found both his wife and mother dying and in a few hours they both passed away. Wife and mother in one day! One can imagine nothing more dreadful. I went on at once to see the poor chap and found him wonderfully calm. I never saw such strength in my life and all based on the sure faith of the Resurrection and being reunited once more and then forever. It taught me a lesson which I shall never forget.*

* The letters in this chapter are from the Atwood correspondence.

June 5, 1884

I hope you know that my friendship for you is v. true and v. strong. I am superficial and I fear somewhat cold, but I have always clung to my friends even after years have separated me from them. . . .

The address on Decoration Day went off fairly well. There were sundry squalling infants in the hall which dampened my ardor.

England, 1887

We stopped at Winchester and went over the School and cathedral there. The quadrangles with their quiet restfulness, the beautiful foliage of the trees and the thick velvety lawns were most refreshing after the boisterous ocean. I regretted, not for the first time, that I had not gone to such a school. It is a more interesting and morally a more healthy place than Cheltenham, but still I daresay it was all for the best. I might not have been as impressionable at Cambridge if I had been a better fellow and under better circumstances at school. . . . We went down to the great Naval Review which was not very exciting, but it was interesting to see the cause and support of England's greatness. The vessels were not beautiful, but terrible in aspect.

1887

It is terrible indeed to stand by the bed of suffering, unable to relieve the pain of the sick or help those who stand by in anguish. One does feel helpless and weak. But it is something both to the sufferer and to the sorrowing to know that one's heart goes out to them and just as the spiritual is more than the physical, so the love and sympathy are of deeper value than anything else can be.

Jan., 20. 1888

Many thanks for the photo wh. you sent me and wh. we all consider very good. . . . The check also was acceptable, not equally with the photo, but still worthy of mention. . . . I feel very strongly indeed what you say about the need of a more personal and more trusting faith. It is the great want of my life. . . . It is a great comfort to me to feel that God has called me to the work wh. I have undertaken and to know that he is behind all the good that is done in the world and will keep it all alive, but what I want to experience is the constant presence of Xt. and the purification of character which that consciousness would bring. If we could only have that how patient and how noble our lives would be and how much influence we would exert for good on those around us. My religious feeling is spasmodic and dependent on occasions, I fear. At times I seem to get a glimpse of the Beatific Vision and then all is earthly and my thoughts as selfish as ever. I was much struck in reading a part of Arnold's life the other day with the reality of his religion. It was implanted in his life and he seemed always to be conscious of it. And then he effected such a vast amount! My own hands seem feeble indeed with such a giant's.

April 6, 1888

I should by all means go to Philadelphia . . . but you must be very careful not to be intense with the young lady.

June 7, 1888

Isn't it a strange thing that the Mother is brought so near to death in order to give a new life to the world? If we could only trust God's love for all these mysteries and fear and hate sin alone we should be stronger and more useful men in this world. . . . It is the sense of being far away from God which is the font of all our unhappiness. Thirty-one years of almost unclouded happiness have passed over me and yet they have not given me the strength of character and the love for my fellow men that they ought to have done. Simply because I have been so selfish and so sinful. One expects the years in some inexplicable, mysterious way to bring peace and righteousness and one finds oneself little better as they go by. In one sense one is further off from heaven than when he was a boy and yet one does have a more confident faith that God will forgive the failings and blunders and sins of his life and make him able to do some good in the world in spite of them.

June 13, 1888 *

Fannie, with that beautiful spirit of hers which finds good in everything, says that even if the little one does not have both eyes he may see more beauty in the world than others do with two. And we must certainly believe that God has some lesson for us in this experience.

May 31, 1889

Very many thanks, my dear old chap, for your welcome letter, which I found this evening on my desk. The years roll by with astonishing rapidity and find one little better as the anniversaries arrive. That is the most discouraging part. Blessings have been showered upon me, more and greater than I ever expected and far greater than I have deserved and my life has been and is full of happiness and yet that real gain in spiritual and intellectual life which one has always thought that time would bring in some mysterious way

* When there was fear that the first baby might lose one eye.

seems as far off as ever. It is a very real happiness for which I am profoundly thankful to know that you think I have helped you. . . . To you I am indebted for much in my own life and career which could not otherwise have come. For you first suggested to me that I had certain powers which I had never recognized and in regard to the existence of which I am still skeptical and yet I have acted on the assumption that you might be right and have gone on and done the little that I have accomplished. . . . I fear it is not built substantially on the only foundation on which solid work can stand. There is so little of Christ in my own life that I fear I can impart but little to others. And yet it may be that, as Arnold says, we may be allowed to come bringing some sheep in our hand. . . . St. Mark's match to-morrow, so I must to bed. Good-night, my dear old boy.

December 15, 1889

I was "right glad" to hear from you. . . . I feel in particularly good spirits because my sermon is done and the exams are the only thing that remain until the Holidays. I am afraid I am a lazy dog. I enjoy the vacation so much. This time I must try to do some reading for I get very little opportunity for it in term time and I am really quite too illiterate for a Schoolmaster. The boys sent a petition signed by the whole School asking my Father to come up for this Sunday and read to them. Accordingly we had a part of that delightful Christmas Carol by Dickens. It is a pleasant sight to see all the boys together in the parlor, clustered around the reader or lying on the floor and to have such ideas of charity and good will given to them in such a persuasive way. There never was a better sermon on the spirit of Xmas time than the carol.

September 20, 1889

With us all is wonderfully prosperous and happy. The old boys have come back in splendid condition. Most of them have been promoted in one way or another and there is a very evident determination on the part of the senior boys to keep up the spirit of the school in the best way. Then we are all well and so I feel like singing a continual song of praise and thanksgiving. There is one sad thing which comes near us. Alex Barnewell, one of our boys, is seriously ill of typhoid-pneumonia and we feel very anxious about him. It is extremely sad that I had almost forgotten it for the moment in the paean of joy that came to my lips.

November 30, 1889

You were prepared for absent-mindness on the part of a man who was duffer enough to say "Florence, wilt thou take this woman, etc." and I am afraid that you won't engage me for your marriage.

107

April 5, 1889

I am quite conscious of the fact that I have owed thee a letter for several weeks, but as in one's home life the nearest have to be disregarded so in one's correspondence. I don't like it. . . . I wish I could rejoice even in rhetorical power in my extempore addresses. They are almost as halting and feeble as they ever were.

The day after the Columbia offer,* came a note from Dr. Eliphalet Potter suggesting I should be "doctorated" by Hobart. It was of course very kind and complimentary, but I rather hesitated and finding that Fannie, my people, and Mr. Brooks shared my feeling, I wrote to Dr. P. saying that I was young and had accomplished very little and so if they thought me worthy in several years I should then gladly accept the degree.

The New York meeting [to raise money] was fairly successful. . . . They treated me in most royal fashion, a most unlenten visit it was, but not altogether free from discipline in its results, for I was pretty fagged out when I got home and outraged nature asserted her protest against continual feasting and abbreviated sleep.

August 5, 1890

On Wednesday I went to Nahant for a wedding . . . and Tuesday I joined the *Mayflower* [Mr. Gardner's yacht] at Newport for the Goelet Cup Races. . . . On Saturday I left the yacht and went to the Whitneys to stay over Sunday. They had a banquet of 20 on Sunday evening, not a very clerical sort of entertainment. . . . Swelldom prevails at Newport and I rather enjoy a day or two of it, just enough to make me feel thankful that I am not in the whirl. The moral tone of the place seems to me good, but it is a wholly material life, not even intellectual, far less spiritual.

November 18, 1892

What a jolly old humbug you are, after all. I have my opinion of a man who suggests the renewal of a correspondence and the sustaining of it in an energetic manner and then fails to answer his friend's letter! . . . I am much interested in the question of the ministry. . . . There is no doubt trouble somewhere that men should not generally look upon the ministry as a possibility as they look forward to their life work. . . . I am inclined to think that there is a certain aristocratic prejudice . . . my point is not so much that there are not many splendid men in the ministry, but that there are very many outside who ought to have been brought in.

* Peabody was approached by Mr. Fish of the Columbia board to ask whether he would consider the presidency of Columbia.

108

Last night I read an essay on the ministry before the Clericus [Club]. It was a poorish paper, but it had a purpose. I hoped to stir the clergy to a realization of the responsibility laid upon them to bring others into a work which every minister thinks, or should think, to be the most absorbing and important in the world. But they did not kindle much . . . altogether, as I thought over the discussion, it seemed to me that there was amazingly little enthusiasm among those men for their profession. All the more does it behoove us who believe in the work to get others into it. I do trust and pray that from among the graduates of Groton there may be many who will take Holy Orders, but I confess the condition of Harvard College to-day restrains my hopefulness and I doubt if you can have anything else so long as President Eliot is at the head!

February 27, 1892

You will be grieved to hear that one of our boys has passed away, a most brilliant fellow, full of promise of mind and character. You will remember him, Morton Postlethwaite. Happily, his parents were both here. We had the service in the Chapel this morning. It has been a sad twenty-four hours. It is an awful thing to think of the responsibility of preparing a boy for eternity. And it was, so far as I am concerned, all so superficial and poor. I ought to have got to know him better and to have helped him more, but I thought we had plenty of time. May God forgive my neglect. I have been trying to write a sermon and have now, at 11 P.M., finished a wretched thing, utterly unsatisfactory as practically all of my work is.

R.M.S. *Majestic*, Queenstown, August 11, 1892

We are waiting in Harbor for the mails, but the ship is throbbing as if she were anxious, like us, to be away to the home of the free. There never was such a ship. She is wonderfully arranged for comfort within and without, has a deck which would soon tire you out sh'd you walk all the way along it. She is furnished luxuriously, at the same time in the best of taste, and is so perfectly ventilated that none of those noxious odors assail your nostrils as you descend to the saloon. On such a ship sea-sickness would seem unpardonable. I have a splendid stateroom, with only one companion, a cheerful person, whom you, with your British snobbishness, would call "one of those vulgar Yankees", but with whom I get on capitally. I still say, as always, England is the place to play, but America is the place to work.

Boston, January 3, 1893

I saw Nash last night. His little girl is better. But there is still much sitting up at night and his wife is fagged out. Now I want you to smuggle in another fifty or a hundred dollars for me for a nurse, as you did before. Nash is so sensitive that I have not sent the money to him direct and yet his wife ought to be relieved. Manage it for me somehow, there's a good Chap, and I will send you a check for either sum, the larger to be preferred.

Groton, February 8, 1893

I was grieved by your letter of last night. It is a trying thing to read over letters which have to do with the old and seemingly happier time. In a way it was a happier time and yet there is growth in character and ability now which one would not care to give up. With you this seems to me to be marked. Only the externals of your life and the deepest things too have been particularly hard and sad. Can't you cast all your care on God, old Chap? I know that it is easy for one in prosperity to say this. But I am so sure that it would solve the whole question for you and bring again a calm and peace which these hard blows have broken in upon so rudely.

Today the weather is glorious and the boys are coasting outside and I am going soon to join.

And yet in spite of all the joy, I feel as Arnold says, a nameless sadness over me steal. And I don't believe that any life which has large responsibilities can get away from it.

Danvers, April 6, 1893

Yesterday I attended the first meeting of the Headmaster's Association which assembled, organized and discussed things in general at the Boston Latin School and afterwards adjourned and dined at Young's. It was rather an interesting experience. The club consists of the Heads of Andover, Exeter, Boston Latin, Roxbury Latin and many prominent public and private schools in New England, New York and Philadelphia and is calculated to have a good deal of effect upon secondary education.

Groton, June 15, 1893

Many thanks for what you say of the Deanship.* You don't know how lucky it is that I cannot consider the place. For I am a sorely over-estimated person.

Groton School Camp, Holderness
New Hampshire, July 17, 1893

I was glad to read your sweet discoursing and to see your old fist once more. I have thought of you much during these days of

* Of the theological school, concerning which Peabody had been approached.

our starting this camp on the lake where we had such a pleasant visit with Whittier in that year long ago. Whenever I row down to Shepherd Hill House I look up towards the wood giants and a feeling of the sacredness of the place comes over me—we have chosen a pleasant sight for the encampment, not the best perhaps but still good enough and convenient to the road which is a consideration when you have large numbers. We had 8 the first week. 10 more came last Tuesday. It was a little hard settling down at first but after a few days the boys discovered 1. That we intended to be their friends 2. That we *would* have order and so they accepted our wishes and all has gone merrily since. It is a great problem as you say, that of the relations between the rich and the poor. Our effect of this camp I hope maybe to show our boys that they can do something for others who are not as fortunate as they. . . . We shall probably invite the same boys each year, the conditions being that we get a good report of each one for the year—and this may enable us to get hold of them and to help them to help others.

November 20, 1893

I suppose that at this moment you are seated at the table in the Thorndike discussing the personality of Satan. I wish I could be there to sit by you and to hear all that you have to say about him. But it was Thayer's turn to go away and I could not leave. I have been here pretty steadily and yet I seem to have been called away a good deal and with Billings off I don't like to leave the brethren very much. Ayrault is doing extremely good work and everything seems to be booming along under full sail—and yet of course there is just a bit more to look after than when Billings is here.

I only wish that I could read a fraction of the books that you accomplish. But alas! my days are spent mainly with the machinery of life. Not that I am unwarily allowing that to overwhelm me—I appreciate that there are far more important things, but struggle as one will against it correspondence and arranging do take up a lot of time. But I won't give up teaching—I am thankful to have a chance to preach, altho I do not half make the best use of my opportunity.

February 26, 1894

I am convinced that a man needs a clear brain to accomplish his best labor, and a clear brain is dependent upon a healthy body. Why not take up the Y.M.C.A. gym again? It really would help you in those many Lenten Duties.

Oxford, July 22, 1894

This Inn is destroying any patience I may have possessed and ruining my sympathy with the working man—One of the waiters is uncivil and the other a drunkard. Neither they nor the maids do more than they are compelled to do. The house is dirty and expensive. Tell your friends far and wide to avoid it.

I wonder if you have heard that W.G.T.* has been unanimously elected Head Master of St. Marks? I have only the fact from him. We are to talk it over and I shall lay before him our need of his services at Groton. But it will not be possible for me to give strong advice against his accepting the position, if he feels that he is able to fill it. For it is undoubtedly a great opportunity.

Westerham, Eng. August 16, 1894

I have thought a good deal about the trouble in regard to the ordination of those men and it has bothered me. I fear as you do that there will be a strong feeling aroused against the [Theological] School and that the Diocese will be stirred by the factions of parties. It is a great pity after these years of peace in which we have got to know each other as men and not simply as ecclesiastics. I share with Huntington an aversion to the extreme radicalism of the broad Churchmen. But I do hate and abominate the sniffers after heresy. Poor Thayer will have one of the worst of them on his Board of Trustees. The report that you give of St. Mark's is not encouraging. Indeed Thayer is going to have a hard time of it. But he is a man of the finest character and I feel confident that he will do excellent work at Southborough. There will be a certain amount of prejudice against him as a Groton Master—but that will be I fancy a small thing compared with the task of raising a school to a high standard of life. We talk things over a good deal and it seems to me that Thayer has it in him to make the school what it ought to be and what it is *not* at the present time.

New York, November 15, 1894

I have had a satisfactory talk with the graduates here and my heart is filled with deep joy at finding some of them dead in earnest about life and eager to do all they can do to purify Politics and to be of service to their fellow men. It is this and not new buildings or long waiting lists which brings abiding pleasure—and I thank God for it all.

Cannes December 16 1894

How distressing the political outlook seems to be! One looks almost in vain for men who are willing to serve their country. Those who are not for themselves seem to be hopelessly bound to their party interests and the country comes in a certain last. Perhaps it is not as bad as I think. You will tell me if I am wrong. It makes me

* William Greenough Thayer.

112

feel like chucking up everything and making a desperate charge in Politics. If some Groton boys do not enter political life and do something for our land it won't be because they have not been urged.

Rome, January 18, 1895

I believe that a change is a good thing for a man. At times I have a bit of an uneasy feeling thinking that perhaps I might develop more fully if I should go elsewhere, but the work at Groton must be much more nearly completed before that and by that time I shall probably be good for little else. Things go on so well under Billings that I feel as if I were not much needed, but there are certain responsibilities which I ought not to shift to others' shoulders, and perhaps this is the work I can do best. I am conscious all the time that it is beyond me in many ways but the school has been so greatly blessed that God seems to have used me for this purpose in spite of my weaknesses. And I do believe that we are now entering upon a time of great importance in the life of the school. When its graduates are coming back to their homes after college and are laying out the lines along which they are to work. If I can be of service in helping them to take a larger outlook than many men in their station of life take it will be something. I am to preach at the American Church here on Sunday and I think that will do me good. I generally preach to myself, perhaps more than to others. Fancy only preaching once in two or three months.

Florence, March 23, 1895

How often have I endeavored to point out to you the unsoundness of that policy of working until you dropped instead of running off for a while and returning in good condition for more effective labor! Hearing Venables the incumbent at the American Church preach each Sunday, I am struck with the exceeding effectiveness of preaching from the Bible when a man has a real knowledge of it, and I have determined to devote myself to it more faithfully than heretofore. The Cambridge School seems to me defective on this point. There is much teaching about the Bible and Biblical criticism and all that—but the number of men who know their Bible and who read it regularly and devoutly is, I venture to say, comparatively small. Perhaps I judge others by myself too much. Certainly I must acknowledge myself an offender in this respect. I had rather a set back last Sunday. I tried to make an address on the Creed, went into the pulpit without notes thinking that I was full of my subject and fresh and able to make a fair presentment. But I got confused and said what I did not intend to say and altogether made a bad failure of it. I am disappointed in myself that I do not preach more effec-

113

tively. It may be that God intends me to do this work better in some other way, and yet I have a strong feeling that I ought to be able to help people in the pulpit and I am not willing to give up that feeling until I have proved by many years experience if I live so long that I cannot.

I am thankful that I am not obliged to live abroad. Life is easier in many ways here and the reports that come about America are not always inspiring, but I believe that all the great social problems lie with us for settlement and I want to have a hand in that in some way. At times it seems as if one could do more in a city and yet the line of duty seems to be pretty clearly marked out at Groton. I do not believe that Dr. Coit's work would have told as it has done if he had left St. Paul's twenty years ago. Some men must stick to the one work where there is so much change as there is with us, and certainly no other life could be as congenial to me or to Fanny.

Wimbledon Park, June 23, 1895

There are two points on which you need reconstructing. 1. the idea that Ohio is to be your permanent home. New England is the place which you love and understand and where you ought to work the greater part of your life. 2. The thought that I shall be wanted elsewhere than at Groton, and if needed that I would go anywhere else. There are great opportunities for developing our usefulness taking the school as a starting point. However it does seem to me that there is no more important work in America at the present time than that of bringing boys into contact with high ideals of life and helping them to see the vast possibilities of their country which they can help to make actual. I can swing the school fairly well (not at all really as it ought to be swung) but it is a most serious question whether I could be of much service in another sphere. Wherefore my beloved Julius, rejoice that we have such a splendid library fund and that we are going to develop the intellectual life more vigorously but that the progress must be slow and that no period of my life will see the achievement of all that the school can be and do.

Oxford, July 24, 1895

There are many letters waiting to be answered but I must write you a few lines from this place where we passed such happy days together three years ago. It made me uncommonly lonely when I first arrived not to find your cheery presence. Do you remember how I knocked Hodges' paper over his head, thinking it was surely you? There is a large company of Parsons some 150 or more all bestocked and broad brim hatted and with ecclesiastical aspect except poor me. I need you to keep me company in the presence of so many who look upon a man with a white straw as a rank outsider.

114

Groton October 3, 1895

Happily the boys are in excellent form and as far as I can see so that there is comparatively little anxiety in regard to the life of the school at present. But I am not at all satisfied with my own teaching and I do not find that sermons come much easier. Which is a disappointment. It may be that I might preach better if I had to preach more frequently and could banish some of the details which almost inevitably throng in upon a Head Master. But I do not see how any radical change is possible. Except a spiritual improvement in myself which I am always hoping for and I trust it may come before I die. Fanny has gone down to the Lindens for the night and I am feeling rather home sick and lonely without her. The thought of possible danger always haunts me at such a time as this when the birth of a child is not far distant. But God will be with us whatever happens.

November 13, 1895

How good it is to think of you as safely launched upon married life. The constant companionship of one's dearest friend is the most satisfying of all earthly joys, and I know what it will mean to you.

December 13, 1895

The worst of your living in that outlandish place [Columbus, Ohio] is that I feel as if I must write you a regular epistle instead of dashing off a few lines as I used to do. But I would rather have you married in Columbus than single even in Massachusetts, which is a piece of unselfishness that I take a good deal of comfort in. Unselfishness not being much in my line. The School goes on in much the same old way. There are hard nuts to crack and I occasionally come near breaking my teeth when I try to crack them with my own jaw, as in my haste I am rather inclined to try to do. When I look at things in the large there seems to be reason for encouragement but at times the results seem to me meagre and unsatisfactory.

May 16, 1896

It has been a gorgeous day. I wish you might have sat alongside of me this afternoon as the baseball match was going on and watched the blue hills in the distance and the exquisite colors all through the valley. It was an afternoon to remember. Riis wrote me the other day that his little child said as she looked at the Sunset "God can paint good, can't he Mamma" and that is the kind of feeling that filled one's heart. If heaven is more beautiful what a glorious place it will be! My mind is not quite free from care tonight. For two boys have measles with temperatures of over 104° and I am a little afraid of pneumonia. But I trust that it may be averted. Several others are in the infirmary with German measles. Both diseases were brought from New York by the brethren after the holidays. I preached on Ascension Day at Cambridge. The Sermon was necessarily simple for I had only a short season for preparation. But I laid emphasis on the need of spirituality in the clergy and an intimate acquaintance with the Holy Scriptures. It does seem to me that the Cambridge School falls short in developing these two things. I love the place and got a lot from it. . . . If there is failure in the lives of these boys it always comes back to me with new weight. If I were a better man I could have helped them to become stronger and more firmly established in the Faith.

December 26, 1896

I should so like to see the little one—: When you say that she resembles her Pa·in the upper portion of her face, I suppose you stop at the brow. Let us hope that her poll will be covered with a more luxuriant growth than that which decorates the paternal pate. I can picture you hanging over the cradle by the hour and discovering all kinds of strange and brilliant qualities in the young one. Do not put her into literature too early. I have been bothered a good bit of late by Billings' trouble with Gladwin. They do not hit it off at all. I have tried to mediate and as is usual in such cases have not given satisfaction to either side. It is the first time I think, that Billings has been seriously disappointed in me. But I cannot make things pleasant by an apology in as much as I have acted to the best of my judgment, and therefore we must simply hope that the sense of Xtian brotherhood will bring all right in course of time.

January 5, 1896

This is our last quiet Sunday together for many a month and we are enjoying it. Frank Thomson and Moncure telephoned yesterday to ask if they might come up and we mustered up courage enough to say no. I have preached at Ayer and called on old Mrs. Freeman. We have read and snoozed in the study, told the children stories and sung hymns with them—now they have gone to tea and I have a few minutes for a chat with you. Your Xmas letter was good to read. It warms the cockles of my heart to think of your happy home. I do wish that I might see it. Don't put down your roots too deep, for we want you back in the East before long.

I wish you would send me a photo of your wife and one of yourself if you have a new one. That combination with you in your top hat was all very well for your intimates (if you really looked at me in that way I would bonnet you in a second) The likeness of your wife was good. But I want something that I can put out in my study. I trust that the chance of war is over. But the idea that we would fight England for such a reason seems simply monstrous. Poor England is getting into deep waters. Believing as I do in Kidd's Theory that the Anglo-Saxon race should be the predominant one for the good of the world, I regret to see other nations trying to block her. If we could only join England in stopping the frightful massacres of the Armenians we should have some ground for satisfaction. This perpetual wire pulling and striving for peace, ignoring all that is valuable materially and all that is sacred cannot but bring a sense of shame to Americans. It simply maddens me at times to be powerless when one sees it going on.

I do not at all like Cleveland's giving out this new loan to Mr. Morgan. Nothing is more calculated to bring out dissatisfaction in the West—and it does not seem to me altogether above suspicion. I can't quite understand a man like Mr. Morgan making money out of his country's need. I hear by the way that Rainsford has broken with him and that he has taken a pew at another church. The fewer of such men we have in this country the better say I. Dullness which is contented with smaller profits is better in the long run.

I 7

GRADUATES AND UNDER-
GRADUATES

AT COLLEGE a Groton graduate realized that he was still one of the school family. The custom of the freshmen going back the first Sunday in the fall term for Chapel, known as Freshman Sunday, began early. It was good to see the Rector in the pulpit once more and hear the familiar, eager voice roll out again, "That's it, my boys." He often preached, too, in various college chapels.

The overwhelming majority of Groton boys have gone to Harvard, Yale, or Princeton in that numerical order. The Rector kept in touch with them in all three places. Naturally, because it was Harvard and Harvard was, so to speak, part of Boston, he kept in closer touch with alumni there than anywhere else. This suited him, because he felt that Harvard men were more in need of counsel and stiffening than those of other colleges. Deep down he loved and respected Harvard and what its tradition stood for, but he observed with concern that Grotonians at Harvard were more apt to get into trouble than at New Haven or Princeton, and he never ceased battling for an improved righteousness in Cambridge. The transition from Groton to the freedom of Harvard was much more abrupt than the transition to Yale or Princeton. No one quarreled with him about that; the Harvard men were the first to admit it. The point of issue was that they stubbornly refused to admit anything should be done about it, while he wanted to do a lot. In general they saw the real difficulty more clearly than he did. He wanted them to join the St. Paul's Society or to convert President Eliot, and he was always goading the parents to help him do away with the evils of drink, gambling, and riotous living. They saw that in a change from a strong paternalism to an extreme condition of *laissez faire* there were bound to be casualties, especially when a lot of Grotonians had a lot of money, an acquaintanceship with all the prettiest girls and most ambitious mammas in Back Bay, a more or less automatic entree to the clubs, and, usually, an instinctive reaction from the rigid restriction and discipline of school.

There was at one point a minor *crise*, when the Rector resigned from the Porcellian Club, of which he had been elected an honorary member. There were many protests, some friendly, some angry, but he had made up his mind it was the thing to do and did it. The graduates went their way; some floundered for a while, but on the whole they did well, amazingly well for boys to whom college life had little importance so far as their daily bread was concerned. If they slipped, the Rector was after them like a hawk. A curt note informed some one that at Groton his performance was not judged to be up to his capacity. On the other hand if he did well, a somewhat longer note invariably arrived congratulating him on his success and making it clear his achievements were admired and appreciated at Groton. Grotonians were never allowed to forget that they were the representatives of the school and its good name.

Every birthday each of them received a card with the familiar handwriting wishing him well and showing he was not forgotten. Many comments tell how alumni learned to look for those cards and counted on receiving them. Apparently nothing was overlooked or unremembered. If the alumni were good sportsmen, they were commended for it. If their behavior was rumored dubious, they were questioned about it.

As an almost instinctive matter they wrote their news or went back in person to report. They told of their griefs, their problems, their engagements. It was taken for granted that they would ask the Rector to marry them. And usually when their sons were born they automatically entered them for Groton in the most expeditious manner possible.

The letters, either to or from the Rector, which follow illustrate these things. As is evident, reactions to his counsel varied. Letters from different periods have been chosen purposely. This phase of his correspondence showed remarkable consistency in all years:

New Haven, Oct. 27 '98

Dear Mr. Peabody:

Your letter came today and you don't know how sorry I am that anyone should get the idea that I was what is commonly known as a "dirty" football player. . . . In the first place as regards the Brown game. The right tackle of the Brown Team tackled me once just as I was on the point of tackling one of their half-backs who had the ball. He naturally spoiled my chance of stopping the play, and I, being very angry at the moment turned around and struck at him but did not hit him. The umpire saw me try to hit him, but did not see the Brown man hold me, so he ruled me off without any warning, which was not exactly fair. . . . Now about my telling the boys at school about the way I padded my jersey and to hold in the line if the umpire didn't see them. I told them that I did not have my jersey padded, because if one ran into a man when one's jersey was padded it was not so easy to block him effectually. . . . I don't think that going without pads to make one a little harder can exactly be called unfair or rough in any sense. As regards holding, I am perfectly sure that I never told any of the fellows to hold or do anything like that if the umpire doesn't see him because there is nothing that the coaches down here are so strict and down on as holding. . . . It is very unfair thing to say of Yale that she sacrifices her honor to win. If she can't win by good, fair, straight playing she does not want to win at all. . . . I don't play any differently now or use any different methods from what I used to, up at Groton. . . .

Affectionately,
F. Gordon Brown Jr.

119

Cambridge
Jan. 23, 1905

DEAR MR. PEABODY:

Now as to the question why more fellows do not join the ministry [at Harvard] it is hardly necessary for me to call your attention to the spirit of independence which is so strong at Harvard. Even the social organizations which are known as fraternities and have chapters in other colleges have almost ceased to identify themselves with the mother fraternity. . . . This spirit of independence does not go so far as to make each man for himself, . . . in fact the spirit of self-sacrifice in a Harvard Club and the loyalty to it and all its members and graduates is very marked. In other words the tendency here at Harvard has been to make the fellows independent of outside influences and loyal only to their clubs.

Mr. Gardner speaks of the simple and wholesome spiritual life we had at Groton—so natural that we did not realize that it existed and so perhaps did not appreciate its value. He speaks of the influence of prayer and the numerous services which we attended. But a far greater influence than these, it seems to me, is the influence of the surroundings, not necessarily of the religious atmosphere, but of the character of the masters and prefects and the purpose in life which all seemed to have. If we Groton boys here at Harvard think of the Church, we think of the Chapel at Groton and our Rector there, . . . we do not feel any tie binding us to the "great church", in fact to me and I have no doubt to many others it is distasteful to hear the church appealing to History to establish its greatness. For in the first place records during the early centuries of the Christian era were poorly kept and it is impossible in many cases to separate legends from history as historical critics now regard it. In the second place from what I have read I do not see that we have any claim to being the only true and lawful church. . . . In the third place even if our claim were well established and admitted by all mankind I do not think such a state of affairs would very much influence a Harvard man, for he would devote all his loyalty to the church in which he was baptized and to the Rector whose sermons he had heard and whose influence he had felt for so many years. I am strongly of the opinion, Mr. Peabody, that most Groton boys who join the St. Paul's Society do so to please you . . . if I really wanted to get a boy to join I would stand much more show of getting him if I told him that such a step would please you. . . . As to the Y.M.C.A. it is needless to say that many things about it will be distasteful to a boy who has been brought up with a prayer book and is used to the service in our church. . . .

Affectionately yours,

——— ———

MY DEAR MR. PEABODY,   November 29, 1904

I think you will be rather surprised when I tell you that my engagement to my distant cousin Eleanor Roosevelt is about to come out. I know you will be glad for my great happiness and consider me a very fortunate man. I had intended going up to School the day after the Harvard-Yale game, but I got jaundice instead and couldn't move from home. I am at the Columbia Law School, trying to understand a little of the work and of course I am going to keep right on. We hope to be married sometime in the late part of winter and we both hope that you will be able to help us in the ceremony—it wouldn't be the same without you.

Always affectionately yours,

FRANKLIN D. ROOSEVELT

DEAR MR. PEABODY: Oct. 23, 1915

After spending months and months in forensics and self-discipline I am engaged to ―― of ――. I also expect really to marry the lady as soon as I get my breath, and can arrange not to starve to death immediately afterwards.

This achievement appears to me to eclipse such events as Adam's eating that original apple or Darwin's discovery that he never did, and I ought to be immensely proud to be identified with such an epoch-making affair; and I am too, or at least I shall be as soon as I recover from fright at the responsibility.

DEAR MR. PEABODY: [Undated]

I know you are deeply interested in the joys and sorrow of all your boys and I need your sympathy and strength very much just now. For two years I have loved a wonderful girl . . . this Christmas I found myself in a position where I could speak and Mr. Peabody she was wonderfully happy. Friday night she died. I had left her only a few hours before radiantly happy . . . and now the hardest task of all is to say "Thy will be done" and to go and live my life as she would have had me do. I can do it for I know her hand is ever on my shoulder and I know too that if I live the pure true life she wants me to I shall go straight to her in heaven when my time comes. But Mr. Peabody there come dark moments when I need the help of the best Christians I know and so I turn to you and Mrs. Peabody.

                                                        New York City
DEAR MR. PEABODY: April 15, 1926

I was electrified by your letter! The things you talked about are

121

the things that we all discuss down here in the unwholesome city all the time, but which we can never get you folks up at School to take any interest in.

I have known the answer to the question of why boys from Groton do better at Yale than they do at Harvard for a long time. The reason is that Yale is a continuation of exactly the same kind of regimen that they are subjected to at Groton, whereas Harvard is an entirely different atmosphere. I do not say which is the better. I am not sure. One cannot tell till the boys are twenty years out of college and the results can be tabulated, but the way boys are treated at Groton is, I believe, the very worst preparation for Harvard that could possibly be devised. You might as well train a boy at Sparta and expect him to shine at Athens. The training is all right of its kind, but it cannot be adapted to certain purposes at all.

Dean —— of Yale came down here and gave an informal talk to some high-brows at a small dinner. They got after him hard about the Senior Societies at Yale. He said: "The Senior Societies have faults, but they are a very powerful weapon to throw at an under-classman who comes to Yale and starts to go wrong." This frank admission of the use of fear as a corrective, of the philosophy of enforced conformity, of the holding up of authority as of more importance than truth, of coercion rather than inspiration, and of the attempt to mould the boys into the desired form irrespective of their capacities or proclivities was of enormous interest to the men present. To train a boy by these methods and then to set him free is to send him into battle naked. As for the "Mollycoddles"—it is not that you are making them at Groton; it is that you do not make them. It takes courage to be a mollycoddle. You are training boys so that they are more afraid of popular clamor than they are of making a difficult tackle in a foot-ball game. What I want to see is a boy produced who will have the courage to say that he thinks foot-ball is nonsense and he won't play no matter to what social tortures he is subjected. If you could produce this kind of courage you would have a percentage of ministers among the graduates that would be the wonder of the country. But you cannot produce ministers if you preach obedience and submission to the voice of the majority, because the majority of the country is now engaged in furiously making money and in self justification sneering at everybody who says that is nonsense.

. . . . .

On reading this letter over I observe it is rather heated. When I say "you" I mean "we". Anyway, it is better to be interested than indifferent. You will observe I am violently interested. I think you would get a great response if you would talk to the graduates about these matters at the dinner. They are all struck dumb when you are round, but quite lively in private—on both sides of the question. I cannot understand why they are dumb, except that every one of them values your good opinion so highly that he is afraid to disagree with anything you say. That really is not fair to you, is it?

Affectionately yours,

GEORGE MARTIN

June 17, 1925

DEAR MR. PEABODY:

The name "Groton" always strikes a responsive chord, gives me a thrill, makes me think of you in particular and the Chapel and I am always glad to contribute to any request for funds to help out something the School is doing, but when it comes to sending my sons through the machine at Groton, as I went through it, both my wife and I hesitate.

I would willingly go through the ordeal of Groton again to get what I did from you and the Chapel services—but I would skip my last year again to be free of it all as soon as possible—to be free of the deadly way that studies were taught in my day to be free as soon as possible from the routine and dress that made us all think and look alike.

You would know from a glance at the relatively poor marks I got the five years I was at Groton that I was either lazy, dull or uninterested in the work.—That it was the last is shown or indicated by the fact that I skipped my sixth form year, went to Harvard a year ahead of my Groton Class, went through Harvard in three years.

Until Harvard, Greek, Latin, French were always an ugly chore— In Harvard I had gone far enough in these subjects to get some fun and interest out of them.—Should it take five or six years of study in French before one may enjoy it the least bit? Must history be taught as a dead language, without interest to the student except after years of toil.—Must history be just a series of dates, names, places, all dead, useless, and soon completely forgotten? (I have in the last few years read "The Life and Times of Cavour" by Thayer, and other works of historical value, and, I assure you, they were so interesting, and I got so much from them, that my previous studies in History at Groton were completely without value by comparison (save for teaching concentration and discipline).

I learned discipline and concentration to the Nth degree at Groton—and both have stood me in good stead—but I was practically taught to hate studying, was forced to hate it, it was made so uninteresting in every blessed course that I can remember (no exception) —and it is only since leaving school that I began to find that such

123

subjects as history had any live relation to the present, were absorbingly interesting.

In some six years in all of French I never learned anything worth mentioning—(can read it now fairly well, but not understand it or write it)—Either I was terribly stupid or the system was wrong.— Couldn't French be made a bit interesting?

My criticism of Groton is that it teaches the studies in an uninteresting way (by comparison with the so-called "Project Method" Schools) and while it gives much of value in teaching discipline and power to concentrate it also teaches a desire to get through with the work at hand as soon as possible, to be rid of it—to be able to forget it because it was not interesting or worth while pursuing further than one had to.

Again, isn't one of the needs of today to get away from form and conventions that prevent one's taking the initiative when needed? Groton teaches boys to think along the lines of their fathers and grandfathers, not to meet the problems of today with a fresh and open mind freed from the cobwebs of convention.

My wife and I have made some study of the so-called Project Method Schools, have our oldest son in one now, and have about come to the conclusion that the children really learn more that will be of lasting value to them there than they ever could in the old-type "grind" school.—(I have a very good friend who went to a Project Method School in Chicago and he tells me the pupils stayed afternoons at their work long after compelled to and had every afternoon finally to be pried from what they were doing and sent home, they were so interested in the task at hand)

I hope to talk further with you on this someday! Faithfully yours,

——— ———

Aug. 2, 1921

MY DEAR ———:

Your record in the entrance examinations was admirable. It is a fine climax to your contributions to the school, for which I thank you heartily. As I remarked several times last year, the intellectual life at Groton needs to be emphasized and this success of yours will do that in the best possible way. I am sure that your people will be pleased at your achievement.

Affectionately yours,

E. P.

July 26, 1921

MY DEAR ———:

My heartiest congratulations upon the birth of the little son! I am delighted to hear of the happiness of you and your wife and of the lad himself, for it is surely a good thing to be born into this world. After a long life, may the earth be the better for his having been here. I am enclosing herewith a blank form of application, or rather, asking Mr. Andrews to do so. Will you kindly fill this out and let the Secretary have it at your convenience?

Affectionately yours,

E. P.

March 5, 1932
MY DEAR ———:
You are one of four Groton boys whom the College reports to be on probation. Your record of History 1 C-, English 28 C-, German A absent, Meteorology 1 D will be as much of a disappointment to your father and your aunt as it has been to me and the other Masters who tried to prepare you for College.

Affectionately yours

ENDICOTT PEABODY

March 8, 1916
MY DEAR ———,
You are right in believing that anything that concerns you is of interest to me, for I have cared for you ever since you came to Groton in 1884.

I feel obliged to tell you that the contents of your letter from Bermuda have brought me great distress. I have been informed that Mrs. ——— obtained a decree of divorce from her husband for some reason other than that of unfaithfulness on his part. This being the case, she was not in my judgment free to contract another marriage.

The step is directly contrary to the teaching of Christ and strikes at the very foundations of family life.

I am of course ready to believe that you take a different view of the matter. To me it is not a question of error but of actual wrong.

I wish I could write differently. Indeed it hurts me, my dear ———, to withhold my blessing—but I am compelled to do so under the circumstances.

I shall always hold you as a friend and follow your course with affectionate interest and stand ready as I have ever done to do any service for you that lies in my power.

Aff yr friend,

ENDICOTT PEABODY

[From another graduate]

[1904?]
MY DEAR MR. PEABODY:
To say I was surprised at receiving your letter would be putting it very mildly. It seems to me very strange that you, after my mar-

125

riage had been approved and sanctified by my parents, should step in and so candidly express your disapproval, especially when, as your letter clearly denotes, you knew nothing of the circumstances which caused me to take such a step. I assure you, Mr. Peabody, I was both surprised and shocked to receive such a letter from you, and I cannot believe that you thought twice about what you said for to my mind it is the duty of a father and a father only to reprimand a boy for a deed which concerns no-one but his immediate family.

Undated, but about 1910

[From a talk to undergraduates:]

This lack of religious life in the home cannot fail in the long run to influence the moral standard. At the present time I believe that there is a better moral condition in the Colleges than there was twenty years ago. This I attribute in part to athletics. A man knows that in order to succeed in athletics he must lead a clean life, he must avoid softness of life, and keep himself in excellent physical condition. Thus athletics ministers to the better life of young men.

I believe that they have had a different effect upon girls. It is no doubt an excellent thing for girls to ride. Girls ride well. They play golf well. They play tennis well enough to play with each other, but this constant association with men in athletics tends to take off the delicate bloom from the peach. Not a few girls remind one of boys who prematurely desire to become young men. So girls smoke cigarettes, and play bridge whist for money, and men, the best kind of men, dislike it. I have an opportunity of talking with many of the prominent athletic men of this country, and they tell me that the condition of society in this respect disgusts them, and when girls go further, and become vulgar, as is not a very uncommon thing to-day, then these men detest their society. They are, no doubt, amused by such girls for a time, but they do not want to marry that kind of being.

A man does not want to marry a doll, it is true, so it used to be said in old times; no, neither does he want to marry a tom-boy.

"A Being breathing thoughtful breath,
A traveller between life and death;
The reason firm, the temperate will
Endurance, foresight, strength, and skill;
And yet a Spirit still, and bright
With something of an angel light."

That is the kind of person that a man hopes for in his wife. One on whose judgment he can rely, and who can understand the depths of his nature. If he does marry the kind of girl we have first described,

126

you know the experience that lies ahead of them; misunderstandings, quarrels,. unfaithfulness, and the natural climax of self-indulgence—divorce.

Think of what this means for the children. It is the beginning of hell upon this earth. This is the dreadful tragedy of life.

Our Lord's condemnation—"Thou Capernaum that art exalted above all the earth shalt be thrust down into hell", is especially dreadful, because Capernaum, which is thrust down to hell belongs in Heaven.

So too the home where love, and joy, and peace, and perfect mutual understanding ought to reign is made the abode of misery.

Do not think that I despair for the future of the world, or of this country. These things are full of menace, but I believe so profoundly in the spiritual nature of women that I am confident that this is only a phase. But let us drive it out as quickly as we can; and we can get rid of it if we will establish religion in the homes.

[To the Alumni at College:]

We have just come to the end of a term which has been so satisfactory in various ways that I feel moved to send you a few lines to inform you of our progress.

There has been unanimity of spirit throughout the School. The health of the boys has been excellent: and all the outdoor activities have been carried on with energy.

Intellectually, there has been a marked advance. The Sixth Form have had an average of eight for two successive months, and as a result are reaping two extra days of vacation.

Each week there have been more than forty-five boys with nothing lower than "B", and some weeks there have been as many as sixty in this class. Always there have been two or three with records of all "A"s.

At Harvard no fewer than six Graduates have won Scholarships— C. P. Curtis Jr. is a John Harvard Scholar, J. Heard, J. W. Suter jr. M. Fremont-Smith, G. H. Roosevelt, H. Josephs are placed among the Harvard College Scholars. R. Williams has been elected a member of the Phi Beta Kappa Society.

From Yale we have a report showing that these eleven men are on the Honor List:—J. W. Clark. V. Webb, R. W. Baker, R Auchincloss, P. C. Bryce, W. A. Harriman, C. H. Marshall jr. A. Whitridge, H. L. Rogers, W. J. Schieffelin, Jr. S. S. Colt. Of these J. W. Clark and V. Webb have Phi Beta Kappa standing and H. L. Rogers is in the first group of his class.

Three out of our ten representatives at Princeton—B. H.'Farr, G. H. Pyne and J. B. Kingsford—are in the Honor Class.

I wish to thank these boys individually and collectively for the credit which their achievements have brought to the School and to urge the others to follow their inspiring lead. It is the greatest reward that can come to us who work here year after year to find that Groton boys whom we follow with constant interest and sympathy, are helping to carry out the ideals for which we have been striving. May we not hope for even greater things in the year that lies before us?

I am,
Affectionately yours,
ENDICOTT PEABODY

And one final anecdote illustrates several things. One of the most loyal and finest of Grotonians and long a Trustee was Pierre Jay. The Rector said of him once, "Peter Jay is the most perfect gentleman I ever knew." To which Jay, taken aback, exclaimed, "My God, did the Rector say that?" When Bishop Atwood dutifully relayed this to the Rector, the latter remarked dolefully, "I wish Pierre Jay were not quite so profane."

18

PERSONAL LETTERS, 1897-1900

E. P. *aet.* 40-43

AGAIN, it is important not to forget that he had a life which did not appear in the school catalogue nor in his official correspondence. He felt deeply, reacted much, aspired greatly, and got around to a remarkable extent. It will be helpful to follow him once more through a series of personal letters to Atwood.

Groton, January 28, '97

I did not get either prayer book, knife or anything else for Malcolm. Possibly I forgot. Probably my proud spirit resented the tone of your letter in which the request was made—or more likely still I was wary in making a large outlay when no money order accompanied your commission. Someday I shall be going to Boston and I will try to purchase some tribute for the boy. The Stanley letters arrived and I am grateful to you for the volume. I have read some of them but this school keeping business knocks ordinary reading. Of the translating of the classics and exposition thereof—I have a large share—But if I were to write to you of the subtleties of Cicero's epistolary style or the beauties of the Virgilian verse it would all be thrown away. Ergo I abstain.

F. and I see each other so little in term time that I feel that I ought not to leave her during the short breathing spaces that we get in vacation—But I love you all the same.

Groton, April 12 '97

Washington is a beautiful city already. It will be a grand place when it is fully developed and when the political life therein is more beautiful, I am glad to have seen it, for politics seem to me much more real now that I have looked upon many of the chief actors therein. We caught a glimpse of Bryan. He looked to me much more manly and simple and genuine than I expected. This present Tariff action of the Republicans seems to me likely to bring in the Bryanites in four years, and I fancy that you and I have seen the highest tide of prosperity that will come in our life time.

June 7, '97

It did seem a tremendous event to pass the 40 mile stone. It means that young manhood has gone. People say that it means the full development of one's strength—But I cling to the hope and the belief that one will grow wiser and better and stronger and more effective until the time comes to lie down and sleep. Surely if character counts for anything a man ought to become a greater power for good as one learns more of men and of God and comes to hate evil more intensely. That was a charming photograph of your daughter. Both Fanny and I liked the little one immensely and admired her and her Pa never looked so handsome. I fancy that the photographer was a sycophant and used some peculiar device to embellish your features. He has succeeded and the group is most attractive. I have had a meeting of a new society not yet named. Percy White and John Alsop, two of the most unselfish boys that ever lived and I constitute the club. We are to meet once a week and read and study sociology—Gradually we shall let others in, if we find boys who are really in earnest. But we shall allow no dead wood. It may be that in this way we can do something to promote cooperation and the right kind of socialism. In any case we are likely to learn a good deal ourselves if we stick to it as we propose to do.

Cotuit, July 18 '97

I am getting in a fair amount of reading. Each day I read one of

129

Robertson's sermons, which are perpetually fresh. I do some Greek Testament. Boissier's Cicero and his friends and thought on the theory and practice of teaching. This week I expect to take up Nash's book against which I shall probably bump my head violently. What a pleasure it is to think of Nash travelling abroad—I know of no man who would appreciate the delights of it half as much as he—I should like to be present at his lectures for the first term after his return. I wonder if he got near enough to the Jubilee to appreciate the glory of it. It seems to me one of the grandest things of the century. One can hardly help comparing the prosperity and the satisfaction of Englishmen with the feelings that we have today in this country. Public life is unlovely with us in these times. But it is a comfort to feel that a man's work tells more here than in any other land and that we are facing in the right direction even if we do get off the line of march.

Cotuit August 10 '97

There are some people who never forget. Among whom number your friend E. P. Ergo, I enclose herewith a check for $30.

I am reading your Jowett with much interest. One is appalled at the mental activity of such a man—As the years go by I do not find myself any better able to lay hold of the deep problems of Philosophy and have to take it in through the popular books.

Cotuit August 29 '97

If you are such a duffer as to send back five dollars when you can come honestly by them I have nothing to say. Money is never a drug on the market with me. I know that the Westerner deals in an ampler way than we in the effete East are in the habit of dealing. The week at Camp passed off pleasantly. Thayer went up with me and stayed two days. He and I had a good deal of School shop to talk over. He is doing excellent work at St. Mark's. Between ourselves Billings was most urgently invited to take charge of Belmont School. Harding has incorporated it and was willing to put the whole thing into B's hands. Happily for us Billings decided that his work at Groton was more important for the present. It would have been a most serious loss to us if he had gone.

This morning I preached at the Union Church in Cotuit. It seemed odd to be introduced as if for a speech and then to stand up clad in ordinary garbs and deliver a sermon. I must say I think we do things better in our Church. But the people listened well and it is always a privilege to get a chance to preach the Gospel.

Groton October 18 '97

I was interrupted at this point as so often happens in a School

130

Master's study. I wish you were here today to enjoy a genuine New England autumn day—such as you used to have in your boyhood. The air is crisp and clear and the colors across the valley are beautiful. One wonders how heaven can be more glorious. I have been uncommon busy these last two weeks. At Harvard I had a gathering of our boys. All but two who were in Cambridge came to the meeting and I talked to them frankly about the temptations of College life and the splendid opportunities which Groton has at Harvard if they will only take advantage of them. It makes me sick at heart to hear of boys becoming vile and foul. No hand is held out to grasp after them at the College. I hope that by going down each term I shall be able to help somewhat. They were a very sympathetic lot of listeners and I was able to let myself go as I have never done before. If I could only do it when I am preaching I think that I should have some effect perhaps.

Groton November 29; '97

Here am I at 40 and I don't know as much nor can I think as straight as Robertson could at 24. If it were not for these collections of Brick and mortar and for a few boys who tell me that I have been of service to them I should consider myself the veriest caricature of a School Master and minister. But God has been so good in sending blessings and helps, one after another into my life that I have no right to be downhearted. I only wish I had studied and read more intelligently all through my life and that I had thus prepared myself to teach better and to influence men more wisely and more deeply.

Just now I have a new scheme on foot—to try to interest the boys in foreign missionary work. It is most reprehensible of me that I should know so little of what our church is doing in the foreign field. I have taken up China with the 4th form in Sacred studies and I am beginning to learn a little about it. I wonder if many of the clergy are as uninformed about these things as I have been? To boys the story of missions ought to be a fascinating thing—I hope that by pegging away at it year after year we shall be able to arouse an intelligent enthusiasm and that by and by some of our graduates will take up the work. I have been remiss too, or rather have not been active enough in urging boys to study for the Ministry—Two of our graduates Egisto Chauncey and Arthur Gray have begun their Theological studies this autumn and there are two boys in our upper forms who hope to take orders. But the life is such a deeply happy and interesting life that we ought to guide many others that way.

I have not read anything lately that I can particularly recom-

131

mend. Just now I am taking up Robertson's life again and find it still stimulating and suggestive.

Groton December 22 '97

The last term was a good one. In many respects the School was in better trim than ever before. I am intending to teach fewer hours next term and hope to get a little more time for study and for investigating the methods of the other masters. We have a fine lot of men but as one of them remarked the other day "they are rather a difficult team to drive."

Groton March 13 '98

The case was a serious one. The Dr. thought the boy had only 1 chance in 10. But I am thankful to say the lad showed great powers of recuperation and already he has gone home to recuperate. Just before he left ―― ―― was taken with pneumonia. He belongs to a delicate family and on the third day he had a bad hemorage. For awhile we feared that he was gone into a rapid decline but he also rallied and is now well on the road to recovery. Such cases as these take a good deal out of me. For the time one feels more than usual one's responsibility. And yet when one looks at it squarely the burden of their health is nothing like the responsibility for their characters. I am afraid, however, that one does not live with this great truth always in mind.

I expect to sail on the 29th of June by the White Star S.S. Teutonic and to return early in August. I hate to leave Fanny at a time when I can see more of her and the children than in School time— but this seems likely to be the only opportunity that I shall get for several years. And I do want to keep in touch with my friends in England. Dear old Arthur has just been through a serious operation. I am thankful to say he is all right again.

Groton April 30 '98

The scarlet fever spread a bit. Two more, making four, came down Sunday night on Wednesday another followed suit. As the cause of the trouble was obscure it seems to me wise to let the lower forms go and two doctors assured me that it was the best thing to do. Accordingly we have come down to the VIth form together with a few members of the upper 4th and of the 5th forms. It was a good deal of a business getting them all away. Parents had to be notified, trunks packed, tickets purchased and all sorts of other things done in order to rid ourselves of the vast throng. But they left us in a pretty short time and are now in their respective homes.

I have been troubled as you are about the war. There would have been no war if the Maine had been blown up in the Harbor of an-

132

other nation. The politicians could not have aroused the people to fight simply by uttering jingo sentiments. I believe 'that the real reason for the war is a determination on the part of the American people that cruelty such as had been practiced for years by' the Spaniards must stop. They did not exhaust all peaceful expedients. I wish they had. But the people became impatient and you cannot hold back a vast multitude when they get excited. For my own part I believe that it is the most righteous war that has been undertaken in this country. The European Nations are military nations. They have no idea of philanthropy or humanitarianism. They laugh at such things. But England does not. She ought to have interfered in behalf of the Armenians. I have no doubt many of the English admire us for the stand we have taken. If Admiral Dewey is successful at Manila I believe the Spaniards will give in and we shall quickly have peace and shall have done a fine thing for the advancement of civilization and Xty.

I am just off with my Frau, who is the best soul in all the world, to dine with the Whartons.

R.M.S. *Teutonic* July 6, '98

We have just received news of the destruction of Cervera's fleet. How skillful our men have shown themselves and what fellows the Spaniards are to brave death. I am saddened at the thought of our great loss by land. We have no particulars of this disastrous fight where so many of our men were killed. I do hope that this may end the war. After that will come mighty questions. I am inclined to agree with the outlook that we can no longer remain apart but must henceforth take our place in the council of nations.

Groton October 31, '98

We have bought a summer place! Where do you think it is? At North Haven about 10 miles from Rockland. North Haven is said to be the one perfect spot on the Maine coast.

Groton December 3 '98

I have got a new interest and enthusiasm in teaching Latin and enjoy the work more than I ever did. During the week I do a good deal of reading aloud—Each evening the boys listen for half an hour to Kipling's new story, on Fridays the Prefects come in for general poetry and Sunday evenings I read Dante (Norton's Translation) to the sixth form. And so I keep in touch with literature, but I should like to get in a great deal more. We had a rare blizzard here, the greatest November snowstorm in the memory of the oldest inhabitants. The roads are piled high on each side with snow.

133

Boston October 1, '99

You may wonder at my being in Boston of a Sunday night. It *is* an odd place for me to be in. But I am passing the night at the Club after the first Service at Harvard. It was what F. Peabody entitles a Syndicate Service. He conducted the prayers, Faunce, new President of Brown, preached and Shaler and I made short addresses. Shaler (Dean of the Scientific School) telling the meaning to him of the daily Chapel prayers, and the good he gets from them. Faunce's Sermon was extremely able, delivered without notes, on the text, "O God, thou art my God." My own preachment was muddling my brain and yet I was interested. The style and the learning of the man impressed me considerably and I felt a minnow among the Tritons. It was an inspiring audience however, nearly filling the building and I was fairly free and seemed to have the sympathy of the people. Especially, perhaps, of the College men. Afterwards I walked half way into town with Bill Burden one of our boys now Captain of the Football and a great duck in the Athletic puddle. I showed him how it seemed to me possible to take advantage of the fresh enthusiasm which has arisen at Harvard caused in no small degree by Athletic success and to use it for the deeper life of the place. Bill agreed that going to Chapel might have the effect of bringing others and is clearly willing to make the experiment. My aim is to get hold of a lot of the prominent men, Captains of teams, Presidents of the classes, leaders in the religious societies and others, and get them to back up the services and make the Chapel the centre of the University as it can be made if they will take up the project with zeal.

Groton December 23 '99

It seems to me that I have not for an age had a chance to puzzle out your old handwriting. The brethren went off Wednesday in high spirits and left us rejoicing at the thought of a holiday. For the last six weeks I have only had occasional glimpses of my wife and children. It is a delightful thing to get with them and have something of family life. My parents and Fanny's come tomorrow for a mild Xmas festivity with us. Dorothy is a person with very bright color and the possessor of a great mop of almost black hair. Which suggests that some ancestor of my wife far back was a colored gentleman and that this is a case of reversion to type. How dreadful are these British losses in Africa. It fills my heart with sadness to think of those fine fellows being mown down in a way which seems so unnecessary. I only hope that the English have learned their lesson and that they will be able under Roberts and Kitchener to speedily bring the war to a close. But the outlook is far from bright. Many of my old School fellows are fighting there.

134

Groton November 5 1900

The [new] Chapel continues beautiful, more glorious day by day. The bells are in place and on Saturday night I hope to have a crew of men come up from Boston to ring a joyous peal. We use the Chapel each day for morning prayers and the boys seem to be unanimous in liking it. We were just a bit afraid that they might consider it too ecclesiastical to go there every morning. To me it is a perpetual inspiration. The School is all agog just now over the St. Mark's football match which is to come on Wednesday. They seem to be a superior lot this year and will probably defeat us. If we are beaten it will be just a bit harder than ever to go away to Harvard for three weeks—for the brethren will be sad at heart. And when boys are dreary they are apt to be troublesome as well.

Groton November 15 1900

Of course I will let you have $1500. Thank you so much for giving me the chance to lend you this. But please do not think of interest. I would much rather not have anything of that kind. It is the part of a friend to allow his friend to serve him. That is 'the doctrine that you have preached and you must stand by it now.

Groton December 7 1900

I did meet Dean Fremantle. 3 times indeed, at my room, at Billings, and at F. S. Peabody's at lunch. The effect of my presence, so far as I could judge was to make him exceedingly sleepy—for he did little else than gape when ever I saw him. The poor old Chap had gout and I fancy he did not feel like a fighting cock. I got my revenge upon him however for I nearly went to sleep in his lecture, which was not bad in itself. but the Dean read it with his nose between the leaves and we might almost as well have employed a phonograph. Hodges is made of steel wire. Otherwise I should think him likely to have nervous prostration after three weeks of entertaining your dean. This is not to disparage your friend. It is only to say that like most Englishmen he talks or not as he chooses and is mighty heavy for human nature's daily food.

135

19
E. P. AND THE FACULTY

MANY of the Rector's most marked characteristics were very evident in his dealings with the faculty. It was a most striking thing, to anyone in a position to observe, that this man, so positive in his beliefs and opinions, so dogmatic in many of his dealings, had a singular capacity for securing and working with remarkably able men who disagreed with him on many minor points and some large ones, but who respected his bigness and integrity and served him faithfully. There can be no doubt that one of the main reasons for the success of Groton School was the caliber of its faculty.

During the first twenty-five years or so the average number of masters was not more than ten or twelve. Of Billings and Gardner more will be said later. Geddes went on to Boston University where he became a full professor. Higley, a real scholar, left Middlebury to come to Groton and remained until his death. Ayrault, Gladwin, Sturgis, Griswold,* Abbott, Richards, Hinchman, Crane, Regan, Andrews, Call, Lynes, Jacomb, and later Thomas, Zahner, Nash, DeVeau stayed for more than twenty years; some of them for thirty, some for more than forty. Thayer left to be head of St. Mark's; Abbott of Lawrenceville. Cushing went into politics and became lieutenant governor of Massachusetts. Arthur Woods departed to be perhaps the best police commissioner New York ever had. Charles Slatterly became a bishop. Ellery Sedgwick was editor of the *Atlantic Monthly*; Julian Coolidge was one of the leading mathematicians at Harvard and master of Lowell House. Remsen Ogilby founded a school in the Philippines and later was president of Trinity College, Hartford.†

* It was Griswold who, meeting a somewhat supercilious British pedagogue who was singing the praises of his own school, asked what the school was. "Eton," replied the Britisher. "Ah!" said Griswold, "the Groton of England, I believe."

† Several who have known Groton long and well agree that four main divisions could be made in Groton history in Peabody's time.
   I. 1884-1904. The founding period. About 1904 Arthur Woods began his
      successful crusade for better scholarship in college entrance.

136

Another thing that one must understand about Groton masters is that they belong to a calling. It was not exactly a profession, although the Rector always inculcated a sense of professional pride, because pedagogy was only part of their task. It was a calling. Of all the texts on which the Rector preached, the one he used most often, not only in the pulpit but in faculty meetings, was "For their sakes I sanctify myself"; and for a Groton master his job was not only a job, it was a way of life. It was not a way of life which would appeal to most men, because it meant giving up many pleasures and freedoms that most men value. For almost nine months of the year a dormitory master, at any rate, lived in a glass house. His life consisted of boys; boys in the dormitory, boys at meals, boys in class, boys in recreation. His day began at five minutes of seven in the morning and usually lasted until about ten o'clock at night. His whole thinking, his whole doing, his whole being was geared to a single object, the welfare of every single boy who came under his care in any way. His own desires, his own behavior, were subordinate to that. One cannot know unless he has experienced it how utterly drained spiritual batteries are after a term of this. One gives all term long with no chance to recharge. Laymen think that a schoolmaster leads an easy, idle life, and point with envious scorn to the long holidays he gets. Those holidays are good and are one of the great rewards that come to teachers, but they are more than a reward, they are a necessity. Further, a schoolmaster is denied one of the greatest satisfactions that can come from most professions. A doctor or an architect can point to a man or a building and say, "Except for me this would not be." A schoolmaster cannot do that. The results he achieves are all intangible. His pupils forget their book

---

II. 1904-1920. The period of crusades; *i.e.*, Woods for scholarship; Abbott for a freer hand for masters; Hinchman for a broader curriculum; agitation for changes in the pedagogical viewpoint by G. Rublee and E. Sedgwick; visit of A. Flexner for purposes of a general survey, which led to considerable changes; a slow but steady broadening of pedagogical horizons, and a slow but steady improvement in scholarship.

III. 1920-1934. The period of fruition. Results of early crusades plus impact of later crusaders (as Tuttle, Zahner, Beasley, and Martin) from the faculty and alumni.

IV. 1934-1941. The period of approaching transition, with a high scholastic tradition established and guarded by the alumni and faculty.

learning and his words of wisdom. What he pours into them vanishes like a beefsteak; it is absorbed, becomes a part of growth and change, but one can't put his finger on it once consumed. And yet, the nature of this calling is such that those who love it love it with a deep, almost passionate devotion. They do not begrudge the world outside nor can they ignore it, since their duty is to prepare boys to live in it, but real life and the deep rewards are at school. Mere teaching ability is not enough. There are admirable college teachers who would be rank failures as schoolmasters. One may say this without qualification, that a man who is to teach school well must love boys and love character and the things that are right.

Of course the dangers of the life are considerable. A man may easily get in a rut. Some men, not many, but some, have done so even at Groton. That is a man's own fault. A man may become a kind of spiritual wastrel and bully, dealing as he does with adolescents who cannot match him in authority, experience, or maturity. The world of a small school is a tiny world and, like an Army post or any small community, subject to minor jealousies, petty feuds, and a good deal of lip-smacking gossip. A man who wants to teach should go into his profession with his eyes open, seeing these things clearly. Then he will find rewards and interests and pleasures which pass ordinary understanding.

Mr. Sturgis, who was at Groton many years, wrote:

In some important ways the relationship between the Rector and the faculty has been completely unchanged from year to year. At the first meeting of each year he outlined his conviction that a master should accept and aim to carry out the highest ideals of his profession, explaining those ideals with inspiring simplicity and sincerity. With this would come also an annual repetition of the value of what the Rector calls "form", i.e. attention to accurate performance of detailed duties. In fact I have always felt he has the most remarkable combination of deep underlying principles with the ability to superintend minor features of the daily regime. This makes it difficult at times for him to delegate unimportant duties to others; as resulted when a "Master of the Day" was appointed to relieve him for bigger affairs. The Rector admitted, without implying lack of confidence in the conscientiousness of the faculty, that he could not help feeling he must in a measure follow up the efficient functioning of the new appointee.

In his personal relation with each master Mr. Peabody is always 100% frank; unhesitatingly critical where in any way he thinks the good of the School demands it, but so obviously speaking from this motive that it gives no possible ground for resentment. I think he has become definitely more tolerant and receptive of new suggestions, even when opposed to his own former prejudices. Though his early training and his slight personal interests in scientific subjects tend to emphasize the traditional classical curriculum, yet he recognizes the wisdom of meeting new educational demands and does his best to appreciate their importance. One great element of the Rector's strength is his ability to decide a question promptly; and if, as occasionally happens, he finds the decision was wrong, he can dismiss it from his mind, knowing he has acted as seemed to him right.

If Peabody could be ruthless in criticism, he could also be adamant in defense. He reserved for himself the right to speak with brutal frankness; but if others criticized a master, or if parents or boys put a master's authority in jeopardy, the master could count on the Rector's backing to the limit. If the master did not belong at Groton, he would go at the end of the year, but while he was there, and sometimes afterward, the Rector believed in "backing him up." Even if basic justice was sometimes strained, this was so. He would rake the master privately from stem to stern, but publicly he would stand behind him unless, as almost never was the case, some question of morality was involved. There were some who thought he carried this principle of loyalty too far and sometimes kept a man on out of affection and sympathy who could have been replaced by a better teacher. It may be so, but if so the case was the exception and not the rule.

There are also many men who could not abide what they call the Rector's paternalism. If a man left the school for an evening or a day, the Rector wanted to know why, when, and where. This was distasteful to some. The Rector's reply to the resentment was simply that the masters got long vacations, that while school was on they were expected to work and work hard, and their first responsibility and his in term time, was to see to it that the boys were taken care of.

He encouraged further study out of term time to improve a man's professional competency. He believed in taking a year off himself now and then and encouraged sabbaticals for his colleagues. When, later, the system of regular repeated sabbaticals was called into question, he was open to suggestions and reasonable requests for time out, provided it was used to the interest of the School, on the part of any member of the faculty.

Copies of his own notes for two of the first faculty meetings at the opening of a year are extant:

As we gather for the first time in the year, I like to remind myself and you, if you will accept a reminder, of the happy situation in which we find ourselves in a world which is pretty well filled with unhappiness. I know partly from personal experience the comparatively uninteresting quality of the life which engages the activities of a great multitude of our fellow citizens. To awake in the morning with the thought of what seems to offer little beyond a humdrum routine connected with things material or mechanical is very different from the experience of the Schoolmaster who is engaged in the absorbing occupation of helping to develop the all round qualities, physical, intellectual, and spiritual, of boys who are to be with him throughout the day.

Of one contemplating the schoolmaster's life, the question was asked—does it not mean a seriously limited field so far as one's own environment is concerned? Are you not, as Shakespeare puts it "cabined, cribbed, confined" by the limitations of your profession? My reply to my friend was that in all callings there is some element of sacrifice. The schoolmaster must abandon the hope of the heights of scholarship scaled by those who can give themselves to research. If a man cares most of all for that and for teaching his subject, he should try to find a place in the college. If his ambition is especially to train boys by instructing and living with them, then he may well become a schoolmaster. With these people he naturally lives through the Term, selecting such times for absence as seem to him proper. But the schoolmaster's mind is set more upon the life with the boys than with outside engagements, and he finds his joy in following it. There is inevitably a great deal of routine in a schoolmaster's life; much, too, of detail, but everything that concerns boys is of interest to him. His desire is to use all the time he can in their service.

I was told by one who knew, that the difference in business between the young American and the young Englishman was found partly in the question asked by the latter whether he could get away from the office in time for a bit of cricket; while the American lingered after his own hours were over to discover what was going on in the office generally with a view to possible promotion as he gained an intelligent grasp of the business.

To the man who is in love with his profession as a schoolmaster generally is, all that goes on is significant. A former member of our Staff who was leaving us informed his successor that it was a mighty interesting life on the whole but that he might find it a bit dull on Sundays. As the successor was a man about to enter the Ministry the chances were against it, but it seemed evident from the first teacher's remark that he had no rightful place in a Church School. He was probably what is now called a humanist, who regarded man as such a lofty creature that he can achieve righteousness without inspiration from on high. He decided wisely, as I think, to take a place open to him on the staff of a university where he has put in a life useful but unconcerned with the responsibilities for the spiritual life of his pupils. The highest in our life did not appeal to him. Just as what seemed the lowest failed to engage the sympathy of another man who complained that a master at Groton was expected to spend much of his time in picking up papers and cleaning up the houses and the grounds generally.

As we have often remarked, there are many details in school life which call for careful attention. All that has to do with the business of the school should be as carefully and as promptly carried on as in a well-conducted office. Reports should be neatly made out and presented at the time that they are called for. I may say that there has been a distinct improvement in this way since the early days. Estimates should be presented as soon as possible after they are asked for. The theory is that masters having their own classrooms and the Memorial Room in which to expatiate will generally be at the Schoolhouse. If a master is to be away from his classroom, I will again ask that he leave a memorandum on his blotter telling where he may be found. I ask this because so much time is otherwise inevitably wasted. Last Term on a good many occasions boys consumed much time in trying to help me to get into touch with men who failed to supply this information.

We asked for increased assistance on the part of all masters in supervising the exercise, that it shall be carried on every day, and that the boys shall be properly clad in both civilian and athletic costume.

I believe that we should do greater service for the boys than we achieve at present if we should all take an interest in the missionary and social work that is done by boys. This would mean attending the meetings of the Missionary Society, the talks of visitors describing the social work that is going on in the cities, and accompanying the boys, when the arrangement can be made, on expeditions to see some of the institutions which are being established in this State for the public welfare.

I would also ask such as are willing to give up a part of their summer holidays to help us in carrying on the Camp at Newfound Lake. The work there is going on well, but it would add to our

141

efficiency if all the masters cared for this part of our outside work and would lend a hand when they might find it possible.

Looking outside of the School, there are conditions which naturally engage the attention of the master who cares for his boys in the large way.

One of our older graduates wrote to me about a son of his who was exercised by the prevalence of hard drinking in his college. He reports that some men are in the habit of getting drunk every Saturday night. The undergraduate to whom this father refers had tried to find out in his scientific way why these men have established this noisome habit. He says that they seem to plan for it as carefully, if not more so, than they plan for their daily work. It would be of value, I think, if each one of us should make a point of investigating this particular condition, especially in the two colleges, Harvard and Yale, to which most of our boys go. If this practice to which my friend refers is pursued by any of our graduates, it would clearly be our duty to take some action with a view, it may be to saving them from themselves or, if that were not possible, keeping them away from the boys who are leading decent lives at the School. It is incumbent upon us to do something to remedy the failures to which we must plead guilty if the situation as described be found among our men.

There are communications concerning a number of boys or about the School which I think will interest you.

The following letters are illustrative of things mentioned above:

DEAR MR. PEABODY:

Sept. 29, 1904

Many thanks for your kind and friendly letter. I think I quite understand what you mean by my lack of form and am very grateful for your criticism which will help me a good deal. . . . I shall always be glad of any criticism, which you may give me. I don't promise always to agree with you, but I will always try to see your point of view. I am inclined to doubt if a year at Oxford would have much more effect on my manners than it would on the color of my hair and as the matter of "good form" seems to me of little importance compared with intellectual activity, I am glad I am going to a place where there is more of the latter, even if there is less of the former.

Sometimes the masters were outspoken themselves:

Rome, April 3, 1899

I have heard that the school has made use of my house as a measle's pest house. I can't believe that you have allowed such a thing to be done without consulting me by cable and would like to hear from you in regard to the matter. Affectionately,

MATHER ABBOTT.

To another headmaster:

MY DEAR MR. ——:

I received last night a letter from Mr. —— which took me completely by surprise. He tells me that you have decided that it is better for him to resign from ——. The reason for your advice, he tells me, is that you have heard rumours of criticism from Grotonians and from me.

As one of the older masters remarked when he heard it, this cannot be the real reason, no Headmaster would get rid of a man on account of vague rumours. In regard to this, however, I have no reason to make enquiry. The point of my writing now is to ask first, whether you told Mr. —— that I had criticized him; second, the nature of the criticisms to which you refer; third, the ground that you have for believing them to be true. I should have thought that both as Headmaster and as a clergyman you would have written directly to one who has been a colleague in education and in the ministry before making a statement of so serious a nature. Even as it is, in the face of Mr. ——'s understanding, I cannot believe that you have accepted a report concerning my views without verifying it.

May I ask for an early reply to this letter, as Mr. ——'s career is of very great interest to me, and I realize how seriously his future is jeopardized through what I conceive to be a misunderstanding.

Very truly yours,

ENDICOTT PEABODY

To a former master, at another school:

MY DEAR ——:

I have this morning received from Mr. —— a letter together with a note from a parent of the —— School boy both of which give me very great distress. This is a quotation from the note:

"I am thankful that you did not advise my taking Mr. —— as tutor, for each day some remark of —— shows the really evil influence he has had, his nightly talks, the whole thing, cynical, sophisticated, sex: it is too bad! you were fortunate to have found him out, and I hope that all this at such an early stage of development will make little lasting impression on ——, for he is so young."

Mr. —— in commenting upon the note informs me that he realized that you were cynical and failed to command the respect of the boys, that the boys laughed openly at you, and that your influence was thought by several of the people at —— to be positively bad.

143

This is a very great revelation to me. I had a high respect for your character as well as your ability, and I still believe that there are in you good qualities, which we found at Groton. It will, however be clearly impossible for me to consider your coming here as a master next year. Such action on my part would call forth unreserved condemnation from the trustees, and there is nothing to be said in support of it.

I need hardly assure you that this unexpected turn of things has given me great pain. Most earnestly do I hope that you will be able to rescue yourself from the defects of character which are indicated by this parent and by Mr. ———. You cannot fail to escape the suffering which will come from the consciousness of having failed to carry out loyally the duties which were entrusted to you at ——— ——— School.

With sincere regret that this action of mine should be inevitable
I am,
Sincerely yours,
Endicott Peabody

To a Groton master:

My dear Mr. ———:

There are two points that have been working in my mind for some time which I want to lay before you. 1. The importance of having a definite and well carried out system for the care of the boys' athletic clothes. At the time of your illness, there was a large quantity of soiled clothes in the confiscation locker, some of them marked, some of them unmarked,—and the boys were, many of them, wearing clothes which had evidently not been washed for a long season. It seems to me of the utmost importance, and I know that the parents must feel strongly about it, that more attention should be given to the care of these clothes which the parents, in many cases find a difficult expense for them to meet. Let us, therefore, next term make sure, FIRST, that every boy knows exactly what he is to purchase; SECOND, that he does not wear anything until it has been marked with his name in full; THIRD, that all clothing confiscated be returned to the school directly it is discovered, the owner being given a fitting punishment for his negligence; FOURTH, that the clothing be washed and repaired thereby insuring the health of the wearer and his decent appearance. I have been a good deal troubled at seeing the boys wearing clothes full of holes and looking worse than any of the public school boys who come up to us for games. Will you please think out a system and see that it is consistently carried through during the year? If necessary, a captain of the gymnasium could probably help you, but I think this is a matter which requires your personal attention.

The second point I have in mind is the decision of the Masters' Committee on Education that we need one of the two morning hours which have hitherto been given up to gymnasium. We are intending to make an effort to improve our scholarship and for that purpose, we require all the time we can get. I realize that you count the two hours for gymnasium valuable for the development of the boys and I sympathize with your desire to retain them. I do not feel, however, that we can spare these hours which all other schools, so far as I know, devote to purely scholastic subjects. For the coming year, at any rate, we will try this system.

Written to a master:

For a long time I have been mulling over the question of the problem of masters' duties and opportunities in our schools. One of the great weaknesses in American education has been the fact that men have given up a few years to teach instead of taking it up as their life work, as they have done in the English schools. The result has been that our schools have, most.of them, acquired very few traditions. It is the masters, as we have often said, who maintain the best traditions of a school and they must, of course, be permanent. But quite often I hear this view challenged. One of the best known headmasters, for instance, is of the opinion that there should be only a few married masters in a school, holding that they are less efficient than unmarried men. This means, inevitably, a weakening of tradition—and I do not think it is true. There must be always, in a school like ours, a certain number of unmarried men to take charge of the dormitories and there will be among these a certain amount of change. This is natural, and, I think on the whole, beneficial. I do, however, hold to the opinion that it is a great advantage to have the larger number of masters permanent and that means, in most cases, married men.

In order that the greater efficiency and greater value, generally, of these men may be established, it seems necessary that they should have a perfectly definite understanding of the situation. From time to time I have tried to enunciate my view of it, but I think I may not have been sufficiently clear. In my judgment, the whole day of a schoolmaster, married or single, should, as a rule, be spent at the school just as a business man's day is spent at his office. That means his arriving in time for chapel Or, if he have earlier duties, as I have in connection with the infirmary, before that hour. The morning being devoted to teaching or study is best spent, as I see it, at the schoolhouse. If a man prefers to study in his own home he should be free to do so, but I think he should realize that time is lost in walking to and fro,

The afternoons should be given to extra teaching, as in the case of the mathematical masters and some others and to playing with the boys or coaching them in sports or encouraging them by being present at their matches. With the ringing of the outside bell, the married master's day ends and he goes home, but there are a good many evenings during the term in which he has either definite or general duties connected with the school. This last requirement may seem over-exacting, but it must be remembered that a schoolmaster has seventeen weeks of vacation which he can devote to home life and study. There are a great many opportunities for maintaining the ideals of the school and influencing the lives of the boys which may be lost unless one is constantly on the lookout to grasp them. I mean such things as unfailing attendance at the chapel services, both week-day and Sunday services; attendance at meetings of the Missionary Society; assisting in the carrying on of our Missions which can be made a much more important feature of our life; taking charge of the summer camp for a week, at least every other year; attendance at lectures and concerts.

The social side of school life is also of much importance; mixing with the boys in the library and schoolroom; taking part in Faculty supper, especially when the Sixth Form boys and the graduates are present, and for the married men there is further chance to get near the boys by entertaining them from time to time at a social meal.

I have jotted down these things somewhat at haphazard, but they seem to me of quite vital importance to the school and to the married men. There is, no doubt, a natural tendency on the part of men to go to their homes and to feel that they must give up time to their families. With this I sympathize, but there is, as I have pointed out, a greater opening than most men have, afforded by our frequent and long vacations and even without these, a man is at his home for a longer time during the week than is the case with most business and professional men. From time to time I talk with such men and find that in most cases the whole of their day and most of their evenings and many of their nights are given up to their work, and this throughout the year, with the exception of a two weeks' holiday. Unless we make a great effort, it seems likely that we shall not be able to persuade others of our own faith that permanent and married men are both desirable and necessary for the proper development of school life.

You will understand, I hope, that in writing this I am not finding fault, but simply making an attempt to arrive at a common agreement with a view to helping us all to render the best possible service to the school.

Note to a master:

DEAR ———:
Would it not be better for this question of the training Camp to be between ——— and me?
You and I do not agree on the question of age and we are quite ready to agree to differ—at least I am.
——— is so determined to carry his point that he is stirring up the Graduates.
I should not like to have him drive in a wedge between Grads and me; but to drive in a w. betw. you and me wd. be too dreadful to contemplate.

Affectionately,

E. P.

And this report gives an interesting insight into school minutiae and shows the type of detail to which the Rector had to give his attention year after year:

Report of Master-in-Charge for week of Feb. 14-21
This report is made simply from a sense of duty, and best interests for all concerned, as I understand the situation.

The Halls. In a note from you last term you mentioned the condition of the halls in the School House, relative to boys going to and from class rooms. The condition is better than it was at that time, but as one would expect, when no one is there the boys rush in crowds to their class rooms, especially at my end of the building, which involves a greater distance to cover than from school room to other end of the upper hall. Much annoyance and confusion has been caused by the man (or men) at the bells: the first may ring on time or not (which is of minor importance) and the same man ring the second bell on time, but the trouble has *often* been connected with the ringing of the third bell; either the same master rings it or, which is worse, the on-coming master rings it when he gets there or as he thinks of it. An eight-day perfect time piece secured to the desk might *enable* the masters to be on time (when there) as to ringing of bells.

Smoking of Cubebs. It is quite certain that this had been done somewhat by the boys while painting scenery etc. I understand that the offence (I infer it is such) has been committed in both B.H. and H.H. Vth form studies. While it in itself can probably not do any harm, is it just to allow it! as most normal boys who would do that are simply drawing the line between "smoking" and "Smoking Cubebs". My experience has been that few boys will stop at that point, and hence are strongly tempted to take the next step.

147

The Diningroom. I refrain from any attempt to make the boys less gluttonous, as previous remarks on the subject have been useless; but since then the orange juice at breakfast has been introduced. I frequently notice boys collecting number of glasses, both near and across the table *before* grace is said, and of course talking if not scrapping. At other meals when you are present the non-talking you see for yourself.

Language. So many times have I wanted to mention this subject, but now feel that I am bound to do so. Many boys say "O, my god", "heck" without the slightest provocation and seem to think nothing of it. . . .

Evening school. Many boys have commented, not favorably, on the manner the evening schoolroom in H.H. is often kept. They say that any correction, remark or even "display of temper" is done *from* the desk in very loud voice, and is more or less frequent, and very annoying to those who want to study, but highly entertaining to others.

Precedence. Recently you announced *emphatically* at coffee, that detention recorded in the detention book was to be served before any other assignments (Sat. the Latenesses and Black marks being an exception). During my week of detention this has been violated several times and in one case most deliberate. Yesterday when I had kept detention for 55 minutes, a boy came in to serve his recorded detention with the excuse that he was told it was all right to come then as he had other things to do first! There were 65 boys on detention yesterday. Having doubts as to some boys serving their detention I found that some of my own latenesses recorded in the book before 9:30 were not on the list, but the climax was reached when two boys came to serve detention whose names were not on the list: I commended them. They said that they knew they had latenesses and were not on the list! I looked over the list and found that 21 boys, having from 1 to 5 latenesses each in the book were not on the list at all. 31 latenesses in all were not served as a result. Some boys said that they had been given at least 4 but none were in the book. I asked the boys as they reported, what they had received their latenesses for and only 6 had any idea at all! Personally I think it is highly demoralizing to these boys entrusted to our care and training, to allow such conditions; they are very quick to see the cause! It seems infinitely better to not have a so-called system than to treat it and the boys in this way. It is not strange that latenesses and black marks have so little weight with the boys, and that boys rule instead of masters in some cases. Boys are quite free to say that all given to them will not get as far as the book, and they run chances of not having enough to summon them to the Rector. The master keeping detention for these offenses can not correctly post

148

his list as boys having enough marks to meet you do not report to the master on detention.

'Phones. It seems rather far fetched to have connecting 'phones between boys' studies.

———

P.S. Possibly you feel that it has been an error to put me on for the week; but what I have touched upon simply and briefly has been done in sincerity.

Letter written to Mather Abbott when he was considering a position at Yale:

I quite realize that there is a great opportunity at Yale for arousing an enthusiasm for Latin, for guiding young instructors into the art of teaching, and for influencing the lives of a great number of young men. Your scholarship and gifts of personality are such that you would certainly accomplish a great deal along each of these lines. The Freshmen would be stimulated to study Latin more earnestly, you would infuse a spirit of eagerness in some of the instructors, and your character would be a power for good among those with whom you were closely thrown. Moreover, if you should continue to coach the Freshmen in rowing, you would make intimate friendships with them.

Having said these things, I must now in some measure retrace my steps.

If you are to become a great teacher, you will have to lead a scholar's life. That means days of laborious study, practically all the working hours being given up to investigation and the teaching of students and instructors. It would, therefore, be difficult for you to find the leisure time which is necessary in order to get into close touch with young men. For a while the Groton boys knowing you would be likely to seek you out, but, after four years, this stream would naturally dry up.

If Yale men are at all like the undergraduates at Harvard, it will not be easy to persuade them to come freely to your home if you are settled in New Haven. A visit to a family is very different from dropping in on a man in college rooms. To an undergraduate it means putting on a stiff collar and presentable clothes and the average student will not do this even to see his dearest friends except on rare occasions. I say this with some positiveness, for I know how hard some of the Harvard teachers have tried to get the undergraduates to come to them freely and how the very best of them and most companionable have in large measure failed.

The instructors will look to you for inspiration and will probably be keen to adopt your suggestions, but there will be among them a great many crude and opinionated young men whom it will require

149

constant forbearance to deal with. Still, there is no reason why you should not be able to handle them. The students are likely to be so multitudinous as to require dealing with in the mass rather than as individuals.

On the financial side, while I do not know exactly what would happen, an assistant professor receiving a salary much larger than the other men of his standing would be likely to arouse a certain feeling of dissatisfaction. It would be stronger, I suppose, with the professors who have given years of their energies to Yale and still receive only a comparatively small emolument.

Perhaps I am drawing too dark a picture. My intention is simply now to tell you the particular obstacles which occur to me. These do not prevent my believing that as I said at the beginning, you would do effective service, nor do they compel me to hold that your work might not be all that you hope for. I do believe, that for the first three or four years there would be great returns, but after that the lions in the path strike me as likely to be dangerous.

On the other hand, for the life at Groton there is the assurance of continued usefulness of a very high quality. You have a great talent for attracting boys, getting to know them well and influencing them as few men can do. Your teaching is much valued by them and helps them not simply to enter college, but having entered to get high standing in their classes. Having sufficient time for the purpose, you can take part with them in the sports and, through coaching in both rowing and football, you can get a grip upon them which will never be shaken off.

At Groton you could find a good deal more time for study than you have found so that the joys of scholarship would not be denied you and as your physical powers decreased you would become more and more efficient as a teacher.

I quite recognize the fact that the choice of this life would seem to the world a sacrifice. It would be the acceptance of a lot less seen of men, but there would still be a great number of people who would look with admiration and understanding at your contribution to education and what is, of course, by far the most important thing, you would be leaving a deep impress upon the lives of young men whose opportunities for great service are unusual.

You and I have been together so much and have known each other so well that there is no need for me to tell you what I personally should prefer; but I should also prefer to have you make your decision without thought of my personal preference. It would seem to me an invasion of your personality for me to ask you to consider my desire, indeed I should hesitate to request you even to consider the need of the School. The point that I should wish to make is that here there is a chance for you to do such permanent work as it is given to comparatively few men to accomplish. Your own conviction as to which is the work intended for you must of course bring the final solution of the problem. I sympathize deeply with you, my dear chap, in your perplexity and wish that I could have complied with your request to say, "Go ahead with Yale work for I believe that you ought to do it". It would not, however, be honest for me to say that, and you want a friend to tell you what seems to him to be true.

20

MR. B. AND MR. G.

TWO men who were with the Rector almost constantly since 1884 deserve a chapter to themselves. Each in his way had a large influence on the Rector, but the way of each was very different from that of the other.

There is not much doubt that the Rector was closer to Sherrard Billings in his daily dealings than to any other man. In a sense, he never opened his heart to Billings as he did to Atwood, or even one or two of his English friends, but Billings was his co-adjutor in the School and in the Chapel, taking charge in the Rector's absence, and sharing the services and preaching with him.

At Groton he was known variously as Mr. B., Beebs, and the Little Man. He was a little man and his size, one suspects he felt, was emphasized by his constant nearness to and inevitable comparison with the Rector. He had a sensitiveness which the Rector lacked and also a sensitivity. Quick to take offense, he, like the Rector made much of small things. It meant a great deal to him to be the first Groton football captain.

He was a better classroom teacher than the Rector; in fact he was a very good teacher indeed, with a knack of making things, especially Latin grammar, memorable. He was a stickler for good manners, good form. Full of mannerisms, he was one of the best raconteurs ever heard and loved to talk. There were certain School occasions, leading the "Blue Bottle Song" on the School Birthday or being chaired around the buildings and bonfire lead-

151

ing the cheers after a victorious St. Mark's game, at which he
was indispensable.

On October 15 came the School Birthday celebration. We all
gathered in the Hundred House Schoolroom. The Rector led us in
a procession winding in and out through the halls singing *John
Brown's Body*, ending at the Dining Room, which was decorated
with flowers and the Groton red, white, and black. After Grace
and a large feast provided by the Matron, Miss Cram, there was a
shout from the VI form for Blue Bottles. Now Blue Bottles is always
sung by the V form led by Mr. B. "Blue Bottles! Blue Bottles" came
the cry and "We want Mr. B."

Mr. B. arose solemnly and swaggered to the table where all the V
were gathered. He put on a robe and took a huge carving knife that
had been provided for him as a baton. He extended his arms for
silence and a hush fell on the room. Then, brandishing his arms, his
moustache bristling, his chin up, and every inch the maestro, he led
them into the old song, very slowly and sedately at first, five bottles
coming off to begin with:

"Twenty-sev'n blue bottles hanging on the wall
Twenty-sev'n blue bottles hanging on the wall
    Take five blue bottles from the bottles on the wall
  Leaves twenty-two blue bottles hanging on the wall."

When seventeen bottles were left, they came off by twos, and the
singing moved faster. When nine were left they came one at a time,
each to a faster tempo. By the time five were left Mr. B. was a
whirling, gesticulating dervish set in flashing steel, but he held his
chorus in strict control. In spite of their speed, he kept them in uni-
son and had a reserve. He needed it, for by the time the last bottle
was reached even the listeners are breathless.

"One blue bottle hanging on the wall
One blue bottle hanging on the wall
    Take one blue bottle from the bottles on the wall"—
Then O so slowly and majestically and ponderously
"Leaves NO blue bottles hanging on the wall."

Thunderous applause. The School stamps and shouts. Mr. B. takes
his bow again and again; is gratified by the appreciation of his art,
congratulates his singers, bows to Mrs. Peabody, who graciously in-
clines her head at him; bows to the Rector who bows back; bows
to Mr. Gardner, who curtseys in return.

Then prayers. And then the prayer for the School written by
Bishop Lawrence and for the Graduates, written by Mr. G.

"Almighty God, our Heavenly Father, who art the only source
of light and life, send down upon this School the rich gifts of Thy

152

Good Spirit, that Thy Truth may be sincerely sought, faithfully received, and obediently followed. Endue its teachers with wisdom, zeal, and patience. Inspire its scholars with the spirit of truth, honor, and humility. May they day by day grow in grace and in the knowledge of our Lord and Saviour Jesus Christ. Grant to all in this School such a cheerful and forbearing spirit, such strength of body, clearness of mind, and purity of heart that Thy work may be heartily done and Thy name glorified. Let Thy blessing rest upon us now and Thy Spirit dwell in this place from generation to generation; through Thy Son, our Lord and Saviour, Jesus Christ, Amen."

Afterwards we all crowded into the Pleasure Dome, where the VI formers read squibs or jokes on the boys and masters, while Mr. G., the owner of the Dome, sat beaming in the corner and knitted on a scarlet, green, and yellow sock.*

He was a remarkably fine preacher to boys. Another gifted preacher, well qualified to judge, called him "the most appealing and convincing preacher in our Church Schools." It would be generally agreed that he was a better preacher than the Rector. Certainly the Rector would insist on it, for no one was more critical of the Rector's preaching than Endicott Peabody himself. Atwood said of Peabody, "He has all gifts save that of eloquence." On occasion he had that, too, but day in and day out Billings was the better. And Billings loved to preach.

For many years he had a strong urge to leave Groton for parish work. He refused several tempting calls, but at last in 1905 when the Rector returned from a year abroad, after many heart-searchings, he left Groton to become associate rector of St. Paul's Church in Boston. Here he threw himself into the work and fell in love with Miss Eleanor Stockton, but he could not get Groton out of his mind, and the heart-searchings continued. After severe hesitation he decided his place was at the school, and in spite of the energetic protests of his parishioners he returned with his bride in 1906. When their little child, a daughter, was born, the mother died. And a few years later the little girl died, too.

Then one saw the true nature and great faith of Sherrard Billings. "A passion of sympathy" as Mr. G. called it arose on behalf of this brave and simple Christian gentleman who in this double stroke of adversity neither wavered nor complained, but showed in his life and courage the love of God and trust in His Son which he had preached in the pulpit.

* Recollection of a School Birthday celebration by a graduate.

At Groton he was the person responsible for many of the details which the Rector could not fit in. Because boys were not as afraid of him as they were of the Rector, they went to him with things that they would not take to "the Big Boss," and this was in itself of importance to the school. Mr. B. was a devout and consecrated churchman, if anything even more low church than the Rector,* but in hearty agreement as to the place of Christianity in the school. As a rule, he and the Rector got along together famously, because Mr. B. was a conformist; a brave and deeply good man, but not an intellectual adventurer. He was intensely loyal to the Rector and to the school which he loved and served with self-forgetful faithfulness these many years.

Samplings of letters tell something of him:

April 26, 1895

I am mad! real mad! —I discovered late in the day that the tenors and basses had been in the habit of stopping on the way home from choir practice to sing songs of their own in the Fives Court! A prefect leading them! Nice warn't it? I was disgusted and aired my views plainly.

Honestly it almost brings the tears to my eyes to think what a good lot of boys we have at Groton. Your absence, do you know, has done good in ways you do not know of. Grafton and Amory have each said how much better they were than when you were here to fall back on. . . . The masters are a most uncommonly good lot of men. Gladwin is a perfect kaleidoscope of inconsistencies, but I make allowance for his extraordinary tendency to exaggerate and so profit by the kernel of truth always in the stories he comes to me with. Amory * nearly killed me the other night. In a spirit of mischief I told him that Mrs. ——— would, I felt sure, want to consult him. . . . He got quite frantic and said if the School did not protect him against weeping mothers he would resign. I explained to him that his very work as a schoolmaster involved relations towards parents the duties of which he might not shirk. He announced in that case he *would* resign and he actually did. I thought I should die a-laughing at him. He wrote out: "Prof. Gardner hereby resigns. He will continue to live in the green house and will give G. S. from time to time such services as he feels like". . . . Isn't it absurd? . . . Smith and Sullivan were up for Saturday and Sunday and much to my disgust *did not go to Church in the morning.* Gardner afterwards romped with them.

* Mr. B. looked askance at a copy of Michelangelo's *Pieta* on a colleague's classroom wall and strenuously opposed a reredos in the Chapel.

* Mr. Gardner.

154

It occurs to me that you have been feeling badly about the matter of salary and have not liked to break the news that the trustees refused an increase this year. Don't ever do that, my dear fellow. I may believe that the master in my position ought to be paid more, but it is not a personal matter and I would not have you worrying about it for anything.

S. B.

DEAR COTTIE: Boston, January 25, 1906

You speak of Groton and you send me nearly into hysterics when you do so. . . . What made [Fanny] think that a year in Boston would be of any manner of use in settling a life problem? It has cleared up some things that perhaps were better off as they were! I have a bit more confidence in myself; I believe I can make this thing go, and can have a busy, pleasant, and useful life in this very job at which I am now working. . . . This is interesting and I think worth while. The mere fact of living in a city is stirring and the feeling of "poscimur", as Philo Sprague says, is very satisfactory. You know all about that, of course; you know what it is, as I have never known, to open your mail and find 3 invitations to preach, to be put on various important committees, to have people coming to ask your advice. You have kept up your connection with the outside world, and have been an important and prominent factor in Church and School matters and you have known the intense interest of that sort of life. But I have a suspicion that never in Boston will my life count for as much as perhaps it has counted at Groton. I am sure you will be known and remembered for what you have done while sitting tight in the saddle at School. And I daresay it is the same with me.

This life is easier, perhaps from the variedness of it and its changing interest—more likely because there is less teaching to do, for teaching on the whole seems to me the most exhausting thing a man can do. And this life on the surface is a broader one. . . . I wonder if in heaven things are easily decided? Affectionately,

SHERRARD BILLINGS.

Mr. William Amory Gardner was an entirely different matter. Called by his contemporaries Amory and by the boys Wag or Billy Wag, he was *sui generis*. He was born a very rich little boy and, his parents dying young, he and his brother were brought up by his aunt, the Mrs. Gardner of the famous museum in Boston, around which they romped as children. It was said of him that he never had a boyhood with or like other boys. At Harvard he was a distinguished scholar. Professor Goodwin said Gardner was the best Greek student he had ever had.

155

Perhaps it was the lack of a boyhood of his own which made him fall so head over heels in love with Groton. That is what he did. From the beginning he had a fanatical, wild devotion for the place and all who belonged to it. Yet—and this is the remarkable quality of him—he saw, as no one else has ever been able to, Groton as it has been and is, both good and bad. And herein, too, was part of his great service to the school. Wag was always talking, always offering suggestions, always criticizing. Because he was always amusing, always stimulating, and frequently right, he managed to get a hearing, if nothing else. He was a perpetual Devil's advocate and for this reason frequently under the Rector's skin. The irritation was increased by a marked eccentricity. At best the Rector might have found difficulty in understanding him, as Mr. G.'s poor health and somewhat frail constitution contrasted with the Rector's own never-failing robustness.

Wag was always putting his hand in his pocket for some worthy cause. His generosity was seen obviously in the Chapel and in other buildings, but much of it is entirely unseen and unknown. He built himself a house large enough to accommodate a huge family. With it he built himself a Pleasure Dome, containing a stage, a small swimming pool, and a squash court, with a maze attached. Here he would serve on Sunday afternoons wisdom, humor, a sticky-drippy-sweet concoction known as google (two colors, but the same taste), and a rock-hard stick of candy known as blackjack. In the house he installed a set of servants, in fear of offending whom he spent the balance of his days.

He loved sports of all kinds from bridge to racing. His big yacht, the cup defender *Mayflower*, was a great joy to him, but he usually had to go below during a race, the strain was so great. He loved good food, ate it heartily, and almost invariably regretted it. In a close rubber of bridge he had to stand holding his heart to quiet his excitement. He rode well, but absentmindedly, and was a great but curious knitter, changing colors and patterns of socks as it pleased him. He read as he walked and kept careful track of his reading, so that his intellectual food might be well-balanced. When his canoe upset in the Nashua, it was like him to "emerge paddling with one hand and with the other still holding his volume of Sophocles before his eyes, while a drenched cigarette still dangled from his lips" as Richard Danielson saw him do. Voluble though he was, and dogmatic, when he was protest-

156

ing against the ordinary custom of things he was fundamentally humble, referring to himself as a molehill in contrast to his colleague Major Higley's mountainous erudition.*

One either got to know him intimately, in which case he

* Another graduate recollection: "One very cold winter day in the winter term a prominent minister came to Groton to preach. He was quite a figure in his own city; admired in the pulpit, and honored as a citizen. After breakfast he wanted to go pay his respects to William Amory Gardner as one of the co-founders of the School. A boy was delegated to chaperone him across to Wag's house.

"The boy had been to Mr. G's for tea once or twice, so knew his way around more or less. They knocked on the door and nobody answered, but there was a noise going on inside, so they pushed the door open and went in. 'Mr. G!' the boy called.

" 'Yes, who is it?' answered a voice from upstairs. 'It doesn't matter in the least. Come up, come up.'

"They started down the hall for the stairs. The voice continued excitedly, 'It makes not the slightest difference that you won the first rubber, my dear boy', it said, 'of course you did. That is *la courtoisie de la maison*. But the laurels of the evening, you must admit, belonged to us. To be sure, in that first rubber we lost a few paltry farthings, whereas you, my poor fellow, owe me several lakhs and a crow of rupees.'

"The visitor was looking dubious as they climbed the stairs. The voice went on. 'Further', it said, 'while it pains me to wound a beloved disciple, I must point out to you, Bertie, that by your unfortunate error on the second hand in the third rubber you forfeited your membership in the Jockey Club of Constantinople and furthermore made our winning so overwhelmingly almost the equivalent of shooting sitting cows with a machine gun. Further still —well upon my word!'

"His discourse was interrupted by the callers entering the bedroom. Standing before the fire naked as he was born except for a voluptuous pair of fur bedroom slippers, toasting his stern and stirring a large plate of porridge as he talked was Billy Wag himself. Holding more porridge and unsmiling in a morning coat was his butler and stretched out on the sofa, with even less on than Wag was Bertie.

" 'This is Dr. ——' said the boy as solemnly as he could.

" 'Of course it is' said Wag, dropping an elaborate curtsey without spilling the porridge. 'How good of you to come. This is Bertie, Dr. ——, one of our alumni. You find us a trifle informal my dear Sir, but if you will give us a moment until we finish our breakfast, perhaps I can persuade Bertie to put on some clothes more suitable for the day. Do be seated.'

" 'I think I'd better get back, Sir,' said the boy.

"Mr. G. bowed low. 'If you will stay and converse I will gladly move over and share the fire with you. I cannot offer it all to you because only my rear is toasted and the front must be warm too this bitter day,' he said, 'if not, will you convey my respects to the Headmaster and tell him that all Groton boys should be made to learn to play bridge.' "

Of such truth were Gardnerian legends woven.

157

would love him, or he would, like many of the boys, look on Wag affectionately as a great character and therefore an ornament to the place, but out of the orbit. If one was not a scholar he would not be likely to think him a great teacher; if one loved books and ideas he would probably rate Wag as one of the greatest teachers he ever knew. If one cared to loaf, it was easy in his class.

Those classes were unlike any others and especially unlike any others at Groton. His recitations were frequently noisy, with Wag furnishing much of the tumult himself. He talked in a queer language, he marked by strange symbols, he grew shrill when distressed, which was often.

A graduate of the middle twenties remembers:

Billy Wag's Greek course was unlike anything I've had before or since. I'm ashamed to say I never did any work or learned any Greek, for he never checked up on us and I was one of those who needed checking when it came to things like grammar. But I've seldom learned so much about so many things. And his classes were enormously funny. Any little thing in the lesson would set him off. Once he gave a description of a ride on and a dispute with a camel. I couldn't tell what got him on the subject, but after he'd made us laugh till our sides ached he spent the rest of the period discussing Egyptian architecture. Another time we hit a passage in the Iliad which mentioned dogs. Wag was off like a bloodhound. He told us about dogs, which lead to architecture in Belgium, the canals of Holland and New York state, various methods of burying the dead, famous epitaphs, the battle of Thermopylae, Aegean steamers, and the unreasonableness of publishers. As we left the room he chanted after us in Greek the twenty line assignment for the day.

Once he had an awful run in with the Rector. Just to start things off we had put his chair on his desk to see what he'd do. He simply climbed on the desk into the chair and began the class. Had we our squibs in order: No, we hadn't, so he did a frantic dance on the desk, pretended to pull his hair out by the roots.

And combined accounts from the *Groton Quarterly* tell of another class:

"Begin translating", he said, "No! No! I can do this, it's quite easy. *And Clearchus said he would jolly well be hanged if he let the king pull his leg. For he considered it infradig to go when the king tried to frighten him out of his seven senses into a pink fit will you keep your eyes on the book and not watch my pretty face?* I'm stuck!" he cried "who knows what οἱ βαρβαροι means?"

158

He looked coyly at us, folding his fingers on the tip of his nose. I ventured "barbarians." Wag shook with emotion.

"Insane, quite insane. Clearchus is telling his men that anyone of them can lick ten Persians. A barbarian is somebody six feet tall with a big club who eats raw meat and can probably lick any civilized man. Nice thing to tell your troops before a battle. No! Clearchus is calling the enemy βαρβαροι; he's calling them wops; wops means somebody dumb that you can kick around. 'οἱ βαρβαροι', them wops—now go ahead."

I went ahead until I struck a snag, a word I didn't know. He looked coy again. "Gentlemen who fail their squibs get zero for the lesson" he said sorrowfully.

"But you didn't write it on the board, sir" said ———.

"O! yes I did. I wrote it up four weeks ago last Tuesday. And anyhow, by applying Rule Five and Syntax Three and the mood sign and the connecting vowel and remembering that the stem double tweakum snatches, you could have found it out for yourselves. So pooh pooh, fie, fie. I shall have to give you zero, too."

"Oh Gee, sir."

"I mark you to please your Mothers, just to please your Mothers, so your Mothers can go around saying: 'Aha, my Jimmy got 80 and your Johnny only 70.' If I mark you on the scale of what I knew at your age you all flunk, if I mark you on what you might know you all get as good as zero; so I mark you on some basis that will give your Mothers a roughly suitable degree of joy or sorrow, and go on teaching in the hope that one-tenth of you may be sufficiently interested in one-tenth of what I tell you to talk it over as you walk to Hundred House and say 'I think the old fool was crazy when he told us so and so.' "

At this point we heard a noise and we looked up to see the Rector in the doorway glaring at Wag, disapproval written in every inch of his large frame. Wag was so upset he dismissed us. We shrunk out, leaving Clearchus to face the music.

Still another alumnus heard about the aftermath of such an episode from one of the Peabody girls:

They argued all the way over to Pa's study. Pa was angry and so was Cousin Amory. Pa said "Amory, it's an impossible situation for the other men when you allow the boys to carry on so." And Cousin Amory said "Cottie, I deeply resent your interfering with my teaching. I seriously object to being treated like a little boy. Either my method of teaching is sound or it is not." And Pa said "No one is interfering with your teaching. The trouble is you're not teaching. You are demoralizing the entire school." Cousin Amory said "I might as well resign right now, but before I do I insist that you allow me to speak to the School and explain why I am resigning and why I heartily disapprove of Groton." Pa said "You know very well, Amory, I will not let you address the School and that furthermore I wouldn't let you resign even if you seriously intended to." I couldn't hear any more because Mother came in and took them both for a walk.

His views on teaching were not the common ones. Here are some of them:

Let the best men, if they are to teach physics and chemistry, be men who know a good deal about Homer, Beethoven, Dante, and Velasquez. If they are to teach classics and history, let them know something of business, trigonometry, how long it takes a hen's egg to hatch. . . . When I taught mathematics I refused to hide truth under silly names that scared the boys until they knew what the names meant. I call a surd a "bizzwhish" and a radical a "boozeboo" until the class sees it doesn't matter what you call it; that a name is just a label for something that is always true. . . . Masters must not shut their eyes to facts. We are all perfectly aware that for a good part of the year the boys are not at Groton. Even here we know that many ideas pour into them from books and newspapers which a normal boy devours just because they are new and totally different from the point of view here. And in vacation many of them live in what seems almost a different planet. . . . It may not be a broader life, but it *seems* broader. . . . Always give reasons— not necessarily then and there, but soon. Never let a boy go to bed with a sense of injustice. . . . Also in deeper discussions always give a boy the reasons which *convince you* of the truth of a matter of religion or ethics. They may be a bit over his head—often will be —they may even set confusion going among the ideas which hitherto have been simple to the boy. There is a real risk. But the gain is great, I believe, in the long run. When the little obedient boy has become the free man, and the tempest and dark hour are upon him he will remember not merely that he was taught to be truthful, pure, unselfish. He will remember that he was taught a lie was wrong be- cause—dishonesty was wrong because—and the because may save him when his anchor is slipping. . . . It takes two to make a teach and there is no sport more delightful than the ever-varying game of adapting the same old learning to the mental curves of the new and wholly different learner. . . . Manual training . . . has real value in stimulating austere regard for truth. If the drawer is a millimeter too large for the bureau, it simply won't go in. If one table leg is a half inch shorter than the other three, the table wobbles. . . . Anyone can tell the difference between black and white, also the difference in moral questions between plainly right and plainly wrong. A sensitiveness to the difference between light gray and just not quite so light gray can be inculcated in the classroom. Later in life muddle-headedness is often at the basis of serious lapses. . . . The fundamental stimulant for the boy should be the desire to equip himself to give. He works that he may be a useful citizen, instead of a consumer; that his tools may be sharp for service, not blunt and useless. Incidentally such a motive renders dishonesty in work absurd, and mediocre effort foolish. . . . Boys are human and at thirteen are seldom philosophers. . . . Boys are very noble animals. . . . It is true that in the great world effort usually receives reward and idleness receives punishment. Unfortunately this is not always true . . . but one need not fear there will be dearth of rewards and punishments. Nature takes care of that and we are all commercialized more or less. It is simply unnatural to be altruistic and nothing else. . . . We should no longer have the absurdity of a zero given to a boy dismissed from class for disorder. . . . The best time to study a lesson is after the recitation.

He also wrote:

Groton School is perfectly incomprehensible to those who have not belonged to it: only partly comprehensible to those who have belonged or still belong. Hence it is peculiarly subject to unfair criticism. The praise and blame bestowed on it by the world are often ludicrously undeserved. It is in almost equal measure over-praised and under-praised, over-blamed and under-blamed. Like all such institutions and in a far greater degree than most, its real essence is a resultant of a thousand little manners and customs and traditions which have grown out of a thousand little episodes of its daily life. The *flavor* of the whole thing—in other words, the *personality* of the institution—is, therefore, something wholly beyond the power of any one to describe in words.

He has been quoted at length because he was a constant force at work on the Rector for many years. Much of what has been quoted is, of course, straight progressivism, well ahead of its time. The Rector believed in and abided by absolutes. Mr. G. always saw the things which are not absolute. There is one more thing which must be said about him and that is that his faith, in its own way, was just as profound and sure as that of the Rector or Mr. B. If one had to pick a single short summary of the man, in which he caught not only his own spirit, but that of Endicott Peabody and Groton, his own Graduates' Prayer would serve:

Watch over our School O! Lord as its years increase, and bless and guide her sons wherever they may be, keeping them ever un-

161

spotted from the world. Let their hearts be warm with the faith of their boyhood's ideals, their faith unshaken, their principles immovable. Be Thou by their side when the dark hour shall come upon them; strengthen them when they stand, comfort and help them when they are weak-hearted, raise them up if they fall. Let the Cross never grow dim to their eyes, but through the struggles and suffering that may attend their steps, let its radiance lead them heavenward, and in their hearts may Thy peace which passeth understanding abide all the days of their life.

Finally, here are a few letters from him to the Rector:

June 8, 1895

DEAR COTTIE:

I fear "culture" is not the Groton boy's strong point. . . . For my part I should be delighted—if the trustees will vote me another $1000 next year, to devote that to an additional master's salary, the remainder to be divided among the other masters. For it is not right that our faculty that increases greatly (by its permanency) in value to the School, should not have this recognized by an increase every year if possible. At present they are really paying for the new building. . . . Their value to Groton School cannot be measured in dollars and cents. They have given life and youth and love and what has been returned to them in happiness has been partly of their own building. . . . I wish the feeling between the boys of the schools [Groton and St. Mark's] were better. They hate us insanely and I am sorry to say our boys while not quite so bad are very silly in their antipathy.

It is one result of the athletic madness of the age. . . . I know my ridiculous attacks of nervous dyspepsia at games make me appear to agree that the nation's life depends on the result. . . . Think of the utter absurdity of the present Harvard-Yale wrangle. A Harvard blackguard writes from the far west injunctions to lay up Butterworth. The letter is picked up on the floor of a hotel and sent to Butterworth's father who apparently reads a letter not addressed to him. This is human but not nice. Yale in a rage sends a demand that . . . Harvard apologize for attacks on Hinkey,—grand ultimatum. Probably no game next year. It makes me sick.

August 19, 1903

DEAR COTTIE:

Welcome home and thanks for your letter. I was a little afraid you would think I overstated things, but your sweet-tempered letter only reassures me that—as I have always known—you are the most modest and fair-minded listener in the world. In fact, do you know, the obstacles which have at times seemed to impede perfect frank-

162

ness have been a curious mixture of tender-heartedness on my part and a knowledge of your humble-mindedness so that I have feared to wound where no cause for fear should exist.

July 4, 1908

I do want to see a crop of young masters arise and stay. Your speech of Prize Day encouraged the idea. It has been everything to me and to the School, I think, this idea of *life work* not *stepping stone* nor *half life*. It is certainly happy and valuable. I feel that we three as having in a sense brought a child into the world must stand by, as I want new men to acquire something of the same idea . . . but matrimony seems to me the most important issue. While we need our quota of dormitory masters, we can afford to be over-officered rather than lose corkers. When I say afford don't forget my readiness to assure $3000 and a house in case a corker wants to get married; i.e. never let that issue be the cause of the loss of the right men, Danielson, Regan, etc. etc. whom we *must* keep.

W. A. G.

[Undated]

I can't give marks as premium for industry without sacrificing my real ability for increasing abiding knowledge. If I shove the weight on the past 24 hours instead of opening new ground, I am constantly confronted with the pathetic industrious boy who wins the battle and loses the campaign. Industry is one of the most valuable things in the world. Morally and spiritually far more important than knowledge, even than trained reasoning powers which is what I aim at chiefly. I can and do preach it all the time. When it comes to rewarding it I shrink, because it so seriously misleads parents who confuse it with digested knowledge and besides I always did hate to reward virtue. I sometimes wish one could give two marks—one an industry mark and one a knowledge mark. The moment a mixture begins there is greater uncertainty and all masters make different mixtures.

I believe I can still give something worth while in the line of general knowledge, development of austere reasoning, fanatical accuracy, international grammar, and day by day sacred studies. What I preach almost daily in Greek class is—I think graduates would tell you—much the biggest abiding part of what I do. But I do not forget that all this is in a sense unsocial. It leaves to others the nurse work and lets me sail the pleasant seas of untrammeled freedom in teaching. I felt a great glow when I perceived four or five years ago that I was teaching at 100% of my powers.

163

My dear Cottie, don't ask me to talk in Chapel. It isn't in my
line at all. I do my preaching daily in class—often out of season
perhaps, but that is where it comes to me spontaneously, and when
it is real and therefore of some use. Speaking on a set occasion
whether at a dinner or elsewhere is simply misery to me and I don't
feel real at all. Of course if the afflatus does blow in the course of
the autumn I will tell you.

I love the School just as much as ever, but in some ways I positively disapprove of it. It is a complex thing I can't express clearly.
If I found myself disloyal I should of course have to withdraw and
I sometimes am worried by doubts on this point; but I still feel that
as long as I heartily believe in the Christian Religion, in Purity, and
in Social Service, my private views as to the morality or wisdom of
the details of leading boys to the desired end are not vital. But they
would of necessity colour anything I might write for publication.
Simply eulogy would simply not be true—where I am out of sympathy with whole codes and systems I can work off my views at
Faculty coffee; but in a book it would do harm or cause sorrow. I
sometimes think you don't quite appreciate as being other than
queer some of the standards I hold, because I say such queer and im-
moderate things. Unluckily a good many little things are to me
symptoms of fundamentals. I talk of the symptoms, but that is because I have lain awake nights over the symbolized fundamentals.

2 1

PARENTS

ONE of the most important phases of Endicott Peabody's
work was his dealing with the parents. To many of
them, as to the boys, he seemed forbidding and fear-
some. It was undoubtedly a factor in his relationship to them
that his school has always been full, with a long waiting list, and
his decisions and comments have been, for this reason, more positive than those of many headmasters. Sometimes real issue was
joined, but not often. The attitude of most Groton parents was
that when they turned a boy over to the Rector they were bound

to trust him to care for the boy properly. His experience was wider than theirs, his view more detached and impartial, and his character unquestioned.

Besides his letters, he sent home reports at regular intervals. His comments on these were usually terse, often monosyllabic. "Good," "unsatisfactory," "very weak in Latin," "excellent." His cast of phrase inclined to the dubious. Heart-warming words of praise were qualified by speculation as to whether the good work would keep up, or morbid suspicions that it would not.

He also on many occasions spoke to meetings of the parents in various cities, as he did to gatherings of graduates. At these times he emphasized the aims and standards of the school and urged on the parents their important part in the educational process. He inveighed against low moral standards in the home, against drinking and smoking (even during the holidays) by the boys, and was especially vehement against divorce, which he abhorred, and which he attacked without regard for the feelings of his audience. In fact he was apt to be most outspoken when a goodly percentage of them were divorced. To him the home was the center of everything, and anything that threatened its unity or mutual love was a great danger and a grievous offense.

These letters indicate his attitude with parents about various matters:

My dear Mr. ———:

It is rather difficult to decide what one ought to say in regard to your proposition. I realize how much an eightieth birthday means, and I cordially sympathize with your wish that ——— should be with you when your mother reaches that stage. On the other hand, the first few days of the school year are among the most important of all, for at that time the classes are organized, and a beginning of a new stage is made in each study. I therefore think it unwise for ——— to remain with you, unless you feel that his presence is of great importance to his grandmother. I will leave the matter in your hands. I am

Sincerely yours,
Endicott Peabody

March 20, 1908
My dear Mr. ———

I do not quite understand the statement which you make in your letter that in the opinion of Mrs. ——— and yourself injustice has

165

been done to W———. It is, of course, quite possible that the views of the Masters who have taught W——— are mistaken.

I have had the boy for several weeks in Latin, and in my judgment he is not in any way superior to the average of the I form; while in English he is not prepared for the School. . . .

If you believe that intentional injustice has been done to the boy by the Masters or by myself I should feel compelled to request that you withdraw him from Groton.

W——— has been a peculiarly troublesome boy; careless and indifferent and idle beyond most of the pupils whom we have had at the School. He has failed to make a position among the boys largely from the defects of his character. . . .

My dear Mrs. ———:

I am sending ——— home this morning because I am unwilling under present conditions to remain responsible for him. It seems that during the whole of the term since ———'s return he has had a pain in the region of the appendix. On Monday this inflammation became so great that he went to bed. In the afternoon I summoned Dr. ——— to ask him if it would be safe to send ——— home. The Doctor found the tenderness so great that he did not think it safe for ——— to travel. On Tuesday morning the boy felt better, and got up. In my absence that day Mr. Billings was in charge, and he advised ——— to see the Doctor again. This advice he did not see fit to follow. He passed the morning in School. At dinner he felt ill, and left the dining room. Shortly after this he went to the river, and bathed. He rode his bicycle, and played ball. On my return in the evening I was naturally a good deal surprised to find that ——— has shown such a complete lack of perception as to how to treat himself, when he was threatened with such serious complications.

Our Infirmary is full of patients with mumps, and Miss ——— was therefore unable to watch ——— as carefully as she would have done under ordinary circumstances. But it is not my idea that boys of fourteen should be followed about by our nurse, and watched from hour to hour. They are expected to have developed some judgment when they have reached this age.

My reason for sending ——— to you is that I fear that he may at any moment be taken with a bad case of appendicitis, and that the operation may be necessary at Groton. At the present time our accommodations are such that an operation of this kind would be not only inconvenient, but not without danger.

You are, of course, the person to decide whether ——— ought to have the operation for appendicitis. But I cannot undertake to retain him at Groton until this operation has been performed, or else I have assurance that the disease is not likely to recur.

I feel bound to say therefore, that I do not wish —— to return to Groton next year in case he has not undergone the operation unless Dr. —— can certify that so far as he can ascertain all inflammation in the vicinity of the appendix has disappeared, and there is no likelihood of ——'s having an attack of appendicitis.

I hope that this will not seem to you an unreasonable position for me to take. I am compelled to it by a natural unwillingness to undertake more responsibility than one in my position is compelled to carry. . . .

My dear Mrs. ——:

I have today received your letter of the 17th of March. So far as I know nothing more has been discovered against —— since he left. . . . There is little use in reviewing this experience which has caused you so much pain. Evidently there was a great deal of discussion about the boy at Newport and I am told that one of the papers published something about him. This would make no difference to me in my feeling about ——: but it does bear upon the question of the expediency of his coming back again as a pupil of the School. . . . You have certainly been most frank and friendly in dealing with us. I regret extremely that you feel that you have not been quite as fairly treated.

I hope that —— will not be so affected that he will hesitate to come freely to Groton after he is established at Harvard. I shall always be glad to see him and to help him in any way I can. I am,

Sincerely yours,

Endicott Peabody

My dear Miss ——,

The Infirmary must be carried on in what we consider the best way for the school.

G—— has now had a normal temperature for some time. There is no reason whatever, in my judgment, for your being in the Infirmary before ten o'clock—except to see the doctor at eight o'clock.

I must therefore ask you to come not before ten o'clock to remain with G——.

There will be no use whatever in your appealing to Mr. ——. I am quite prepared to stand by this decision to the extent of having —— withdrawn from the school.

Very truly yours,

Endicott Peabody

This letter to the Rector reflects the indignation he sometimes met:

167

Dear Sir:

I am in receipt of your letter of February 1.

Since I subscribed to the Groton Fund, several things have happened.

My boy who was in the Fourth Form, and by his reports was doing fairly well, was sent away from Groton without the slightest warning to me, and no valid reason given except that he was too old for his form. He was sent away at the Easter vacation, 19—, at a time in the year when it was impossible to get him in any other school, which forced me to send him to one of those tutoring places working a very great and serious detriment to the boy.

Under these circumstance, do you think I have any feeling for Groton, when I firmly believe that their unjustified action has done more to ruin the boy's chances in life than anything that could have happened to him?

Yours very truly,

——— ———

Dear Mr. ———:

Knowing as you do that I have been a good deal troubled by our inability to collect payments for accounts sent to you in the post you can easily realize that the question presents itself very forcibly to me as to whether it is well for ——— to remain at Groton. The money problem is not the only fact that influences my mind. The boy's preparation has been so poor that it is not at all improbable he will have to repeat the I form. He has evidently been under slight discipline in the past, and his conduct is not particularly satisfactory. The most important consideration is that if he should remain at Groton he would be associating with boys whose means are for the most part greater than his are likely to be. This is only a slight disadvantage in the case of boys of substantial character but in ———'s case I think it might make for serious harm. In view of all these considerations I would suggest your careful thought upon the expediency of transferring ——— to a smaller school, where he would receive more individual attention than we can give him, and where the expenses are not so great.

In the event of your deciding that you will wish him to remain at Groton we can keep him here for some time longer; possibly, but not certainly for the rest of the year.

I think it highly probable, however, that at the end of the term it will be incumbent upon me to ask you to withdraw him from the school.

I am, yours very truly,

Endicott Peabody

November 18, 1903

DEAR MR. PEABODY:
I feel that the size of such an offense as writing the meanings of words in one's Virgil depends on the standards of conduct in the school where the offense is committed. If you undertake the difficult labor of making your boys strictly honest in their methods in recitations, of course I will back you so far as lies in me. You seem to make character at Groton that is incomparably the finest fruit of school training. I don't want G——— to miss anything that is coming to him from you in the way of character, and I will invite him to be heartily ashamed that he has violated the moral law of Groton School. That seems to be all I can do. I trust G——— now, and expect to trust him very much further when he goes to college and I want him above all things to be absolutely honest. I think he is honest, will be trustworthy, too, please God.

Any schoolmaster will find a familiar note struck in the following:

November 28, 1902

DEAR MR. PEABODY:
——— reached Boston safely yesterday, without an overcoat, by the way, but wearing a rubber coat. He says his light brown overcoat has been lost. I hope it maybe found. . . . Last evening I had a talk with ——— in regard to his progress at school and his blackmarks. He tells me he has made an appeal on some of his blackmarks which he thinks were unjustly given and the master now has the matter under advisement. In regard to studies, ——— says that he is troubled about his mathematics upon which he says himself that he is very slow, and needs much explanation. . . .

Often the parents wished to be helpful:

November 10, 1905

DEAR SIR:
When Mr. Harriman returned from Japan he brought with him several Japanese boys some of them proficient in the art of Jiu Jitsu and some in fencing. They are anxious to learn to speak English and it occurred to Mr. Harriman that perhaps you might like to take one of them in at Groton and let him instruct the boys there in fencing or Jiu Jitsu. . . .
Secretary to Mr. Harriman

Sometimes he encountered resentfully fierce criticism:

DEAR MR. PEABODY:
Sometime ago I received enclosed bill. It is so badly stated that it

is impossible to know what the items mean, but assuming that it covers all indebtedness of myself and my son I send a check for the balance claimed.

I am amazed that this bill should have been sent, but in my desire to make an ending of my connection with Groton School I pay it, and ask you to return the bill receipted to me here.

I should have been glad to pay this without comment had I not feared that my doing so would be used to emphasize the reports spread from Groton that I had "exonerated" you and had "withdrawn" all charges of carelessness.

Knowing as you do how thoroughly I blame you for the maiming of my unfortunate boy, you owed it to yourself as well as to me to make your Masters and friends acquainted with my views: nor should the presence of my son at Groton as Mr. Gardner's guest have been used as a proof of such reports.

If candor had impelled you to confess what was evident from your own statement, that you lost your head and failed to show presence of mind reasonably to be expected from a man in your position, or had you confessed regret that you had failed to keep your repeated promises to me to notify Dr. —— in case of accident to my son, my views of your conduct would have been materially modified. . . .

The reply to the above, which referred to a tragic accident to a boy in which the Rector was absolved from blame by impartial judges:

My dear Mr. ——,

I met you at the house of Dr. —— in order that I might explain to you the course that I pursued at the time of ——'s accident. It was perfectly evident that you did not approve of my course. I spoke of our interview to very few persons and they were fully aware of your attitude. I know nothing whatever of the report which has reached you that I considered that you exonerated me.

I am very sorry now that I did not communicate with Dr. —— For I realize that it would have made you feel differently. At the time I did not see that it was the proper thing for me to do. But it is not well to open up the question again.

The whole experience brings me profound and lasting regret.

I write this thinking that it may bring some relief to you in your pain.

I am, sincerely yours,
Endicott Peabody

Dear Mr. ——:

I am sorry to be obliged to report that —— was untruthful this

170

morning. He was manipulating a pen in connection with the lid of his desk in such a way as to prick the boy in front of him. The master, thinking that something was wrong, called ——— up and asked him what he was doing. ——— replied that he was doing nothing. On being more closely interrogated, he admitted that he had been attempting to touch the boy with his pen.

On being sent to me, ——— told me that he answered thoughtlessly; but it is perfectly evident that the boy was unconscientious about this, and it is of great importance that he should have it very definitely impressed upon him that a boy must be absolutely frank in all ways.

I have not punished ——— for this, as we have no penalty for moral offenses. A boy must make up his mind that he intends to tell the truth if he is to be an acceptable pupil at Groton.

It is fair to add that ——— has struck me as being generally a truthful person. I have no doubt that a definite word from you will be a help to the boy. . . .

Dear Mr. ———:

I am sorry to tell you that I find that ——— has been betting at Groton. Hearing something about it, I questioned the boy. He tells me that last Christmas he was challenged by a St. Mark's boy, and feeling that it was rather a loyal thing to do, he backed Groton in the foot ball game of 19— to the extent of two dollars, that afterwards, when he realized that the Groton team was not very strong, he hedged by betting against Groton to the extent of one dollar. Apparently he did not realize the inconsistency so far as his supposed loyalty to the school was concerned.

I have no doubt that other boys have been guilty of similar action, and they would probably plead as ——— did that they were backing up their school by betting on its eleven.

I am well aware that betting is common in the colleges and in ordinary society and that it is not looked upon as a venial offense. I am quite determined, however, that so far as the school goes we should have none of it at Groton; and I have told ——— that he must make up his mind absolutely if he intends to remain in the school. He assures me that he is determined to resist any temptation of the kind in the future, and I believe that his intention is right and that he will carry it out. . . .

[To the same:]

Since writing you the other day, ——— has again been reported for ill manners at table. I confess to having been a good deal annoyed by his offending so soon again, and I compelled him to report to me frequently and to pay other penalties. I also gave him a very

171

definite talk. His punishments are over this evening, and he assures me that he intends to conduct himself properly hereafter.

In a way I am glad this has happened, for I think that we understand each other better and —— realizes that he must take real pains hereafter. . . .

Dear Mr. ——:

I agree with all that you say as to the effect of the theatre upon boys and I should like to have your ideas brought before the parents. In this circular, however, it seems to me wise to lay stress upon the worst result of these miserable plays, which is to degrade their ideas of marriage and their reverence for womanhood, and to make them look upon impurity as a slight thing. If we had plenty of time, we might compose a letter which would be more comprehensive, but we believe it to be most important to get this out well before the Christmas holidays in order that we may keep some boys at least from the gross temptations induced by the problem plays and suggestive vaudevilles.

We found, last year, that fur coats were used so injudiciously by the boys that it would be wise to eliminate them from the school. I therefore gave a notice to the effect that no new overcoats of this nature should be introduced. . . .

Dear Mr. ——:

The spirit of your letter is so different from that of those that I received from parents for many years that I hardly know whether it is worth while to attempt to explain further about ——. In enclosing to you the memoranda made by the master concerning ——, I mentioned the fact that they were jotted down hastily and that the master had not expected that they would go any farther. I sent them forward to you because I supposed that you would be glad to get the view of a man who was dealing with —— in the details of discipline. The master would undoubtedly agree with you, as I do, that the memoranda touch upon very slight offenses. The reason why they have value in my eyes is that they show that the boy, even when on probation, continues to fool in an aimless, silly way and does not get down to steady work. Instead of taking the memoranda for what they are worth and allowing that even if exaggerated they might be of some value to you, you criticise severely the master who wrote them and defend your boy. Granted that each one of the peccadilloes is slight in itself, still I believe that they do throw light upon the situation.

You say that it was some time ago decided that Groton was the best place for ——'s education. That decision was of course based upon the hypothesis that —— would develop in a normal way. Unfortunately, he still remains an individualist who has little in common with his surroundings. At the faculty meeting yesterday, a master who has ——— in his class remarked that the boy was an "undesirable citizen." Another master, one who had made an especial effort to befriend ———, told me only a few days ago that the boy was so cheap in talk, so flippant, and so unpleasant to deal with that he felt very much like giving up all connection with him in out-of-school hours.

I quite appreciate the wisdom of your contention that all boys should not be run into the same mould, and I am ready to believe that we have erred in this direction; but unless a boy cares for the place and shows a desire to get on with his teachers and to form friendships with his school fellows, it is an open question whether he is in a place which is best suited to him for his education.

——— has certainly earned better marks this month, as the report will show you, and for this he deserves some credit, although he was compelled to do this in order to stay with his form; but the question still remains whether he would not get more from a different school. It may well be that in a smaller school where he could have more individual attention, he would be happier and would make more progress in every way. I am not desirous to press this question at the present moment; but I think it fair to you to say that it is in my mind, and it seems to me justice to ——— that it should not be looked upon as closed until the good that he is getting from this school is more manifest than it is at the present time. . . .

These letters are nearly all stern. They have purposely been chosen as such in an effort to make clear the granite core of the Rector's headmastership. It would be misleading, however, not to point out that his correspondence abounded in many letters of a very different kind, and that, indeed, the letters given are of a type which is rare in this parental correspondence, filled as it is with admiration for him.* The parents trusted him, often feared him. His form of expression was not always tactful, but happy, genial letters to and from parents could be quoted in abundance. They sought him out, not only in vacations when their boys were still in school, but long afterward when he came their way. There can be no doubt that his relationship with most of them was extremely cordial. When any member of the Groton family, which included boys and parents, experienced joy or grief, word was almost sure to come from Peabody. When a boy did well,

* See Chapter 45 and elsewhere.

173

his parents usually received a note of satisfaction, whether the achievement was in school or after life. He made a particular point on Prize Days of publicly calling attention to notable performances of individuals during the preceding year, either at school or in college. If he was unyielding in "punishing wickedness and vice," he was unstinted in praise and acknowledgment of virtue.

22

TWENTIETH REUNION

E. P. *aet.* 47

IN 1904 there was held the first of the four great reunions celebrating additional decades in the school's history under Peabody's headmastership. Plans were laid far ahead. Theodore Roosevelt was then in the White House and had two sons in Groton at the time. Naturally the Rector and trustees wanted him for the principal speaker. He and Peabody had been friends and correspondents for many years. They had occasionally differed as two strong and determined men must do, but they never lost their mutual respect and admiration for one another. For instance, in 1894, following a talk he had given at Groton, Roosevelt wrote:

November 16, 1894
DEAR COTTY:

I have just received your very sweet letter, and I feel quite ashamed about the check. I shall take it, but on the distinct understanding, old man, that this is the last time I ever do. I really can't consent to be paid for a pleasure as great as my visit to Groton was. I would not have missed it for anything. I have always hitherto regarded the fact that my boys had to go to school as a necessary evil. I now feel that I would not have them miss Groton any more than if they wished to go to Harvard I should have them miss Harvard. My whole stay with you was unalloyed pleasure.

I fairly laughed when I came to the line where you said that you sometimes longed to be in the larger world of men. I don't think you understand how much good you are doing. You *are* in the larger world, in the very highest and best service, and I can say quite conscientiously I don't know any one of our generation who I think is making so permanent a mark for good.

Give my warm regards to Mrs. Cotty:

Always faithfully yours,
THEODORE ROOSEVELT

And so, when he was officially invited to speak at the Twentieth Prize Day, he answered:

September 1st, 1903

DEAR COTTY:

Indeed I accept with pleasure and am genuinely glad to have the chance to be with you on Prize Day, in the twentieth year of the life of Groton School. I have two boys with you; I hope to have two others; I feel that Groton stands for the hopes and beliefs and aspirations, and above all for the sturdy, resolute purposes, which represent all that is loftiest and truest in our American life; and moreover I feel that all who are giving the best there is in them to the training of our boys in body and mind, and above all in soul and character, make the whole people their debtors. So I shall esteem it a privilege to come.

Faithfully yours,
THEODORE ROOSEVELT

Shortly afterward, when the Rector wrote him a somewhat discouraged letter, he replied:

Oyster Bay, N.Y. September 15, 1903

DEAR COTTY:

. . . You say that at times you feel depressed. It is the penalty of doing hard and active work, old fellow. No man ever did good work yet save at the cost of experiment and effort so intense that there was bound to be a certain quantity of error or mistake in the work done. If, in addition, his work is genuinely important, he must expect to be misrepresented by a large number of base men, and to be misunderstood by a much larger number of ignorant but well meaning men. All of this he must expect as part of the penalty of what he does, and part of his effort to work in effective fashion for the achievement of results worth achieving. If, at the end of twenty years of effort, he has as much to show as you now have for your twenty years of work, he may well count himself thrice fortunate.

Ever yours,
THEODORE ROOSEVELT

The announcement that the President would speak brought the reporters down on the Rector's head. They found him difficult. To one who wished data for an article on one of the Roosevelt boys Peabody wrote:

I should be very glad indeed to assist you in your enterprize if I could find it consistent with my duty. It is very clear to me, however, that the boys are entrusted to my care to be educated in a quiet country school and that one of the objects of the parents in sending them to Groton is to avoid the publicity which might otherwise attach to them. I am quite sure that this is the view that would be taken by President Roosevelt. It will therefore be impossible for me to assist you with the article concerning Archie Roosevelt by allowing the school or the boy to be photographed.

It was a gala occasion. Yale had made the Rector a master of arts with the citation: "What strength is to weakness, what experience is to ignorance or blind confidence, what light and faith are to darkness and doubt, what courage is to trembling fear, what the spiritual potter is to the pliant clay of youthful character, what Paul was to Timothy—that, all that, is the Head Master of Groton School to the young manhood blessed with his devoted instruction and companionship." And Harvard, which he so loved and with which he so battled, went one better with a doctorship of sacred theology and the citation: "Endicott Peabody, graduate of the English Cambridge, clergyman, head master of a school for boys that stands for purity, manliness, and helpfulness."

A hundred and six of the brethren were back. Bishop Lawrence preached. There was a huge feast in the school dining room, which was profaned by very good cigars. Form after form was called and stood up amidst thunderous applause. The Bishop, speaking for the Board of Trustees, announced that Mrs. Peabody's portrait was to be painted by Miss Lydia Emmet and given to Mr. Peabody. The Rector himself was to be painted by Sargent for the school. Silver paper weights, known as Milestones, were given by the Trustees to Mr. B. and Mr. G. and Mrs. MacMurray, the matron who had been at the School from the beginning. Mr. Higley read an ode. The Prize Day address was made by the President of the United States, who had two sons in the school. Theodore Roosevelt said, among other things:

You are not entitled, either in college or in life, to an ounce of privilege because you have been to Groton—not an ounce, but we are entitled to hold you to an exceptionable accountability because you have been to Groton. Much has been given you, therefore we have a right to expect much from you. . . . I was glad to hear the Rector when he asked you to be careful not to turn out snobs. Now there are in our civic and social life very much worse creatures than snobs, but none more contemptible. . . . The interest you take in him is, can a given man accomplish anything? If he cannot, then let him give place to some one who can. . . . I believe with all my heart in athletics, but I believe in bodily vigor chiefly because of the spirit that lies back of it. . . . It is a mighty good thing to be a half-back on a varsity eleven; but it is a mighty poor thing, when a man reaches forty, only to be able to say that he was once half-back on a varsity eleven. . . . Be truthful; a lie implies fear.

Groton had grown up. It was an adult school now; a new school no longer.

23

SUCH GREAT FAITH

NO ACCOUNT of the Rector would be complete which did not deal with the religion which was such a dominating force in his life. Yet, in a sense, it is a difficult thing to write about. He was not a theologian.* Fine points and subtle critical distinctions simply did not interest him and he never bothered with them. Except for his sermons, his religious writings were very slender. His reading in ecclesiastical fields, except for the Bible and a few books to which he returned again and again, was slight, not because he intended it to be, but because he felt that the great business of living was life, and life for him was full and engrossing.

The fact is that he cared greatly for persons and not much for ideas. When he preached in Chapel he did not preach theology but the simplicity in Christ to boys. As has been said, he had a

* The Rev. J. Thayer Addison, who knew the Rector intimately, who was perhaps more familiar with the religious cast of his mind than any one else, and who is a teacher of long experience in a theological school, made the following comments on reading this chapter before it went to press: "The Rector is not primarily intellectual, but this section gives the impression that he doesn't know what theology is all about and has never read any. . . . He reads and understands more theology than the average clergyman does!"

mind that was content with absolutes. He absolutely believed in God and in His Son Jesus Christ. It is doubtful if the necessity for proof of the existence of God ever seriously troubled him personally and it upset him when any one else seemed to want or need it. He mistrusted that approach. Skepticism is never attractive to the true believer; doubts lead to questions and thence to more doubts. Which may explain why boys at Groton sometimes complained about "near arguments as to the existence of God." Good friends and staunch admirers of the Rector sometimes wondered what the effect on him of a single great and overwhelming sorrow in his life would have been. He saw as clearly as anyone how great had been his good fortune, and was devoutly grateful for it. That was one of the charming and disarming things about him; great blessedness made him at once confident and humble. But he was indeed blessed. He had marvelous health and strength, wealth, worldly success, a job he loved, the best of wives, the happiest of homes. His six children all grew up into fine, strong people. He never lost anyone really close and dear to him until the death of his father and mother, and when they departed they had had long, useful, good lives past the allotted time and were ready for departure. Rarely has the problem of evil affected a human with so little immediacy. It is no wonder that his life was a song of praise, no wonder he often wrote in his letters *Laus Deo*.

Therefore, liking persons and holding personality and character the most important things in the world, it was natural for him to adore and live in Christ, whom he regarded as the sum of all character and personality. It was natural for him to ignore ontological and teleological arguments for the existence of God, natural to ignore the question of the virgin birth, and natural to attack immorality and weakness and faithlessness wherever he found them with all the power of his being.

His churchmanship was broad. It was inevitable that he should leave the Unitarians, feeling as he did about the divinity of Christ. It was equally impossible for him to consider Rome (not that he ever did) because of distrust of the elaborate and the ritualistic. He chose the church, as he has chosen everything in his life, in which he could be his honest self. The Episcopal church is dignified and has a moving and beautiful, but simple, ritual. It has two great traditions, that of succession and that of

Protestantism. It is eminently a church of nice people. And it is a broad church.

It may well be that of all his functions at school the two which meant the most to him were celebrating the Holy Communion and preparing boys for Confirmation. Yet it is interesting that in his invitation to the Holy Communion he always issued the invitation to "all those who love the Lord Jesus Christ," and, much as he wanted all boys to be confirmed, he welcomed all to the Lord's Supper, whether they were confirmed or not, provided they were sufficiently mature.

Again and again in his letters he mentions how much the sermons of Frederick W. Robertson meant to him.* If one examines some of these great writings, it is easy to see why they appealed. Their clarity, force, honesty, and directness are as steadying and inspiring today as they were when they were written eighty to one hundred years ago. It may help in understanding Peabody's religious life to give a few short excerpts:

Men are awakened from coarse rude life to the desire of something deeper; and the god or spirit of this world can subtly turn that aside into channels which shall effectually enfeeble and ruin the soul. Refinement—melting imagery—dim religious light; all the witchery of form and color—music—architecture; all these, even colored with the hues of religion, producing feelings either religious or quasi-religious, may yet do the world's work. For all attempt to impress the heart through the senses, "to make perfect through the flesh" is fraught with that danger beneath which Greece sunk. There is a self-deception in those feelings—the thrill, the sense of mystery, and the luxury of contemplation, and the impressions on the senses: all these lie very close to voluptuousness—enfeeblement of heart— yea, even impurity . . . the education of the taste, and the cultivation of the taste, and the cultivation of the feelings in undue proportion, destroy the masculine mind. An education chiefly romantic or poetical, not balanced by hard practical life, is simply the ruin of the soul.

. . . . . .

* The Reverend Malcolm Strachan, who knew the Rector's intimate spiritual life in later years and who had unusual opportunity to know of his reading and thinking, feels that John Frederick Denison Maurice also had great influence on the Rector and that in Maurice's sermons and writings is found possibly the best of all reflections of Peabody's religious thought. Mrs. Peabody implied to Strachan that she also felt this. Strachan supports Addison in thinking that the amount of regular reading the Rector did was remarkable. It was done in small quantities, but steadily year after year.

If anyone ever felt the beauty of this world, it was Christ. The beauty of the lily nestling in the grass—He felt it all; but the beauty He exhibited in life was the stern loveliness of moral action. The King in His Beauty "had no form or comeliness"; it was the beauty of obedience, of noble deeds, of unconquerable fidelity, of unswerving truth, of Divine self-devotion. The Cross! the Cross! We must have something of iron and hardness in our characters . . . an inward, not an outward beauty, which rejects and turns sternly away from the meretricious forms of the outward world, which have a corrupting or debilitating tendency.*

The Church is the kingdom of God on earth, and the whole fabric of the Christian religion rests on the monarchy of Christ. . . . He taught not by elaborate trains of argument, like a scribe or a philosopher: He uttered his truths rather as detached intuitions, recognized by intuition, to be judged only by being felt. . . . The truth of Christ is true to the unselfish; a falsehood to the selfish. . . . Purity is good, because my heart is so made that it feels it to be good.

Brother men, the truer you are, the humbler, the nobler, the more you will feel Christ to be your king. . . .

The first qualification is to *be* true. . . . Truth lies in character. Christ did not simply *speak* truth: He was truth: true through and through; for truth is a thing, not of words, but of life and being. None but a Spirit can be true. . . .

The next qualification is integrity. But by integrity I do not mean simply sincerity or honesty; integrity rather according to the meaning of the word as its derivation interprets it—entireness—wholeness —soundness: that which Christ means when He says, "If thine eye be single, thy whole body shall be full of light."

This integrity extends through the entireness or wholeness of character. It is found in small matters as well as great; for the allegiance of the soul to truth is tested by small things rather than by those which are more important. There is many a man who would lose his life rather than perjure himself in a court of justice, whose life is yet a tissue of small insincerities. We think we hate falsehood when we are only hating the consequences of falsehood. We resent hypocrisy and treachery and calumny, not because they are untrue, but because they harm us. We hate the false calumny, but we are half pleased with the false praise. . . . Now he is a man of integrity who hates untruth as untruth.†

The brotherhood of which we hear so much is often only a one-

* From "The Grecian," in *Sermons Preached at Brighton*, by Rev. Frederick W. Robertson; Harper and Brothers, new edition, pp. 134-135.
† From "The Kingdom of the Truth," *op. cit.*, pp. 216 ff.

sided brotherhood. It demands that the rich shall treat the poor as brothers. It has a right to do so. It is a brave and just demand; but it forgets that the obligation is mutual. . . . It requires that every candid allowance shall be made for the vices of the poorer classes, in virtue of the circumstances which, so to speak, seem to make such vices inevitable: for their harlotry, their drunkenness, their uncleanness, their insubordination. Let it enforce that demand; it may and must do it in the name of Christ. He was mercifully and mournfully gentle to those who through terrible temptation and social injustice had sunk, and sunk into misery at least as much as into sin. But then, let it not be forgotten that some sympathy must be also due on the same score of circumstances to the rich man. Wealth has its temptations, so has power. The vices of the rich are his forgetfulness of responsibility, his indolence, his extravagance, his ignorance of wretchedness. These must be looked upon, not certainly with weak excuses, but with a brother's eye by the poor man if he will assert a brotherhood. . . . It is not brotherhood to say that the laborer does wrong because he is tempted, and the man of wealth because he is intrinsically bad.*

"To believe is to be happy; to doubt is to be wretched. But I will not urge that. Seventy years—and the most fevered brain will be still enough. We will not say much of the wretchedness of doubt. To believe is to be *strong*. Doubt cramps energy. Belief is power. Only so far as a man believes strongly, mightily, can he act cheerfully, or do anything that is worth the doing.†

But the man who had the greatest influence of all on Peabody was Phillips Brooks. Here the written and spoken word was given power by personal contact. To him, more than to anyone else, Peabody looked for guidance and inspiration; from him, more than from anyone else, stemmed his gigantic faith and his broad churchmanship. The following quotations give a glimpse of this:

A noble principle or thought, like the widow's barrel and cruse, is never dry. We draw on it for our daily life, we drink of its power in our weakness, and taste its power in our despair; but God's blessing is on it and the fulness of his truth is filling it, and so it never fails.‡

When we gain a victory, moral or mental, when we subdue a passion or achieve a thought, let the conquest be decisive. Let the ques-

* From "Christ's Judgment Respecting Inheritance," *op. cit.*, pp. 204-205.
† From "The Skepticism of Pilate," *op. cit.*, p. 234.
‡ Allen, *Phillips Brooks*, Vol. I, p. 186.

tion be settled, the idea mastered, the doubt decided forever. Let there be no fear of future difficulty. If the serpent lie across our path and we must kill it to pass, let the blow be quick and straight and strong. . . .*

Saints, as we often think of them, are feeble, nerveless creatures, silly and effeminate, the mere soft padding of the universe. I would present sainthood to you as the strong chain of God's presence in humanity running down through all history. . . . That is the true apostolical saintly succession, the tactual succession of heart touching heart with fire. . . .†

I stop a moment and think of that great pastorship, of all it meant to countless souls; and to have lived in it and carried it on as he ‡ did seems to me to be an indescribable, an inestimable privilege. A great pastorship is the noblest picture of human influence and of the relationship of man to man which the world has to show. It is the canonization of friendship. It is friendship lifted above the regions of mere instinct and sentiment and fondness, above all thought of policy or convenience, and exalted into the mutual helpfulness of the children of God. The pastor is father and mother both to those whose deepest lives he helps in deepest ways. His belonging to his people is like the broad spreading of the sky over the lives of men and women and little children, of good and bad, of weak and strong, on all of whom alike it sheds its rain and dew.§

Then there are sermons written by the Rector himself. The text of the one quoted in its entirety here was a favorite one of his from Isaiah 6:8: "Then said I: Here am I, send me."

This is religion, according to the Old Testament. "Then said I, here am I, send me." The New Testament has the same definition, only enriched. It has in it the elements of joy and strength.

Duty is a great word to conjure with. A great poet of England sang of one of her greatest sons:

> "Not once or twice in our rough island story
> The path of duty has been the way to glory"

But you get tired of trying to do your duty. The musts are so frequent and they are formed on such different grounds. You must do this because it looks badly—you must do that because it is gen-

* *Ibid.*, Vol. I, p. 194.   † *Ibid.*, Vol. II, p. 191.   ‡ Rev. A. H. Vinton.
§ From "Memorial Sermon on Dr. Vinton," quoted by Allen, *Phillips Brooks*, Vol. II, p. 306. See, too, Brooks's notes on "Religious Convictions," Allen, Vol. II, pp. 346-356.

erally done—you must do that because it is good for you. It is your duty to keep up a good reputation for yourself and your family: it is your duty to take good care of yourself. It is your duty to do right. And, I say, sometimes one gets tired of it; of duty. It is an abstract idea. It is fine, but it lacks a personal quality.

But religion is all alive with personality. It is God's will for you. He wants you to do this. He does not compel it. You may refuse if you like, but He desires it mightily in His great love for you.

You cannot please Him in any other way. You may offer sacrifices of various kinds, as the Jews offered the blood of lambs and goats and other creatures. You may observe Fasts and Feasts of the Church and give away money. The real thing is the answer of the Lord Jesus Christ "Lo, I come to Thy Will O God."

Behind God's will is God's power waiting for the man who desires to obey Him. Joy—"my meat is to do the will of Him that sent me"—and strength. And belief and obedience go together. "All things are possible to him that believeth."

This is the first consideration which comes to my mind as I start to speak to you about the subject which I have chosen for this morning.

There is a joy in life. Do not lose it. A man can find great happiness in the world. "My life has been supremely happy" Theodore Roosevelt told an audience.

There is a reservoir of strength from which a man can draw without limit. One may say with confidence that it has been the source of the power of many great men.

This is preliminary to the subject of vocation, which I want you to think about with me for a short time. "Why don't you talk to boys about what they are going to do in life?" is a question frequently asked me. The usual hypothesis in the case of boys, that they are not old enough, is I believe not correct.

Some years ago I was looking over the records of a leading English school and there I found tabulated the professions or activities which had been chosen by members of the upper forms. They were boys 18 and 19 years of age. The boys must have been thinking of their choices for some time before they stated them. Our boys are not necessarily less mature than the English. It is largely a matter of habit that they should put off selecting their life work or even considering it and should find themselves even at the end of their college career sometimes drifting aimlessly. "I guess I'll do this" or "I guess I'll do that."

If a man guesses at the supreme moment of his life and guesses wrong he is lost, so far as joy and power are concerned.

There is such a thing as vocation. It is a real present fact to-day. It means calling, the calling of God to an individual to do a specific

183

thing. It is a personal appeal to a man's soul. "Whom shall I send? and who will go for me?" Then said I "Lo, here am I; send me!"

How can you know what God desires for you?

There are different ways. There is the immediate touch of God with the soul of man. The man does not know why nor can he explain how. It is not a thing to be analyzed, but he is sure of it—This is His call. Or there is the gradually forming conviction that He calls one—through the increasing interest in a particular subject or a particular kind of work. There is further the call that comes from a great need that may exist for a certain kind of work to be done or certain people to be served.

At this moment of the world's history and speaking to young men some of whom at any rate care to know—if not to choose God's will, I should select the last thought first.

What is needed most? Food and wealth and physical prowess? Enjoyment of the rest and luxuries of peace? "Let us eat and drink?" Let us enter into the gaieties of life which we have made secure for ourselves?

Or shall it be a determination that this Nation shall be that which we know She can become, a self-controlled, clean living people ready to respond to the ideals of democracy and Christianity?

That is what is at stake to-day. I see the two things working in our cities—the same old routine of Evil—over-eating, over-drinking and resulting immorality. Men and women finding their excitement in trying to debauch others. The young looking on with inquiring minds, wondering if all this simulated merriment is not really life, not willing, quite, to believe it has no joy in it and yet in their hearts knowing full well that the laughter of the dissipated man or woman is but the crackling of thorns under a pot.

On the other side I see people who have been profoundly stirred by the life and death struggle between Good and Evil.

It is a magnificent challenge to the Youth of America.

I cannot believe that as you think of your own future as an active member of Society you are going to be willing to ask the old questions—

What can I get out of it?
How can I make the most money?
How can I acquire fame?
How can I have the pleasantest time in life?

I do believe and pray that you will try to find what you are called to do. I was once talking of a man's work in life with the head of a great University and he remarked "A man should do what he can do best." My feeling was and is that he should do not what he can do best, but the *best* thing he can do.

184

You and I who are strong would make efficient porters or useful cowboys, but our environment and training and the hopes that our parents have entertained for us have made us conscious that we are capable of better things.

To do the best of which we are capable:

To learn the greatest need and supply it in some measure if you can.

To stand for the spiritual things instead of materialism which has nearly been our undoing.

To listen for the voice of God coming direct to your soul or indirect through persons or conditions.

To hear Him say, as He has been saying through the generations "Whom shall I send? And who will go for us?"

And then to answer with all one's heart aglow "Lord God, Here am I: send me!"

That is religion. It is life, life piled on life indeed. Renewed each day and still forever new because it is lived in the power of the Almighty and Everlasting God.

Vocation will be found for each of us through honestly desiring to know God's will. That will becomes known to the man who tries to obey His Commandments:

To be pure
To be true
To be unselfish
To be a Christian

So living we become altered, to receive the message that is sent us.

As you think on these things and as you listen there may come to your ears a call for help which is in the air to-day and comparatively few men are hearing it. You speak of joy and strength coming into men's lives. How are they to be found? I find in myself and in others a haunting spirit of fear of failure and resulting weakness. What shall I do to be saved from it? And the answer is: Believe in the Lord Jesus Christ and thou shalt be saved. There is none other name under Heaven whereby men can be saved.

It is to tell of that salvation that God is looking for men to-day. In the ministry there is an accession of these things, joy and strength. "There is no career that can compare with it for a moment in rich, satisfying relationships and the deep and interesting insight which it gives him into human nature and in the chance of the best culture of his own character." So spoke Phillips Brooks to an audience of young men gathered in a Theological School.

God is calling for you to-day. Once more, "Whom shall I send? and who will go for us?" Is there anyone who will answer the call to that specific work? "Here am I—send me!"

185

An example of his interest both in the graduates and in the ministry as well as an illuminating sidelight on his own attitude in later years is given in this letter written to John Crocker in 1927:

Groton, Massachusetts
November 12, 1927

MY DEAR JACK:

Thank you so very much for your frank and interesting letter of November 9th. It pleases me immensely to know that you realize that I care very much for everything that concerns you spiritually and mentally and in all other ways.

The account that you give of the trend of the teaching at the Yale Divinity School surprises me somewhat, but knowing, as I do, the tendency at the Union Seminary, it does not seem to me extraordinary. There is undoubtedly a great danger of the liberal school going astray, as we believe, in pursuing the higher criticism, in their attempts to persuade the world that there is no opposition between Science and Religion, and in their studying a psychology which is tinged with materialism, so giving up the old landmarks and losing the enthusiasm which characterized the early Church. Apart from the Incarnation there seems to be no power to "turn the world upside down", and I heartily sympathize with you in withstanding the tendency towards Unitarian views that you find in the Divinity School.

I am not greatly troubled by the thought of your finding yourself more in sympathy with Bishop Gore and his followers in theology. "Lux Mundi" was largely his work. It brought much sorrow to Canon Liddon who counted it heretical. I suppose that Gore has become somewhat more conservative as time has gone on, but I should regard him as a sound thinker.

I also believe in a visible catholic church as an ideal. My conception of it may be somewhat different from that of Bishop Gore, but I should be sorry to be written down as simply a Protestant.

I agree with you in considering Dean Fosbroke a man of broad learning and sound judgment. I think he had upon Malcolm more influence than any other man when Malcolm was at the Episcopal Theological School. About the other teachers at the General I have no information. Years ago there was a party spirit there which expressed itself on one occasion, I remember, as putting down Dean Stanley as "no Christian" because he did not believe in their view of baptismal regeneration. Perhaps things have changed since those days.

Some time during the year I wish you would have a talk with Angus Dun and, perhaps, Dean Washburn. They seem to me to have a high conception of religion and a love for our Church as being best fitted to express it.

I like to think of the pleasure that Betsy and Rachel Carnegie are going to have in seeing you and Mary and passing the night under your hospitable roof. My love to you both,

Affectionately yours,

ENDICOTT PEABODY

John Crocker, Esq.

In connection with the ministry the Rector has said elsewhere:

The call to the Ministry may be the result of a slow and steady growth towards it, or it may be a sudden experience as it was largely with me. In any case it is the movement of one's personality towards the service rather than the outcome of philosophical thought. The intellect, of course, must not be disregarded, but it is rather, as Tennyson writes, "All my nature makes towards Thee." That was the way, I think, in which the Apostles were enlisted under Jesus. Jesus called each one, "Follow me and I will make you fishers of men", and they instinctively obeyed him.

It was at times a sore disappointment to the Rector that more of his boys did not enter the ministry. Statistically, as a matter of fact, the representation was about normal, but in actual numbers it was small. One suspects it was hard for him to understand that to most boys he was not an ordinary minister; he was the Rector, and to urge young men to follow him did not seem to them at all the same thing as urging them to follow the ordinary paths of the ministry.

As to his views on the Episcopal church, there is a revealing letter written in reply to one of the graduates who did enter the ministry and was a very high churchman:

Feb. 13, 1917

MY DEAR ———:

I have today received your interesting letter and while the questions that it raises are clear in my mind, I will try to answer them.

Before making the attempt, I am fully conscious that the answers will be unsatisfactory both to you and myself for my views are not of an absolutely definite nature which characterizes a person who counts himself a Catholic in the sense in which you use the term. I confess to finding the Broad Church Party in some ways one-sided. In their search for truth they seem to me to have dwelt upon the intellectual and to have neglected in some measure the devotional.

I always have tried to avoid labeling myself a "Party Man." No doubt I am regarded as a broad churchman and certainly if Phillips

187

Brooks is fairly so called, I should not be unwilling to be included in the class, for I admired his character and found myself in sympathy with his views. I have been, I suppose, more influenced by him than by any other man. At the same time I should very much prefer not to call myself by any party name.

I am a churchman, and desire to be a Christian—I am not prepared to put it the other way. There are many Christians who are not churchmen. In my judgment indeed the Catholicism of which you speak is very far from being coextensive with Christianity. I find in its followers defects far more serious than those which I discover in the adherents of the other party. And the real heresy that seems to me not uncommon in the former is that there is something greater than character. They seem to make the Holy Communion and ecclesiastical doctrines ends in themselves and not means for holiness. . . .

One of the fundamental errors of the Catholic party lies in their belief that there is a life higher than the family life. This seems to me, psychologically and spiritually unsound, and I am quite sure that a lot of harm is done by it. . . .

You speak of the atheism which is found in New England as a result of Protestantism. How do you account for the dreadful condition of the morality in South America? You have probably read something about it. I listened to the account of a man who went to South America in order to examine social and religious conditions and the story that he had to tell us was too horrible. . . . If it be a question between character and sacerdotalism I should not hesitate, and I fancy that we should agree in our choice. . . .

When it comes to the finest representatives of either system such as King, or Gore and Paget (whose life I am now reading with keen interest) or Brooks, Huntington and Maurice, I find little to choose, except that the opinions of the latter group appeal to me more.

I have been greatly interested in the work that Dean Rousmaniere is doing at the Cathedral Church in Boston. He has established a class in Personal Religion and holds devotional services which are largely attended and which evidently satisfy a great need.

If we were to thrash this thing out, as we cannot do on paper, I fancy that we should reach these conclusions—you, that devotion is first and character second, while I should hold that character is the great end with devotion as a necessary means to it.

There are a thousand other things that one might say. This letter is not intended to be a logical setting-forth of my views, but simply some of the thoughts which are started by your letter.

The glory of our Church, to my mind, is that it is Catholic; that is, it can hold not only you and me, who differ from one another in many details, but it welcomes also, all who "hunger and thirst after righteousness", and are willing to accept our Lord's invitation to come to him.

Affectionately yours,
Endicott Peabody

He never forgot, for all his own love for his own church, that it is a minority body in America, and as far back as 1897, when there was a move to change its title, he wrote, "I do sincerely trust that so great a calamity as the adoption of 'The American Church' * may be averted. It would be an act of arrogance which would alienate men and clergy inside the Church and out."

Religion, to him, could not be disconnected from life. At the opening of a school year in Chapel he said,

> As those, who have plighted their troth to one another until death stand before the altar, the prayer goes up for them, "that they may love, honor, and cherish each other, and so live to-gether in faithfulness and patience, in wisdom and true Godliness, that their home may be a haven of blessing and peace." Home—alas for the broken home—and such homes we must confess are numerous to-day. It is our part, that of masters and boys, to emphasize the fact that on the sacredness in which the home is held are found the blessing and peace we pray for. On it the stability of the nation depends.

A most important part of his religious life and influence was the regularity of worship. A short morning Chapel service each week day; family prayers each evening; and on Sunday, Morning and Evening Prayer and Communion either early or, on the first Sunday of the month, at the eleven o'clock service. The effect of this repetition of great prayers, great lessons, great psalms was cumulatively very far-reaching. Incidentally, it may explain why most Grotonians have a sound vocabulary and an ability to use the English language which is above the average.

Bishop Atwood said Peabody lacked the gift of eloquence. There was at least one kind of time when this was not so. Once in a while, when he had something pressing on his mind, he would speak to the school in Chapel, not from the pulpit, but from the chancel steps. Then he was always brief, perhaps five minutes, always deeply moved, and deeply moving. His words and being took fire. He found instinctively the words he needed,

---

* *I.e.* as a title instead of "The Protestant Episcopal Church in the United States of America."

knew it, pointed his finger and said, "That's it, that's it, my boys," and one knew that was it. At these times he had a power and an eloquence often lacking in his prepared sermons.

In all his preaching, however, what has held and moved the boys and the graduates who have listened to the Rector for sixty years is the man himself. If preaching has been rightly defined as "the presentation of religious truth through personality," surely the religious truths which he has held with such burning conviction have seldom been delivered through a personality more ardent and compelling. When you listen to him you are not likely to criticize oratorical and rhetorical defects; nor do you think of yourself as acquiring knowledge or even as absorbing ideas. What happens is that you are kindled; you *catch* something, because a share of his power has become yours.*

The Groton Sabbath for many years was a strictly Puritanical day. Even in the earliest days there were some protests at its strictness. Change came slowly and has never come wholly. The nature of the transition is indicated by Billings' description of his own emotions when an alteration in the rules was made allowing the boys to skate on Sunday. "We were of the old fashioned type of religion," he wrote;

that is, we believed in the Bible and a rather literal interpretation of the Bible, and we believed in the Ten Commandments tremendously. One was keeping the Sabbath Day holy. I shall never forget the change that came when we let the boys skate on Sunday. I suppose for twenty years no boys had, but on the first Sabbath it was allowed I thought to myself that if boys were allowed to skate, I might as well skate, too. I went down to the pond and put my skates on, and never to my dying day shall I forget the sensation. It seemed to me the Lord would strike me dead.

A gradual lessening of severity took place. Later boys could, in addition to skating and canoeing, play golf and tennis, indeed any game which was not organized. But blue suits and stiff collars still prevailed. If one wished a newspaper he had to walk half a mile and read it there. The Rector's own attitude in recent years was indicated by the following letter:

MY DEAR MISS ———:

In these days, I think we are obliged to change somewhat our

---

* This paragraph was written by the Rev. J. Thayer Addison. To the author of the book it is truer than Bishop Atwood's opinion. See also discussion of the topic in Chapter 30.

Puritan ideas of Sunday observance. Some branches of the Christian Church have never agreed with the Puritans in their idea of what they call the Sabbath. Sunday is not the Jewish Sabbath Day. It comes as the first day of the week and is a weekly remembrance of the Resurrection. We are, therefore, in my judgment moving towards a more Christian view when we try to make Sunday a cheerful day. It ought to be different from other days. Primarily it should be a development of the spiritual life. My feeling is that work is out of place on such a day, but not actually wrong.

If a person goes to Church in the morning then it seems to me in the afternoon they should be fairly free to choose their activity, always bearing in mind that it should not be such as to shock the feelings of other people. In this particular I should be inclined to let the boys do their work inasmuch as it [is] in the nature of an emergency, but I should also think it well to remind them that Sunday is not intended to be a work-day. If any other questions occur I should be very glad indeed to try to answer them.

Sincerely yours,

ENDICOTT PEABODY

In addition to the Groton Chapel, which is officially St. John's Church, the Rector has been responsible for the parish which includes St. Andrew's Church in Ayer and missions at Shirley and Forge Village. The first vicar at St. Andrew's was Dr. Thayer.

Outside the immediate field of Groton, the Rector has been a considerable joiner of causes that seemed to him worthy.* For many years he has been a vice-president of the Watch and Ward Society.

* He is recorded as belonging to the following organizations (1933): American Association for Labor Legislation, American Forestry Co., American Museum of Natural History, American Peace Society, American School Hygiene Association, Audubon Society, Boston Childrens' Aid Society, Classical Association of New England, Consumers' League, Drama League of Boston, Episcopal City Mission, Essex Institute, Faith & Hope Association, Groton Historic Society, Headmasters Association, Joint Committee on Social Service, Massachusetts Civic Alliance, Massachusetts Civil Service Association, Massachusetts Child Labor Committee, Massachusetts Biographical Society, Massachusetts Peace Society, National Association of Audubon Societies, National Economic League, National Municipal League, National Institute, National Conservation Association, New England Association of Colleges and Church Schools, New England Association, Prospect Union, Public School Art League, Playground & Recreation Association of America, Religious Education Association, St. Luke's Home, Society for Prevention of Cruelty to Children.

Finally there is this paper which he wrote on "The Relation of Religion and Life in a Boarding School":

A gentleman of the Jewish Faith was interviewing the headmaster of one of our Church Boarding Schools. "If I send my son to this School" he asked "may he be excused from the Chapel services?" "That would be impossible" was the reply, "the boys all go to Chapel together. It is an integral part of the life of the community. If a boy were to give up attendance at Chapel, he would still have evening prayers at the house; if he were absent from those there would still be Sacred Studies; there would remain a Christian atmosphere, which, we trust, pervades the place, and from this he would find no retreat." The father considered the question for a week and finally concluded his son would become either a Christian or an atheist if he attended the School, so the boy was sent elsewhere.

It is to be hoped the father was right, so far at least as the danger of his son becoming a Christian is concerned and that his reasoning was based upon the assumption that after eliminating the visible signs of Christianity there would still be a residuum strong enough to influence the lives of those who come to a Church School.

The paramount consideration is that of the atmosphere which is breathed all the time by the boys. It is an indefinable quality, but recognized where it exists. The outward and visible means to production of it may be briefly reviewed.

There are first of all and most in evidence the Services of Chapel. They are the services of our book of Common Prayer which we believe to be the best expression of the religious life for boys as well as older people. These contribute greatly to the upbuilding of religious enthusiasm if the boys enter into them heartily as they can be led to do. Boys delight in singing hymns to-gether and they enjoy taking part in the chanting and responsive readings when they are educated thereto. There must be continuous, active participation in the service in order to inspire them. The Sermon in the Chapel, if preached by men who sympathize with boys and understand them, will be given serious attention. One of the striking portions of *Tom Brown at Rugby*, to an older reader at least, is the tribute paid to the power of Arnold's preaching.

The great opportunity of a Master, who is also Rector of a School, comes when the boys are being prepared for confirmation. Then he can talk to them very frankly of all that concerns their lives. He can point out to them that to a boy at least conduct is ¾ of life and that Service to the Master and Brethren is contained in the principle of life of Jesus. "For their sakes I consecrate myself". At such a time or at any other when one is conferring with a boy concerning the

192

deep things of life, the boy has as a rule, comparatively little to say. It is not natural that he should talk much. He is learning the meaning of Christ's religion, he is trying to be *truthful* and *pure* and there is very little he can express. Indeed may there not be great danger of unreality and of subsequent reaction if he attempts to express the emotions which flood in upon him at the moment or those which it seems to him the proper thing to describe because they are what he ought to feel? No—it is enough, for a beginning of a boy's conscious religious life that he should try to follow the Master and should get from Him help to follow— The time to speak of a deeper spiritual experience will come later. The Services of a Church in their largest significance minister to the religious life. Along with them must go that which in modern pedagogy is known as "interior self activity". The Services of the Church must lead to the Service of the boy. The inspiration, if there be any, in the School life should lead a boy to desire to do something for others. A live eager, successful missionary will arouse tremendous enthusiasm in a boy's heart. Many an instance might be quoted of a desire to die a martyr's death in Africa on the part of a boy whose people have no higher aim for him than social prominence or financial success in Wall Street. The aim should be to harness Pegasus. It is an awful thing to quench the ardor of youth, the willingness for sacrifice, the wish to be of use. Men call it boys' enthusiasm, Quixotic, and destroy it, and the result is the commonplace which is the tragedy of so many lives of tremendous possibilities. There is a chance for service just when the boy is in the School. Never again in all probability will he have such an opportunity. Let him do things now for the Brethren. Boys are great Missionaries for good or evil, or for indifference, which is also evil. And if an older boy, one who has begun to realize the meaning of the Christian life, is encouraged he can strengthen weak hands and guide doubtful feet and save lives which are drifting into bad kinds of ways.

A School boy's religion like Charity begins at home and home for him during five or six years is a School. He may get great help by extending his Service to the dwellers around about. Every boarding school is a store house of greater energy than the biggest power house of an electric railway. The possibilities of influence of such an institution are incalculable. The problem of a School Master is how to bring the power to bear upon the community in which they live. Experience shows that boys' clubs and missions and Sunday Schools may be carried on by the joint efforts of boys and Masters. And that the people who in the country have got into the habit of not coming to the Church are glad to have the Church come to them. And that the service thus rendered by members of a school blesses those that give as much as those who receive.

Services—Service—the one the activity of the Church the other the activity of the boy these two things combine to create a religious atmosphere in a School. The third large important factor is the influence of the Masters. There is a new relationship between Masters and boys similar to that which now exists between Parents and Children. There are probably people who view this with regret. There is very little *Ex officio* respect today. A man must make good his claim to leadership and he can get little help, if any from his position.

The Master, especially the lay master who can talk simply to a boy of his own religious aspirations and of the help that Christ has been to him in his life, can win the confidence of a boy to a peculiar degree and can help him to enter into the services of the Church and to volunteer for the Service of the Brethren, which combine to create the atmosphere of a Christian community.

24

THE DAY'S WORK, 1903-1909

E. P. *aet.* 46-52

ANYTHING connected with either education or religion was grist to Peabody's mill, as was anything that directly or indirectly affected the welfare or smooth functioning of Groton. Occasionally his feet strayed into unusual pastures, as when he corresponded with Professor Charles Eliot Norton about the appropriateness of a suggested design for a seal of Groton School. Norton took counsel with Mr. J. L. Kipling, the father of Rudyard Kipling, who happened to be staying with him at Shady Hill. The Rector considered their suggestions gratefully, but eventually adopted another design. He also had a correspondence with Norton in regard to the selection of busts for the fine new schoolroom.*

The following random letters illustrate some of his other interests:

* The list finally selected was: Homer, Demosthenes, Dante, Columbus, Newton, Shakespeare, Milton, Goethe, Scott, Franklin, Hawthorne, Emerson, Grant, Hamilton, Lincoln, Socrates, Caesar, Washington.

To Walter Camp: Nov. 23, 1909

. . . In my work at Groton I am convinced that foot ball is of profound importance for the moral even more than for the physical
development of the boys. In these days of exceeding comfort, the
boys need an opportunity to endure hardness and, it may be, suffering. Foot ball has in it the element which goes to make a soldier;
and we must have it or some similar advantages, especially now
when we are working for peace and hoping for the cessation of
wars.

Foot ball can never be made a gentle or an altogether safe game;
but there is a feeling abroad—and I confess to sharing it in some
measure—that the chances for serious injury are too frequent to-day.
Even if it were an accident, the fact that there have been twenty
deaths from foot ball this season would be sufficient to create in the
mind of many people a desire to abolish the game.

To a parent: Dec. 3, 1909

We established the scholarships partly because we desired to have
a set of boys who had already begun to study seriously and to show
high promise of intellectual development. We thought that such
boys would naturally set a good lead to the other students and
would therefore materially assist us in acquiring and maintaining a
high quality of scholarship. In order that we might have boys without reference to the incomes of their people, we offered to assist in
a pecuniary way such boys as might need it. In the event of a
scholar's failing to fulfill what is expected of him, it would be natural to insist that he must make an effort not to do so, and failing
this, that he should no longer retain his scholarship. This is what I
have in mind in ———'s case. As we reached ———'s name on the
regular list this year, he would have a right to admission on his own
application, and therefore we should be perfectly willing to retain
him as an ordinary student, but it would not be quite fair to the
school, in my judgment, to carry him or any other boy after they
had ceased to do their part in keeping up the standard of scholarship.

To a college officer: Dec. 16, 1909

MY DEAR MR. ———:

Your diagnosis of A——— is so accurate that very little can be
added to it. It may throw a little light upon the boy for you to
know that he is the son of a Mrs. A———, a New York widow who
has been rather successful herself in combining the worldly and the
spiritual. But what has worked for her has not been equally success-

ful in the case of her son. She lives in noble state, garbing her domestics after the European fashion in knee breeches, etc, with all that it implies. She has tried to keep the boy straight in spite of his lavish surroundings and an environment of self-indulgence. A——— never went in for vigorous games at the school and never really entered into its spirit. He is an amiable boy who has not yet yielded to the temptations which will come to him with increasing power. If you can possibly get him to refrain from approaching things which look evil, you will do him a great service. I still hope that he will become a good man. At present, he is simply negatively good.

In regard to B——— the situation is clearer. Last autumn it came to my knowledge that he and C——— had taken for a ride on the scenic railway there two girls whom they met at Revere Beach. As soon as I heard of this, I took it up with B———. He assured me that he and his friend had only talked with these girls for a short time, and that there was nothing that was not in every way proper. He acknowledged at that time that he had taken for a turn in his automobile two girls to whom he had been introduced by some friend and whom he believed to be entirely respectable. As a proof of his opinion he told me that he had driven them perfectly openly in public and had made no attempt at concealment. I was naturally obliged to accept B———'s statements and I thought it fair to him to do nothing more than to remove him from all participation in the responsibility for the care of the school.

Mrs. B———, to whom I communicated all that I knew, was greatly agitated and assured me that she considered the discovery of these indiscretions would be a great source of safety to the boy in the future.

She is herself a woman of some character, but not, I think, particularly wise, or judicious, or strong in dealing with the boy.

At Easter, she and I fell out because I would not allow her son to take an extra vacation in order to go with her to Bermuda, and from that time, I think she has had a feeling of some antagonism toward me.

Reply to an invitation to Professor Copeland (of Harvard) to read to the boys:

15 Hollis Hall, Cambridge
Nov. 30, 1908

My dear Mr. Peabody:

I did, indeed, send you a letter which you never received. But all is right now. I shall be very glad, indeed, to read from the Bible on our first Friday evening; from Shakespeare on the second; and from Dickens on the third. Glad also to pass the night, as I know that I am not to be billeted on some one for breakfast.

Will you kindly advise me as soon as possible about trains? I should like, if I can, to reach Groton in time for a nap before dinner; and if I could get there at 5 o'clock, that would be possible. My voice is always fresher, and my reading better under those conditions.

Believe me, with kindest regards,

Yours truly,

C. T. COPELAND.

And the Rector's comments:

MY DEAR ——:

I have already written to your eccentric friend telling him that selections from the Bible, Shakespeare, and Dickens would be entirely acceptable to us. It was quite incidentally that I discovered that he proposed this programme, for so far as I know, he got no farther than thinking that he would write to me. No letter of his has crossed my threshold for several months.

It seems a pity that he should stay at Groton Inn. The one and only time that he was here, he partook of faculty supper in a cheerful frame of mind and came down to breakfast the next morning like a little man. We can, however, very easily keep breakfast for him when he comes down at a late hour, or my butler, Tommy, can carry the food to him on a silver tray. If you dare approach the gentleman with these suggestions, I shall be much obliged to you, and still more grateful if you will let me know how they strike him.

In reply to a request for endorsement of a school:

March 4, 1909

MY DEAR MR. ——:

I should like very much to be of service to you in the development of your school work. I am afraid, however, it would not be consistent with the replies that I have given to others on the same subject if I should allow my name to be placed in your school catalogue when I am not intimately acquainted with the school and its teachers. I have adopted this policy because I have felt I ought only to appear as a reference where I could speak from actual knowledge.

In reply to a request for his views on liquor:

Sept. 25, 1908

. . . My feeling is that it is best for a boy not to drink at all during the freshman year. If he does drink, I advise him to confine himself to a beer that contains a 'comparatively small proportion of alcohol. Our drinking habits in America are of the worst possible nature. We drink a lot of hard liquor and that between meals. I wish very much that we could establish the fashion of drinking at

197

meals only and then taking either wine or beer. This is a very important question in a young man's life, for the drinking of hard liquor at an early age means drunkenness sooner or later, and this almost inevitably leads on to impurity.

Concerning a proposed book on education:

Oct. 7, 1908

I hardly think that I could write a book at all. If I should succeed in compiling you a sufficient number of words, they would probably be a repetition of the things that I have said and written during the last twenty years. My gift, if I have any, does not lie in either analysis or expression. Truth to tell, I believe that I am lazy as well as uncertain about myself; and perhaps I ought to make an attempt.*

To his brother Francis Peabody:

My DEAR FRANK:

Oct. 9, 1908

. . . I am afraid that you are right in regard to the lack of sportsmanship in this country. It may be that there has been deterioration in manners and morals during the last twenty or thirty years, but there has also been advance along many lines. The Englishmen are more honest sportsmen largely because their traditions are better; but I am not at all prepared to say that they are generally more honest men than the Americans. In the English schools, which I visit pretty frequently and where I come closely into touch with the life, I do not find the boys more moral or finer than ours; in fact, there are a good many evils in English schools which are not found here, and my experience leads me to think that the manners of Englishmen, especially of young Englishmen, are shockingly bad. My friend Arthur, of Cambridge, told me that there were no manners left at all at Trinity. I have found this true in the case of the son of ———, the Bishop of ———. . . . He was as unmannerly and selfish a young cub as I have ever come across, and yet he passed among men as a thoroughly acceptable member of the community.

Nor do I believe that the trend of politics in England is a bit more encouraging than it is here; in fact, it seems to me that we are on the whole on the up grade while England is beset with difficulties and dangers of all kinds, which they are, for the most part, unable to deal with.

I hope very much that we may see you all here on the fourth of November.   I am

Affectionately yours,

ENDICOTT PEABODY

* The book was never written. The nearest thing to it was a chapter, "Academic Influence," in a volume entitled *The Education of the Modern Boy*, published by Small, Maynard in 1925. Peabody was one of several contributing headmasters.

To the Boston and Maine Railroad:

1906

I am informed by the master who went to New York yesterday in one of the special cars which you supplied our boys, leaving Groton at 7:44 A.M. that there was no heat whatever in either of the cars and that in consequence all the members of the party suffered severely from the cold. The master complained to the conductor who kept promising to relieve the situation, but did nothing whatever in this way. The cold was so great that the boys sat in their heavy winter overcoats and even then were uncomfortable. The consequences of a long ride under these circumstances may be serious, and I have no doubt that many of the parents will complain bitterly of the treatment.

It seems to me inexcusable that we should have been treated in this fashion, and I hope that you can assure me that it will not happen again. The parents of many of our boys are prominent railroad people, and I am quite sure that they would bitterly resent such neglect on the part of your road.

Explanation of a newspaper account of an address:

Nov. 17, 1908

If you gained an idea of the address from the New Haven paper, I am glad to have an opportunity to tell you that the brief report in that journal did not give a correct idea of my main theme. My purpose was to point out to the Yale men that gratitude is a finer motive in the development of character than fear. In the course of my remarks, I mentioned incidentally that the idle rich—who are, speaking in the large, the vicious rich—are on the whole the most harmful element in our community. The New Haven paper took up this remark as if it were the chief point of my sermon.

To a friend wishing his son to go to Oxford:

[Undated; c. 1908]

I think that you may have a somewhat exaggerated idea of the excellencies of Oxford. It is a charming place where men may pass three happy and useful years. The atmosphere is perhaps a little clearer and finer than it is at our colleges, but there is also a dissipated set at Oxford which in profligacy runs far ahead of any class of men that we have. It is only a few years since one of our masters was staying in Oxford, and a graduate of Yale came to him in the evening and said that he had broken away from an undergraduate dinner party which was so disgraceful that he could not endure it. I believe that such a condition of things would not be found in any one of the three American universities to which I have referred.

To another headmaster:

Nov. 24, 1908

Your remark concerning H—— and cigarettes had not reached me, but it is almost certain to do so in the course of time. The world is small and the misdemeanors of Groton boys nearly always come back to me after a time. I am disappointed that H—— should have lacked self-control in this respect. At the end of this term, I am intending to lay down pretty drastic regulations in regard to smoking in the holidays; and I think that we shall reduce it to a minimum. Our great difficulty is that parents have not sufficient moral courage to deny their children any wish they may express.

To another headmaster:

Nov. 24, 1908

MY DEAR DIMAN: *

Winsor † and I have got together and written this open letter to parents for which we are asking the signature of the headmasters of the schools described in the accompanying list. It would have been more satisfactory to have a meeting of the headmasters; but this was impossible, owing to the shortness of the time. The suggestion was made to me only the other day, and I jumped at it.

Theatre-going has become almost a curse to our boys, and I hail any plan which promises to reduce the evil.

We are hoping to get the letter out in the course of a few days. Will you therefore be good enough to telegraph me if you are willing to have your name appear among the signatures, and how many copies you would like? I am intending to send a copy to the parents of each of our boys.

To President Lowell of Harvard:

Feb. 22, 1909

My theory has always been that the head of an institution can do more than any other officer to influence persons. I have thought, for example, that much of the trouble about foot ball might have been obviated if the president had taken the head coach into his confidnece and worked with him over the purifying of the game.

I feel confident that the reforms, social, moral, spiritual, which are needed in college life can be effected by you in a comparatively few years if you are able to give yourself in large measure to them; for there is already a large number of men among the undergraduates who would back you up.

I quite realize that there are a thousand things which will have

* Headmaster of St. George's School.
† Headmaster of Middlesex School.

your attention and care. To me the greatest interest in the world is the development of the lives of young men; and it seems to me that you now have the opportunity to do great and lasting work to this generation and to the many who shall come to Harvard.

Some day I should like to talk this all over with you. I am moved to write to you now by the death of young ———, which strikes me not simply as a dreadful tragedy but also as a call to us older men to bestir ourselves to vigorous action.

I am ever

Sincerely yours,

ENDICOTT PEABODY

And a letter to Peabody from an old friend:

[1904 ?]

You are absolutely the most generous of men.

I always think and believe there were two stages in work of Jesus. The first, what is commonly called the work born of early enthusiasms (the days of splendid faiths and splendid ventures when the great sifting work is done) . . . the second, when the great carrying on and holding up work is done of which He said "I must work the work of Him that sent me while it is day for the night cometh when no man can work". This is not tiredness, it is not disappointment, it is not loss of faith: but it is the consciousness of the limit of time and opportunity which comes to all earnest men as they grow older. . . . Blessed, I say, is the man who knows the meaning and does the work of both these stages. I am preaching, who have never known either, but who has longed for both and who hopes the mere longing may be counted to him for righteousness of some kind. God will bless you at Jerusalem as he has at Ephesus, who can doubt it? And thousands will bless the day that gave you to America and to themselves—and I amongst the number.

C. GRIFFITH

25

SCHOOLMASTER IN A RUT

E. P. *aet.* 44-54
1901-1911

ALTHOUGH Peabody's professional life was centered in Groton and his intellectual energy was devoted to secondary education and the church, he found time for many friendships and interests which had no connection with either. Like most headmasters he was much more restricted in term time than his contemporaries in other callings. Whereas, even if they worked hard at the office or on the job during the day, they were usually free in the evening, his evenings were busy, too. But the vacations were his, and he used them vigorously. He was apt to be vigorous even in relaxation, but a trip or a summer in Maine was a change which he always enjoyed.

Often, too, he would be away to preach or marry or speak during a term and this nearly always meant he went someplace where he met interesting and stimulating people.* Often such people came to visit him at Groton. And as he grew older the graduates began to do increasingly interesting things about which they wrote him or came to tell him, so that vicariously he was more in touch with the many phases of the world in his time than most men.

Let us follow his major peregrinations over a period of several years. In 1901 William Endicott informed him that persons unknown wanted him to sit for a portrait by John Singer Sargent, adding that it would probably be necessary to go to England to meet the famous artist.† The Rector felt Mrs. Peabody needed a change and was desirous to go. He was full of the joy and strength of life, but as usual his birthday and the congratulations it called forth awoke in him the awareness of time's hurrying chariot, and on May 31, 1901, he wrote:

I shrink from growing old in a certain sense. And yet I have

---

* He invariably put any fees given him by grateful graduates into a scholarship fund.

† For various reasons the Sargent portrait was not done until 1904. See Chapter 23.

nothing but gratitude in my heart for all that God has given me. It is all wonderful and all undeserved. If I had only made more vigorous effort and worked harder to develop myself spiritually I could have accomplished a great deal. For no man ever had a better opportunity given to him.

The words "Brethren: the time is short" have been in my mind off and on—one cannot expect very many more years. If one can only gain a deeper and more constant faith and a more eager love for Xt one can hope to bring men to Him here, and in the next world please God we shall have a still better chance to know Him and I trust to help others towards righteousness.*

That October he went to New Haven for a Yale celebration:

New York, October 24, 1901

For two days Fanny and I have been at the bicentennial of Yale. We stayed with Prof. T. S. Woolsey—the International Law man. (Son of the former President). Ex. Rep. Gilman and his wife and a Prof. Bacon and his wife were there. Such a grand assemblage of distinguished men as met on the stage for the Honorary Degrees would have delighted your heart. I couldn't help thinking how much more you could appreciate it than I. Cap. Cowles said the one undignified thing of which the President [Roosevelt] was guilty was getting up and waving his hand at me when we caught sight of each other. F. and I had a good talk with Roosevelt in the afternoon. He is a good deal annoyed by the row over Booker Washington and would entertain a thousand darkies in his present mood. B. W. was at Yale and was given an enthusiastic reception, so was Hay, so was Choate, so was James C. Carter, whom Hadley spoke of as the Nestor and the Chesterfield of the Bar. You would have revelled in it. The spirit was the Yale spirit intensified and took possession of me.

In many respects 1902 was an anxious year for him as these letters show:

Groton, February 5, 1902

I haven't written to you for a long while: We have been through deep waters since you left. Last Saturday week Carroll Hodges was taken with pneumonia. It developed into meningitis, then blood poisoning—and he died on Sunday at 5 o'clock. His poor Father and Mother arrived four hours after he was gone—and their distress was heart-rending. We had a service for the little fellow in the Chapel on Monday morning. Last Saturday Billy Gammell—whose

* This letter and others in this chapter are taken from the Atwood correspondence.

203

people you know—came down with pneumonia and is now seriously ill. This morning Howard Potter was found to have it and has already developed a well-defined case. It is bewildering—an anxious time—but we are in God's hands and he will do what is best.

Groton, April 29, 1902

My dear Father has been laid low with what must be acknowledged, I fear, to be a stroke of apoplexy. He was found lying on the floor in his room in the Hotel at Hot Springs the morning after his arrival. They write us that his left side is somewhat numb and his speech indistinct. This happened last Tuesday morning. Jack is there with my Mother and Father and assures us that there is daily improvement. It certainly looks as if he would recover—largely—from this—but we cannot tell when a second shock may come. The sad part of it is that his splendidly vigorous active cheerful life has come to an end. I cannot bear to think of him as an invalid but that it seems he must be henceforth until God takes him home. My poor Mother is very brave, but Jack writes that she is dreadfully tired, has a bad cold and we feel much troubled about her. Strange that so suddenly the strength of their lives should be taken from them.

But his father rallied more than had been expected, so, at the urging of the trustees (the Rector had written, "The great question is that of support. It is no slight expense to go abroad with five children, leaving the sixth in an expensive school"), he went ahead with his plans. By the time he reached Dresden he was at work:

Dresden, October 12, 1902

I generally manage to get in for a Sunday of work wherever I may be. You do the same—don't you? The Incumbent of the American Church is still off on his vacation and so I have accepted the invitation of the vestry to preach today. I came over for the Holy Communion at 8 o'clock: but no one arrived for the Service. They gave me breakfast in the Rectory, and now I am waiting in a spacious but rather cold vestry for the 11 o'clock service. I have also read with especial interest Munsterberg's *American Traits*. He draws too fine a picture of his country but he is generally right. The Germans have had more time to think and to order life after a rational, restful fashion. We are in too much of a hurry and do things any old way.

Weimar, November 23, 1902

Fanny is gaining, I think. She didn't sleep at first. This place is more bracing than we expected it to be. But now she is doing better

204

in this way. And if all goes on as it is going I expect to see her begin to gain weight. We did enjoy the Dresden Gallery very much. The Sistine Madonna I visited several times and found it inspiring. The child with its deep glowing eyes is a wonderful being. Just after Xmas we hope to spend a few days in Dresden. We shall probably stay at a hotel near the gallery in order to be able to drop in there each day. Our weather has turned cold at an early date. The days are glorious. The Sun is as brilliant as it is at home. I wish you were here now. This is a splendid place for walking and we could have some grand tramps together.

Today the Germans observed as a sort of All-Souls Day. For the last two days they have been carrying wreaths of evergreen brightened with artificial flowers to the cemetery. As we went through it this afternoon the whole ground was brilliant with color. The Germans take more care of the graves of their friends than we do. It is a fine custom. They are a curious mixture aren't they? of sentiment and sentimentalism. Goethe was not an admirable character do you think?

Weimar, November 30, 1902

In early February I expect to go to England to see Mrs. Johnson,* Cochin, and old Arthur and other friends, and also to select some place for our summer residence. Shortly after Xmas we shall go with the two older children to Dresden for a few days.

From Germany they went on to Italy:

Near Florence, March 21, 1903

At times during this sabbatical year I have had a guilty feeling of being a skulker for it was not necessary for my own condition that I should go abroad. But a change did seem important for Fanny. And I hope that the new scenes and manner of life may have the effect of making me in some way a more useful man. The time is drawing on, isn't it? Here I shall be 46 years old in May. One cannot look forward to very many years more and it seems as if life and work had just begun. I hope and pray that in the years to come I may be able to throw off the self-consciousness which has hampered the early years and that I may be far, far more devoted to God and the service of our fellow men. It seems to me fairly certain that the rest of my days will be spent at Groton and I feel that I ought to and that I can do much more for the boys than I have done in the past. The buildings are practically done and paid for

* Mrs. Johnson, formerly Miss Sterling, was somewhat older than Peabody and a devoted friend of all the Peabody family for many years. The friendship dated back to boyhood days when S. E. Peabody was in business in London.

and now I hope to be enabled to build up the intellectual and spiritual life of the place far more effectively than in the past. It can only be done through becoming a finer and stronger man myself and that I hope to strive after much harder.

Florence, May 4, 1903

For some extraordinary reason yet to be discovered, my usually imperturbable temper seems to have me wrong today. At lunch I have been quarrelling with Betsy and making things generally uncomfortable. You are far enough away to make it impossible to pick a quarrel, so I shall have a chat with you before I tool off on my bicycle and try by exercise to dispel the unwelcome visitor. It's probably stomach or weather. You pays your money and you takes your choice.

By summer they were back with friends in England, but too busy, as was Sargent, to tend to the portrait.

Kent, June 14, 1903

Last Thursday I passed with Arthur in Cambridge. He has lodgings in Jesus Lane and dines at Trinity. He supplements his income by taking pupils and has some very warm friends among them. I met two or three fine fellows there. Young clergymen who were fine scholars and delightful companions. A kind of product of University life commoner a good deal in England than with us. The public schools are full of defects, but they do have first rate men as teachers and the outcome of them is far ahead of anything we produce. Don't think that I am become Anglicized. I am simply reporting to your private ear what I see.

We are to go to Cochin's on the 25th. The 26th he and I are to be at Cheltenham for Prize Day and for the old Cheltonian dinner. It is great fun going to these old haunts. At the same time it is rather sad to find oneself a stranger where one knew everybody in the old days.

At Groton the year is closing after a most successful season. Billings has done well—Now I want him to go off on his Sabbatical, but the Masters are anxious to keep him at home until 1904. It will be much easier for him to settle down as asst. again after being away. So I think. But it may be that my wish will not be carried out. In which case I must exercise the patience which I have been trying to acquire during this year off.

Kent, August 15, 1903

Billings has been here and we have had long talks together. He has managed the School well, but it has been rather a hard year and I fancy that there will be need of the brisk energy derived from a Sabbatical year to get things into really good shape again.

Peabody saw to it that Billings did get a sabbatical promptly:

Groton, November 13, 1903

You have doubtless learnt before this that Billings has refused the call to Holy Trinity. It is of course a great relief to us. It would have been very hard to fill Billings' place. He is a good preacher, an enthusiastic teacher, and a man who understands well how to handle boys. The qualities he possesses are not commonly found among the Clergy of America. Now, however, he is off on his Sabbatical. I have urged him to go, for he is tired and I want to get his vacation over and have him back settled in Brooks House. It will throw rather more work on me, but I am fresh after my year off and quite ready to carry things along with zeal. The School has started off well. I have been rather savager than usual in dealing with the boys, but they were inclined at first, I thought, to be a little restless under discipline and so I administered discipline in large doses.

In the autumn of 1904 Peabody inaugurated the long series of successful conferences of masters of church schools. The success of these was largely instrumental in the establishment of the Secondary Education Board later on.

Groton, September 27, 1904

The Conference of Church School Masters was an astonishing success. They fell into the spirit of it at once and we had two and a half days of most profitable and delightful intercourse. They were a fine set of men, alive and up to date and were unanimous in feeling that an association such as we contemplate may be of great value to Church education. Lots of men have written thank you notes that have been most gratifying. The work has begun very happily. I don't think that we have ever had so friendly a spirit right through the School.

He never forgot his friends.

Groton, December 31, 1904

This is the last night of the old year. How strangely it is going out. But I trust that the new year is going to bring fresh strength to your dear wife and that He has great blessings in store for you. And blessing will surely come if we can only put our whole confidence in Him.

I stretch out my hand to you across this great continent, dear Friend, and grasp yours in eternal friendship.

207

Often, for instance in April, 1905, we find him spending the spring holidays in the south. "I suppose I told you," he wrote, "that we were really off for Jekyl Island, called by the initiated Shekel Island. It is really an enchanting place." In other years Bermuda enchanted or Florida. He loved an occasional social interlude as he loved an opportunity to loaf energetically. Wherever he went his correspondence followed him.

By July of that same 1905 he was back in England, visiting the Chamberlains:

I had an interesting week-end there. The guests were political allies of the Chamberlains. Lord and Lady Minto, Gerald and Lady Balfour and several others. One did not get the same insight into things political that one gets at Washintgon. Roosevelt speaks out freely all that is in his mind. While Chamberlain, as you know, talks only to the individual and that in subdued tones.

From Kent he had to go to London to sit for his portrait, work on which had been delayed.

Sargent is getting on capitally . . . He is taking me standing up dressed in a Doctor's gown with a crimson hood, arms folded and looking a little to the left. The picture strikes me as good, like me so far as I can judge, but idealized.*. . . Sargent has been most friendly. I find him an interesting talker, sympathetic and chatty and decidedly inclined to make the best of me. The English, like all good people, take you up where they left you. It has been a great pleasure renewing old friendships.

He was back at Groton before the summer was over because Billings had accepted a call to St. Paul's Church in Boston. The Rector hated to lose him, but "he has been unsettled for some time and I am inclined to think that he had better try parish life, much as we should miss him." Peabody himself was also much interested in Theodore Roosevelt's efforts on behalf of reform in football and had indeed been prodding the President for some time to take the lead in the matter. "You may look upon your little friend as the originator of a great scheme," the Rector wrote.

In early November, "I have been preaching to-day at Princeton and a most interesting experience. President Wilson, with

* It now hangs in the school dining room at Groton. Mrs. Peabody also owns a charcoal sketch of the Rector, which many prefer to the oil portrait and others refer to as "Six Blackmarks."

whom I stayed, is a first-rate man. We made great friends together."

Here then we see that within a few months he had hobnobbed with American plutocracy, stayed under the same roof with Joseph Chamberlain, where he had met the latter's sons, Austen and Neville, had made friends with the most distinguished artist of his day, had been in cahoots with Theodore Roosevelt, and had visited Woodrow Wilson. It was the sort of thing which happened to him many times.

It had to be tucked in. Towards the end of November he wrote from Groton: "I am busy as a nailer—to-night faculty meeting—to-morrow to Boston shopping. Thursday a speech at one of our missions. Friday a lecture here. Saturday the Yale game to which I take 40 boys. Sunday a sermon and in the afternoon I go to Middlesex School to preach. So the days go by." And just before Christmas he wrote in a shaky hand, "I am ez full of work ez an egg is of meat and I have just been thrown off a beast of a plug which Frank lent me so that my wrists are exceedingly groggy, otherwise I am all right, thank you."

In January, 1906, he was rejoicing. "Isn't it good that Port Arthur has fallen at last? I hope it may be the beginning of the end. The humanity of the Japanese is a lesson to us Christians, isn't it?" *

The following July he married Billings. "He is a happy man. His wife is a strong vigorous hopeful right minded attractive girl who ought to be a great help to him. She has an objective way about her which will counterbalance [his] tendency to introspection and occasional despondency. He has done extraordinarily well at St. Paul's." From the wedding Peabody went on to a Northfield conference.

It was interesting. There were some 600 or 700 college and schoolboys there and I found them very freundlich. My addresses were not particularly impressive, I am sorry to say, and I had to leave after so short a visit that I hardly got the full flavor of the place. But it was decidedly invigorating. Mott is a remarkable person. One of the strongest men in the Church today. . . . Sunday is a rather busy day with me. . . . I rise at 7 and finish preparing my sermon before breakfast. Have Sacred Studies with the Sixth 9:30–10:30. Chapel with sermon at 11:00. Interview parents or graduates

---

* It perhaps needs to be pointed out in 1944 that he was here expressing the practically unanimous opinion of Americans in 1906.

until 1:30 when we dine. Then comes Faculty Coffee and then a pleasant hour or two off. Tea at 6:00. Reading to boys 6:30-7:00. Evening Chapel 7:15-8:15. Talks with boys until 9:20. Faculty Supper for masters and grads and missionaries and a bed about 10:45.

Sometimes his journeys were sad ones. In the summer of 1907 he wrote from Maine: "My heart is very sad to-night. I am on my way to join poor Billings at Groton. A daughter was born to them yesterday, but the same envelope which contained the message of the birth of the little one had also a report of Eleanor's death. . . . May God help us all to comfort and love one another and to trust him. . . ."

He loved to visit other schools and nearly always brought ideas back to Groton with him from them. For example:

Boston, February 17, 1908

I am on my way from Exeter, N. H. where I passed Sunday. Some 100 odd of the Academy boys attend the Service. I may say that the Sermon was rather poor. Oddly enough it was a sermon which I particularly enjoyed preaching at Groton and Billings thought it one of the best I had delivered for a long time. For some reason or another. it did not go well. I suppose that it was not particularly fitted to that congregation or that I did not get into it as I ought. It is strange—isn't it? how the same words have different effects on two congregations. Amen, the Principal of the School, took me all over the buildings and grounds and was exceedingly kind: So were all the other masters. They called and dined and supped with us at the Rectory and we with them. I do not know when I have talked so much, in private and public. In the evening I preached to the Y.M.C.A. We had a large gathering. Some 200 or so, and as it was a purely voluntary audience I enjoyed it greatly. Afterwards a lot of them came into a smaller room and I spent ¾ of an hour talking to them. The morning I spoke to the School as a whole in their. assembly room. I urged them to fight the battle for America—mentioning B. Washington and T. Roosevelt as the 2 great Americans for young men to back up. It seems to me that T. R. has struck rock bottom. The real question is whether this country will care for Honesty 1st or Prosperity 1st. Whether we are prepared to seek 1st the Kingdom of God believing that all these things will be added. I believe that it is a vital time in the history of the Country—and I cannot understand how honest and patriotic men can oppose the President. There are doubtless mistakes in definite acts and proposals: but a man, who is intelligent and spiritual, ought to be able to see the great principle which is at stake.

And in the same year:

Hartford, Conn., March 9, 1908

It is so natural for you to feel what you speak of—the "finality of death"—Death is final here for a few years: but it is an incident which in the next world will have lost even the association of finality. And the time is short. The thought of it must comfort and at the same time, stimulate. I must work the works of Him that sent me, while it is day. The night cometh when no man can work. It does my heart good to think of your Sanitorium and of the blessed help which it is bringing to those who are in dire need of help. I am just on my way back from Hotchkiss—a School in N.W. Connecticut—It is a very interesting place. Last night I went to a Prayer meeting of the St. Luke's Society. It was attended by 100 out of the 200 boys. They got up, one after another and spoke upon "the Will" (which was the topic of the evening) of the nature of it, of their own need of strength of will and of their determination to get new strength of will. It was really inspiring to see these boys—of about 16 or 17, stand up bravely and express their aspirations and confess their sins. The speakers were all listened to with the utmost courtesy. Buehler, the Head Master (a very good chap, by the way) told me that the Society has a tremendous influence for good upon the life of the School. I wish that we could get something of the warmth and simplicity of personal religious life into our Church School boys.

Sometimes there were suggestions that he might be something other than headmaster of Groton:

New York, April 25, 1908

Your letter anent the Episcopate * was friendly and encouraging. Since I wrote you last not a word about Washington has come to me and I fancy that the whole thing may have been the outcome of the imagination of a few friends. Fanny and my Children would have nothing of it for me: and I fancy that it would be my duty to the School and the Masters to remain at Groton. Even if I should be called. There is attractiveness in the thought that a change might call out latent powers. The School life is very rich, however: and it may be that one ought to consider how one can do more for others without reference to one's own development.

Anything to do with religion interested him. He gave his interest full rein when he returned to England for a summer:

* Of Western Massachusetts. He was also mentioned for the Episcopate of Washington (state).

Windsor, July 12, 1908

The opening of the Lambeth conference at Canterbury was splendid. Mrs. Lawrence could not go and so I had her ticket for the Choir. There was a most impressive procession of Bishops in their best go-to-meeting gowns. The Archbishop sat in his historic chair and gave an address of welcome in which there was much that was modern and looking to the future. At Westminster the next morning, Dean Robinson preached a sermon on Church Unity which must have stirred a good deal of adverse comment in the minds of the extreme Brethren. It was large and Xtian and fine in my judgment. Again I saw a lot of Bishops at the reception of the American Ambassador at Dorchester House. Mrs. Reid was cordial and invited me to lunch at D.H., but I had an engagement. I have visited schools —Winchester, on the way from Southampton, Wellington a new school founded, you remember, by Benson. Walter Lawrence's boy is there and so I motored down with Lady Lawrence. Now I am passing Sunday at Eton with Lyttelton. We have just had a good walk through the lovely country with the magnificent ancient Elms in the foreground and upon the hill the massive gray towers of windsor Castle. I tell you, it's a great thing to be educated in a place which is so beautiful and so rooted in the heart of English History. I have seen many people—The Lawrences, the Griffiths, the Blaines, old friends at Lords at the Oxford and Cambridge Cricket Match.

In the election of a new president of Harvard he saw great hope:

Groton, January 14, 1909

What do you think of Lawrence Lowell's election to the Presy of Harvard? The selection seems to me a wise one. Lowell understands Harvard all to pieces. He is progressive without being radical. More human than Eliot, and, I think, more interested in the development of Institutional religion in the College. I hope to get hold of Lowell before he begins his work as President. The 2 great things that they need at Harvard are

1. Social unity. There is a great rift between the haves and the have-nots. Such a condition is bad in the University.

2. A more spiritual atmosphere. Men who go there either find no enthusiasm and give up their own or else struggle on without much of any aid from the President or older men. For these reasons there is, I believe, a setting away from Harvard. Much the better half of our VI form goes to Yale this year and several fellows who were directed towards Harvard have swung off to Princeton.

He never joined any order (except, of course, the church),*

*And in later years the Groton Rotary Club; if that was an order.

212

but he could see opportunity for good even where he disapproved:

Groton, April 13, 1909

I am inclined to think you have made a ten strike in joining the Elks. I have always had a feeling that Freemasons and such like formed an artificial society which interfered with the large Brotherhood of the Church—and theoretically I fancy that this is true—but one can not find ideal conditions: and I can understand your being brought into touch with Brother Elks in such a way as to give you a splendid chance to influence them. The work that you have been accomplishing quite puts me to shame. I do not get through the half of it. Your Protestant Confessor appeals to me. Then I think of the kind of people who go in for the confessional in our Church and the kind of effect the exercise has upon those who are tied to them—and I will none of it.

One exciting rumor, which proved unfounded, arose in 1909:

New York, October 23, 1909

You will be amused to hear that Woods [Arthur] came up to school the other day with the proposition I should go to London as Ambassador. Bob Bacon had discussed it with Woods and had apparently been earnest in his desire that I should be appointed. The fact that I am a clergyman is sufficient in my judgment, to prevent its being considered by the authorities. But what fun it would be, for a few years! You must come out and stay with us and be introduced to Edward VII and other dignitaries.

It was in this year, too, that he first encountered personal grief through the loss of one near and dear to him:

Boston, November 1, 1909

On Saturday evening my dear father went to his rest. I was summoned from Groton, but owing to lateness of trains I did not reach Kernwood until it was all over. I am thankful that he did not suffer much—at 2 o'clock there was a spasm of pain. They gave him some soothing remedy. Then he became unconscious and breathed his life away. We have been dreading the end in the fear that it might bring agony and that he was not called upon to endure. You can imagine that the feeling uppermost in our minds is that of relief for my father. His splendid vigor and activity and determination to have a share in all that men were doing were imprisoned these last 4 months by a weakening body. Now he is set free, and in some other sphere he is able, I trust, to have the joy of life which he knew in this world for so many years. His life was occupied largely with busi-

213

ness. He enjoyed the excitement and haste of the mart. He delighted in doing things. But he was first of all a father. His great joy in life was in his children, for them he worked and for their happiness and prosperity and future he cared more than for anything else in the world. And so his children are today drawn very close together through their love for him. My Mother is calm and sweet. Her mind is not in a condition to grasp the situation. For that we are thankful.

A few days later he wrote:

Groton, November 11, 1909

There was a very nice article about Father in the Globe of last Sunday. The writer spoke of the numerous acts of kindness and generosity which he performed. He hated publicity and these acts are not known. Frank tells me and/or George—that Father was inclined to help along almost any poor Chap in business who came to him with a project which might be successful if it were taken up by some one possessing means.

About a year afterward he was on his travels again, this time for a full sabbatical. He began in England and Germany, then wandered far afield:

Cairo, January 18, 1911

It makes me homesick tonight, alone as I am in this strange city of Egypt to read of your having gone through that deeply solemn service of consecration without my having anything to do with it. But I am just a little sad to think of your belonging to a different order of the ministry from that of which I am a member. But that last is, of course, superficial. I am really heartily glad that your faithful unselfish life work has been recognized by the Church at large and that you now occupy a high position which will place you among the most influential in the Church.

I do read a bit—hitherto rather with the idea of getting into the atmosphere of Egypt than of learning the History in detail and I look hard at the street life hoping to understand the people whose ways are so different from ours. The Mosques are, a few of them, impressive and in some ways beautiful—but they have not the uplift of our Cathedrals or their individual features, which keep them distinct. One is impressed by the frequency of prayer and by the consciousness of the being of God which characterizes these people. It is much the same in Roman Catholic Countries. While there is much of superstition and while they fail often to connect between the spiritual and the moral, they do use their Churches and they do retain the spirit of worship which is too frequently lacking with us.

214

Don't you agree? How inspiring it would be if we could go into Trinity and there find 40 or 50 people saying their prayers and others coming and going all through the day.

Florence, May 7, 1911

It is a delight to be in Florence again. Perugia was beautiful and we had a most interesting time at Assisi. But there is something about Florence that draws us very close to it. I suppose the early impressions, way back in 1895 are renewed.

Tremezzo, Como, June 2, 1911

Well I am 54 years of age, old Chap. I am just a little ahead of you, am I not? They have been years of almost unclouded happiness, but the record of accomplishment is far from satisfactory. The work has been superficial in large measure. There has been in it too little of personal service, too little of intellectual spiritual life. But, please God, some time yet remains, and I am going to try to let Him work through me instead of making the effort of working for Him.

You would be amused if you could see the number of letters that I have received making suggestions as to how I could accomplish more satisfactory results. Men propose many things that are not possible: but they nearly all agree in wanting me to give up as far as possible the business part of the Institution and giving myself more to personal intercourse with the boys and masters. And this I believe to be good advice. The fact is, I have done a good many things myself because men to whom they were assigned did not perform them well, and I ought to have been more patient and taught them how to accomplish them. I come of a race of business men and that part of the work is easier to me than thinking and writing and even talking with individuals. The views of the masters differ a good deal as regards results. Some think we have lived in a Fool's Paradise and that much is unsound. On the other hand the authorities at both Yale and Harvard have written this year speaking with much appreciation of the influence of our Graduates The best thing, after all, is to do as wisely and as bravely as one can and to leave the results with God. The difficulties connected with our especial labor do not diminish as time goes on—the materialism of many homes drags down the children at an early age or else slows them up after we have perhaps helped them somewhat to see the spiritual side of life. But the fundamental trouble lies with us. I know full well that if I had been a better man these 25 years the lives of many of our graduates would be much finer than they are today.

Shortly after the Peabodys returned from this grand tour

215

their son Malcolm started for the other side of the earth to join Remsen Ogilby at Baguio School in the Philippines:

Groton, October 2, 1911

Malcolm left us last Wednesday. He is due in Vancouver tomorrow and should sail by the "Empress of India" on the fourth. I had a talk with him shortly before he left, and made it quite clear to him that the thing I desired more than anything for him was that he should enter the ministry. I think that he has understood this right along and that he would be glad to give me the pleasure; but he is conscientious and would therefore not contemplate taking up the work unless he felt a pretty definite call to it.

And almost immediately afterward Peabody suffered a second great personal loss:

Kernwood, October 12, 1911

You will have heard, perhaps, before this letter reaches you of my dear Mother's death. She passed quietly away on Monday night just as the clock was striking the hour of midnight bringing in her birthday. She would have been 83 years of age. It was good to think of the day's being the beginning of her new life in Paradise. We were all there. Jack and Frank and Martha and Fanny and I as Mother would have wished. There was no struggle, no pain. Just a quiet falling asleep after an active, almost strenuous life in the Service of others. My Mother was not demonstrative, as you know. She was too much a part of the New England soil for that, but she disregarded herself and cared only for her children and grandchildren. Her life was almost entirely happy from beginning to end. There was in her nature a beautiful mingling of perfect sincerity and courage together with great sweetness of nature. It would be difficult to find two people who were less touched by the littleness of the world than were my Father and Mother.

He wrote Atwood suggesting a memorial to her:

Groton, November 14, 1911

Thank you so much for your letter of sympathy about my Mother. In a way one misses her more as time goes on: and yet there is a happy feeling growing of their being settled. My Father and Mother with George and those who were dear to them in the next country. I want to give a thousand dollars in their memory— and I naturally turn towards your work. It would be nice to have it go into some definite thing which would be a memorial—such as a small cottage or something of that kind. But I daresay you are hampered by conditions in gifts and so I should prefer to have you use it for whatever would be of greatest service in connection with the Church or with the Hospital.

26

SILVER SPOONS

A MATTER which perplexed many of his friends more than it did him was the growing reputation of Groton as a snobbish school.* He pointed out that the boys lived a simple, in some respects an almost monastic, life; they washed in tin basins, they were allowed very little money indeed, and few privileges. But the world outside knew that Groton was hard to get into and that the great bulk of Groton graduates were sons of wealthy families. Not knowing that admission to Groton was controlled by long-established policy, they resented being told the rules would not be changed. Such suspicion was heightened by the Rector's sympathy for things British, by his intolerance of the press and all forms of publicity which he considered detrimental to the school or to individual boys or simply in bad taste. Many strangers set Groton down as a rich man's, exclusive school and let it go at that, while at regu-

* It was a prejudice which began early and endured late. For instance, in 1943 an alumnus devoted to the Rector and with real affection for the school wrote: "The greatest weakness of the school—coming largely from the Rector —is its implicit and explicit identification with the over-privileged upper class with all its manifold petty snobberies, complacencies, prejudices, and' patronizing superiorities. The intellect can thrive only when the social atmosphere is relatively classless, but such an atmosphere is even more important in the development of character, and character should keep step with intellect. . . . [These are] evils that have hung about the greatness of Groton, which has been a little Anglican island—'unspotted by the world' of heterogeneous American life."

This expresses a common prejudice—or criticism. The Rector would have pointed to the performance of the graduates in rebutttal and rested his case there. Cf. Chapter 37. His defenders would add that even if the criticism were justified in individual cases, the responsibility lay much more in the homes from which the boys came than with the Rector.

lar intervals the press joined with Peabody's friends and foes in offering gratuitous advice either directly or by implication.

There can be no question that Peabody had a very high percentage of boys from the upper social strata and that this fact affected his problem and his results. A random sampling of classes, for instance, shows that in the early years over 90 per cent, in the middle years about 85 per cent, and in later years about 75 per cent of the boys were from families listed in social registers. This is the roughest sort of estimate, which might not tally with any given year. In some years it dropped considerably lower, but a survey of the Groton alumni list indicates its general truth. The Rector would have been the first to scorn this as an index of anything worth indexing. In more than sixty years he was never heard to pay even lip service to society in the sense of the social page. For many of its goings on he frequently expressed a thorough disgust. A family background lined with notoriety of that sort was a definite handicap to applicants for admission, and numerous cases could be cited in which it was an actual bar.

Nevertheless, it indicates how many boys came from families in which good food, adequate clothing, gentle surroundings, and general care and training above the average were accepted facts; in which it was fair presumption that no matter how watered the stock had become, someone at some time had somehow had intelligence, ability, and drive above the ordinary. It also meant in many cases a large chance that competition and incentive had been almost entirely lacking.

It is exceedingly difficult to weigh the two tendencies in the Rector's problem. On the one hand, priceless advantages of heredity and environment; on the other the lack of motivation to take life earnestly when it was so patently and contagiously unnecessary to do so. One can say only that to ignore either factor is to becloud any attempt either to weigh the problem or to evaluate its solution.

In a general way the Rector was aware of the suspicion and hostility. The simplest answer would have been to make Groton a big school, but on this he would not budge. The largest number of boys ever there in his headmastership was 194, and the average number in the final years ran nearer 180. He did take scholarship boys, and to the writer's knowledge no scholarship boy who ever went to Groton was ever made to feel that he was different or less fortunate than his fellows in any way. Indeed there was what amounted to a conspiracy not to have scholarships known about. They were never announced nor publicly discussed. The boys who held them constituted a real leaven in the lump, but they, again, were not known about and their presence did not dispel the common suspicion. Popular opinion filled Groton with polo ponies and fur coats.

Akin to this feeling that it was a snobbish place was the idea, in large part justified for many years, that its clientele came entirely from the eastern seaboard, notably Boston and New York. That this in itself made Groton exclusive, as compared with a public school which takes children from a single city district, is obviously questionable; but the Rector agreed heartily that a wider geographic spread was desirable, and in 1915 he sent Mr. Billings on a missionary journey through the west. Such efforts were moderately productive, though sometimes unintentionally vitiated as when the Rector wired a parent in Indianapolis that there was an unexpected vacancy available for boys living west of the Mississippi. As time went on there did come to be a higher percentage of non-Easterners, but Groton remained in the majority an Eastern school and a school supported mainly by well-to-do families.

Peabody and Groton were Hamiltonian and not Jeffersonian. He was a patrician and believed in patricians. If it is not the popular kind of democracy today, it is a very genuine kind from which the modern fashion originated. It would have been understood by Sir Harry Vane or Washington or the Adamses or Gladstone or Winston Churchill. It was a theory of democracy which holds that all men are entitled to justice before the law, with equal opportunity for equal talents as an unrealized goal rather than a realized fact. It made no pretense of considering all men equal since, it held, experience and common sense proved they were not. It believed that democracy was the hope of the world, with free speech and the rights of conscience, but it also believed that the only hope of democracy was its ability to produce an ever devoted and intelligent and honest aristocracy. It objected to the theory that the average or mediocre is as good as the best.

There were times when the theory fell foul of its own supporters.

Sophisticated persons know that it is not enough to be right. In this world, it is necessary to be successful also. This is often resented by closet theorists . . . but wise men accept the universe, and get on with their knitting. Of all this the Rector was fully aware. . . . This attitude is conducive to an urgency, which tended to push boys a little further along the road to success than they would have got under their own steam. Unfortunately it did not induce any increased discrimination in the selection of occupations, and the graduates took to finance as eagerly as to medicine. The Rector saw this very clearly; but his only weapon of opposition was exhortation. He urged the boys to go into the professions and keep away from Wall Street. He lectured on vocations in Sacred Studies: and they asked him how an Army officer could possibly send his son to Groton. . . . T. R. came up, when he was President. . . . He urged the boys not to take champagne or butlers with them on camping trips in the Adirondacks—honestly, that is what he said. It sounded awfully pukka at the time; but long afterward many wondered what it was all about.*

The other side of the case was stated by a parent who had two sons at the school on scholarships (*n.b.* he was an army officer). In an unpublished article written in reply to an attack made on private schools in a magazine, he wrote:

It is said that there is no justification for an English public school, expensive, snobby, and exclusive in a democratic nation like America. I presume that by exclusive the gentleman means that the school sets standards for entrance and for performance afterwards and sticks to them. A private school is expensive, yes. So are many things. The question seems to be not 'Is it expensive?', but 'Do you get your money's worth?' In general one pays in life for what one gets. It is also said that private schools are snobbish. Doubtless there are many snobs in them, but I doubt if there are more than in the public schools I have attended or known in various parts of the country. In a school such as Groton, there is a high percentage of families to whom snobbery might come very easily, but snobs are like Army officers and bankers and parsons; all sorts. Snobbery is a relative thing, an unpleasant one, but a very human one. To assume that a rich man is by the mere fact of being rich unlike other men or that poor men are never guilty of the vices of rich men is to go through life blindly. In the Army I have never noticed a colonel's lady asking Judy O'Grady in for dinner or cards. They may be sisters under their skins; I rather think they are, but they are not social equals. You may say that this is rank, and I agree, but rank is nothing but one form of social demarcation that divides snobs into

* George Martin in his *Preface to the Biography of a Headmaster.*

levels the world over. I was raised in a little mid-western town, as democratic a community as ever existed on the face of the earth, but even there the nice families lived in one part of town and the rest of the citizens in another and my family were concerned when I played with certain friends because, they said, their families were trash. I have observed the same phenomenon from Boston to San Francisco.

The reasons I sent my sons to Groton were that I wished them to be gentlemen and scholars. The former word is much abused, but I know what I mean by it. It means a gentle man, a man cultivated in mind and spirit, courteous, bound by unwritten, but immemorial standards of behavior and by very ancient, but very honorable traditions of duty and responsibility towards his family, his friends, his nation, and his world. I want them to be scholars, or at least cultured men because I believe that is an honorable estate, not only because it is likely to bring them lasting pleasure and profit, but because if they are well-read they will be better fitted to defend themselves from injustice and wrong-doing either by themselves or others. My investigations convinced me that their chances of becoming gentlemen and scholars if they went to Groton and held their own there were excellent. I was willing to pay a large price for that investment.

Further, I wanted the boys to have to stand on their own feet. It's risky with children, but in many respects of all the forms of education that have practical value, the acquiring of self-dependence and common sense by experiencing responsibility, learning initiative, and self-control seem to me the most important. Therefore I picked a boarding school. The argument that home is always the best place for a child won't work, in my opinion. I know lots of homes, some of them with fine people in them, which are the very worst possible place for a child. It isn't a question of home or school. A boy can have both. My sons have had both and are better for it. And so far as education goes, I imagine Dr. Peabody has forgotten more than I'll ever know. What's more, he looks at my boy with an impersonal affection, which I can't do.

Which brings me to my third main reason, which is that I believe the most important factor in education is personality. I believed and believe now more than I ever did that Dr. Peabody and his masters and their wives are the kind of persons I want to have influencing my boy as he grows up. If they insist the boys go to Church, that is all right with me. If, afterwards, they decide against keeping up the practice, that is up to them. If they wish to set rigid standards of behavior and discipline, that is all right with me, I believe in them, particularly when they are based on love and honesty. If they wish to adopt certain English names and customs, perhaps I would not, but

221

I do them the justice of assuming they wouldn't adopt them unless they had proved good and workable. If they have also a few ideas and ways which don't meet my personal approval, I try to apply to them the same charity I like to have applied to me.

And lastly I picked Groton because I like a small school. I mistrust size in anything. Bigness is impersonal and I'll take persons. All our systems and theories and philosophies are precisely what people make them. Men and women are the only things that count, whether they're good or bad.

Peabody himself never considered the desirability of quality as against quantity debatable. There is a record of a conversation following his request for the withdrawal of a boy whose father had given a considerable sum of money to the school. Commenting on the episode the Rector said:

The difficulty with ――― was that he believed being a gentleman is something which happens, whereas, of course, it must be accomplished. There is a most awful amount of rot talked about it today. A lot of people seem to think that because poverty is dreadful and laboring men are badly treated, it is wrong to have good manners and be decent and live up to standards. The idea of apologizing for being a gentleman! It is almost as bad as talking forever about one's possessions or family. The worst thing of all is to be a drone, to do nothing, and boast of it. Being a gentleman is a responsibility, that's what it is.

He went on:

It used to grieve me when I made mistakes or failed in an intention. At last I realized that if one does the honest best he can, that's all he can do. If that is wrong or inadequate, there is at least the comfort that one affords endless satisfaction to numerous other people by it.

27

END OF AN ERA

E. P. *aet.* 55-60
1912-1917

PEABODY followed with great satisfaction his son Malcolm's progress toward the ministry by way of teaching experience under Ogilby at Baguio School. "He has grown deeper and broader, I am sure, through his experiences in the Philippines. Every day I give thanks that he has decided to enter the ministry. It is the greatest blessing that has come to us in our married life and we have had a multitude of blessings. This afternoon I beat one of our graduates at squash. If my mind and character were equal to my physical powers I should be greatly satisfied." So he wrote in the spring of 1912.

He kept his friendships alive. "I am afraid of being writ down an unfaithful friend, I who *depend* so much upon my friends and think so much of friendship." He did not allow increasing years to formalize old relationships, as witness this response to a summertime invitation:

North Haven, July 8, 1913

Rt. Rev. Atwood dear Sir
      yours to hand
    In reply wd. say—

That as one of the inferior clergy the subscriber feels compelled to obey your arbitrary summons to
Grindstone Neck.

He will therefore present himself for your inspection on Friday next, July 11, taking boat from North Haven (State of Maine) on that day, jolly early in the morning.

In return for your tyrannical treatment he counts it just
1. That you meet him at Bar Harbour. . . .
2. That you and your daughters should visit his lovely thatched cottage at North H. on or about the first of August.

And he begs to sign himself
Your Lordship's
least distinguished servant
ENDICOTT PEABODY

P.S. The above will remain until Tuesday provided the provender hangs out.

As he grew older he became increasingly interested in national and international affairs. Later in 1913 he asked: *

What is to become of the Philippines? These Democratic friends of yours may commit one of the most hideous mistakes by giving them up before the people are prepared for self government, and thereby inject a fresh opportunity for war among the nations of the East and West. These Anti-Imperialists are simply preposterous, in my judgment, in their attitude towards Cameron Forbes. He has given up money and time and health in his services for his country.

* Unidentified letters in this chapter are from the Atwood correspondence.

Through great ability and sterling character he has initiated and carried forward a splendid work of civilization among the Filipinos.

The nation is so prone to think all public men guided by selfish motives that many people, I hate to say most people, believe that every public servant is seeking his ówn private advancement. Forbes has got around him a splendid lot of young men, the kind of fellows that the English have made use of in the Colonies; and it tries my soul sorely to think that their work may be cancelled by a lot of people who have inadequate knowledge of the situation and are unable to grasp the ideal many of us have cherished of making a nation capable of self-government, and then of giving them an opportunity to carry it out.

He also took heart in the increasing evidence that his boys were doing well in the world as they, too, grew older.

We have a capital lot of new boys. George Rublee has been drawing up a finance bill which has greatly impressed the knowing ones in Washington, and now Pete Jay writes me that he has been appointed the Government representative of the reserve banks in New York on an equality with the President of the Board. It is gratifying that these and other important things should be done by our Graduates now, for people have been saying that Groton boys do not "amount to much" in after life.

Soon with him, as with others, the outbreak of war was a vital concern.

The war is with us, as with you, an all absorbing subject.

It seems to me impossible that the Allies should not prevail in the long run, and yet Germany is putting up a tremendously stiff fight, and the success of the Allies can be achieved only after there has been a frightful amount of slaughter. I cannot quite make out where our duty lies in regard to our own country. To increase our armament and raise a large army and navy would arouse the fighting spirit which we all deplore and yet, it is perfectly certain, I suppose, that we should be trodden under foot by Germany or Japan if we should fall out with either of them.

The Mexican question seems to be almost as far from settlement as ever. I admire the idealistic spirit which Wilson has shown here. It cannot be logically defended on diplomatic grounds, but I should say that the justification of it can come only from success.

We have been much pleased at Grafton Cushing's election as Lieutenant Governor. He ran far ahead of his ticket as you know. It seems to me the triumph of a man who has been quietly serviceable to the state, and his election a proof that social position is not counted against a man if he is personally acceptable to the people.

And again:

The awful devastation and woe which are overwhelming Europe ought to have a sobering effect upon the people of this country and I think they have. If this is the case, we ought to take every possible advantage of it. We have lately received news of the death of three Groton boys who were at the front. This has not been confirmed, I believe, but there seems little reason to doubt the truth of it. We still have two boys actively engaged in the war. Norman Prince is in the French Aviation Corps, and has twice been decorated. There was a report that he had met with disaster, but this seems to be without foundation. Arnold Whitridge is serving with the British somewhere in Belgium.

The execution of Miss Cavell has aroused a very bitter feeling in the east. It cannot be justified by any laws of modern warfare. Lawyers tell me that it is very doubtful if a man committing the offence, of which Miss Cavell was guilty, would be put to death and that certainly in no civilized country would a woman be condemned to be punished in this way. It is another incident of the awful degradation to which Germany has sunk. Tomorrow the Clerical Association of the Diocese is going to meet here. I have it in mind to suggest the signing of a protest against this dreadful crime and send it, to either the President or the Bishop, with the request that it be forwarded to persons in some way responsible for the crime.

There were two or three pacifists who protested against the remarks that were made by Tayler, Drown, and me, but I think that the large majority of men were of the opinion that a great principle is at stake in this war and that the triumph of the Teuton forces would mean the destruction of liberty and civilization for many years, perhaps centuries.

I am sorry that you dissent so completely from this view. The moral issue seems to me so clear that it is difficult for me to imagine any person siding with Germany, nor can I understand neutrality of mind in a question of such profound importance to the world.

It is just possible that I may go across the ocean in May or in the early part of the summer holidays.* Rose is studying nursing at the Presbyterian Hospital in New York with a view to taking a place in some hospital in France. I cannot of course let her go alone. It is possible that the Germans may enter upon a course of submarine warfare involving the destruction of all ships without reference to the nationality of the passengers. If this should happen, I should naturally be unwilling for Rose to run such a risk. At the present time things are so uncertain that one cannot make definite plans. If

* Of 1916.

I should go, I should wait for three months on the other side until Rose had finished her nursing service. In that event, I should probably take some kind of work, either in Church or camp, under the Bishop of London or the Dean of Westminster.

War came closer. Numerous graduates were fighting and more were going to training camps. Four, Henry Farnsworth, Dilwyn Starr, Bertram Randolph, and Norman Prince were killed in action with the British or French forces long before America entered the war. The Rector was heart and soul with the Allies. Things such as the sinking of the *Lusitania* he rated as the worst sort of atrocity and barbarism. The war colored his sermons more and more.

He was justly proud of what Grotonians were doing to help get the country ready to fight. In 1915 he had a letter from General Leonard Wood:

> You have every reason to be pleased with the work of the Groton contingent at the college camps. Groton sent probably seven or eight, perhaps ten times as many students in proportion to her available total (age limit) as any school or college. They all did well. I congratulate you again upon this showing. It is an answer to the criticism that is sometimes made against schools of the Groton type, namely, that they tend to a self-satisfied, narrow spirit and do not build up ideals of public obligation.

And another one from Theodore Roosevelt: "I wish you to know how well Groton has done. General Wood told me that Groton had made, in numbers and individual achievement, a markedly better showing than any other school."

It was the same when the Plattsburg idea started. Groton's representation and performance was outstanding. The school was in on the ground floor there, and all took great pride in what the graduates were doing. Some of the boys began to grow restless and talked of leaving school to enlist.

Ordinary matters were not neglected. Peabody's zest for athletics and keen satisfaction in good Groton teams were unabated.

> You have probably gleaned from some of the numerous papers that you have read, that we were successful in defeating St. Mark's at football the other day. We had a rather remarkable team and they secured a victory which was a real help to us psychologically. For three years St. Mark's have been too much for us, and the graduates have been asking whether the spirit of the school was as vig-

226

orous as in the old days when all Groton teams vanquished their opponents. The question was asked so often that the present boys were beginning to lose confidence in themselves and so I hailed this success with a good deal of pleasure. It was not that St. Mark's was weak, for they played a pretty strong and a very courageous game, but our eleven was quite a remarkable team for a school and the graduates went away realizing they had themselves never played on such a well-trained and effective team. The boys are somewhat fatigued today, but in a very happy frame of mind. I am almost ashamed to acknowledge to myself the help that athletic victories bring to schoolmasters. A succession of defeats makes the boys inclined to discontent and criticism, while success causes them to look upon the school with an intense loyalty. It seems to me wrong that this accidental influence should have so great an effect upon the views of some people.

Other letters spoke of things besides the war:

Groton, March 27, 1915

Billings has just returned from a trip among the great cities of the central west. He was sent on this tour by a committee of our graduates who were anxious to have our plan of competitive examinations much more widely known. Billings was almost unwilling to undertake the job and started out with a rather heavy heart. He has had the time of his life, as I suspected he might, and has apparently done quite remarkable work for the school. At one city a member of his audience said afterwards that when western people sent their sons east, they wanted them to be associated with eastern boys, and he thought there was a danger of Groton becoming too much a Western School! This was, I believe, said with entire gravity, but the danger does not loom up too high upon our horizon at present.

Groton, May 13th, 1916

The diocesan Convention took place on Wednesday and Thursday. Lawrence was in great form, giving an interesting and stimulating account of his work in connection with pensions. He was so natural and so simple that all the clergy were drawn to him and the Convention was on the whole the most friendly and most sociable gathering of the kind that we have ever seen. This may have been partly due to the fact that no serious issues came before us, but I think that in any case Massachusetts is rather singularly free from the odium theologicum.

You will doubtless have heard before this of Mr. Higley's death. The beginning of his final sickness was so characteristic. He was taken with a bad cold, but for two days he insisted, in spite of Mrs.

227

Higley's entreaties, upon going on with his work. On the third day he was obliged to allow her to send for the Doctor who found his lungs badly affected and ordered him to bed at once. For several days he held his own, but on the Thursday he became worse and Dr. Shattuck, who was called in for consultation, told me that he considered his condition grave. The next day he was somewhat better until the evening when he suddenly stopped breathing and before the nurse could apply any remedy he was gone.

He had sent in to the Trustees his resignation so that we were expecting to go on next year without his active co-operation, but we had hoped that for a good many years we might have the privilege of asking him questions and getting him to lecture to masters and to boys on sundry topics. For him it is a fine thing, for he would have hated to gradually lose his powers, but it is a shock for all of us and a dreadful blow to his poor wife.

Higley was so easy as a disciplinarian that the boys sometimes took advantage of him, and did not work as faithfully as they ought to do, but with few possible exceptions they appreciated before they left Groton the kind of man he was, and I am quite sure that his scholarship and his magnificent character had a deep and lasting influence on most of them. It has been a privilege to have him as a colleague for over thirty years. I only wish now that I had made a point of seeing him more frequently and talking more with him, for he was a mine of learning and was always ready to enlighten one on the problem that one might bring to him. He was one of the most lovable of men. I am afraid he did not know how much we cared for him, but perhaps it is clearer to him now.

A graduate who had been critical of the school for many years and sent his son elsewhere wrote Peabody at this time:

June 12th, 1916

Dear Mr. Peabody:

Thanks for your letter. You are quite right that men and women and character are the only things that really make any difference in the world. Wealth is merely a by-product of effort and intelligence, on somebody's part.

I have often felt, and recently particularly, that the N.E. was getting too rich and too luxurious. That wealth was corrupting folks pretty badly. I have felt that a school like Groton was handicapped by having too many boys of wealthy families. But as I look back I think I value more highly than anything else the high ideals that were taught there and particularly the sense of obligation and service. You were pretty orthodox and uncompromising, there was a good deal of the old puritanism in it all, but it was manly and virile

228

and commanded respect. I know I kicked against the orthodoxy, not only religious, but of conduct, but I see now the tremendous value of such training.

It's not hard to train boys who have to make a living and who want to get ahead in the world because they are denied so much, but it is terribly hard to implant high ideals in a lot of boys who don't have to work and who have many influences at work on them that tend to destroy their moral fibre. I think that Groton has succeeded wonderfully in the standard of good conduct it has set up and if everybody who graduated hasn't measured up to them it only means that a small proportion of people anyhow make good, that the wastage of nature is enormous.

Knowledge and experience are necessary to success but high ideals are the bed rock. One must have them to build on. I think that you and Groton have supplied them generously.

Next year I will have two schools on my hands and about 400 boys and girls in them. They will both be public schools but the building and shaping the policy for them both will be in the hands of only two or three people. The responsibility has made me think a good deal more than ever about the Groton training I got and to value it more. The schools will of course be very different from Groton but their objects will be to train citizens—and I take it there is no higher object that any school can have.

I should be delighted to have you and Mrs. Peabody come down and visit me during the coming winter. I think you would both be interested in the schools and the whole section of country. It's the last place in the world I ever expected to land in and work in but it seems to be the place I was intended to land in and so I am not sorry.

With kindest regards to you both and best wishes for a pleasant summer,

Aff'y,

———

And this letter to Dean Briggs of Harvard shows Peabody's continuing concern with football and athletics:

November eighth, 1916

MY DEAR DEAN BRIGGS:—

You will, perhaps, recall a report which was handed in by a committee of Yale men at the end of last term. In this report they recommend, as I understand it, the abolition of professional coaches of all branches of athletics. Such a move as this seems to me to promise much for American Youth. As thing are at the present time, there is a ludicrous disproportion between the salaries of some of the university coaches and the professors of the universities. That in itself is bad. There is also, of course, the disadvantage which cannot be altogether separated from the professional coach, that it is his business to procure victory. I am inclined to think that the spirit in the universities is somewhat more sportsmanlike than it was fifteen years ago. At the same time there is little of the real fun in University football at least—possibly in other games as well—and there is present in the minds of all the players and coaches the conviction that they must win or else the series will be a failure.

If we could do away with professional coaches there might be trouble at the start. The standard of the varsity teams would probably be lowered, but the element of recreation would be brought in and we might have a much greater number of men taking part in the games.

I wonder if this jumps with your judgment. I believe you could bring it to pass if you should undertake the task of making our amateur sports amateur.

Ever sincerely yours,

ENDICOTT PEABODY

He wrote to Dr. Drury * in regard to training camps:

January 18, 1917

MY DEAR SAM:

I wonder if you have reached any definite view in regard to the effect of Plum Island upon your boys. Some of the military authorities have written to ask me what impression the camp left upon our candidates, and I am feeling round with a view to answering their question.

At the present moment I am a good deal affected by the fact that we had last term more profanity and loose talk in the Sixth form than we have ever had before in the history of the School. This was found chiefly among the boys who were at Plum Island.

In talking with them and with others who know about the situation at Plum Island, I find that many of the boys were inclined to go with the regular soldiers who were a pretty low-down lot so far as talk is concerned.

From the boys coming from various parts of the country they heard a great deal of profanity and much else that was objectionable. Unconsciously they imbibed a good deal of this kind of thing, and I fancy that unthinkingly they desired to become democratic and so fell in with the general tone of the boys and of the place. Fortunately I discovered these things in time to tackle them and I think we about eliminated this sort of thing from the school.

The question, however, is whether it is worth while for us to work against such disadvantages.

* Headmaster of St. Paul's School.

230

The Groton boys in the past have been in the habit of giving up one week or two weeks to the School Camp, where they have had an opportunity to serve the small boys who come there from Boston. This experience has been universally good. Some of our boys have gone to either Northfield or Blairstown where they have also received benefit.

I confess that I hardly like the alternative which seems to be set before us now of having them go to a place which is not particularly wholesome and where indeed the training is not greatly beneficial. I say this because I find that physical instructors generally, and our own in particular, are of the opinion that the military training is rather narrow, not to be compared to the training which is desired by the modern system of all-round development.

If the boys at these schools have four or five years of military training in the school, two years at Plum Island and then two or three years at Plattsburg they will simply be grinding over the same grist in a large measure and will become heartily tired of military training. That is the way it strikes me at the moment.

I should like very much to know what you think about the matter.

You will recognize a certain kind of halting style as a characteristic of this letter. I may say that this is actually to be attributed to your influence. I have just taken up the Dictaphone and I am learning to talk into it. It is not as easy as it seemed to be when I saw you handling it at St. Paul's. I hope that I shall learn to do it better. Meanwhile you will pardon the queerly disjointed style of this epistle, I trust.

With love for my cousin, I am
Affectionately yours,
ENDICOTT PEABODY

He sent this wire:

Groton Mass., April 29, 1917

To the President,
White House,
Washington, D. C.

Believe it of utmost importance for interests of our Nation, economic, social and moral, that National Prohibition should be established for duration of the war. Earnestly hope you may decide to carry this through.

ENDICOTT PEABODY,
Headmaster, Groton School

But it was the war that mattered most. Not only did Peabody, like many Americans, feel that the eventual entrance of the

United States was inevitable; with him the struggle before we entered meant the loss of friends and sons of friends. All his affection for England came to the front to reinforce his conviction that issues larger than national interests were involved. "Better that the world should go to its death than that Germany should come out victorious."

In spite of his horror of war Peabody welcomed the President's war message with relief and admiration. "There is doubtless much selfishness and evil in the Allied States, but the primary conflict seems to me between tyranny and freedom—and the tyranny becomes more obvious as the war progresses in the heartless and bestial crimes perpetrated by the central powers."

On March 17, 1917, he wrote:

I wonder if you are rejoicing as some of us are, at the revolution in Russia? I am glad to find myself in sympathy with the foundation principles of France and Great Britain—that is, in liberty and justice. With all their faults, these nations seem to me to stand fundamentally for those two things. Russia was the destroyer of liberty and I did not care to have us in alliance with her. Now that she has declared herself determined to destroy the corrupt rulers who have been holding her down, we may hope for a new future for the world. If only Germany would rise and put the Hohenzollerns behind the bars, we might have the full burden, which is oppressing us, lifted from our shoulders.

I saw enough of war in France last summer to make me hate it more than ever, and yet I am thoroughly convinced that the complacent satisfaction of a certain portion of our population which rejoices at prosperity and shrinks from war because it would interfere with our money-making, is far worse than war. There is nothing uplifting about it, while in war with all its hideousness, there is a splendid spirit of the utter forgetfulness of self.

As soon as war was declared he set about making Groton's contribution as large as possible:

Groton, April 27, 1917

We shall not be free in our vacation until August comes, and then perhaps for only a short time. We have undertaken to plant a great deal more ground than we usually till. Our plan is to plant twenty acres of potatoes, five of corn, and five of beans. The ploughing, harrowing, and planting of this land will be done by the men. What is known as the cultivating will be done by the boys. They will stay here in groups of twenty or twenty-five during the whole of July and will come again early in September.

Our boys are willing to come back, give up their holiday and to grub in the soil. The graduates are enlisting in the Army, Navy, in Aviation and in nearly everything that one can think of. I feel quite sure that whatever else may be the product of war, the outcome will certainly be an increase in patriotism. I believed that this feeling existed in the hearts of our people, but it has long been latent.

I wish that you could regard the entrance of this nation into the war with the same enthusiasm with which I look upon it. It seems to me that we are aligning ourselves with the forces of righteousness against the worst power developed in the world since the beginning of history. The Hohenzollerns are altogether degenerate as far as morality is concerned. They are hostes humani generis. I am glad that we are going to help to turn them out. When they are ousted, then Germany will come into line and Peace in the world will be possible.

His own family was involved in the struggle:

Groton, October 19th, 1918

Malcolm has at last received his commission from the Government. At last accounts he was staying at Boulogne to break in Moulton, who will succeed him in the Hospital Unit. He was expecting then to go to some place for a while for a short rest before joining his company. I am glad that he is to have the experience of ministering to men in active service, and would not for anything try to deter him from it. At the same time one must face the fact that it means pretty constant exposure to danger. We shall, however, be with many of the rest in carrying this burden. Rose, also, is close by the front, in places where shells and bombs come more than occasionally. She is showing a fine spirit and is counted, I think, a really useful person. Helen is doing well at Saumur, well away from the battle front, so that we naturally feel easier about her.

When at last it was finished, he wrote Atwood joyfully and hopefully:

Boston, December 4th, 1918

We have not told each other how happy we are that the war is over—have we? Isn't it a blessed relief! It's such a comfort to get up in the morning and think that the killing is not going on. Now may we have a League of Nations or something that will weld the Allies together and prevent war forever. I am one of the few in this part of the world—among my pals at least, who approve of the President's going over.

28

GROTON IN THE FIRST
WORLD WAR

E. P. *aet.* 60-61

GROTON and the Peabody family were very much in the war. The Rector himself went to France in the summers of 1916 and 1918. In addition to Malcolm, Helen, and Rose being abroad a future son-in-law, F. Trubee Davison, was a pioneer in volunteer naval aviation and was seriously injured in a plane crash. Mr. Billings at fifty-nine volunteered as Chaplain in France and served devotedly for more than a year. When he returned to Groton, tired but victorious after serving his country and his King, he was given a royal welcome.

By the end of the war the total number of graduates, masters, and former pupils who did not graduate but left with good records was 740. Of these in 1917 at least 100 were over 40 years old. Many were married; about 60 dead. At least 100 were still in college. 475 men were in service, surely an honorable percentage of alumni.

Sons of the school received 160 decorations or citations. There were 5 Navy Crosses; 7 Distinguished Service medals; 24 *Croix de Guerres*, 8 with palms and 2 with stars; 1 D.S.O.; 9 Legion of Honors; 4 Military Crosses; 5 Distinguished Service Crosses; 2 *Medailles Militaires*; 2 Order of St. Michael and St. George; and one or more awards of other British, French, Belgian, Italian, Montenegran, Chinese, Japanese, Portuguese, Serbian, Rumanian and Polish decorations.

Six graduates were killed in action; 18 died on war service. 36 were wounded, gassed, or injured. Grotonians were entitled to the Mons Star and were in action all along the front when the Armistice was signed. They included a general, an ace. They had been in the Lafayette Escadrille and one had given his life there. Out of the total in the armed services 399 had commissions.

Incidentally, in connection with the service, when the NC-4, the first flying boat to cross the Atlantic, soared toward Europe, a Grotonian was in the crew. The famous Wright Whirlwind motor was designed by another Groton graduate, Charles Law-rance.

One need not be an advocate or admirer of war to believe that the country's danger tests the devotion, training, and ability of the graduates of an educational institution. If this is so, Groton graduates met their first test satisfactorily, at least in the opinion of General Pershing, who wrote a commendatory letter about it to the Rector when he saw the final report prepared by Henry Richards.

When the news of the Armistice came there was a whole holi-day and a wonderful *Te Deum* in the Chapel. When the news proved false and later true news came, the process was repeated.

29
BETWEEN TWO WORLDS

E. P. *aet.* 61-66
1918-1923

DURING the war years Peabody's correspondence, as may be imagined, was extraordinarily interesting and large. The alumni kept in touch with him from all over the United States and most of Europe. He began a collection of their pictures in uniform, and this collection always hung on the walls of his study until retirement.

When the Armistice was signed, he and Groton, like the rest of the world, theoretically returned to the normal paths of peace. He placed great hope in the League of Nations, and when it finally went down with Wilson he wrote: "I am sick at' heart this morning. The action of the Senate was not unexpected, but it brings bitter disappointment all the same. We are committed to a policy of aloofness which destroys the great purpose for which we went to war. I don't know which is the more to blame, Lodge or Wilson. My instinct is to wish a plague on both their houses. They have given America over to materialism and self-ishness."

Theodore Roosevelt's death in 1919 grieved him sorely:

Groton, January 17th, 1919

Many thanks for your letter which came yesterday. Yes, it is a great loss to all of us that Roosevelt should have been taken just at this time. I thought him wrong in his view of the League of Nations which I pray may come to pass. But in the great question of re-construction of our economic Social system I trusted him completely. For I think he was both great and fearless. Wilson's ideas are fine, with nearly all I find myself in agreement, but I do not have entire faith in him as a man, and after all it is to the great and true man that one wants to tie in these bewildering days. Pray God the Peace Conference may put an end to war. I am dreadfully afraid that the Latin races have not sufficient altruism to bring about the great ideal which we have in mind. I went to Oyster Bay for Roosevelt's funeral. I was impressed in its perfect simplicity; almost austere it was indeed. It was an answer to the people who have accused him of always courting publicity, taking the center of the stage, and all that. As a matter of fact he mingled with men and came forward on public occasions because he thought it necessary in order to serve the country which he loved. But his delight was in living at Oyster Bay among his family and friends. He was always most affectionate and sympathetic whenever I was with him and I shall miss him all the rest of my life.

Concern for the nation mingled with thought for the school and his ever beloved ministry: .

We have been travelling along at the usual rate, perhaps a little bit more rapidly than we are wont. Chauncey Stillman has given us some new tennis courts and endowed all our courts. Two friends have promised enough to enable us to purchase the house which we now rent for Mr. Tuttle, and to endow that as well. Two entrance gates have been promised. One of them, to go near the cage and Hundred House, is to be a memorial to my father, to be given by my brother Frank, my sister Martha, and me. The other gate will be at the avenue that runs between the Chapel and Brooks House. I am now setting out on a quest for funds wherewith to build the second wing of the School House, to contain a museum, biological laboratory, class rooms and business office. Amory Gardner is for allowing the coming generation to add to the plant. My hope is to leave it such that our successors may give themselves more completely to teaching and intellectual pursuits.

I wonder what you are thinking of the Ku Klux Klan? There is an astonishing tendency among some of the respectable people in this part of the world to justify their existence on the ground that the Jews and Roman Catholics are taking possession of the country. To

236

my mind the existence of a secret lawless society for the purpose of establishing democratic ideas is simply preposterous. I hate the secrecy of all secret organizations, and I view with grave misgiving the increase of lawlessness on the part of educated people as shown in the breaking of prohibition laws, condoning lynching and the extension of these secret associations. The Protestant ministers in Boston spoke out plainly the other day advocating repressive measures, but there was not one of our men who gave an opinion. Why is it that the Episcopal Church is always the last to get into any democratic or progressive movement?

Battle Creek, Michigan, Oct. 23rd, '23

As you may have guessed, I left Boston before William Lawrence's anniversary. His sermon is to be published and we shall know better what he had to say after we have read it. Personally I am glad that he could give reassurance to people who question the fact of the Virgin birth. Carnegie, so Malcolm tells me, does not agree. He thinks it is dishonest to repeat the creed when one does not believe each fact stated therein. He discriminates between this and the interpretation of various clauses which he thinks must be left to the conscience of the individual.

I am greatly troubled by the turn things are taking in Europe. The breaking up of Germany is in itself a most serious matter and one cannot tell what other nations will become involved. I wonder if the French have not all along had it in the backs of their minds that the occupation of the Ruhr might result in a buffer state? From the beginning I have disapproved of their military movements. In my judgment they ought to have submitted the question of Germany's financial possibilities to an International Commission. If they had done that we should have known where we stood, whereas now the whole thing is largely a matter of guess work. It seems to me not impossible that the whole world may again be involved in war. There are, however, many things which may happen to prevent this and for these we must most earnestly pray.

He began to see his function and that of Groton more clearly. He began to speak, no longer just for himself and his own small school, but for a whole way of life and belief which he sensed was in peril. This was illustrated by his remarks at an educational conference he attended after the war.

At the conference someone began with a discourse on self-expression. The Rector looked resigned. Then someone got up and pointed out all the ways in which studying Latin is a waste of time. It was hard to tell whether the Rector was mad or perplexed. There was an intermission and he got in a wrangle with some fellow practitioners about whether the colleges should give a point for work in art. The discussion grew confused until it developed that the Rector didn't understand about points. He never bothered to count them up. If a Groton boy finished his school course, naturally he was ready for college and took his examinations to prove it, but he studied things because he ought to know them, not to get points.

After the intermission a young English teacher took the floor and delivered a harangue against censorship of books in school. Let any boy read anything he wants, was his thesis, and he mentioned Rabelais and *Candide* as cases in point. When he had finished, the Rector stood up and moved to the front of the room so he could look the gathering in the eye. He stood there, his hands in his side pockets, and his chin up. The gist of his remarks ran this way:

The purpose of a teacher is to teach. And teaching which teaches what is bad is not good teaching. No one can defend a man or a woman from evil and cheapness, but one prevents a child from wallowing in mud or dabbling in filth. It is as important to keep a mind clean as it is a home. Merely to teach the things that are honest and true and of good report there is barely enough time. Why complicate the problem with muck? He was not up on modern literature and did not profess to be a critic or connoisseur. He heard a great deal of talk about self-expression and creativity. In his experience a single life based on the principle "for their sakes I sanctify myself" was worth the whole lot of it. People were complaining about discipline as though discipline were something bad. In his experience a man or woman who had been disciplined invariably thanked God for it and those who hadn't been disciplined rarely amounted to much. For himself and his school, he believed in discipline and in the classics and in teaching what was worth teaching. He wound up with a quotation from Kipling:

The 'eathen in 'is blindness bows down to wood an' stone;
'E don't obey no orders unless they is 'is own;
'E keeps his side-arms awful: 'e leaves 'em all about,
An' then come up the Regiment an' pokes the 'eathen out.

All along o' dirtiness, all along o' mess
All along o' doin' things rather-more-or-less,

All along of abby-nay, kul, and hazar-ho,
Mind you keep your rifle and yourself just so.

Of all 'is five years' schoolin' they don't remember much
Excep' the not retreatin', the step and keepin' touch.
It looks like teachin' wasted when they duck an' spread an' 'op
But if 'e 'adn't learned 'em they'd be all about the shop.

'E's just as sick as they are, 'is 'eart is like to split,
But 'e works 'em, works 'em, works 'em till he feels 'em take the
  bit;
The rest is 'oldin' steady till the watchful bugles play,
An' 'e lifts 'em, lifts 'em, lifts 'em through the charge that wins
  the day.

The Rector paused a minute and looked them all straight in
the eye. "I prefer," he said, "until something demonstrably better comes along, to keep away from dirtiness—keep away from
mess, 'All along o' doin' things rather-more-or-less,' and I suggest that we will be better teachers and better men if we learn
to keep our rifle and ourself just so."

It was the end of an era, for him and for the world. At Groton, as elsewhere, the nature of the change was not suddenly
evident nor did it follow the lines most people expected. The
most interesting thing about the new era at Groton was that
whereas most of the world changed by throwing ancient landmarks into the bushes, the Rector devoted his giant's energy to
preserving them as reliable guides to the road.

30

DEFENDER OF THE FAITH

THERE is a good deal of evidence, written and reminiscent, that the period extending roughly from 1905 to
1915 was the period of the Rector's greatest severity
and intolerance. He had achieved both success and security in
his school. He had built a magnificent plant and an enviable
reputation. He had far more applicants for admission than he

could take. His work had been recognized and crowned by the two universities whose approbation meant most to him. There had been intimations that if he wished great place in the ecclesiastical world it was his for the seeking.

This very success may have led him into an unconscious restlessness of which he was himself unaware and which in turn he met with an intense drive for performance by himself, his colleagues, and his boys. He was now in the prime of his life. It might have been past the prime for men who were less strong, and he sensed that the time had come when he must either choose Groton until the end or leave Groton while there was still time for some great work to be done. There was no point at which a sudden final decision was reached, but there is the feeling of a slowly increasing impetus to perfection which alters, beginning about the time of the World War, by almost imperceptible gradations to a broader, deeper, and more understanding mellowness than he had ever had before. This change was accomplished without any loss of strength. It was rather as if a great promontory were rubbed smooth by time, wind, and tide of its jagged and forbidding boulders and outlying reefs, to stand rounded and softened in outline to a more majestic shape. It is safe to say that after the war he was never seriously tempted to leave Groton.

As one follows him through the years, however, one cannot help marvel at his steadiness and endurance under the constant wearing of criticism. Some of this was angry, some vindictive, some genuinely friendly. Like all positive men he had his bitter detractors. One could imagine him without effort resisting all such. But in addition to these, all his professional life he was subjected to a constant torrent of friendly disagreement and criticism by those who loved and respected him. The boys may have been in awe of him at school, parents may have vied to get him to take their sons, but an extraordinary and increasing number of them went out of their way to instruct or reform him as to methods of running a school, as to art, literature, drama, morals, and kindred topics. They wrote him frankly as he wrote or spoke to them and some of these passages at arms throw a most clear light on what he thought and felt in those years.

The fact of the matter is that Peabody was more a Roman than a Greek. Culture as such meant less to him than civilization. He was too busy to be a wide reader; too much a pragmatist to be concerned with intellectual subtleties. When he went to a play, he went to be entertained; when he looked at a picture, he wanted it to be a good likeness of something or somebody worthwhile; when he read a book, he wanted to be instructed or edified, not stimulated or perplexed. He built all his houses on firm rock, built them to stand and to be lived in, and furnished them simply and durably.

As time went on he and Groton became more tolerant and broader. For himself, this was partly the result of the steady wearing process already mentioned. Because he was so outspoken himself, so ready to pounce on the smudge or the doubtful purpose or the off-color performance, he developed in his boys a rather unusual capacity to think for themselves and to stick to their opinions. He never yielded in any essential, but he did, as time passed, become more forbearing and less rigid. It was not the least of his great achievements or characteristics that as he grew older he became broader, more understanding, more gentle, and did it without sacrificing his integrity. As he mellowed, the school did, too, but this was accomplished vicariously. There was a time when the Groton boy who was artistic or interested in nature or genuinely inclined to read widely had a hard time of it. Two or three real artists definitely suffered for their love of art. As late as 1916 a boy who cut a baseball game to go hunt insects and frogs was very close to being that worst of things, an outsider. For many years there was what amounted to a Groton *Index Purgatorius* which included such books as *Tom Jones* and *Stalky*. *Tom Jones* the Rector thought indecent. *Stalky* was not indecent, but it was a book about a kind of school of which the Rector heartily disapproved and he did not choose to have it in circulation. Gradually this changed. It changed so noticeably in the period in which Emerson Tuttle, Walter Siple, and Louis Zahner rose in the school, in which Twining Lynes flourished, and in which the Peabody girls grew up and brought back the outside world to their father, that one suspects more than coincidence. What they began was carried on by others, and within ten years after the war art, music, nature study, manual training, and extraordinary pedagogical achievements in literature and history were commonplace. It was again characteristic of the Rector that as he grew older and reached the age when most men harden and shrivel, he won the support of able men who could make his school alive in these things for which he himself

241

had no particular interest, but which he judged good because those he trusted thought them good.

Meanwhile, even in transition, he hammered at what Mrs. Peabody called "the minor morals." For instance he wrote to a graduate:

What you say about the tendency on the part of boarding school boys to drink and smoke is a very serious matter. One of the boarding schools, as you possibly know, was compelled to send away several boys for drinking. I heard of one of our boys having taken some hard liquor in the vacation, and I informed our fifth form at the end of the year that if any body did that kind of thing, I intended not to allow him to return to the school. This seems a somewhat drastic position to take, but one must act definitely when this kind of thing has come among boys, especially when their parents set them an example as they do today. For years I have urged our boys to refrain from smoking on the ground of loyalty to the school, and I think that more than three-fourths of the boys comply with my request.

Whenever he got the chance, at Prize Day or at an alumni dinner or a parents' meeting, he stated and restated his belief that manners and behavior were important, that self-discipline was good. Often he complained to such gatherings that Grotonians were falling short of reasonable expectation. Sometimes he would send a graduate a book he thought might be helpful, and often he would get a searching reply, as this from a graduate in 1924:

Dear Dr. Peabody:

I am very grateful to you for Dr. Drown's book, and particularly for your friendly reassuring letter.

In regard to the sentiments expressed by yourself in your last letter—I should like to know *one thing* (I think I asked you this question before—after the N. Y. dinner last year—but I am not clear on it yet—) When you speak of the indifference on the part of Groton graduates for spiritual things—are you judging them by definite standards (i.e. the part they take in Church affairs, missionary activities etc., the number entering the ministry: enthusiasm for Dwight Hall and Phillips Brooks House etc.) or by a general impression derived from intimate conversations with the boys who have matured?

When you say spiritual things—would you allow that the intensity and sincerity with which men wrestled with the problem of

242

their relationship with humankind and whatever they may judge the Divine—was an index of their spirituality?

How would you rate a fellow Grotonian of mine who doesn't believe in the Creed but reads the New Testament constantly and is frequently troubled and perplexed by problems of spiritual values? He's had certain mystical experiences on which he places great significance—or the other type, the robust fellow who dives into cold water every morning, goes to Church every Sunday, believes that all's well with the world and has no doubts. Tolstoy or Roosevelt. The Mystic or the Wholesomeminded?

In other words I believe there are probably many Grotonians, who are spiritual-minded but do not exhibit it,—who have all the sentiments and instincts of the finest Christian personalities without the public avowals and decorum to make them conspicuously noteworthy for their religiousness.

Again, in other words—given the type of boy that goes to Groton with his home environment, I don't see how anyone could have possibly done better than you have done. . . .

Affectionately yours,
HARRY A. MURRAY.

To this Peabody replied:

It is hard for me to answer categorically your question about my idea of spiritual minded men. I should agree with you in counting as spiritual all men who are seeking for the truth and living accordingly. I have no doubt that there is a very large number of Groton graduates who are doing this, indeed, I could, and to outsiders I generally do, speak of our Graduates as a remarkable body of men. I do, however, miss their co-operation in the church, first of all for their own sake. The Christian religion is a social thing. There are undoubtedly choice souls here and there who can commune with God apart from their kind, but most men need the brotherhood. You have that in medicine, I suppose; probably you belong to societies and associations which get together and instruct and encourage one another. A doctor who separates himself from the great body of physicians would probably miss a great deal. This is true of political life. We need to encourage one another in patriotism. It seems to me still more true in regard to the life of the spirit. One may not get anything from a particular service and may come away depressed by the sermon, but in the long run the worship and the listening to a man who believes and wants to tell what he believes does have an effect upon one's spiritual development. It is equally important in connection with one's influence. The man who identifies himself with the church, which is the great company of people who believe in Christ, encourages them and identifies himself with the movements against evil and for righteousness. Organization is necessary for effectiveness in business and in war. It is equally necessary for the great purpose of establishing the Kingdom of God in the world, which was the reason for the coming of Christ. I have always rejoiced that Theodore Roosevelt loved the Bible, and said so. That he went to church and gave his reasons for believing in it. I am quite sure that his power for good throughout the country was greatly increased thereby. I have in mind a friend who was in some ways quite equal to Roosevelt, perhaps superior, but had no interest in the church and therefore was not identified in people's minds with spiritual activities. He would have done a lot more if he had joined the brotherhood.

And to the same graduate, Dr. Harry A. Murray, he wrote later:

Taking up some of the points of your article, after assuring you that I appreciate the interest that you show in the school by writing at length about it, I am making the following comments:

Regarding the importance of teaching boys to think:

In this I agree with you, of course. It is more important that they should be instructed in this than that they should have their minds filled with knowledge. I wonder if you are not judging the school from the standpoint of your own age, after having had training and experience which have at least given you this faculty. We do not succeed in teaching boys to think as we ought to do. We have not approached our ideals in any way, but I am inclined to believe that Groton boys are as well trained in this way as the pupils of other schools.

I wonder if you have not rather taken it for granted that the methods pursued in 1909 for instance, are exactly those which we use today? An instance of a change is that in the teaching of history. Some one sent me an article by H. G. Wells recommending "new methods" in the study of history. I replied to the sender that these were practically our methods, and Mr. Ayrault, the head of the history department, informs me that we are actually using the new books which Wells recommends. There are changes in practically all the departments.

Chapel Services:

Would it be wise to make them voluntary? At present the boys go to Chapel as naturally as they go to dinner or to recitation. It is a part of the common life from which their education comes. To raise the question of compulsion, which is not at all uppermost in their minds today, might be unwise. The immediate effect would be to create much discussion, and on the part of some of the boys, to promote the habit of not going to Chapel at all. I realize that many

244

of our graduates do not continue to go to church after their school life is over and no system at a university has developed the church-going habit so far as I know, and I have talked it over with many of my friends who are responsible for the religious life at the different colleges. The voluntary system is almost a failure and nothing particularly promising has been devised. At Harvard a very large proportion of the men never get religious instruction and never take part in common worship during their college life. The excuses for absenting themselves from church are various: 1. They were obliged to go to Chapel during their school days and got enough of it; or 2:—Their people did not go to church and so they did not get the habit of it. We find that boys at whose homes there is an interest in religion and whose parents are in the habit of going to church, and who receive the training of church schools, continue to go to church when their freedom of choice has come; or 3:—chapel services were arranged for boys and they like them, but they find that in churches in the cities nobody takes part in the singing or responses, and they do not get anything out of attending them.

Curriculum:

We have made a good many changes, introducing science, advanced mathematics, manual training, drawing, and music, as alternatives to certain studies. We still regard the classics as an important part of a boy's education, but where a boy has shown himself unable to grapple with language, we do not require Greek; we assign him to some other subject. The need in American schools is not so much a perfect curriculum as a higher quality of teaching. It is more important that a boy should come into contact with a scholar's mind than that he should be instructed in some subject which particularly interests him, by a man who has excellent methods of teaching, but lacks the quality which comes from a first-rate, all-round, scholar.

We do not believe in self-government, but in co-operation. So far as I know, the experiments in self-government have not been successful. Co-operation is our method, and we find what seems to me a remarkable response from our boys. The prefects are interested in the school and in the individuals, and talk with me and the other masters as freely about things which touch the life of the place or of the boys, as they talk with their companions. All the boys are ready, almost without exception, to do anything that one asks of them, either in the way of definite tasks or attempting to influence boys with whom they have a special power.

And again:

The disappointment of my own life came from the indifference to spiritual things on the part of those for whom I am responsible.

245

With them I am not annoyed, I hope, but I am always conscious of my own fault in having failed to give them the intellectual and spiritual impetus which they should have had when they were boys.

To the same in regard to religion:

I think you are a bit severe upon the people who go to Church even in New York! While there is undoubtedly a great deal of formalism and a failure on the part of churchgoers to embody the principles of Christ in their lives, these are the people after all who stand for the organized righteousness of the community; e.g. when a man like Grenfell desires sympathy and assistance, both personal and financial, for his great work in Labrador he goes first of all and most regularly to all of the Churches. There he finds the great mass of his supporters. I know full well the splendid services which have been rendered in Labrador by doctors and men of science. Whether they believe or not, such men receive the commendation of Christ, "Inasmuch as ye have done it until one of the least of these, ye have done it unto me." But that spirit of Christ and the knowledge of him have been kept alive through the ages by the Christian Church. I realize that, as you say, the Church has stood against progress, especially the discoveries of science. Many Churchmen would acknowledge the intense conservatism of the Church as a defect; on the other hand, today the Church is, on the whole, more progressive in its attitude towards the problems of Labour and Capital than are many of the people outside the Church and any one who is radical in his view of the economic situation is bitterly criticized and often persecuted by the World.

I quite agree with you in condemnation of the Roman Catholic institution of the confessional. I count it a most harmful thing that the priest should be permitted to pry into the affairs of the individual and the family. On the other hand, I do think that there is an inherent desire for confession in human nature, and I am inclined to think that the clergy have an equal share with the doctors in the voluntary confessions of their people.

Needless to tell you that I believe that science and religion are fellow-workers in the search for truth. Coué I have read with much interest. As he himself remarks, his system is not at all in opposition to the Christian religion; indeed I believe that it can be made a very great help, only, like all other new discoveries, it needs to be administered with care.

To the same, in reply to further questions:

Lincoln's dictum about what he considers the ideal Church appeals to one strongly. The Unitarian Church—so far as its creed is concerned—comes nearest to his definition. It is a striking fact that the Unitarian Church while it has developed a great number of philanthropic individuals and many fine characters has not grown since its early days. There is a strong effort on the part of some Unitarian laymen to increase its membership today, but clearly there is something lacking in its composition. I have no doubt that Unitarianism has helped to widen the horizon of other Churches and has stood for the human side of Christ.

Can you eliminate theology from Christianity? Is there not in every department of thought a philosophy which is an integral part of that department? In Christianity, for instance, must we not try to get some definite idea about the sacrifice of Christ as well as ethical life, and must we not try to discover the essential nature of his personality? Furthermore, must not a Christian deduce his idea of God from the revelation of Jesus? After all, is not Lincoln's demand met by the Jews as well as by the Unitarians? I have much sympathy with the desire to simplify the Creed, but I have no idea that a Church without a Creed would prove acceptable to mankind. Even in the case of the Unitarians they refused some years ago to admit to their Church all who believed in Goodness, and on the other hand they would not, I fancy, accept as one of their ministers a man who believed in the Trinity.

Do not think that I wish to attack Unitarianism. My people on both sides were, as you probably know, members of the Unitarian Church, but I think from the experience of that Church one sees the necessity of a Creed more characteristic of Christianity.

A constant source of worry to him was that his boys sometimes went through stormy times as freshmen and sophomores at college, especially at Harvard.

In 1944, after the Rector had retired, one of his warmest admirers and most vigorous dissenters, George W. Martin, who had graduated in 1906, wrote an article on Peabody which was published in *Harper's Magazine*. Martin had been at school in Peabody's most unrelenting period; he had later been editor of the *Groton Quarterly* and had had many contacts of various sorts with the Rector in the twenties. He wrote in part:

Education is one of those subjects, like divorce or constitutional law, on which everyone has an opinion. . . . The Rector never sold out to any one school of thought in this connection. Sometimes he was sure education ought to be connected with discipline; sometimes he thought well of science, but more often not; and as the world changed, he changed too. This capacity to change was referred to by his admirers as "growing." His detractors noted the

changes, but considered them the irrational results of outside stim-
uli; the unconscious response of intellectual inertia to current pres-
sures. The conclusions of any particular person in this respect are
observed to be heavily influenced by the investment of time and
effort in any particular department of education. When one has
labored long years at Latin and Greek, one is scornful of the educational value of engineering. And anyone who has put years of work
on studying chemistry is apt to describe that subject positively as
the way to the good life—although chemists make a rather comic
noise in the ears of "educated persons." When the Rector supported the thesis of the advocates of science they considered him
intelligent; when he opposed the emphasis on science the scientists
thought him a mossback. As an actual fact he was not profound;
but he was alert and intelligent and completely devoid of any shame
about changing his mind when he was wrong. This was disconcert-
ing. Indeed, it is hardly fair. He never spent any time or effort proving he was right yesterday; he simply went on to the next thing.
He never tried to get even with anybody, nor bore any grudge.
Thus he saved so much time life appeared leisurely.

Martin continued:

The Rector had a great talent for firing incompetents. He did not
fire boys often: he worked over them. But he was entirely aware of
the strong and weak points of the masters, and those who did not
measure up to requirements he eliminated. This kept the School
from becoming a Home for Indigent Incompetents. . . . He may
have had great faith in human nature, but it was a kind of general,
impersonal faith. . . . He was just, but not particularly sympathetic.
It was sometimes felt that a clergyman should have cultivated a more
trustful nature which could be imposed upon.

As to his teaching Martin said:

He taught First Form Latin. The boys learned no Latin to speak
of, and picked up no interesting information on the side. He was not
unkind, but the children were ill at ease . . . whenever the Latin
suspended for an instant there was a kind of Peter Parley talk which
bored the kids. . . . Besides this Latin class Mr. Peabody undertook
the instruction of the Fifth and Sixth Form in Sacred Studies. . . .
Somehow the subject would get turned around; and it would seem
as if the class were enamored of Mohammed, and on the verge of
embracing Islam. And this, of course, was quite all right if only
these exuberant explorers were openminded enough to see, before
the end of the hour, that Christianity was best, after all. But sometimes it was just touch and go whether they could be brought back

248

into the fold and the gate shut safely before the clock struck. It was nervous work. Buddha was disposed of without difficulty. Apparently Nirvana excited no interest, and Gautama no converts. But when Zoroaster came along, there were ten short minutes spent on him; and for the other fifty minutes the faithful St. Bernard dogs were searching the Alps for the yodeling Parsees straying far from the company compound.

And of Chapel and ethical instruction:

Certain phrases [in the Rector's sermons] recurred continually: "the dyer's hand is subdued to what it is dipped in" . . . "sanctify yourselves for their sakes." * . . . The boys wanted to live dangerously and see life. The Rector wanted them to be pure in heart, and to keep unspotted from the world. These objectives are not inconsistent; but you cannot capture the imagination of boys by talking of goodness, or self-sacrifice, or strong silent heroism. What the beggars wanted was to excite the admiration and astonishment of the other monkeys. . . . After St. George killed the dragon he was very popular and it is obviously up to the proprietor of a large stable of boys to provide dragons right along. Now, there was something phony about Mr. Peabody's dragons. Instead of getting into some old clothes, and sneaking up on the dragon, and grabbing him by the neck, and sinking your teeth in his jugular vein, while he roared and writhed and breathed out clouds of smoke—but you hung on; it wasn't like that. . . . In the first place you had to go into training; and then, when the dragon was brought around, it appeared you were to *talk* him to death, or set him a good example or something, more like St. Georgianna than St. George.

It was a continuous puzzlement what kind of man the Rector was. The way he walked was incompatible with the way he talked; and the boys believed their eyes rather than their ears. . . . He was determined to be liberal—if it killed him. And so, of course, he was not really liberal, he was only determined.

* There is no doubt that the Rector used certain phrases repeatedly. Mr. Martin perhaps overlooks, however, the importance of this in preaching to a transient congregation of boys. Each year a good part of the school would be composed of new boys to whom the phrases were new. Furthermore, to assume that a boy will grasp an idea hearing it once is the fondest sort of optimism. He needs to hear it again and again so that years later he may be able to use it. This repetition may be somewhat wearing for the faculty, who hear it year after year, although it is not indisputable that hearing a thing once is sufficient even for adults. There are two possibilities: First, Peabody used a few ideas repeatedly because he didn't have any others. Second, he used a few repeatedly because he thought they were basic and was more interested in quality than in quantity.

And finally:

The Rector complained a good deal about the vacations—especially the short vacations at Christmas and Easter. He said [the boys] . . . spent their time at the theatre, and later discussed, not the merits of character portrayal, nor the problems presented, but "the beauty of actresses."

He just had not thought this out. Any boy of seventeen who was more interested in the technique of drama than in feminine pulchritude would have been an object of suspicion to the Rector at first contact. But he was right in complaining about the vacations. They were too violent. The boys reacted from the cloistered existence at Groton like sailors getting shore leave; and though the damage was not permanent, it was unnecessary and exasperating. The role of the parents was difficult. If they were rich they took their boys to Jekyll Island, and thus supplied a sterilized playground from which there was no escape. But if they had to live in New York or Boston, the boys ran themselves ragged. The Rector exercised a kind of remote control which operated to involve the parents in collusive and clandestine breaches of unenforceable ethics. . . . No satisfactory solution was ever evolved. The young continued to be interested in actresses.

These opinions of Martin have been quoted at length because, in addition to being witty, they represent the type of criticism to which the Rector was subjected for more than fifty years.*

3 1

SEARCH FOR TRUTH

BUT it gave an untrue picture for all that, or perhaps not so much an untrue picture as an incomplete one. All the criticisms may have been true up to a point. The Rector was intolerant; the Rector did have many rich boys in his school;

* As has been suggested, Peabody had severe critics as well as ardent defenders. To get more fully the taste of blame and praise it would be instructive for those interested to read some of the chapters in *Views from the Circle*, a privately printed collection of reactions to Groton by individuals who knew the Rector in various circumstances in different periods of his career. Especially informative are the articles by H. H. Richards, George Biddle, Arnold Whitridge, Walter S. Hinchman, Christopher Rand, Louis S. Auchincloss, and George R. Clay.

the Rector may not have been profound; the Rector was often brutally outspoken and severe. But if the Rector was intolerant, he was so in an age, after the war, when it was fashionable "to tolerate anything but intolerance." He was a notably intolerant man perhaps in the Harding administration and the revival of the Ku Klux Klan and the Coolidge bull market and the days of flaming youth and boogie-woogie and Aimee McPherson and Father Divine and Al Capone and Huey Long and the rise of Adolf Hitler. If he lacked the subtlety and resilience of a willow, he had the uncompromising strength of an oak. If he had many rich boys in his school, he inoculated them with a desire to be useful citizens and with a sense of obligation to serve. If he had material to work with which was both difficult and above average, he got results from it. If he was not profound, he was sound, and if he seldom read Byron or Shelley, he was permanently familiar with the Ten Commandments and the Fifteenth Psalm. If he was sometimes ruthless, he was most often so with himself and with his family.

He said once: "I am not sure I like boys to think too much. A lot of people think a lot of things we could do without. Manifestly the world is full of evil that we all encounter as we go along. Nobody denies that. But why emphasize it ahead of time?"

That can be plucked out of the content he gave it as an example of narrowness. But in his usage the argument might have run that he wanted to build a good ship; a good, strong ship, built to last for years, carry good cargoes, and weather any storm that came. Some said that since the ship was going to get her bottom fouled and have rats and vermin aboard her and rusty boilers and worms in the planking, it was wise, in order to get her ready for that, to expose her to barnacles before she was launched, to install some pedigreed rats in the hold, to weather her boilers so they would be rusty while still new and to build wormy planking into her decks. The Rector's theory was it was better to build her just as staunch and true as he could, using nothing but proved and tried materials, and then send her to sea to meet whatever storms and calms awaited her.

And this whole discussion leaves out the warmth and charm of the man, for he was very charming. If his forthrightness made him a few enemies, his inner wholesomeness and outer grace won him friends and admirers of all ages. It was a touching thing at an alumni gathering to see faces light up when they saw him; touching to hear the way in which old boys spoke of him. Mention has already been made of the loyalty of the masters to him, even many of those who left. It was matched or surpassed by that of the boys. One wondered, sometimes, whether any school was loved the way Peabody's school was. Nor was this loyalty confined to masters and boys. His helpers in the office were there for many years; Fred Torrey, Miss Ames, Miss McConnell. The author had this, which he knew, confirmed when he went to Groton to seek material for the book. Faces lit up there, too, remembering the Rector and what he was personally to other persons. The men on the place, known to the boys, typically enough, as the Sons of Rest—George Meyet, Joe Cleary, Tom and Tim, "St. Peter"—or the maids who served the school year after year, all were devoted to him.* No less great and enduring was the gratitude and admiration of the parents. A few were hurt and bitter, but the Groton addressbook is filled with names that occur over and over again, a sure sign of loyalty. Brothers followed brothers, sons fathers, and before the Rector retired there were grandsons.

The preceding chapters emphasized the positive, rugged sides of Peabody's character. This is proper, because without that formidable determination shown in many ways neither he nor the school could have become what they became. Again, however, the picture was incomplete. Adventurous souls may have strayed from the compound in sacred studies, to the anxiety of the Rector, but most boys, forgetting, as time went by, the details of sermons and courses, were held steady by what he had been to them. They may have remembered that Billings was the better preacher, but they remembered what the Rector told them was right and wrong. Here is a recollection of a Confirmation class written down by a boy in after years:

The talks came in the Rector's study. He sat at his desk with the light on his face. He was very simple and earnest. Of course, I can't give you exactly what he said in the whole series of talks, but it was something like this:

---

* "One waitress would never wait on the St. Mark's team when they were at Groton and St. Peter bet his savings on the Groton football team the first year I coached. All the men did. They had a pool with their opposite numbers at Southborough."—Extract from letter of H. E. Tuttle.

252

The greatest joy in life is to give oneself utterly to Christ, who is everything that is good and true and beautiful. It is necessary to give. It is not enough to wait. One can prepare his mind for giving by studying, reading, and thinking and his spirit by prayer and thanksgiving. We all need help for life. No matter how strong and sure and safe we are the time always comes when our strength is not enough. The wonderful thing about having Christ to turn to is that He is so charming and so alive with vivid personality. And when we turn to Him, we consecrate not only ourselves, but others, since we turn partly for their sakes. Baptism takes us into the Church, but that is usually done for us by others, they consecrate themselves for us. The glorious thing about Confirmation is that it is our own decision, made carefully and publicly when all the evidence is in, to take our stand by the side of a Master who is brave and wise and holy. By His example He showed us all the way, the truth, and the light. Being a man He repented and having repented, He was forgiven. Being forgiven, He was strengthened. "Make me a clean heart, O! God, and renew a right spirit within me." A life without the power of Christ and God in it, is only a man's little life. To join our life with God's of course means renunciation. Nothing worth while is ever done or gained without giving up something. A naval officer gives up home; a doctor time and comfort; a great lawyer leisure and everything except the service of justice: so a Christian gives up the world, the flesh, and the devil. The devil is a personal spirit of evil, as Christ is the personal spirit of good. The devil is subtle and poisonous. He plays on pride and vanity and lying and envy. A man can disarm him only by becoming as a little child and saying "My Father." The devil is irreverent and a sly tempter. He gets us to tempt others and so captures us. He leads us to sin and gambling, to get something for nothing. We have to renounce him and all his works. No half measures will do. When we have taken the first steps then the great rewards come.

I cannot remember it all, but it seemed so simple and indisputable as he talked to us sitting there, the firelight flickering behind him. He showed us that a man must have faith as he goes through the world, faith and trust in God, who made heaven and earth, and in Christ His Son. He made us see there what a tremendous thing it is for a man or a boy to be able to say "I believe—Credo." I came to see that a life without purpose, kindness, and usefulness is a kind of blasphemous thing.

Of course I got religion. When I left one of his lectures I didn't want to talk, just be quiet. I knew ——— felt the same way. We left the Rector's and walked over to Brooks House arm in arm without saying a word. It was a deep blue winter night, studded with bright stars. As we went in, ——— turned and lifted a hand to the sky in a kind of salute. Then we slipped up to bed with no more than a brief good-night.*

Then there was his humor. He had an abundant store of it. Perhaps it was a bit old-fashioned. George Martin said in this connection, referring to a matter mentioned in an earlier chapter:

If anyone will look through the bound volumes of *Punch* . . . a great light will break upon him. For there are all the jokes, the preoccupation with playing fields, the impatience with vulgarity, the social dilemmas of the well-endowed dowagers, the total ignorance of life on any other plane, the complete confidence in the morality of property, the feminine women, the protective and possessive man, the swells and the bounders and the snobs—in short there is portrayed the benign complacency of a ruling class which had no regrets for the past and no fears for the future. Brought up in this society, the remarkable thing is not that the Rector was inscrutable and different from home-grown, grass-root Americans, but. that when he finally came back to Boston he was endurable at all. He was endurable. He was very popular.

He rather liked practical jokes. A master told of riding to Boston in the train in the early days with the Rector and a group of other masters. In the seat ahead of Peabody was a serious-minded member of the faculty who was inclined to being dignified and proper. The Rector took his stick and tipped his colleague's straw hat. The hat was restored to its proper angle. The stick tipped it again. The owner of the hat moved huffily to another seat. "What, not leaving us old man?" ask the Rector sympathetically.

He used to tell stories on himself, as of the boy who was sent to him by a master to report that he, the boy, had called him, the Rector, "the Big Swede."

---

* Even when he was away from school, Peabody's thoughts were at school and he was alert to note anything that would be of use to him there. The Rev. Malcolm Strachan, an intimate of his in later years, tells of notes for confirmation lectures jotted down on all manner of stationery in all manner of places; phrases and ideas on hotel writing paper, on odds and ends of various sizes and shapes. The Rector also gave Strachan numerous of his books and asked Strachan to help in the arrangement of others. Strachan was struck by the regularity of the Rector's reading. No day passed without a stint finished. In the margin of a book he would make a notation as to the date on which a particular section was finished.

"I was rather relieved," the Rector said. "I could think of so many things worse than that."

Occasionally his early training in games caused an impasse between him and the boys. He never really approved of baseball, with its chit-chat and gum chewing and counsels as to avoiding baby carriages. He felt it wasn't quite cricket. If a pitcher got in trouble, the Rector felt he deserved silent sympathy or even honest encouragement; certainly not raucous innuendoes. Often when a batter would strike out, the Rector would call from the bench, "Well tried, old man!" to the despair of the more ingrained players. But the point was that he could see that this was funny. He never really changed his point of view, but he never really minded if people laughed at him because of it.

Everyone knew he was humorous. It was a quality the boys prized in him, but it was an Olympian humor at school. Only when he was away from school did he fully relax. Then he could be jaunty and carefree. There is a description, by a boy traveling with the Rector by train, of an interchange between Peabody and the waiter in the dining car. It had to do with the ordering of a chop, which the Rector insisted must have come from a hippopotamus. The whole affair was conducted in high good humor and mutual appreciation by both parties.

Everything interested him; everything, that is, which was not shoddy or mean. Ignorance of a topic on his part was no impediment, it simply made him the more eager to hear about it. If he was a vice-president of the Watch and Ward Society, he was also a contributor to Roy Chapman Andrews' expedition to Mongolia to look for dinosaur eggs; if he believed firmly in Prohibition, he was also deeply interested in the Zionist problem.

"He makes me think," wrote Walter Hinchman,

of Carlyle's sentence about Ruskin, "No other man . . . that I meet has in him the divine rage against iniquity, falsity, and baseness that Ruskin has, and that every man ought to have." This sincerity and faith does something magical to his sermons. His single gesture—one large hand in a rather awkward patting movement—is not impressive; but you believe his sincerity so wholly that you believe what he says. And another thing, while we're discussing assets, we've left out the biggest of all. The Rector's first and greatest virtue is Mrs. Peabody. I'm sure he would agree. I wonder if you boys ever realize how much the Rector demands of his wife, how much he subordinates her to his work? Of course, he never does demand it and she is never subordinated. But she has been singularly able to identify

255

herself with him. She is not "second fiddle"; she is part of him and his life, indissolubly so. They are a great team. Furthermore, if this does not seem important, think how much of the Rector's success depends on his single devotion to his cause, his school, and consider the disaster implicit in any other type of wife. Plenty of wives help their husbands, many subordinate their own interests. Few are capable of such complete identity.

Other qualities, by no means minor, are his simplicity and his humility. He is so far from cunning that he is almost easy to fool. Once or twice I have been amazed at seeing the Rector swallow the vaporings of persons who knew how to put a plausible veneer on their disingenuous views, but this credulous quality is the defect of his simplicity. He is not uncompromising because he thinks he is right, but because he believes himself the agent of a principle he believes is right. In fact, he is so humble personally, that strange as it may seem to many who see only his positive, assertive side, I think he actually lacks confidence in himself and has been saved for greatness, perhaps on that account, by a reliance in something larger than himself. A more complicated or more analytical mind would always have been disturbed by doubts and fears. The Rector's simplicity and humility liberate him—at times, possibly, into mistakes others would avoid, but, in the measure of the years, into a cumulative habit of devoted service to a high calling.

Some of the older graduates say that "the Rector's views on education are instinctive rather than reasoned." It may be. He is certainly suspicious of ideas which imply a change in his scheme of things. He is inclined to condemn what he cannot understand. But that doesn't mean the Rector's idea of a school is not worth promoting! It has been one of the great contributions to American education. Essentially Thomas Arnold's innovation at Rugby, a compound of drill in the classics, athletics and muscular Christianity, it found other expression, in America before Groton was founded, notably at St. Paul's; but the Rector was the first to make friendship between boys and masters a natural, accepted fact—a condition now taken for granted in most schools, but almost unknown in 1884. Further, he abolished the clique-forming house system and, by keeping the School small, he stressed the family feature as the larger institutions cannot do. Graduates, who visit in great numbers year after year, do not go back just to visit the old school, but to see the Headmaster and his wife.

In all these things Mrs. Peabody aided and abetted him. He asked the guests to Groton, and enjoyed them; she had to entertain them. She molded her life to fit his and was unwearying for his welfare. She, too, enjoyed *Punch* and believed in it. She, too,

256

was capable of a serene stubbornness. For sixty years he tried to make her hurry, and she was at no time hurried.

Periodically somebody, a boy or a master or a parent, would get mad at the Rector. Nobody ever got mad at Mrs. Peabody. Jokes abounded about her as they did about the Rector, but there was a singular lack of meanness in them. One, which was probably apocryphal, but which all who knew her felt might perfectly possibly have been true, told of her being on a crowded train one day and, seeing a back which looked to her familiar, addressing a strange middle-aged gentleman, to his astonishment, by a Christian name which was not his. In the face of his evident amazement, Mrs. Peabody remained unruffled. "Oh!" she said, "I thought you were one of my children."

Mrs. Peabody, too, for all her gentleness and serenity, believed in and insisted on manners and minor morals. At her own table or in the school dining room, at tea, at "parlor" (when, twice a week, she had younger boys into her house to play games), she insisted that behavior be courteous and decorous. One boy remembers playing crokinole long ago, stubbing his finger, and saying aloud, "Dad gum it!" Mrs. Peabody came over quietly, but swiftly. He remembers her voice sounded like steel wrapped in velvet. "T———, I cannot have such language in my house. If you choose to speak that way, I must ask you not to come again."

No one resented this setting of standards. At heart all were grateful, and there would have been no surer way of infuriating the school than for someone to be rude to Mrs. Peabody. Her rebukes to boys were very rare, because there was so seldom need for them. And always if a boy was sick or tired, it seemed she knew it and had counsel and rest at hand.

To see Mrs. Peabody at her finest one had to attend one of the state occasions, most of all Prize Day. Hundreds of parents, past, present, and prospective, each expecting, and getting, the personal word, the individual question that meant so much; graduates, trustees, friends, faculty, all milling about, trampling through her house, making themselves at home in her rooms, expecting her to know all the answers and to be neither ignorant, impatient, nor weary. Somehow she contrived to make old friends and strangers alike feel that they had come, even in that big gathering, to her home as her guest, and all this while apparently unfretted that five hundred people had to be fed and

257

watered and moved in the mass from one function to another. And there was another thing with the Peabodys. Not all appreciated it fully because, in the dispensation of fortune, not all knew grief or sorrow. But those who did discovered how marvelously kind and sympathetic they could be. One knew it instinctively of her, of course, but it was an amazement that he, who could be so adamant and stern, should have such a deep capacity for gentle and understanding tenderness. A single example of this will suffice. A winter morning word came to the school that a graduate, whose brother was still in the school, had been seriously injured in an accident. The Rector told the boy the sad news after morning Chapel. The mother was ill at a friend's home in Boston, the father far away. The Rector and Mrs. Peabody with the younger brother went at once to Boston to join the mother, while the father hastened to the injured lad. He got there too late. But all that day until he could reach the stricken mother and brother, the Peabodys stayed by, doing the little things that mattered, talking simply and naturally of the boy who had gone, and the Rector offering prayers from the wounded simplicity of his heart. One does not forget these things.

Later there was a memorial service in the Groton Chapel for this boy, and the sermon the Rector preached is so typical of the preacher and tells so much of him in so many ways that it may well serve, in its entirety, to close this chapter.

St. Luke 11.52. "And Jesus increased in wisdom and stature, and in favor with God and man."

Three weeks ago I spoke to you of the great experience of Jesus' boyhood, when in the temple at Jerusalem there was borne in upon him the energizing truth that He was in the world to be about His Father's business.

It was a stirring call at a time when "he heard the years before Him and the tumult of His life."

He might have been tempted to get to work at once—you and I would certainly have been—preparation is so long drawn out, so tedious, so tame. But Jesus went back to His quiet home at Nazareth, there to spend many years with His parents, waiting for the time to come when He should enter upon His life work. Those were happy years. The statement can be made quite positively, even though we know comparatively little of the particulars of the daily round. But we can be sure they were happy years because they were years of *growth*. That is the source of all contentment in

258

youth, in middle age, in the declining years. "I am growing—in one way or another. A greater world is opening up to me. The vision of what may come 'for me and for the world grows larger year by year." Any boy or man who can say that has the root of happiness in himself.

And so we say that we are confident of the happiness of Jesus in those "blameless years he lived beneath the Syrian blue," because one who knew wrote of Him, "He increased in wisdom and stature and in favor with God and man."

What would that mean in some detail? It would mean, first of all, that He was getting what we call His intellectual education, at first in the village school, then, not at the university, but in the synagogue from the teachers there. It was what we should count a rather narrow curriculum, and yet it touched on the great subjects of study of all time. He would learn there the history of His people from the very beginning when they were called in Abraham from the far-off East to dwell in the little Land of Canaan, up to the time in which He was living; and the knowledge of the perseverance and courage and faith of His people would create in Him an intense patriotism. How completely that can take possession of a man you know from this great war. This last week you heard it expressed in words of fire from one who spoke to us of his beloved France.

There in Nazareth he would be instructed in the law of His people, the great principles underlying their relations to one another, the things which the Jewish nation had declared to be right or wrong, the science of their government. He went to the Law School.

He would become familiar also with the noble literature of His people, not so extensive as that which is at our command, and yet nothing finer in literature has ever been written. "When I travel," a man of unusual culture once said to me, "I carry just two books—Shakespeare and the Bible." And Jesus had a complete knowledge of the Bible of His time. He would learn, further, religion and the philosophy of religion.

As He walked about the hills of His native village, looking far off to the plains and the sea, there would be borne in upon Him the great spiritual truth which had been revealed to the chief of His country's prophets, of the deliverer of His people and of the world. And this is the picture of Him: "He is despised and rejected of men, a man of sorrows and acquainted with grief: and we hid, as it were, our faces from Him: He was despised and we esteemed Him not." It was the background of all the truth of life—that men can be saved only with suffering, that he that loseth his life, only he can save it; that the way of the cross is the way of Him that would save the world.

259

History, law, literature, religion, theology—these were 'the things on which He depended for His education. They produced a well-trained brain, taken into the mind of One who was pure in heart. They produced a power to see into the meaning of things, to understand the working of the human soul, to *know men*, which is described as an increase in wisdom.

"Judge not by the appearance, but judge righteous judgment." That is the end of education in the twentieth century as much as it was in the days when Jesus was studying at Nazareth.

He increased also in stature. I am glad to lay emphasis upon that fact. Too often, in mediaeval art, which was affected by the spirit of asceticism which despises the body, Jesus is represented as a poor, delicate, rather effeminate person who has no appeal for red-blooded men except the appeal of pity. He was not that at all. He was a strong man physically, muscular, sinewy, enduring. He drove the plane and wielded the hammer and carried the timbers, and did the heavy work of a carpenter. He walked great distances. He was a commanding figure of a man. He drove out of the temple with a small whip a great multitude of men who were overawed by His impressive personality. He was growing strong, with exercise and outdoor life, all those early years.

Then He increased in favor with God. How could He do that? God had sent His Son, the son of his love, on the first Christmas day. How could he love Him more: It was perhaps not greater love, but a *deeper satisfaction* year by year, an ever growing delight in His development, at times of great crises in His life, at His baptism, at His transfiguration, declaring, "This is my beloved Son, in whom I am well pleased."

And He increased in favor with man as well. How they must have loved Him in Nazareth! We are not told about that time; but we know how great is the attractiveness of a strong, unselfish, sympathetic boy and youth, and we can certainly understand their feeling of affection for Him, even though there may have been something in His thoughtfulness and His reticence as He pondered over the future, which they could not understand.

"He increased in wisdom and stature and in favor with God and man."

A scientific man of the present day has said that this is the best description ever given of the development of an all-round youth.

It comes naturally to our minds at such a time as this when we gather to pay reverence to the memory of him whom we have loved and lost awhile.

It is good to assure one another, as we have done in our service, that our dear friend is with Him who in heaven and earth is the God, not of the dead, but of the living. It is good to thank Him for

God, not of the dead, but of the living. It is good to thank Him for that life which has touched ours and will not be wholly separated from our thought until he greets us with his happy smile in the other land. It is good to highly resolve that we will, with God's help, endeavor to perform the kind of service here in this world which he gave promise of doing—this friend of ours, ——— ———, a name which you will, many of you, pronounce with reverence all the days of your life.

What manner of man was he whom we deplore, and at the same time thank God for, this morning? One who was growing in much the same way in which the Master grew in Galilee.

He was increasing in stature. Large he might have become, but his power lay not so much in his size as in the quality of his muscles, in the energy which was perennial, in his nervous force. How great they were you, most of you, realize, when you recall his athletic achievements at school, on the eleven, on the basket ball team, as a fives player—while his skill and effectiveness in baseball have already becomes a tradition of our athletic history.

There was in him that exuberance of life, that thing which the French call the "joie de vivre" which comes from a healthy and a vigorous body.

"How good is man's life; the mere living
How fit to employ
All the heart and the soul and the senses
Forever in joy!"

He must have understood and sympathized with those lines.

In wisdom also he increased. Already his judgment had much effect upon a great number of those who looked to him as a leader. You accepted his decisions as Prefect because you knew he was fair-minded. No great experience of life had he known—he was still so young; but there was a native truthfulness of mind, and instinct of justice, a sense of values. You felt that his judgment was just, because he sought not his own will, because he wanted to do right. "He was always a dependable person," so one of his classmates said, "for his character was strong and sound, and he never failed to follow unswervingly the right as he saw it." It was a gift this—consisting of a clear mind and natural power of insight. It was the result also of the doing of duty day by day—studying, and studying to good purpose—a scholar standing high in his form.

He increased in favor with man. How well you boys know that. He was a popular boy, a popular man, someone may say. He was far more than that. He was one who was beloved vividly and deeply, with a love more intense than comes to the lot of ordinary men. Why did you give him your devotion? "I think it was because

261

he was so gentle in his nature," one has written of him. That gentleness was not indicative of timidity, for he was fearless, a hater of shams and all evil things! It showed itself in a subtle sympathy and in a charm of manner which was constant—"It never had to be assumed when in company with strangers;" so a friend declares, "and never waned when in the constant company of friends." .

Closely akin to this was the cheerfulness of his nature. He met life as he met his friends—with a smile; there was sunshine there, "real sunshine, I mean," says one. There were difficulties in his life, and trials. No life is free from them; but they were borne so sweetly that they were not trials. "He seemed to me," another told me, "to fulfill the prayer we use in Chapel that we may live to the good cheer of our fellow men."

Together with this gentle nature which radiated cheer, there was an enthusiasm which was contagious. He was interested in all kinds of things—the small things as well as the great,—in all sorts of persons, the quiet and the demonstrative, the obscure and the prominent; people of all kinds were drawn to him, through his gentleness, cheerfulness, enthusiasms. Yes, through all of these, but still more through that which combines in itself all these and much besides— *what we call love.*

That was really it, my boys, was it not? He was loveable. "How proud I am to have been his friend!" A general testimony that— "because I found this in him, or that"—was it not really because he loved? He gave himself; he had no *things* to give. He was not possessed of this world's goods, but he loved, and love is the only gift in which the giver gives himself.

"He had a great love for all men." "He was a good companion, a great friend, an excellent mixer." "He sweetened life for all who knew him and he has sweetened death for some." Do not these descriptive words of many friends bear witness to his growth in favor with man? He was much loved, we say, because he loved so much.

"And every one that loveth is born of God, for God is love." So wrote the Apostle who is described as the disciple whom Jesus loved. This young man also, when Jesus saw him coming to Him, Jesus must have loved.

You remember why the Son of man placed some on the right hand of the Throne of His glory?

"I was an hungered, He said, and ye gave me meat, I was thirsty and ye gave me drink, I was a stranger and ye took me in; naked and ye clothed me; I was sick and ye visited me; I was in prison and ye came unto me." And when in their perplexity they asked when they had done such things to Him, He made reply, "Verily I say

262

they had done such things to Him, He made reply, "Verily I say unto you, inasmuch as ye have done it unto one of the least of these my brethren, ye have done it unto me."

It was not food or drink or any thing this boy gave you, my friends; it was far more than that; it was a good lead in life, it was uplift and hope for yourselves; it was his friendship and his love. And doing these things to you—things that are greater far than food or raiment—he did them unto Christ.

"They that be wise", it is written in the Great Book, "Shall shine as the brightness of the firmament; and they that turn to righteousness as the stars for ever and ever."

It is a blessed encouragement to us who live and work in this place to be told by the father of this noble son that "the happiest years of his life were his Groton years, and he had no unhappy ones, the most useful years of his life were the same, and he lived none but useful years." And to have the first part of that confirmed by his own statement made to a friend only a few hours before his death.

And so we have come together my friends, to revive his memory, to do honor to his name, to tell one another of our love for him, to offer our grateful thanks that our lives have been enriched through his having been born into the world.

Can we do better now than that which he himself would have done had he been here today? Gather at the table of the Lord whom we have chosen as our Master and whom we would henceforth serve more truly if we may?

You—we—need the deep things the Master alone can give— comfort. You need it. "I don't think I ever felt anything myself so much," were the simple words of one writing of his death. Where can abiding comfort be obtained? "Come unto me all ye that labour and are heavy laden and I will give you rest." "Only the infinite pity is sufficient for the infinite pathos of human life."

We need to learn again the way of life, the way of Him who laid down his life for His friends, who will teach you and me, so far as we will try to learn the lesson that it is unselfishness, and giving of self, and love which make the world a wonderful place to live in, that he who loseth his life, he only shall find it.

We need, as a consequence of the love of Christ, and as the result of this boy's friendship and example, to offer and present unto the Master "Ourselves, our souls, and bodies to be a holy, reasonable, and living sacrifice," together with the prayer that we, the young and the older ones as well, we also may "increase in wisdom and stature, and in favor with God and man."

263

32

THE EARLY TWENTIES

E. P. *aet.* 65-69
1922-1926

THE Rector's fame was spreading. In 1922, New York University made him a doctor of humane letters. Chancellor Brown said: "Endicott Peabody, the law was your schoolmaster and led you to the Church. You have had need of both law and gospel in your chosen task of educating American boys, to which you have devoted well-nigh forty years in a single school. But, added to these, you have brought to your task a deliberate and reasoned purpose and a personal art of teaching, through which you have made your life work a conspicuous service to your country and Humanity."

He was much on his travels; going to educational and religious conferences, preaching, marrying, and burying. All fees he received from graduates he put into the Scholarship Fund. At home he had good cause for contentment. He had a common operation in the early twenties, from which he speedily recovered; otherwise he and Mrs. Peabody were in remarkable health. The children were sources of pride. Malcolm, rising steadily in the councils of the church, was happily married to Mary Parkman, a close family friend of long standing, and the eldest grandchild was an Endicott Peabody. Rose and Dorothy were happily married, and Helen was shortly to marry R. Minturn Sedgwick, another much loved Grotonian. Betsy became a real authority in the field of remedial reading and in the course of time the only woman on the Groton faculty and a real force in the school. Margery studied nursing and made an admirable career for herself in the Boston hospitals and as visiting nurse.

There were changes at Groton, of course. Slowly the veterans began to drop out. Abbott went first to Yale, then as headmaster to Lawrenceville. Ayrault and Jacomb retired. Gladwin and Crane died. Some of the best of the younger men moved on. Tuttle went to Yale where he became master of Davenport College. Siple went first to the Fogg Museum in Cambridge and then to the Cincinnati Art Museum as director. Several others

264

went to college faculties. Yet the quality of teaching at Groton probably improved, and at least one man, Louis C. Zahner, started on the career which was to establish him as one of the outstanding teachers of English in American schools.

Peabody kept in touch with his faculty even in vacation. The following letters are typical of many. The first was to a master on sabbatical:

North Haven, Maine, July 19 '21

I was delighted to get your letter of the 7th of May. As the years increase we must keep in closer touch with one another. The sad part of growing old is that one's friends and relations gradually slip away. We are both finding that as a personal experience, and it does not make it much easier that we knew years ago that this would be the case. So, please be sure to jot down your thoughts on paper and send them to me from time to time.

The boys gave me a great welcome on my return from California.* Instead of taking out the horses and dragging the carriage, they took me out of the motor and carried me on their shoulders to the school steps. It was only a small thing, but I was greatly pleased at their friendly feeling on my coming home.

Since the vacation began I have been posting about the country officiating at two or three weddings of Old Boys, talking at Speechday of a school founded by a graduate, and making sundry visits. Now we have settled down in our island home off the coast of Maine. There is abundant opportunity for exercise here in the way of golf, lawn tennis, small boat sailing and rowing. I affect the last especially, for I like to get hard and fit against the coming year's work. I wish you might have come to this part of the world. There is a wonderful combination of sea and mountain and the resulting climate in which you would have rejoiced. At present, my wife, Helen, Betsy, and I are the only occupants of our cottage.

To a prospective master:

July 17, 1923

Our forms are not altogether on a level of the English public schools. They are distinctly behind in Classics, but ahead in Mathematics, Science, and English. You will find, I think, the general average higher than that in England, and the standard of scholarship lower, in fact, we have very few scholars who can compare with those of the English schools. This runs through the whole of American life. In nearly all things we have a great body of more than fair

* He had been away for the winter term.

265

performers, while the excellent and the very bad are not numerous, the "Duffer" being as conspicuous by his absence as the accomplished scholar. The boys in the third form are fourteen or fifteen years old. Promotion comes each year unless an individual falls below the mark required.

To Mr. Gladwin, then librarian:

Northeast Harbor, Maine, July 17, 1923

A thing on my mind: 1. The translation of the Odyssey, that is in the library. This has been used from time to time by the boys without permission of you or of their class master, and I think we better withdraw the book. Will you see that it is taken away?

To a graduate inquiring about the teaching of Sacred Studies he replied:

Northeast Harbor, Maine, July 21, 1923

MY DEAR JACK:

We are entering upon a new plan in regard to Sacred Studies. It may seem to you a bit of exaggeration to call it a new plan when it is simply having two recitations a week instead of one. If you knew how hard it is to get men to teach Sacred Studies, you would sympathize with me unanimously. My idea is to try Sacred Studies in a somewhat more objective way than we have done hitherto, and to put the subject on the same level as other studies, marking them regularly and counting them in the monthly average. It becomes more important than ever to get a good course laid out.

This is what we did last year:

First Form: Stories from the Old Testament, Soare's Heroes of the Old Testament, passages from the Bible learned by heart, something concerning the use of the Prayer Book.

Second Form: Life of Christ.

Third Form: The Acts. The Christian Church during the Apostolic Period.

Fourth Form: Some Epistles of St. Paul; Christian Nurture Book, Course 10; The new life of the Church; The beginning of Christianity in England, etc.

Fifth Form: Theoretically, the Life teaching of Jesus in detail. Actually, Mr. Billings taught them, "How We Got Our Bible." After that he taught Hodge's O. T. History and some of the new Testament.

He is of the mind that the boys got a fair amount of information, but I think the course was a very sketchy one.

Sixth Form: 1. Jesus' History, Glover. 2. Jesus in the experience of men, Glover. 3. The Apostles' Creed of Today, Drown. 4. The Episcopal Church, Hodges.

A former master was editor of a magazine in which appeared a photograph of a famous actress. The Rector wrote protesting against it. In reply the master wrote:

I am sorry you found it suggestive or pornographic in character. I am a publisher and I take my calling seriously, I daresay as seriously as you do yours. I have no intention whatever of publishing anything that could harm young or old. I am disturbed, however, that you and I should be so far apart on what is harmful. That picture wasn't printed to stimulate anybody, not the way you mean. It was published because I thought it remarkably pretty. I still think so. Frankly it never occurred to me it would be a temptation to anybody. Apparently we disagree as to what is a matter of temptation to boys. . . . I think that boys and girls to-day are a much saner, nicer, healthier crowd than we were, and part of it is because a hush hush conspiracy is being broken up. Bustles and crinolines were fundamentally obscene, but there is nothing obscene about a bathing suit or that picture. . . . After all, modesty is a relative and not a positive standard, as you know, Sir, from your travels. . . . I think Miss ——'s back is a pretty back, but not a temptation, not suggestive. If you tell a boy it's suggestive he has a right to answer "What of?"

Which did not prevent the Rector from thinking it was suggestive and frowning upon that or similar magazines in the school.

And to a request from an educator for information about Groton:

Northeast Harbor, Maine, July 24, 1923
MY DEAR MR. FISKE:
Before answering your letter of the fourteenth of July, let me say that Mr. Siple, one of your committee, is leaving this country for his Sabbatical year, and will, therefore, not be at Salisbury for the Conference. I venture to suggest your asking Mr. C. S. Griswold to take his place. Mr. Griswold has done a great deal of work, as you know, in connection with the unification of entrance examinations, and he could, I think, render valuable assistance in this connection. His address is always Groton School.

To take up your questions:

1. We have established separate curricula at Groton. Beginning with the third form, however, there is a liberty of choice which in-

creases each year, so that there are practically two courses which might be called Modern and Classical. There has been a reduction in the number of hours devoted to studies in the fifth and sixth form. In the latter form there are boys required to take only five courses, and in some few instances this has been reduced to four.

2. There has been no systematic change to provide for extra curriculum activities, but the able boys find opportunity for this without interfering with their duties. We try to regulate the number of interests of this nature, in the case of the individual. No change has been made in the vacations. We have thirteen weeks less two days at midsummer, two weeks and three days at Christmas, and two weeks at Easter. I believe this is different from the arrangement of some of the schools.

3. Many of our elective courses have no reference to college preparation. Throughout the year we have various lectures of an educational nature. Last year there was a course of lectures on Current Events.

4. Our boys carry on the stationery store, the athletic store, some assist in the Office. To all these boys pecuniary stipends are attached. Our scholarships are given to boys who maintain a high standard of performance in all respects. The Prefects co-operate with the masters in regulating the school life, and they are vested with large authority.

5. Our forms are divided into two, sometimes three, divisions. "A" division contains the abler boys, and they go more rapidly than the others.

6. We have employed the new plan of admission to college, ever since it was established, and have found it satisfactory.

7. In particular instances we have had boys examined by psychologists, but we have not yet adopted the intelligence test. We are in correspondence with the Harvard Department of Education, and expect to adopt some system of this nature.

8. We have accepted the report of the committee establishing uniform admission, and have embodied their recommendations in our entrance examinations.

9. We are in touch with our community in the following ways:

I. Masters and boys teach in our two school missions.

II. This past year we have taken part in four community services on Sunday mornings, in the Town of Groton.

III. During May we carry on evening services in the Town Hall of Groton, inviting various clergymen of our church to make the addresses, the school leading the singing.

IV. The Missionary Society has a Christmas tree at the School and Christmas trees at the missions.

V. During the summer vacation the Missionary Society carries on

268

a camp to which are invited city boys who could not otherwise have holidays. This camp is manned by masters, graduates, and present boys. The funds for it are collected by the Missionary Society.

VI. Clothes that have been outgrown are contributed by the boys and sold at reduced prices to the neighbors.

VII. Our masters fill certain offices in the Town, one of them being Chairman of the Public Library Committee, another Chairman of the School Board, a third directs the Forum, which was established by him.

VIII. This vacation, the grounds of the school will be used by the Massachusetts Farm Bureau, for their annual outing.

IX. The lawn tennis grounds and golf course are free to neighbors who desire to use them. The Chapel is kept open during the holidays, in order that it may be seen by visitors, a great number of whom come to Groton for this purpose.

The English department provides a list for summer reading for each of the forms. Boys who are behind in any subjects are required to make it up during the summer.

If there are any other things about which you would like to ask me, I shall be very glad indeed to try to answer them.

Sincerely yours,
ENDICOTT PEABODY

Occasionally there was confusion in the mind of a correspondent:

North Haven, Maine, July 19, 1921

MY DEAR MR. RANDALL:

I am sorry that I could not fulfill your request for an article about Groton School. This is the school which I represent and not St. Mark's School which is at Southboro. I think you may have got both these schools confused with St. Paul's for you speak in your letter of my possibly not being at Concord. As a matter of fact, your letter did not reach me until I arrived at North Haven on the 14th of July. I am writing this line because I do not wish to appear to have intentionally neglected your request.

Sincerely yours,
ENDICOTT PEABODY

His voluminous correspondence with graduates continued:

Northeast Harbor, Maine, July 3, 1923

What you wrote in your letter about Mr. ———'s opinion of Groton interested me. Your explanation was, of course, correct. I do not remember the exact incident, but generally when people sit next to me, I am inclined to point out boys whom they are likely to know or with whose parents they are acquainted. If the B——s would examine the lists, say of prefects, for the last ten years, they would find that boys were given high positions in the school without reference to the financial standing of their parents. The inference of young ———, that his people were not pleased, therefore he was sent to St. Paul's, and his brothers to Lawrenceville, is incorrect. These boys were not on our lists at all, and so we could not have taken them even if Mr. ——— had been pleased with the school.

It is the fact that parents have been annoyed with us for not taking their boys for whom they have made their petition, which gives rise to a great deal of criticism of the school. I write all this to you because it seems fair that you should understand the situation as far as I can explain it.

We are sending you a good lot of boys this autumn. I hope that they will give as good an account of themselves as you men have done. Our standing at Yale, both intellectually and socially, (in the larger sense of the word), is all that one should desire. A pleasant summer to you and my kindest regards, please, to your father.

Affectionately yours,

E. P.

The following has to do with a book by a graduate about the war:

DEAR MR. PEABODY:

I only just received your letter as it was sent to Bermuda and then forwarded here where we are living at present. I am glad you liked what I said about Mr. Billings and Ham Coolidge.*

As for the rest, I feel justified in saying a few things in its defence.

As I wrote you, it was my earnest desire and intention to portray the events and characters and spirit of those days as they actually were: to mix in the true proportions the various elements that existed. To do this there is bound to be a certain amount of profanity, drinking, coarse humor and acts of lust and violence as well as the nobler qualities of heroism, comradeship, earnestness and idealism.

I have very little sympathy with writers whose sole purpose seems to be to show the ugly side of life. But neither have I with those who conceal the truth in order to draw a picture, not of what really exists, but of what they would like to have.

It is useless for anyone to pretend that such things do not exist among "single men in barracks" in war time in a foreign land. I am

* Capt. Hamilton Coolidge, a former senior prefect, who was shot down in his plane over France just before the Armistice. He was an ace.

270

afraid my picture of the airmen is a true one. (Any overseas flyer would agree). Yet Bishop Brent was probably quite correct in his statement. There was, I feel sure, less drinking and immorality among our men than in the other armies. (Read V. M. Yeates' book, Winged Victory, just out, on the English airmen)

But to pretend that many of the Aviators did not get drunk and swear and sing bawdy songs and go out with women is ridiculous, because they did.

But that they were a depraved set of men, I deny. There are far coarser and more immoral things described in Shakespeare or in the Bible than in 'Riders of the Sky'. The "heroes" of the Old Testament are a sorry lot beside the American Aviators. Abraham and Isaac and Jacob were mean and cowardly and treacherous, and David and Solomon as immoral as could well be. Moses was the only redeeming character, and he was punished above all the rest.

Besides, if we paint a picture of war in ideal terms are we not acting contrary to the best interests of the world that is trying to prevent future wars?

I hope you will forgive my going into such detail, but I have always felt that you were so fair-minded about things, even if you did not always agree, that I wanted to explain my reasons for writing as I did.

Affectionately yours,

LADDIE BREWER

To which the Rector replied:

MY DEAR LADDIE:

Thank you for writing me at length concerning my words, which might seem critical of "The Riders of the Sky". I quite appreciate that it is important to be truthful in attempting to draw a picture of a particular epoch or event; and my point would be that an author might do well to indicate conditions, however unpleasant, rather than enter into details of wrong-doing.

I am not very familiar with the fiction of the present day. I wish I had more time to examine it. My impression is that there is a tendency to deal with things immoral in a way in which a person who was at the same time truthful and sensitive would not do. In dealing with a boy who has done wrong, for instance, I should count it better to take it for granted that we both realize the evil of his conduct, rather than dwell upon the minutiae of his offence.

Matters of this kind must, of course, be treated according to the views of the author, or of the person dealing with misconduct. Thank you for writing me at length on this subject.

Affectionately

ENDICOTT PEABODY

This, from a graduate who had been seriously ill, makes plain another vein in which they wrote him:

MY DEAR RECTOR:

It was very sweet of you to write me as you did while I was in the hospital and I greatly appreciated the kindly thought. Now that I am up and about and making what is really an extraordinary recovery I can answer all the letters which were sent to me and yours is one I have wanted to answer for some time.

That I am here at all today I can only attribute to the hand of the Almighty. I suppose that I am not the only one whom pain and suffering have brought to the foot of the Cross. I fought against it for a long time through pride since for years I felt that like Henley I was the Master of my Fate and the Captain of my Soul. But I see now that I was mistaken—that no one is in reality and that without God one isn't anything at all. At any rate like the Prodigal Son I came humbly back to my Father and now that I know I am forgiven I have felt more at peace and happier than I have been for years.

This last year has been a perfect nightmare to me and why I didn't make way with myself I hardly know. Perhaps it was the affection I bear for my wife (and what I have owed to her during this last year I can never repay; I have practically lived on her strength all through it) and the reflection that it was the act of a coward. At any rate I stuck it out and now that the skies are clearing I can begin to rejoice that I can still "feel dawn, see sunset's glow, love and be loved" instead of lying in ——— churchyard.

At any rate, my dear old Rector, you will see, the next time we meet, a man who has been changed a good deal and I hope a better one for the trial of fire through which I have had to pass. I fear that it will be a long time before I am up to much and for this winter I shall have to regard myself as a good deal of an invalid. My strength is coming back very slowly and I cannot do much yet.

Thank goodness, I have sufficiently recovered to be able to do some work so I am hard at the proofs of my next book which the Champions in Paris are publishing and which I hope will be out by next spring. If for no other reason I am jolly glad that I did pull through because it always mars a book if someone else than the author has to put the final touches to it.

Please give a great deal of love to the Madam and thank her for the interest she has displayed. I shall hope next spring to get a chance to run up to Groton. This summer on our way to Bar Harbor in the motor we did spend a night at the Inn and went into the Chapel the next morning, but of course there wasn't a soul in the place except the workmen and caretakers.

272

My wife sends her most cordial regards to you both.
Affectionately yours,
—— ——

As does this:

Dear Mr. Peabody,
About ten days ago when our little daughter —— was very ill indeed (she had been operated on for Mastoiditis, had a "general pneumococcal infection," followed by pneumonia and threatened Mastoiditis in the other ear), and things looked very dark indeed. My wife and I both wanted very much to have prayers offered for her in Church. I suppose we could have asked the Rector at ——, where we have been staying (indeed I believe he was good enough to do so of his own accord), or our own church at ——, but there was no particular link of sympathy with either of these; and we were both so anxious that it should not be just a perfunctory business and we wanted to ask a friend, who would care, as well as a clergyman. I felt that you always take such an interest in all your graduates and that you and Mrs. Peabody have always been so kind to Elizabeth and myself, that you would understand, in fact, I wanted to ask you particularly. So we decided to cable you asking for prayers for —— and it was a great comfort when we had done so.

From another graduate to Mrs. Peabody, who received letters too:

Dear Mrs. Peabody:
How very good of you to write me! You can have no idea of the consolation which my friends have given me by their letters and yours I appreciate most deeply.
I bless Groton every day of my life for what it gave me and find it a solid rock of support just now.
My love to the Rector. I do hope he is quite well again—and to all, and thank you again from my heart for your beautiful letter.
Affectionately always,
Joseph C. Grew

From a graduate doctor:

June 4, 1924
Dear Mr. Peabody,
Many thanks for the birthday postal card. It aroused in my spirit again the desire to come to Groton some time, perhaps, in the near future and talk over some of the matters in which you know I am

273

interested and from which through rumor you may have gained the impression that I am not altogether in sympathy with the school. The situation contains a paradox which revolves about the fact that institutions are one thing and individuals another. One can easily entertain the highest admiration, respect and affection for the individuals who establish and direct an institution and at the same time make a critical and impersonal analysis of the institution and its influences. However, I would much rather talk the whole matter over as it has appeared to me through the extraordinary experiences which have come to me in the past three or four years in the shape of boys in trouble, rather than to write at length.

Please give my love to Mrs. Peabody and believe me as ever,

Affectionately yours,

———   ———

An older alumnus wrote:

DEAR MR. PEABODY:

Now that I have passed the half century mark, it seems as though your postals of kind greeting come closer together, but perhaps that is entirely a psychological effect. They are, however, just as welcome as ever and always make me pause and think of my school days and all that you and Mrs. Peabody did for us at that time.

It must be wonderfully interesting to you to watch the difference in the development of the boys of those days. Even I find that my classmates at Harvard show a most extraordinary variation in development in the last twenty-eight years. I do not think that the majority of them seem to grow old; on the contrary they get old all of a sudden, and this seems to take place at any time, even as early as ten years after they are out of college; but I think I can frankly say that there is no one who shows less signs of advancing years than your good self. Please keep it up—

With kindest remembrances to the Madame and all your family, as always,

Affectionately yours,

———   ———

Still another said:

It sounds very trite to congratulate a person on the life he has led but that is what one has to do when they write to you about what a fine school Groton is. Your life is so closely interwoven with the school and the school so clearly expresses your character and your ideals that it is all one and the same thing. By you I of course include Mrs. Peabody for I know what a large part she has had to do with it all.

274

I suppose we all have criticized Groton at one time or another. I know I have felt at times that the school was handicapped by the fact that so many of the boys came from one or two localities and belonged to only one or two strata of society. But, of course, you have realized that better than anybody else and have done a great deal to correct it. However the positive virtues of the place stand out in my mind more strongly as I get older and see more of life and people and realize more clearly how important the ideals Groton stands for are to the world.

I think that courage is a fairly common quality, both physical and moral courage. Truthfulness for its own sake is far less common. The spirit of justness and fairness, the willingness to give the other fellow a chance is, so far as I have observed, very uncommon. In fact I only know a very limited number of people that I would trust to be fair when their own interests are at all vitally affected. Yet I would expect this quality from most graduates of Groton and I think that in most cases I would not be disappointed. I believe that you have instilled this idea of justice that I speak of into most of the Groton boys and if they don't always act on it they at least will recognize it if they are appealed to.

I don't know of any other quality that is more needed in this grab and take and hold world. If we are going to get anywhere with the government of our own country or make any progress with international relations we have got to proceed with some regard for the other fellow's point of view and interest. If we don't our party system will degenerate into a brawl of blocs each out after its own selfish end and there will be another international war just as soon as the nations have paid off a little of the debt on the last one and stored up some guns and ammunition.

I believe that this spirit of fair play and consideration for the other fellow; putting his interest ahead of your own if justice demands it, is the dominant idea of the school. You may give it a different name but it boils down to the same thing. And it is, of course, the greatest quality that a man can have. Certainly no man can be called truly great who hasn't got it.

If I don't always practice it, and I try to, it's not because I didn't learn justice at Groton.

I guess that about covers what I think about the school.

I am glad to learn that you are well after your operation and I trust that you won't have any more trouble. Please give my love to Mrs. Peabody.

Aff'y,

___ ___

Often a parent picked up the thread:

275

My dear Dr. Peabody:—

On Thursday last I was in New Haven. While waiting for Stewart to finish his morning recitations, I called on Dean Jones whom I had never met to find out how the lad was doing.

When I stated my errand he sent for the boy's record and after looking it over said. "He is all right. Your boy's marks for this year are 80, 80, 80, 65 and 60. He was captain of his Class crew. Tell him to hit up the stroke on that literature. The fact that he is from Groton is in his favor. Those Groton boys are the best we get. The Rector must be a very fine, man."

It was such a spontaneous tribute that it gives me much pleasure to repeat it with my thanks for all you did for my boy.

I am,

Very sincerely yours,

——— ———

From the time the Eighteenth Amendment was adopted the Rector was interested in the enforcement of the law. As was his custom he met the question head on, seeing it as black or white. He was hailed by the law-abiders, vilified by the rest. Many of the graduates were especially vociferous. George Martin, whom the Rector had asked to be the first editor of the *Groton School Quarterly*, a magazine designed to keep alumni and parents in touch (which, parenthetically, had become a most stimulating, lively, and interesting magazine, outstanding of its kind), wrote an unsigned article pointing out the case of the anti-Prohibition-ists. It was a cogent, brilliant statement which many readers at-tributed to Peabody, who was promptly deluged with congratu-latory letters praising his courage and discernment. Although understandably embarrassed and annoyed at being quoted, in Chicago, San Francisco, and elsewhere far and near, as having said not only what he had not said, but what he vehemently dis-believed, he took no public step save to insist that the *Quarterly* make clear that he had not written the article and patiently to explain to his suddenly augmented public that he was neither hero nor turncoat. His faith in the advantages of complete free-dom of speech was not strengthened.

Some of the correspondence in regard to the *Quarterly* is amusing:

1924 [exact date missing]

Dear Mr. Peabody:—

I am today in receipt of a letter from my class-mate, ——— ———,

276

in London, in which he says that he is forwarding to you a letter which I wrote him—after some considerable correspondence—about his subscribing to the Groton Alumni Fund. I cannot remember exactly what I said in my letter to ———— and I have no copy of it. Whatever it was, it produced a check from him accompanied by a letter that I am certainly not going to show to you.

If he sends you the letter, I want it. I am going to send the whole correspondence to Frank Polk.

Please summon your sense of humor. I am too mad at the moment to do anything but froth at the mouth. I suppose ———— is a bad egg and takes dope. And I am a good deal of a crank myself. Rejoice, O Israel, for the Philistines have fallen out among themselves!

Affectionately yours,

GEORGE W. MARTIN

May 26, 1924.

DEAR MR. PEABODY:

Thank you for your letter. ———— ———— is partly crazy. I am partly crazy myself, but in an entirely different way from ————. I made the mistake of thinking his lunacy was like mine, but it is not in the least.

Now, about this Quarterly: that is causing me unexpected perturbations. I told Pierre Jay that I would get out the four copies next year and see that it was properly done. So I will. Then I began thinking about what was to be put into the paper, and concluded that reading matter was desirable provided it was read by anybody.

The most interesting question connected with the school is whether it educates anybody. But all the cranks talk about this very secretly—not being of one mind at all—and wherever two or three are gathered together no one talks about it for fear of being considered unloyal. This seems to me to be the wrong attitude. If the school is an avenue to Truth then it need not fear what anyone says about it. If it is not, the quicker we find it out the better.

The danger is in this case that if I write a provocative editorial on the subject calculated to smoke out anyone with any thoughts on it and prod him into the correspondence column, I shall hurt your feelings. This prospect causes me to oscillate somewhat in my orbit and is uncomfortable—in fact not the proper attitude for a real radical at all. The prospect for an acrimonious and diverting discussion, however, is excellent, and vast interest in the school should result.

Affectionately yours,

GEORGE W. MARTIN

You know, I am not "going for" you or anybody else. I am interested in freedom with a great passion and only constant vigilance will preserve it in the world. Education leads to truth, and truth to freedom; and so I come to be interested in education.

But, as I told Pierre Jay last summer, I can play only on one string and know only one tune, and I think I shall soon exhaust my audience; and just *before* that happens Jay should get a new piper with a new tune.

We do not show you the pieces beforehand because we do not want to involve you in the responsibility for them, but leave you quite free to condemn and repudiate if you like.

> Affectionately,
> GEORGE W. MARTIN

After enduring the long rolling barrage from the *Quarterly*, which he felt ventured into peculiar pastures, the Rector suggested that the editor go to Groton to see for himself, with the following result:

[undated, but about 1925]

DEAR MR. PEABODY:

I listened a great deal over the week-end, and so derived considerable profit from a pleasant visit. I see very clearly that one of the most important functions of a Headmaster is to keep up morale; and, after discussing various plans for the improvement of mankind and modifying some of the immutable laws of the universe, the principal impression I have carried away is that it is due to your imperturbable common-sense that the school does not blow up nor dissolve into mush. As for the technique: You know I am not modest about making suggestions, but I do not think of any important detail or policy which could be altered without entailing consequences the ultimate effects of which are not foreseeable at present.

As for the *Quarterly:* one of the objects of the editors was to rouse the graduates to an interest in education and in the school. I like to think that it has accomplished this to some extent—although I am aware that it has been partly at your expense. There are a lot of graduates who are entirely out of touch and in a frame of mind always to believe the worst. If a semi-official organ voices their worst apprehensions, perhaps they will appreciate that they are not really unique in their wisdom but that what is in their minds is also being taken into daily consideration by those responsible. I have tried to steer a course between being quite impersonal and yet sufficiently specific to arrest attention, and this—perhaps inevitably—has resulted in an occasional impression abroad that I was "making an attack" on your policies. Well—I have always appreciated that for

278

me to "make an attack" on you had a humourous resemblance to a little boy throwing pebbles at a whale, and from your indulgent patience with the performance I am confident that you have felt the same way. No unbiased critic can conclude but that discussion is free at Groton and there is nothing to conceal.

In the next issue there is a rather tart letter from Francis Biddle, which some of the editors didn't want to print. It was polite, and it seemed to me we should not censor it because of its subject matter, so it went in. It will rouse those on the fence to your defence; and I hope it will amuse you.

Affectionately,
GEORGE W. MARTIN

Regeneration, however, was only partial:

February 24, 1926

This is a secret. While we are waiting for the next number of the *Quarterly* to come out, I will tell it to you for your amusement.

The Editors of the paper agreed that an apology should be published on account of having involved you in the authorship of the prohibition piece. I wrote the handsomest apology you ever saw, and submitted it to the rest of the Board. Three of the remaining four concurred with me in thinking it was magnificent, but the fifth refused positively to apologise at all. That was curious, wasn't it? After an hour's hard work he was cajoled and threatened into agreeing to the form which will be published—which is the lamest, grudgingest acknowledgment of a mistake imaginable.

Well, that is tough luck. I like to do everything in the Grand Manner—even in apologising. It embarrasses the other party if you apologise without qualification or hesitation. Now you won't be embarrassed, and that is too bad.

Affectionately,
GEORGE W. MARTIN

November 24, 1925

DEAR MR. PEABODY:

Here is another of your graduates taking a fall out of Bishop ———, —not actually in one of the School publications, however, though I rush to tell on him anyway. [He enclosed a clipping]

You know—the world is changing very fast. You used to turn out respectable solid pillars of the state, who sold bonds, got rich, played polo, and always supported the status quo.

Now come these rotten reds like Freddy Allen and me who vulgarly pillory all the most sacred cows of the Victorian Age. These

279

fellows are accustomed to be disposed of by subtle insinuations that they are drunkards or divorcees or crooks. But it is difficult to condemn this crowd on the old lines. Many of them are quite decent. What interests me enormously is the fact that these men are coming out of Groton and they did not used to. You must be putting something in the beans that didn't used to be there. And what also interests me is to know whether all this ferment agitates you somewhat or whether it makes you laugh. It is hardly fair for men who are honest and sober and faithful to their wives to spend all their spare time running spears into the Great Ones and yelling for a re-deal. It becomes rather difficult to shut them up by calling them soreheads—which is the treatment the old manual called for.

Affectionately yours,

GEORGE W. MARTIN

Martin, writing some years afterward, said:

Prohibition came along. It proved completely unenforceable. Practically all the graduates of the School became criminals. Admittedly the noble experiment operated to breed corruption, to teach girls to drink gin, to flout the law, to create disorder, and to produce a host of ills. When one consulted solemnly with oneself, it was evident that, measured by any frame of reference that made sense, the situation demanded resistance as clearly as the imposition of Ship Money Taxes by Charles I. To comply was to co-operate with tyranny.

The graduates, from the first, saw this clearly and saw it whole, and contributed steadily to the breakdown of enforcement. The Rector went through a slow mutation. He first fell under the influence of Mr. Horace Taft, who persuaded him that to be a criminal was the worst thing that could happen to his boys; and so he started out to compliance.

Then someone called him the Vicar of Bray, and said he had sold out his real convictions for a mess of pottage called "law and order". All the criminal graduates came up to School, and for the first time in their lives felt morally superior. The biographies of great rebels were pointed out to him. The worst of it was everyone was kind and solicitous about it; and the amount of interest taken in the New Testament was prodigious. Even the stock-brokers were reading it.

This was a wonderful and chastening experience. For once a moral question got so complicated that it was not instantly apparent what was the proper course. And though many a graduate had an attack of the dry grins on observing the Rector's predicament, not one had any thought that he was cowardly or taking the easy path. And when the Cromwellians finally won, they admired him for sticking

280

it out all by himself; and they knew he never did really think any less of them even if they were criminals.

It may have been a wonderful and chastening experience, but it was no fun for the Rector. He did not enjoy more than other men either being misunderstood or the opposition of friends. Whatever the rest of the country thought of Prohibition, the great majority of the Rector's friends were violently opposed to it, both in conviction and emotion, as they were later opposed to Franklin Roosevelt beyond the realm of argument. It took courage to stand almost alone against them and one's own self interest. Further still, if the graduates and friends could see clearly the harm that came from Prohibition and the lawlessness that followed, so could the Rector. But he felt he saw further, saw that the evil came not from Prohibition, but from the national mood, following the war and the general collapse of standards, that made general lawbreaking possible and welcomed in, with protests against tyranny and blue-nosed Puritanism, the opportunity which the Eighteenth Amendment provided for making lawbreaking and the ignoring of standards respectable. He made it clear that what he favored and had practiced was temperance and not prohibition. But he believed Prohibition was better than license, and a step which might lead to temperance. He held it a law passed legally. Even if it were a bad law, he thought it should be abolished legally, and he feared the results of general disregard of the law far more than he feared the hardships of prohibition. It is not yet wholly apparent that he was wrong. At the time he thought the ladies and gentlemen did protest too much. For every sincere John Hampden and Tom Paine he saw many cases of violent indignation among citizens the calm of whose civic complacency had never been ruffled until they envisaged the dry specter of an existence without liquor. Peabody followed his invariable role in matters of conscience. He decided what he thought was right and stuck to it.

The *Groton Quarterly* was established in 1924 as a forum of free opinion in the Groton family at large. The Rector always wrote a letter, usually brief, dealing with current topics and reporting on school affairs, but he turned the editorial and other pages over to the editors and any contributors they might produce. The result was a magazine of opinion unique among schools, and many regretted the circulation was not larger. The

281

Rector's blood was frequently spilled, however, in printed quarrels and opinions with which he held not at all, yet which appeared, inevitably, to rest under his aegis. These, too, he bore patiently, and merely did his best to find a succession of able and interested editors. But it was a good many years before the *Quarterly* was entirely a source of comfort to him.

The dangers he saw in breaking the law he saw in many other aspects of American and international life as the third decade of the century rolled along. He thundered louder and more frequently than ever against divorce, at the annual alumni dinners in New York or Boston, always well attended, at Prize Days, at parents' leagues. Unwearyingly and often untactfully he hammered in his minority report that standards begin in the home, that standards are essentially religious and spiritual matters, and that whether one breaks a law or a Commandment or a vow, God will sooner or later call him or her into judgment.

To him "being a bad influence" was a real thing. He had sudden feelings about people, feelings which he trusted, as when, while he was Easter vacationing in Bermuda not long after the war, he decided that a certain fifth-form boy, the leader of his form, popular, influential and a relative of Mrs. Peabody, a boy whose father had contributed to the school in the past and promised further contributions to the Endowment Fund, was a bad influence in the school and should go. He was not allowed to return after the holidays, and his father was very angry when asked for his contribution to the fund. Another time a mutual friend, a clergyman, told the Rector of a graduate who had behaved very badly, but who had reformed, been baptized, and wanted to return to school. The Rector was dubious. "——— has acted badly," he said. "He has not been a good man. I am not sure I want to see him."

Old friends were always faithful:

29 Draggott Avenue, Kenton-Harrow, Msex.
Christmas Day

MY DEAREST PEABODY:

There is really no end to yr. kind thoughts of me and I cannot find words by which to convey to you in any degree adequately my gratitude to you. What I am now wishing especially to thank you for the cablegram which reached me on the 27th. I didn't know what it meant when it reached me for it wasn't in a Postal Envelope, but when in the course of the day I did realize what it was my heart really overflowed with love and gratitude to you and all yrs. and I was made happy, yet more than happy, by feeling that I was in such v. close and near touch with you. The cablegram you may be sure will be treasured by me and moreover my dearest Peabody it did me real good to receive it for I am v. tired with a bad cough and cold and think sometimes it is the beginning of the end, and your love and sympathy are more than I can describe to you. I trust that dear Mrs. Peabody, you and your children are having a happy family gathering this Xmas and that all Xmas and New Year's blessings may be given to you one and all. While I think of it, let me say I wrote as I promised I'd do a line to Griffith last Monday when I was feeling more able to write than now. May all be going on well with him! I must stop now and give you once more my v. heartiest thanks for the cablegram and its love and devotion to a v. old friend. My v. best greeting to Mrs. Peabody, you and all yours as always.

Yr. most faithful, most grateful and most affectionate old friend,

P. ARTHUR

And loyal:

December 16, 1924

DEAR COTT:—

I am concerned about the Housing problem at Groton. You may have the feeling that, if *Nash's* family-in-law do not want to build a master's house, you would like to put *Minturn* and *Helen* in *Brooks House*. If that is the most convenient arrangement, you must decide on that without regard to me; for while I admit that I should like a few more years in my present quarters, I could not endure the feeling that I was in any way an *obstacle* at Groton. Isn't it awful to be getting old! How I hate these uppish young people!!

Yrs. in the Cause,

S. B.

May 31, 1926

DEAR COTT:

Many happy returns of to-day or yesterday according to your preference. This scarf you probably won't wear, but you will believe it shows feeling. I have a lot of feeling about this last birthday in our present decade; but I can't express it even on paper without giving way to tears. For 19 long years—ever since my Eleanor left me—I have had to repress emotion all along the line, as indeed I shall have to do the rest of my life. Repression is not very Christian; but I guess it is the only way by which some men can keep on playing the game. I can be glad for you that no flood of sorrow is dammed up in you ready to break out if gates are opened.

You will have many good years at Groton yet, I am confident. I too look forward eagerly to some more years—if what unregenerate boys call the "pump" keeps working.

This is a nice, cheerful letter to write a pal on such an occasion! I am much more cheerful really than this. That first Chapter of Genesis is theologically sound—I wish I knew who wrote it! God looked at everything, and behold it was "very good." It's so—it's all *very good*.

Afftly, always

S. B.

33

PLANS AND PROGRESS

WHEN the war was over, the Rector had paused briefly to survey the condition of the school. The plant was in good shape, but not completed. His trustees were able and genuinely interested. The original group had passed on or resigned except for Bishop Lawrence and himself, but their places had been filled, principally by graduates, who were devoted to him and to the school. The faculty, in spite of serious losses, was stronger than ever, with a good percentage of new fresh blood. The waiting list for boys was longer and stronger than ever, and he was more able than ever to fill all his places with first- and second-formers.

He set in his mind four main goals and set about their realization. The first was to leave to his successor a completed and, as nearly as he could manage it, perfect plant, so that the Almighty Wall would be built for many generations to come. Secondly, he wanted an endowment large enough so that his successor would be, not only free from financial worry, but able to face with equanimity any hard times that might come. Thirdly, he wanted to establish a scale of pay and living for the faculty which would make schoolmastering at least as attractive as any other profession from the point of view of comfort and security, not only at Groton, but, by example, at other boarding schools. And lastly, he wanted to bring the instruction and training of boys at Groton to such a pitch that its standards would be recognized as tops in the colleges and in after life. To the achievement of these goals he set first his thought and then his actions.

While these goals were probably not exactly formulated in his mind until after the war, they had all been in his consciousness for many years, and his own inclinations had been kept glowing by being constantly breathed upon by the trustees and Mr. Gardner. For instance, as early as 1886 he secured the Anna Dickinson Scott Fund of $5000, "the income to be used in the discretion of the Trustees for the general endowment of the School," this in addition to another $15,000 used for payment of debt. In 1889 the Sarah Lawrence Brooks Trust Fund of $5000 was received, "the income to be used for the benefit of poor scholars." In his Headmaster's Report the Rector said, however:

The first $5000 (a Scholarship Fund), which has been presented by Mrs. Gorham Brooks, has been borrowed temporarily for the building fund. This establishment of scholarships promises to be of great value to the School in raising the standard of scholarship, as only those who are in earnest, and successful in studies will be admitted to this foundation and they will lead the rest of the School to higher pastures.

This first scholarship gift was augmented by the Clarence Seymour Wadsworth Trust Fund of $6000 in 1894.

Money raising for other than building purposes began in earnest in 1898 with the first Endowment Fund of $72,000. The Headmaster's Report said:

The money subscribed for the Endowment Fund has been used to extinguish the debt. We are now in a position to increase the teachers' salaries, possibly to present them with some token, even though slight, of our appreciation of their remaining with us when many of them might have received much higher payments. . . . As an indication of our indebtedness to them I might cite the remark of a member of one of the largest school publishing houses in this country, who told one interested in our work, that "Groton was one of the best schools in the country and paid its masters the lowest salaries."

The trustees' records go on to state, somewhat tartly, that "no authority could be shown upon the Records for having spent this money in extinguishing the debt."

Also in 1898 came the first installment of the William Amory Gardner Trust Fund of $10,000, "the income to be devoted to the payment of larger salaries to the masters." Mr. G. added $10,000 to this in 1906 and again in 1909. These latter two gifts were more specifically to be applied for the increase of salaries to married masters and, in the case of the last, to building a master's cottage. And in 1916 Mr. George H. Crocker established a fund of $25,000 to provide income to be added to the salary of a master during his sabbatical year. Mention has previously been made of the anonymous gift of $90,000 in 1903 which finally did "extinguish the debt" once and for all. It should also be kept in mind that between 1884 and 1916 plant and equipment worth well over a million dollars had been obtained. In 1917 and 1918 more than $160,000 were made available in two Headmaster's Discretionary Funds to be used for such purpose as he desired.

Here a word should be said of the relationship between the Rector and the trustees. The two most striking facts are the caliber of the trustees and the extraordinarily small number of them. Between 1884 and 1940 there were only twenty-eight. Understandably, as time went on, the membership of the board increasingly was composed of graduates. Mr. Gardner was elected in 1913. Such men as Pierre Jay, Ellery Sedgwick, George Rublee, Redmond Cross, James Lawrence, Francis Higginson, and afterward Vanderbilt Webb, Arnold Whitridge, R. Minturn Sedgwick, William Blair, Hugh Auchincloss and Henry S. Morgan knew and cared for the school deeply and gave freely of time, honest affection, and wisdom to its welfare. The principle of continuity was further helped by the presence on the board of Bishop Lawrence, long president, from the beginning. He started with the Rector and resigned the same day. Such other friends as Charles G. Washburn and later Reginald Washburn and Robert H. Gardiner loved and served the school as though it were their own.

From the beginning there was a tendency to let the Rector have his own way. A running battle of many years went on between him and the first treasurer, William C. Endicott, who invariably addressed him in letters as "The Rev. E. P., dear Cotty." Endicott had scruples as to authorized procedure and the letter of the law, neither of which bothered the Rector much. At regular intervals the Rev. E. P. would receive a communication, touched with asperity, informing him that he either had done something he had no right to do or had left undone something he should have done. For instance he was required by the Articles of Incorporation to present to the trustees twice a year a written report on the condition of the school. Usually it was invariably pointed out its absence and asked for a copy. Neither party, over approximately thirty. years, gave any evidence of changing his habits, and the work went serenely on, zestfully peppered with somewhat stern and outspoken correspondence. Mr. Endicott had one ace in the hole, a prize which he offered for a specific purpose. Whenever the Rector suggested or attempted another purpose, the donor got after him.

The trustees performed an enormously important function. They, as a group, trusted, admired, and loved the Rector, but they required him to submit to a barrage of questions, criticisms, and doubts. In the main, as has been said, he had his own way, but before he had it he underwent the scrutiny of keen, experienced, and independent minds, who because of affection and trust rarely completely crossed him, but who nevertheless constituted a guiding and restraining influence.

His methods were sometimes unorthodox. If he thought a debt should be extinguished before scholarships were granted, he extinguished the debt and consulted the authorities afterward. His instinct was to plunge toward the main chance, the greater danger. He did not hesitate to commit himself to projects if it was expedient at the moment, even if the commitment afterward fell short of performance.

This, then, was the background when he undertook his final money raising and building program. It is interesting to note the order in which he set about the parts of the work involving expenditure.

His first goal was an endowment fund of such colossal proportions for a small school in a single drive that it seemed an almost fanciful idea. The goal set was a million dollars. But working with Peabody was perhaps the greatest money raiser of his time, William Lawrence, Bishop of Eastern Massachusetts. Bishop Lawrence held it a kindness to inform a rich, or even a well-to-do, man or woman of an opportunity to give to a worthy cause. He considered it a privilege to be able to give wisely and well, and believed most people were grateful for information and guidance. If they were not, they simply did not need to give. It was in this spirit that the campaign was launched.

The goal was attained in 1927 and slightly more than a million dollars was raised. The most generous donor was Payne Whitney, who gave very liberally. This new endowment was joined with nearly fifty other previous funds, large and small, to establish a combined fund with a value of well over a million and a half.

287

When Payne Whitney, a graduate, died in 1929 he left the school another enormous gift of over a million and a half dollars, which was set up as the Payne Whitney Fund. Meanwhile the Rector had been steadily adding to the Masters' Pension Fund and the Employees' Pension Fund, and a satisfactory scheme for retirement pay of masters and employees had been set up.* Mr. Clarence Dillon, a parent, also gave a Clarence Dillon Scholarship Fund of more than $50,000. It was now possible to proceed on long-distance planning.

The building plans had also made great progress. Significantly the least appealing, but possibly most necessary, job was attended to first. The Rector set great store by the matron, Miss Edna Cram. It was said she was the only person to whom he never said no. She needed space and equipment, so in 1922 a large servants' wing was added to Hundred House, solving a problem which had long been vexing. In 1926 Mr. Dillon, the giver of the Scholarship Fund, also gave the Hall, an auditorium complete with stage, movie booth, piano and all other requisites for formal or informal gatherings. In this hall and in the school dining room portraits were placed of masters who had been with the school for many years. In 1928 and 1929 long-needed additions were made to the infirmary, which was not only enlarged but brought thoroughly up to date, with even X-ray machines available. In 1931 the Gymnasium was enlarged and modernized. In 1932 additional dormitory space was added, with improved accommodation for single masters, both to Hundred House and Brooks House.† In this general period several new married masters' houses were either built or bought, and numerous improvements made in athletic facilities. Finally, in 1933, the Schoolhouse was enlarged. Better office space was provided. Every master had a classroom of his own; facilities for art and manual training were notably improved. Then he rested from these labors.

* It was very satisfactory at the time, far in advance of most schools. But all financial matters and figures must be considered in reference to particular periods. For instance, Mr. Whitney's gift thirty years later would have represented at least three times as much as when made. The Rector established a basic principle as to pensions: the actual cost was to increase greatly as the years went on.

† Some additions to both Brooks House and Hundred House had been made in earlier years.

Meanwhile he had been at work on the problem of the faculty. Once the money was in sight, with the enthusiastic approval of the trustees he called in expert counsel in the person of one of the board, Professor Roger B. Merriman of Harvard, and Dean Holmes of the Harvard Graduate School of Education. A careful study was made of the whole problem of salaries, not only from the point of view of Groton but of the independent schools as a group. In June, 1924, the committee made its report.

Stating the two aims—to make such further salary increases as the improved school finances would allow, and to establish a better standard of masters' pay in terms of permanent policy—the report said:

The committee has studied both of these questions and has had the benefit of conferences with Professor H. W. Holmes, Dean of the Graduate School of Education at Harvard. In his report to the headmaster on the subject of teaching at Groton, Professor Holmes says:

"My reaction to the suggestion that Groton establish a new standard of payment to school masters is naturally extremely favorable. The teacher is the substance of education. The two main ways in which we can get men of power to go into teaching are, I believe, these: first, make teaching a more independent, scientific, constructive kind of work; second, pay better salaries. As to the salaries, it seems to me not so important to make initial salaries large, as to make final salaries large. Men are not deterred from going into law or business by the fact that they can not earn much at the beginning. They are sometimes attracted into teaching because for a while it provides a relatively high return. But men who look far ahead sometimes avoid yielding to the temptation to teach for $1,200 or $1,500, because they know that they cannot make $15,000 or $20,000 at the end of their careers. I believe Groton can do most for the profession by establishing certain masterships with unusually high salaries for teachers who have proved their power. If this is done, together with a general raising of the salary schedule, it ought to be accompanied by provisions for retirement on pension on a contributory basis, and also by a scheme for stimulating and exacting personal and professional growth. A young man who comes to Groton for his first experience in teaching ought to be told of the opportunities that lie before him in a career at the school. He ought to be told that he will be expected to continue his studies in the subject he is teaching and also in professional subjects. Arrangements should be made to permit him to complete his work for a higher degree. He should know that he is expected to be a scholar, a man of influence and vigor, and a trained technician in teaching. The

289

school should take no one, even as a beginner, who has not had at least an apprenticeship in teaching, and some preliminary study of education. Groton can do a service of the very highest order to the teaching profession by working out a plan of this general sort."

The committee has reached unanimous conclusions, and having found the trustees at the last meeting in general accord with these conclusions, it now presents the following definite recommendations.

In brief summary, the recommendations introduced the principle of, and provided a system for, including the value of rent, board, and incidentals in expressing salaries (and accordingly, in computing pensions); established as the maximum master's salary $8,000, equal to the top at Harvard or Yale for professors other than holders of specially endowed chairs; proposed a new salary schedule in which cash payments would total $94,040 for 1924-25, an overall boost of $12,960 over 1923-24,* including a substantial increase for the headmaster; and suggested that for pensions (contributed to by masters and the school jointly) the goal should be an annuity amounting to at least half of the master's total salary (cash payment plus housing etc.) at the time of retirement.

In recommending maximum salaries corresponding to university professorships, the report said:

The committee realizes, of course, that teaching in schools and teaching in universities are very different things, and that the qualifications for success in the one are by no means identical with those in the other. But it is strongly of the opinion that the dignity and importance of the schoolmaster's task are fully equal to those of the university professor's. It therefore desires to put before the young men who come to teach at Groton the possibility of ultimately attaining as high a rate of compensation as if they went into college work, and thus remove all financial hindrance to a perfectly free choice between the two callings.

It also suggested:

That in connection with the establishment of a maximum salary of $8,000 the following statement of qualifications should be adopted, to govern not only the advancement of any master to the maximum salary, but also any increase which may be made hereafter in the salaries of masters generally.

* Compared with the $52,800 total of ten years earlier (1913-14), the new schedule was higher by $41,240.

(a) Character and personality, sympathy with boys, and an abiding interest in their development and welfare. These are the indispensable foundations of success in a teaching career, and at Groton they may be considered a sine qua non.

(b) Proficiency in a chosen field of scholarship, and in the art of teaching it, combined with ability to inspire boys with a lasting interest therein.

(c) Continued intellectual growth and development; comprehensive grasp of the major educational problems and of the latest developments in the chosen field; devotion of parts of vacations and sabbatical absences to study.

(d) Increasing general usefulness and value to the school.

(e) Length of service, but only when combined with the foregoing.

It is the view of the committee that only those should be considered for advancement to the maximum salary whose qualifications under (b) and (c) are outstanding.

Pension Contributions. That hereafter pension contributions by both the school and the masters should be based on the cash payments plus the value of the incidentals, instead of only on the cash payments as at present. This will require somewhat larger annual contributions by both the school and the masters, and will increase correspondingly the amount of the annuities the pension plan will provide. It should be the aim of the school, as far as the funds at its disposal may permit, to provide pensions of not less than one half of the cash payment, plus one half of the value of the incidentals the master is receiving at the time of his retirement.

The Trustees adopted the committee's proposals unanimously. They as well as the Rector believed that in taking this step they were rendering a service not only to Groton masters, but to schoolmasters everywhere, and they earnestly hoped their example would encourage others to follow.

This disposed of, there was the question of graduates' sons, who were applying for the school in ever increasing numbers. Again a Trustees' Committee delved into the matter thoroughly and presented a report, which was also adopted, in March 1926.

Report of Committee on Admissions

The committee considering the problem of admissions reports that, according to Mr. Andrews, the following numbers of sons of graduates are entered on the List for the twelve years beginning next Autumn.

1926	15	1932	28
1927	26	1933	22
1928	29	1934	33
1929	36	1935	20
1930	30	1936	30
1931	24	1937	22

or a total of 315.

On the assumption that at least three per annum should be dropped for death, illness, change of parents' plans, or failure to pass the examinations, 36 should be deducted, leaving 279 sons of graduates who may want to enter the school during the above period.

On the assumption that an average of 33 places per annum will be available, we have a total of 396 places. Subtracting 279 from this figure, there will apparently be 117 places which must be filled by sons of non-graduates. This is 29.54% of 396, as against 30.3%, representing the 10 sons of non-graduates out of 33 that have recently been taken by means of competitive examinations.

It thus appears that all sons of graduates who are able to pass the entrance examinations can be taken care of and that in addition the total number of boys admitted through competitive examinations over the twelve year period need not be reduced below the present level, provided the principle of flexibility is introduced.

The committee recommends that the number of boys taken by competitive examinations each year be not fixed at a definite number but varied in accordance with the number of graduates' sons desirous of taking the entrance examinations for that year. Graduates should be notified and, so far as possible pinned down, two years in advance, and the competitives adjusted accordingly.

There are only two years when there seems any likelihood of having the entire group of new boys or perhaps a form composed only of graduates' sons.

The committee recommends that the present list be maintained.

The committee also recommends that consideration be given to the possibility of broadening the candidacy for competitive examinations with the purpose of securing a larger element of diversity than at present, both individual and geographical.

The school was somewhat larger now. For several years the Rector said 183 boys was the ideal number, with a·faculty of around 25. The idealness of any number tended to vary, and there were even a few years when the school reached 190 or over; but this was never really ideal, and building arrangements, general thought, and practice always stopped definitely short of 200.

He was not idle in other ways. In 1925 he asked Dr. Roger Lee and Dr. Haven Emerson to visit the school for a detailed survey of the medical, sanitary, and hygienic condition of the school. He was also concerned with the plight of "Russian generals and others."

For some years he had been considering the advisability of founding another small school. In 1925, with the help of Mr. Billings, he took steps to bring the idea to fruition. He gathered together a board of trustees, selected a name, Brooks (after Phillips Brooks), decided on a headmaster, and issued a prospectus stating the new school would open in 1927. No sooner was Brooks launched than Peabody also went on the board of another new school, Millbrook, founded by a Groton master, Edward Pulling.

His basic ideas as to boys had not altered. He believed in keeping boys busy; working them hard and playing them hard. He was uneasy when they were idle or unoccupied, and he still had forebodings as to the dangers of too much inquiry by an immature mind. He never cared much for originality, and his whole nature distrusted skepticism. This gave force to Bishop Atwood's contention that Peabody was the last of the Puritans. He had a Cromwellian capacity for insisting on his own rights of conscience, and a Cromwellian defence against those who disagreed with him.

34
LARES AND PENATES

DURING all these years daily life at Groton had gone on with a gentle, dignified, and urgent constancy. There were few, if any, days that were really idle. When the boys were there, one day was very much like another for five decades. When the boys were away, there was always the pressure of business to be caught up with.

The Peabody house was part of Hundred House, the largest building in the school plant. It was connected with the sixth form corridor by an unlatched door. One entered, coming from the corridor, a rather narrow hall which opened on a broader hall which, on the right, led to the front door, and on the left to the Rector's study. As one entered by the front door the dining room was on the right, the parlor (little used in daily life) on the left. The parlor was white in tone and seemed more formal than the other rooms in the house. It felt less lived in. Going on toward the study one had on the right the faculty room (where coffee was served after lunch each day for the men, tea later in the afternoon for the sixth form and visitors) and the "boudoir" on the left. The boudoir was as much Mrs. Peabody's sanctum as the study was his, except that it was much less private. It was a small room, looking out on the library wing of the school and woods beyond; it was remarkably full of things always, and it was frequently remarkably full of people. One does not remember any other room of equivalent size which invariably had so much in it and yet was invariably tidy. The Madam's desk (a piece of furniture expressive of herself—dainty, busy, and just so) stood in one corner beside the fireplace. There were always two other desks in the room; used by various of the girls. Books filled cracks and crannies. Wherever books left an opening there were pictures of the family and friends, with a large water color of the Lindens. As time went on the gallery grew, overflowed the mantel and crept over the walls beside the larger sketches of each of the children. Sons-in-law, a daughter-in-law, their children, found space. There were knitting bags and sewing kits; parcels and publications; heaps of correspondence; and all of them were in order. It was in this room that Mrs. Peabody did her business. She was, like him, an active correspondent. It was here that the faculty ladies gathered after lunch for coffee to exchange gossip, prejudices, and small talk even as their husbands did across the hall. If prejudices were exchanged, it was in a kindly fashion. The Madam would not tolerate anything else, and indeed she was so good and gentle herself that meanness would have been out of place in her presence. To the boudoir also came parents and graduates to sit and talk in the evening as well as during the day. It was a room one remembered; one of those rooms that affects many lives.

At the end of the hall was the study. This was a big room, a rectangle approaching a square, with heavy beams overhead, a big fireplace, and windows on three sides. It jutted out from the main bulk of the house. The space between windows was filled in large part with bookshelves, and there were more shelves lower down and more books in revolving stands. To the left of the fireplace was a full-length portrait of Mrs. Peabody. To the right, after the war, were pictures of all the alumni in their uniforms. In later years a picture of Franklin Roosevelt stood on the mantel. A large bench rested in front of the fire. Right in the middle of the room were two big desks placed back to back. Sometimes he worked at one; sometimes at the other. It was a matter of opinion whether it was more perturbing to open the door after knocking and hearing him say "Come in" (very slow and heavy on the "come") and find him facing you, or to find him with his back turned. The two desks gave him a lot of drawers, each with its own particular neat contents. In the middle of the desks was a fenced-in paper holder. His favorite pens were miniature oars with the Groton shield on them. Also on the desk were photographs of Mrs. Peabody and the children.

This was where he worked in the afternoons and evenings. During the mornings he was always in his study in the School-house; a small room opening off the main hall, opposite the schoolroom on one side, opposite the faculty room on another, and next to his classroom on the third. It was ideally situated to enable him to emerge promptly to quell traffic, to see to it that study hall was going as it should, to lay hold on any boy or master suited to his needs. His mere appearance in the hall had a salutary and quieting effect. He carried his work over with him in a green baize bag. Often he bicycled. A boy took his homework back to Hundred House for him before lunch. He used to counsel young graduates as to the desirability of doing things in order, one at a time.

Upstairs in the Peabody house the family's rooms were on the second floor, opening off a balcony that ran around the stair well. On the third floor were guest rooms, also opening off a balcony; Mrs. Peabody's attic (a general catch-all); and the "Grad Dorm," which consisted in several cubicles and a lava-tory, available for any graduate at any time.

When graduates returned, or when they met him elsewhere, even long after, the ingrained habit of obedience persisted. One of them wrote, speaking of the mid-thirties:

A few years ago a graduate, who had been out of school approxi-mately ten years, and his wife, and my wife and I were aboard the

Monarch of Bermuda, returning from a brief visit to that island. As the ship was being warped away from the dock in Hamilton, we climbed to the boat deck to wave goodbye to some friends on shore. F——— climbed to a point of vantage, and proceeded to get out on the end of a life-boat davit. At the precise moment when he reached his perilous objective, the Rector, who was returning from one of his Bermuda vacations, came striding down the deck and sighted F———. Without a word to any of the other three of us, the familiar voice said "Come down off that davit, F———." F——— did not even turn round. With an abject "Yes, Sir," he scrambled down with a degree of alacrity that would have pleased the Rector in a First Former. In any event, the Rector did not even pause and continued his promenade.*

The thoughtfulness of Mrs. Peabody was proverbial. One characteristic instance took place when a master, who had long been ill, returned home from the hospital, still convalescent. Having no maid, his wife had to care for the house as well as the invalid. On the day of the husband's return Mrs. Peabody sent the wife a complete roast chicken dinner, with gravy, vegetables; all cooked and hot, ready to be served.

The interest of all members of the Peabody family in all details of school life sometimes led to curious commissions. Mrs. Peabody once sent for a master and instructed him to obtain a new set of tail feathers for the stuffed eagle in the school dining room. She had noticed the bird was looking shabby and did not propose to allow him to get away with it.

When arrangements were made for President Roosevelt to attend the Fiftieth Anniversary, great plans were made to treat him with the dignity to which he was entitled. Mrs. Peabody was especially firm about the importance of protocol. He was to be addressed as "Mr. President," etc. On Mr. President's arrival, to everybody's delight, she demolished plans by darting down the steps, kissing him, and exclaiming, "Franklin, dear boy, I am *so* glad to see you."

On numerous occasions when there had been a death in a boy's family, a dormitory master was excused from all duties in order that he might offer help and companionship to a boy preparing to travel home. On his return to school a boy would be asked to the Peabodys' frequently for meals, games, or quiet talks. One boy, whose younger brother had died tragically during the summer vacation, received a note from Mrs. Peabody late in December advis-

* From a letter by Thomas Robins, Jr., January, 1944.

ing him not to attend the final reading of *The Christmas Carol*, as she realized the death of Tiny Tim might prove emotionally upsetting.*

The Peabodys saw one another day in and day out, but they had almost no time alone together. The familiar goldfish, so often cited as the exemplar of those who have no privacy, lives a somewhat secluded life compared with the headmaster and headmistress of a small boarding school conceived as Groton was. Boys, parents, faculty, friends, and visitors had free access to the house. They came for breakfast; they stayed during the morning; they were there before, during, and after lunch; they dropped in for tea. In the evening the Rector habitually did much of his most important work. Sometimes she could slip in and sit beside him while he labored at the desk, but even this quiet pleasure was subject to frequent interruptions.

His enthusiasm for exercise has been often mentioned and was always evident. He and she rode together frequently until both were nearly eighty; she always sidesaddle, he astride. In addition to this, he played fives for many years. Doubles he liked especially and still played when he was seventy years old. It was fun to play with him, but rather embarrassing. He was very large and when planted in the court represented a considerable obstacle. Since he liked to take a position well forward (an entirely legal procedure), and since it was not in his nature to get out the road of anything, particularly boys, his opponent was confronted with the awkward alternatives of not seeing the ball or of making physical contact with the Rector. The latter choice was undesirable both for reasons of policy and because collision naturally meant that the less ponderous object suffered more.

He was not a great walker. He enjoyed riding anything, but one felt that walking was not active enough. In a large way he approved the beauties of nature, but individual flowers and birds held no great attraction for him. He loved sunsets and sunrises (he could well have been an authority on the latter); he loved mountains, moors, and valleys, but he loved them in the large, not in the particular. He had no great knowledge or love for music, except that he liked to sing old familiar songs.

* Recollection of Acosta Nichols, Jr. *Cf.* also note sent on the morning after the game to a captain of a baseball team defeated by St. Mark's: "We grieved that we had to lose. We can stand it, but we would like to have won for your sake, dear boy. Affectionately, F. Peabody."

At Sing Songs in the library he would announce the songs and join the singing, while boys, spread over floor and furniture, would fill the big room with *A Capital Ship, Solomon Levi, Ivan Petrovsky Skivar,* or *John Peel* and the *British Grenadiers.* Best of all was John Farmer's wonderful Harrow song, *Forty Years On:*

Forty years on when afar and asunder
Parted are those who are singing to-day,
When you look back and forgetfully wonder
What you were like in your work and your play....
Routs and discomfitures, rushes and rallies
Bases attempted and rescued and won,
Strife without anger and art without malice,
How will it seem to you forty years on? . . .
O! the great days in the distance enchanted,
Days of fresh air in the rain and the sun,
How we rejoiced as we struggled and panted
Hardly believable, forty years on!
Forty years on, growing older and older,
Shorter in wind, and in memory long,
Feeble of foot and rheumatic of shoulder,
What will it help you that once you were strong?
God gives us bases to guard or beleaguer,
Games to play out, whether earnest or fun;
Fights for the fearless and goals for the eager....
Twenty and thirty and forty years on!

It was a pleasure to be with him. Partly, perhaps, because there was a sense of permanence about him that was reassuring, but even more that he was a delightful companion, irrespective of the age of his company. He was amusing and amused, full of comments, queries, and recollections. Certain phrases and words flavored his conversation and correspondence. *"Te duce sequar"* or *"Seniores priores"* (shoving you through the door ahead of him); "Age before beauty"; "Did you ever hear of the Scotchman who had so much to do he went a-fishing?" "He's a rum chap." For breakfast he used an enormous coffee cup which was inscribed, "It isn't that I'm greedy; I just like a lot."

His humor was active; his wit, though less common, sometimes flashed. Once when a sixth-former conducting a missionary service at Forge Village began to read a lesson with the interesting statement "Here beginneth the first chapter according to St. Genesis," the Rector's comment was that the harvest was likely to be more plenteous if the laborers were a little more intelligent than the flowers of the field. In a discussion of a formerly prominent headmaster of whom he disapproved the Rector chuckled, "He had everything but character."

In an excellent, but unfortunately unpublished informal study of the Rector, Acosta Nichols, Jr.,* who graduated from Groton in 1930 and taught there from the autumn of 1934 until after Peabody's retirement, records the following anecdotes:

At faculty meetings he often introduced a light touch into business. "X's mother wrote that he was a Catholic who attended St. George's Church in Stuyvesant Square. This looks like Church unity to me." And in the same meeting, of a boy accused of spending too much time in polishing shoes: "That boy had better shine his brain rather than his shoes."

Stories of the Rector's sang-froid under trying situations are almost as numerous as those of the awesomeness of his wrath. When a maid in the school dining room dropped a tray full of dishes almost everyone else looked up and stopped talking. The Rector continued to eat unmoved. "Five dollars worth of crockery", he remarked without taking his eyes from his plate.

In June 1939, when Mr. Peabody was awarded an L.H.D. by Yale, one of his companions at the ceremony was Walt Disney. When the Rector returned from New Haven he remarked "Everybody at the ceremony was saying 'Look, there's Walt Disney, walking arm in arm with Mickey Mouse.' "

One day when lamenting the number of interruptions that had occurred when he was seeking to do some work he said "I can imagine only one harder fate for a schoolmaster than undergoing so many interruptions, that would be to have such relations with the boys that they would not try to interrupt his work."

Two habits he had which were little known and always aroused interest when boys learned of them were smoking and whistling. For some reason no one ever seemed to think of the Rector as a smoker, although he indulged mildly in pipes (usually corn-cob),

* See Chapter 40.

smoker, although he indulged mildly in pipes (usually corn-cob), cigarettes, and cigars (only the denicotinized variety, however). He was an inveterate whistler. . . . Sometimes he sang to himself in the same way. One night, after a concert by a Russian basso which he had particularly enjoyed, Mr. Peabody regaled a large number of graduates gathered about the table at Faculty Supper with an imitation of the singer's manner of rendering his arias.

Disloyalty in any form was something that infuriated Mr. Peabody. In 1938 and 1939 a custom developed of Groton and St. Mark's boys wagering their school ties on the outcomes of football and baseball games. Those who knew of this custom regretted the betting principle involved, but no one felt that fundamental disloyalty to the school entered in until the Rector denounced what had occurred in the strongest terms. To give up the tie of one's school was, he said, on a par with surrendering the flag of one's country. Each institution demands utter loyalty, and it is unthinkable to treat insignia lightly.

He always maintained that one of the most vital duties of a headmaster is to be ready to say "no" at all times. . . . Consciously or unconsciously he developed this reaction himself, so that knowing ones seldom broached a question directly, but led up to it slowly, and persuasively. The Rector in turn often prepared the ground by saying laughingly "The answer is 'no' " before a boy had a chance to say a word. He was well aware that the possibility of being sent to see him was a deterrent to certain kinds of conduct or absent-mindedness. A greeting he sometimes used on such occasions was "You are looking for trouble? Well, here I am."

Perhaps the single quality of Mr. Peabody that most impresses those in contact with him is his calm faith, his uttter confidence in ultimate triumph of the good in man over the evil. As has been said elsewhere, the greatest secret of the success of his preaching lies in the personality of the man himself, which carries such absolute conviction. Apart from the pulpit, however, there are many episodes in the daily life of the school where the same faith appears. One instance was noticed not long ago, when a distinguished visiting lecturer, speaking on the current international situation, confessed himself unable to see any light.

"It is a thoroughly black picture," he said, "and I regret to say that I see no way in which it may be improved."

Several boys who were near the Rector heard his aside to Mrs. Peabody: "There is a way out. There is! And I know what it is."

And the following morning Mr. Peabody opened the Chapel service by reading St. Paul's great argument against discouragement and defeatism.

Forthrightness is so essential a part of Mr. Peabody's nature that it is inconceivable to him that others should be less frank. One of the few actions a boy can take that prejudices the Rector against him is to appear to be a conspirator. "I don't like the attitude of that boy. He always seems to be whispering," is a remark not infrequently heard.

In Faculty Meetings, the Rector's remarks about boys are often memorable and quotable epigrammatic word pictures. Typical of such characterizations was the observation: "Whenever I see X, he makes me want to say 'Don't.' "*

Much amusement was caused after the Rector's operation by the reasons he gave for not riding his bicycle. To most people it would have been understandable if a man of 82, recently recovered from a major abdominal operation, had merely stated that riding a bicycle was too great an exertion to undertake. Mr. Peabody's explanation was that the surgeons had removed so much tissue from one side of his body that his balance might be seriously affected, the excess weight causing him to tip to the other side. One received the impression that it would have been safe to cycle only if he had carried a ten pound counterweight in his right-hand pocket.

The boys were also long amused by the Rector's habit of addressing his bicycle as though it were a horse—"Whoa, Boy!" was his standard advice to it when he dismounted.

Not all of his teaching was limited to Groton. Dr. Henry Pennypacker of Harvard used to tell the story of a boy at the high school of which Pennypacker was then head, who carried off some equipment from Groton after a game. Pennypacker sent the boy to Groton to see the Rector in person. The boy went into the study terrified, prepared for a lecture, threatened arrest, and so on. The Rector asked him to sit down and pulled up a chair for him. Peabody said he was sorry it had happened, that it wasn't fair of Groton boys to be so careless about their things, that everybody was tempted and most people make mistakes once in a while, but the important thing is not to make the same mistake twice, especially when the mistake involved one's personal honor and the reputation of his team and school. The Rector didn't scold or reproach. He thanked the boy for coming up; said it was very decent of him, and that he was sure it would be a turning point in the boy's life. Neither Pennypacker nor the boy, said the former, ever forgot the lesson.

* He told a story himself of a II former whose name was read out to see him at the end of school. The boy, greatly worried, sought counsel of an older friend. "I can't think of anything I've done wrong," he said. "I just hope he wants to tell me some relative has died."

Another time, Groton was scheduled to play a football game with a small school not usually on the schedule. For some reason the Groton coach called the game off without warning. The headmaster of the other school was upset and communicated with the Rector. Peabody summoned the Groton team and said briefly that they had promised to play the game, they would play it, if necessary, the day before St. Mark's. He then got in his car, drove across country to the other school, asked the other headmaster to call all his boys together and proceeded to apologize in person for the bad manners he felt Groton had shown.

He could not abide poor sportsmanship. One day a boy got angry in a scrimmage and slugged his opposite number. The Rector saw it, sent the boy in, and would not let him play for the school in the next game. On the other hand, when a boy broke his wrist, and the doctor said he could play if he wore a heavy cast from his elbow to his knuckles, the Rector approved his playing even though it was technically illegal. "He's all right," said the Rector. "He'll play fair and it will hinder more than help him." And the boy played the rest of the season.

Many times his was the mediating and decisive influence between a boy and his family after the boy had left school. He was particularly eager to turn men's thoughts to the ministry. "What a life it would be," he wrote John Crocker in 1928, "if one might be a Parish Priest and a Missionary and a School Master!

It may be that in the next world we shall have chances to fill all these roles."

A graduate who wrote to the Rector of his engagement was sure to get a joyful letter back. "I am perfectly delighted to hear of your engagement. There is nothing in the world so beautiful that God gives to a man as the love of a true woman and I am sure this has come to you."

He wrote this from a full heart. One could understand, seeing them together. Somehow he and she were welded, yet each remained distinct. On all fundamentals, so far as one could judge, they thought and felt as one, but she was quite independent as to details, as was he, and each was quite content it should be so, respecting the integrity of the other. She was loyal with a great loyalty and would not consent that anything he did or was should be open to criticism, and yet she never spared to suggest and criticize herself when she thought it would help him.

In later years, as the grandchildren came, there were many visits to be made to the various households. The grandchildren called him Doodoo. Sometimes they would make him fretful with their romping, in which case Mrs. Peabody would gather them under her wing out of the way, but he loved them and they loved him.

His correspondence unfortunately contains little in connection with some of his greatest battles. One might think that his struggles were limited to Billings and Gardner. This was not so. He periodically "drank delight of battle with [his] peers," and his opponents included the J. P. Morgans, father and son; Theodore Roosevelt (a fierce running fight, reaching a climax over whether one of the boys could go to a dentist in Washington and terminating in the President's sending a dentist to Groton.)*

Perhaps to the loss of posterity these were for the most part private and verbal contests, conducted in the full panoply of war, but discreetly as between gentlemen. One sensed the "thunder of the captains," but never saw the gore; only certain unmistakable results in what happened at Groton to boys or to causes which served as pawns.

* Mr. Billings once acted as the Rector's emissary to the prominent parent of a boy who had been severely disciplined. Mr. B. not only convinced the gentleman of the propriety with which the case was handled, but came back with an anonymous check for $90,000 to pay off the school debt!

R. M. Sedgwick recollects: "In 1938 or '39 Mr. Peabody was reminiscing to me of the early days of the school. He told me that after Brooks House and Hundred House were complete, he decided that the next secular building that the school needed was a school house. He retained Peabody and Stearns to draw rough plans and when they were ready he went to New York to raise the money. The great J. P. Morgan was a member of the Groton board and it was on him that the Rector called first.

Mr. Morgan was cordial and at once evinced a keen interest in the projected school house. He then asked Mr. Peabody if he had some plans. The Rector produced them and the great man studied them with care. Presently he looked up and said, 'I notice the building is only two stories. Would it not be much more economical to make it three?' The Rector agreed but said that to harmonise with the other buildings, it was desirable to have it two stories, and, further, that there was a very slight fire hazard in a three story building. Mr. Morgan was not impressed and argued strenuously for a three storied building. After a few minutes he paused and said, 'Look Cottie, if you will make it three stories, I'll give you the building—otherwise, I am not interested.' The Rector thanked him, said he appreciated his position and added he was very sorry he must insist on two stories and then took his leave. History does not record Mr. Morgan's reaction but it is probable he must have come close to fainting from surprise. The Rector had no serious difficulty in raising the necessary funds elsewhere."

At Groton he was always addressed as Mr. Peabody, never Doctor Peabody. He never encouraged the use of the title which had come to him with his various degrees, but which he felt he had not earned by his own study. His more informal appellations were varied, as: the Big Boss; the Boss; Umboss; the Big Swede; Peabo. The one title, however, stood above all—The Rector. That was he. It was understood that the Rector was just one person, no other, as if one said "Caesar" and let it go at that.*

35

THREE SCORE YEARS AND TEN

E. P. *aet.* 70-72
1927-1928

HIS graduates stretched over a large age group now. Many of them were grandfathers; many of them had died. His interest in their affairs and characters went on undiminished. On the same day he might write to one who was president of a bank and another who was a college undergraduate. Their letters to him continued to come with each mail.

"It was good of you to send a postcard. Thank you," wrote one.

For the approval or disapproval of most people I have learned to care nothing, because I know how ready they are to judge by appearances . . . but your opinion does matter to me. You see I respect you. . . . My mental attitude used to be . . . a childish sort of defiance. I shall be forty years old this year. . . . I have matured enough at any rate to want to talk out with you your judgment of me. . . . In one of his sermons while I was at Groton, Mr. B said "We are all only stepping stones for our children." This at least I have tried to be as far as I could.

* R. M. Sedgwick noted: My father was only a few years younger than Mr. Peabody, and they had been friends since early manhood, yet my father always called Mr. Peabody "Rector" and not Cottie. I don't think it was apropos of this in particular, but I do recall Mr. Peabody once saying to me, "I wish my nickname were not Cottie. It sounds so diminutive that many of my friends will not use it and Endicott is too formal so they avoid that as well and stick to Mr. Peabody." I think he would have liked the older graduates to call him by his first name.

A deluge of letters came for his seventieth birthday. He eventually answered them personally, but it took a long time as it was a big chore, and not wishing to seem unappreciative of such an outpouring he wrote a general word of thanks on June 10, 1927.

DEAR ALUMNI:

I wish it were possible for me to express with my own pen my thanks for the letters I have received from the Alumni and other kind friends.

It is a great encouragement to read such words of affection on the occasion of my seventieth birthday, to be doubly assured of the Old Boys' devotion to the School and to know with certainty that the School will be fully looked after in the coming years.

For myself, I realize how far I fall short of the commendations you have so generously bestowed upon me. I shall try to be more worthy in consequence of this great experience. It is an undying interest that I have in our great school family. Grotoniensis sum et nihil Grotoniense a me alienum puto.

It has been a forty-three years blessed with prosperity and friendship. For the earlier years I have equal cause for gratitude. I have lived, seen God's hand in a lifetime and all was for best. Whatever lies ahead, we may be sure that our love for one another cannot cease, and that the school, like the Scotchman's tree, will be growing while we are sleeping.

With love and gratitude, I am

Sincerely your friend,

ENDICOTT PEABODY

He neither looked nor acted his age. He exercised regularly, principally on horseback. Graduates returning after a long absence found him as they had left, so far as they could remember. The only outward change was that each year he and Mrs. Peabody left Groton before the end of the winter term and sometimes returned a week or so late. In 1921 he had spent a whole winter term in the Far West, but he had had no sabbatical since 1911 and showed no inclination to take one.

Nevertheless, 1927 was an active, difficult year. In the fall term, following various minor troubles at school, several boys stopped in, after a Harvard-Yale game, at the rooms of graduates and took drinks, although they behaved themselves well otherwise. It was the climax to a contest that had been building up, and the Rector decided to put an end to it. He promptly expelled six sixth-formers and just as promptly received strong protests from parents and alumni. He strongly urged the boys be accepted at other schools, but none of them remained at Groton.

It was a restless period at the school. For two or three years the older boys were critical, and the problem was aggravated by many faculty changes. Numerous people observed with satisfaction that their gloomiest prophecies were fulfilled; the Rector should have resigned when he was sixty-five or sixty or before the war. One of the most thoughtful summaries of the situation came from one of the graduates of this period, F. Vinton Lindley, 1929, who wrote the Rector in part as follows (he had just received 100 in an English examination for Yale):

It is entirely to the School that I owe any such ability and knowledge as might have fitted me for that test. It is not so much to the actual teaching of English as to the atmosphere which pervades the School. . . . I have been to [other schools] many times when those schools have been in session. I know intimately a large number of boys from schools all over the country. And, perhaps foolishly, I have examined and analyzed them all hypercritically. It is with no sense of conceited superiority that I find them all infinitely inferior to Groton, above everything in a certain indefinable tone, in those qualities which an educated gentleman has perhaps in excess. Together with this there has been an intellectual broad-mindedness and stimulus which, I believe, has never before been present except in a University. . . .

Our form, I suppose, was rather a problem. I gather that the Faculty as a whole did not think very highly of it. . . . In the first place during its last two years about twelve new masters entered the Faculty. This made the situation difficult in that our form knew better than a large part of the Faculty what were the customs and traditions of the School and above all understood the Unwritten Code of Honor which is an intangible, yet extremely important factor . . . as you, of course, realize more than I do. . . . Our form was critical not because it was Bolshevistic by nature nor because it hated the School, but just the opposite, because it loved the School, was deeply interested in, and wished to improve, the School. [Here followed a detailed estimate of the teaching ability of every member of the Faculty.] We cannot help feeling that as a principle the censorship of books and magazines is wrong. Desirable as it may seem to keep boys unspotted from the world, yet in this modern age it is artificial in the extreme to prevent them from reading Voltaire at School when they find their parents and even grandparents reading novels which are of infinitely lower moral standard at home. . . . It was this censorship more than any other one thing that gave

306

our form the feeling of sullen resentment which they held at one time. Boys are essentially just minded. They can see the necessity for discipline, for having no week-ends, for Chapel, for studies, for compulsory athletics, for everything in fact but the almost medieval quality of censorship.

Other letters received were neither as discerning nor thoughtful, but the Rector answered them all in painstaking detail. He knew the problems well. One of the largest of them was building for his successor a faculty which would be sure to carry the school safely over a difficult transition period. For the Rector, if he would not admit that he was growing old, realized that other men were.

There was also, early in 1927, a difficulty about his new school, Brooks. The idea of establishing another small school had been in his mind for several years. Originally he wished to stipulate that the headmaster should be a clergyman. When the man selected felt he could not accept the position if so bound, the Rector agreed, feeling the desired result would come. It did not, and this, coupled with other factors which disquieted him, particularly a growing feeling that the prospective head "lacked humility," led him to insist that he go to Oxford for two years of study, preferably of religion. Since boys had already been accepted, masters engaged, and buildings built, the new board of trustees differed sharply. The majority were in favor of going ahead, and the Rector, once overruled, accepted the decision and, typically, dropped the question and gave his wisdom, energy, and loyalty to the school. He was instrumental in bringing to it funds amounting to more than $200,000 for plant and equipment. When the original gift of land was made, however, the donor, Mr. Richard S. Russell of Boston, stipulated in 1926:

In order that there may be a definite and clear understanding of the situation I wish to say that it would give me great pleasure to deed to the new school the land . . . to-gether with the buildings thereon . . . on or before March 31, 1927, provided that between now and then, as your plans are definitely worked out, there develops sufficient support, financial and otherwise, to reasonably and conservatively assure the success of the new undertaking. It would seem essential that such adequate financial support should include:
1. The raising of an endowment fund, as suggested by you, of not less than $150,000.
2. Contributions of such an amount (now roughly guessed as

$75,000) as may later be estimated by the architects to be necessary for changes. . . .

3. The reasonable expectation and assurance of an additional $150,000 by April 1, 1928, to be available for a new permanent building, to-gether with necessary expenditures for sewage disposal plant, athletic facilities, and so forth.

On June 11, 1928, in his Treasurer's report, Mr. Russell said "The treasurer also wishes to call the attention of the Trustees to the fact that the Endowment Fund, now amounting on the books to $14,000, should be increased to at least $150,000, the minimum contemplated in the original financial requirements of the School."

There was a voluminous correspondence on the question. The Rector steadily pointed out that ample funds had been raised to enable the school to go ahead. Russell equally steadily pointed out that the conditions on which he had made the gift which made the school possible had not been met. The matter was complicated by the fact that his son had been among the group of boys sent away from Groton in 1927, within a few weeks of his original offer. Meanwhile the school was opened, new buildings erected and contracted for, and the school immensely in the debt of both men in terms of interest and energy. The final solution was further gifts by Russell, with continued devotion to Brooks, and no endowment fund in terms of the original bargain, although money raised either directly or indirectly by the Rector eventually approached the figures first agreed upon.

Further correspondence throws an interesting light upon the varying points of view of the businessman and the clergyman:

Rev. Endicott Peabody,
    Groton School,
    Groton, Mass.   October 31, 1927

DEAR DR. PEABODY:
    Your wisdom and foresight when we first talked of Brooks School, nearly two years ago, in considering a small endowment fund as an essential at the start, is very evident at this time. My feeling on that subject then was so strong that my offer of April, 1926, was very definitely made contingent on the raising of an endowment fund of $150,000, $75,000 for reconstruction, and the reasonable expectation of an additional $150,000 by April 1, 1928. This made a total of $375,000. The problem of adapting the buildings made it wise to anticipate part of the expenditure contemplated

308

for 1928 by increasing the immediate expenditure from $75,000 to approximately $150,000, so that $75,000 of the $150,000 anticipated requirement for 1928 has already been provided. The result is, however, that no progress has been made to date on the $150,000 endowment fund.

Last spring, when the Trustees voted to proceed with the construction and opening of the school, I called their attention during the meeting to the fact that the conditions made by me had not been met. My interest in the undertaking was such that I did not wish to stand in the way of immediate progress. I realized that I was deéding the property prior to the fulfillment of the conditions I had made, but felt that those conditions were so obviously fundamental to the welfare of the school that I did not need worry about their prompt fulfillment.

In your letters during the summer, you have referred to the endowment as something which need not be counted a necessity at the present time, but which could be gathered in by and by, and that for the present we should be satisfied with supplementing the deficit year by year. I can say most positively that if I had felt that your views as to the advisability, necessity, and possibility of raising this fund might change, I should certainly have considered it wise to delay the start of the undertaking until this had been accomplished. The failure of the school to get the expected 20 pupils by the opening day means that the school income is $19,600 instead of $28,000. This makes inevitable a deficit of perhaps $12,000 to $15,000 this year, which proves conclusively how absolutely vital to the welfare of the school the raising of this endowment fund is.

My feeling from the very beginning has been that you were the only one with the acquaintance, standing and ability to obtain the necessary subscriptions. I still feel this to be the case, and have entire confidence that a reasonable amount of time spent by you during the coming winter would very promptly supply the relatively modest fund required.

I trust you realize and enjoy the satisfaction and delight everyone constantly expresses about the school, its location, plant, and staff. Its outstanding success seems assured.

Sincerely yours,
RICHARD S. RUSSELL

November 3, 1927
DEAR MR. RUSSELL:
Everything connected with Brooks School seems to me to have gone forward as well as we could have expected; in some ways better even than I had hoped. . . . The number of boys is somewhat dis-

309

appointing. I think this may be due partly to the fact that there was some slight doubt about the time of opening the school until a rather late day, and that then we did not advertise quite as freely as we might have done. There are enough boys, however, just now to give the masters an opportunity to show their mettle, and from what they tell me they seem to be marching forward bravely.

Our first estimate of the cost of preparing the buildings was, as you will recall, $75,000. We have raised $162,000—I am speaking in thousands just now—the balance amounting to $77,000 may fairly be looked upon as the beginning for the endowment of $150,000. We add to this the subscriptions of Mr. and Mrs. Pyle, Mrs. J. T. Pyle, Messrs. J. P. Morgan and J. S. Drum, amounting to $9500, and the subscriptions of Mrs. Brown and Mr. George Whitney and the $2000 promised by my sister amounting to $8000. These combined make $94,500. This would be a good start towards the $150,000 endowment which we had in mind. For the additional fund of $150,000 which in your judgment will be required for new buildings and extension or plant, we must work, as well as for the balance of the endowment fund. It is fair to bear in mind that we had good reason to believe that Payne Whitney would subscribe at least $50,000, for he assured Mr. Billings that he was interested in the enterprise and asked Mr. Billings to come to him in 1927. If we had secured this $50,000 we should be short of the first $150,000 by $5,500.

Taking it altogether I do feel that we have no reason to be discouraged or even disappointed thus far, although it is possible it may take a longer time to get the money than we expected in April 1926.

Sincerely yours,
ENDICOTT PEABODY

November 8, 1927
DEAR DR. PEABODY:—

I am delighted you expect to get substantial assistance from friends of Groton.

That which you can do very readily would be impossible for anyone else. With the $150,000 endowment fund in hand, the School will have an 'essential back log, necessary both to ensure the stability of its operations and to fulfill the conditions upon which the School was founded.

I note your calculations showing that we are in a sense $5,500 short of the needed $150,000 endowment fund, but of course of your several sums only $8,000 is real, as we have not received the additional $50,000 from Payne Whitney, the $9,500 from Morgan, Drum and Pyle is included in the $152,000 subscriptions raised, so cannot be counted again, and the balance, or $77,000, has been spent. Unfortunately this theoretical fund will not yield us income to meet expenses.

The true situation is that there has been raised $150,000 of the $225,000 for buildings and $8,000 of the $150,000 endowment. With prosperity as widespread as it is and with your ability to put before individuals the opportunity for productive employment of surplus funds, I am perfectly confident of success in meeting the annoying but unavoidable financial need by next year, providing you can set aside a reasonable amount of time for the undertaking.

Sincerely yours,

RICHARD S. RUSSELL

The points of view remained unaltered seventeen years later.

Now and then a graduate would send his boy to some other school than Groton. Usually in such cases a letter came explaining why. To one such the Rector replied:

December 11, 1930

MY DEAR ———,

It is disappointing to me and it will be to all of your old friends at Groton not to have your boy come to us. Kent School is undoubtedly an excellent institution. I like Father Sill and I admire the ability which he has shown in developing his school. I can quite understand your being favorably impressed with the self-help plan which he has carried through so successfully.

As we say in the language of the street, "that's that".

Some day I should like you to come to Groton just as a graduate and find out what is doing here. You speak of "older established schools with older methods". Two and one-half years ago Pulling, who afterwards taught at Avon Old Farms School, and another Master in our History Department went to a so-called Progressive School Conference in St. Louis. When they returned both of them assured me that we had been pursuing for some time the methods which the progressive people presented as ideals to be aimed at. I mention this to show you that men who are themselves progressive count us well up with the modern methods of education.

Touching the question of expulsion from the school, it would be interesting for you, if you cared to do so, to discover the number of boys expelled from, say, the five outstanding private schools. I should be very glad, indeed, to explain to you or to any graduate the reasons for our sending away six boys four years ago. One could not form a fair judgment without a knowledge of details and I am sure that you wish to be fair. Apart from this incident, the

311

number of boys dismissed from Groton in the middle of the year can be counted on the fingers of one hand or, at any rate, one and one-half hands. That fact is perhaps also not known to you. I have no definite information in regard to the practice of other schools. I recall that when Abbott went to Lawrenceville, he expelled some thirty or forty and, I fancy, that there is a pretty definite loss from expulsion in other places, but of this I am not certain. We have also a good many things to show you when you come.

With best wishes, I am,

Affectionately yours,
E. P.

One by one his old friends were passing, in America and abroad. Thayer, who had been closest to him among the head-masters, was about to retire, as was Stearns of Andover before long, leaving Peabody and Horace Taft as the elders in the profession. Cochin Griffith was dead, and "dear old Arthur's" last message had come in the form of a notice from his executors. "We are writing to inform you that by his will, the late Mr. Pellew Arthur bequeathed to you the sum of £10 with a request that you should purchase some little token in remembrance of him." Peabody's way was to be both more lonely and more prominent from now on.

He and Horace Taft were very fond of one another and full of mutual respect. A typical letter from Taft, who was a lovable person and a great headmaster, read:

April 27, 1927

My Dear Cotty:

It is long since your good letter came, but I have been too busy with the shingles and other pleasures to keep up with my correspondence. The trouble is of course, that I was put behind in my work, and then when I came to try to catch up, the doctor and anxious and officious friends kept jumping on me and trying to prevent my "getting tired", as they called it, which meant doing anything at all. However, I am pretty well altogether, and expect to say good-by to the shingles in the course of a week or ten days. In any case, I am not accepting invitations to talk on law enforcement or to do anything else not connected with my school work. Roberts constantly complains that I indulge in too many extra-curriculum activities.

I agree with you that there is something in the new education idea. The trouble is that they have carried it so far that they have taken all the back-bone out of a boy's training. I remember stirring a man up who was on that side, and getting from him the reply: "We believe in hard work just as much as you do". I said: "I do not care what you believe in. The only thing that you have succeeded in getting into the minds of the half-million half-baked high school girls who are doing the teaching for the country is: Make it interesting, and the only way in which they can possibly interpret this is: Make it easy." The Lincoln School is whaling away with an exceptional set of highly paid experts. I am unable to judge what the results are. I hear violent opinions both ways, but I feel certain that methods that might produce good results with such exceptional teachers, would be calamitous when used by ordinary teachers. On the other hand, I am sure that a good many boys are subjected to the training of our orthodox schools who ought to have something different. The trouble is that the only other schools, as a rule, are schools with patent methods, often fraudulent.

I am tickled to think that you still "pack a hefty wollop." May you continue to so pack for many a year. As for me, I do not begin to have your vigor, though I am a little your junior, but I insist that it is not time for my friends to be selecting wreaths, as I suspect some of them are planning. I tell them I am going to go on head-mastering for ten years yet.

I have a good deal of fun with Stearns and Perry,* telling them I wish I were at the head of a big school and could drop around for salary day, and for the rest of the time cavort over the country. Their search for funds has taken them far afield.

Please give my kindest regards to Mrs. Peabody.

Yours as ever,

HORACE D. TAFT

Even when he was away from school, masters and alumni kept him in touch:

March 23, 1927

DEAR E. P.

The term ended quietly for all except S. B. who scented conspeeracy in the very weather (which was balmy). "*Very disco*ncerting weather" he remarked to me on St. Patrick's day. He telephoned HEP the night before and said, "*T*omorrow is Saint *P*atrick's *day*, Saint *P*atrick's *day* yes—a*nd* I am a*f*raid that the *bo*ys may want to wear *g*reen *ti*es. I wish you would see that none of the *bo*ys in your *do*rmitory wear *g*reen *ti*es *t*omorrow. We must *ni*p it in the *bud.*!"

* Principals of Phillips Andover and Exeter Academies, respectively.

313

A graduate wrote him:

DEAR MR. PEABODY:
Many thanks for your card on my birthday. It is a stimulating thing for me, I can tell you, to have such continuous encouragement from you. I've never felt happier than I do now, though I do feel an impatience to get to work now and then. Mary and I were talking only tonight of the extraordinary harmony that is possible in a minister's life. The satisfaction of both the active and the contemplative life are his; he more than others, I think has the excitement of conflict without the pain of rancour or selfishness; through him, it seems, God dispenses the one sure means of strength, the one never failing comfort, hope, and joy; the privilege of creative work is surely his to the greatest degree. I'm beginning to understand what too few young men seem to appreciate, that the minister is the happiest of men. I can't thank you enough for helping me to see this truth. Certainly I owe you more than anyone in this matter and it would be strange if I did not feel grateful.

Mary sends her love to you and Mrs. Peabody; do please give her mine too.

Affectionately
JACK CROCKER.

And there were other compensations, as this:

July second, 1927
DEAR MR. PEABODY:
I was at the Yale Commencement this spring and was greatly impressed with the honors of various kinds awarded to Groton Graduates. The three College honors announced on the program all went to Grotonians, namely, to Pierson and Bingham. The only formal address from outside of the Yale official family was given by Trubee Davison, another Grotonian; and among the honorary degrees which received the most enthusiasm was the one given to Charles Lanier Lawrance for the invention of the Wright Whirlwind Motor, who, I believe, is also a Grotonian. I have no doubt that there were other Groton boys on the scholarship lists, indeed, I remember noticing one to Wardwell, for two year honors.

This was a very remarkable record for one Commencement, and reminds me of the splendid record that Groton has always made at Yale for moral character, and the remarkable record that it has made in recent years in scholarship.

I am no longer, as you know, officially connected with Yale, but I must send you this word of very sincere congratulations. I doubt whether any school has ever had more conspicuous achievement on

314

the part of the graduates at any single Commencement, especially when it is realized that Pierson's scholarship record was the highest in the history of Yale College.

Always sincerely yours,
ANSON PHELPS STOKES.

He wrote one of the trustees of Brooks School his ideas as to the proper status of a headmaster:

My plan for the school is that which I have always held for Groton, that the master shall have a free hand and that he shall be retained at the school so long as he carries on to the satisfaction of the trustees. That is better, in my judgment, than either attempting to interfere in the details of the working of the school or looking upon the headmaster as necessarily a permanent fixture.*

Surveying his own incumbency one was left in doubt as to what constituted permanency.

36

THE COLLEGE RECORD

THE war was a sudden emergency which tested the Rector's system and theories. But what of the more prosaic business of year-in and year-out performance in terms of preparation for college and performance in college? †

At Harvard, from 1890-1905, 148 candidates were admitted. There is no record of 28. Those reported took 1580 examinations. Of these 6.1% received highest honors; 11.4% honors; 9.4% failed. Between 1906 and 1932 at Harvard there were 2560 papers of which 193 were highest honors; 553 honors.

At Yale, from 1887 to 1932, 2947 papers were taken of which

* In earlier years he had resigned from the board of trustees of Lawrence Academy because he felt the headmaster was not being given a free hand.

† Detailed statistics in regard to college entrance and other records will be found in *Fifty Years On, a Short History of Groton School* by F. D. Ashburn; the Gosden Head Press, 1935.

315

754 were honors or highest honors. But close examination of figures shows a steady rise in performance. For instance after 1903 there were only 4 failures out of 238 papers. And in English since 1904, 4 out of the only 6 papers to receive 100% were written by Grotonians! All were given after 1928. Between 1912 and 1932 only 10 papers were taken in chemistry, but 9 were honors; in physics there were 22 honors out of 50 papers. In mathematics, between 1918 and 1932, on the Cp. 3 paper there were 95 papers and 66 honors. And in Latin on the most advanced examination, Cp. 4, there were only 4 failures, and 51 honors, out of 143 papers.

Finally, at Princeton, the third college in order of entrants, between 1921 and 1930 there were 64 papers, no failures, 39 honors and 12 highest honors.

In 1932 total candidates for Harvard, Princeton, and Yale took 112 papers. Of these 51.7% were honors; 14 were highest honors; 44 honors. The percentage of honors by subjects was: English, 53.5%; Latin, 70.9%; history, 75%; French, 50%; German, 25%; mathematics, 25%; physics, 44%. In this class one boy received 100% in English; one two highest and two honors out of four examinations; three received three honors and one highest each; and one three highest honors.

Between 1890, when the first graduate finished his college course, and 1932, 30 Grotonians were elected to Phi Beta Kappa at Harvard; 35 at Yale; and 7 at other colleges.

In addition to this, 56 won either John Harvard or Harvard College Scholarships, and 11 others prizes or scholarships at Harvard. At Yale, Grotonians won 71 prizes or prize scholarship awards.

In other undergraduate activities at Harvard there were three presidents of the *Advocate*, three of the *Crimson*, three of the *Lampoon*, and one of the Debating Union. At Yale there were three chairmen of the *News;* three of the *Yale Literary Magazine;* four presidents of the Dramatic Association (in 1923, 1924, 1925, and 1928); two presidents of Dwight Hall; two of Phi Beta Kappa. In 1924-25 the elected heads of the *Crimson*, the *News*, the *Yale Lit*, the *Advocate;* of the *Yale Dramatic Association*, the Harvard Union; and the captain of the Harvard football team were all Grotonians.

Athletically, forty-seven won letters in football at Harvard, of whom four were captains; in baseball twenty-two, of whom four were captains; in crew thirty-two, of whom two were captains. Five won hockey letters and eleven track. Eleven were Freshman captains in various sports. At Yale six won football letters, one a captain; in baseball only three; in crew twenty-two, with five captaincies. There were four hockey letter-men and two in track. Six were Freshman captains in various sports.

Groton was also represented on an Olympic crew and had two national squash champions.

But perhaps the most interesting feature of all is that these two lists, athletic and nonathletic, coincide as to names to a remarkable extent. There is a feeling of balance in the total result, as of athletes who were scholars and scholars who were not grimy with the oil of the lamp.

Lastly, it may be pointed out, that however desirable or undesirable such concentration of graduates in two or three colleges may be, the scholastic and prize records, Phi Beta Kappa, for instance, were at least as hard to come by in Harvard, Yale, and Princeton as at any other three colleges or universities in the country.

37

NON SCHOLAE SED VITAE

DISCIMUS

WHAT of the big world, of Life with a capital L, for which he had been preparing boys for nearly fifty years? There had been about a thousand boys. Many of them were still young; nearly a hundred and fifty still in college. Of those who were thirty years old or more there were perhaps five hundred living. What had they been doing since lege at the time of his retirement. What did they do after they left him?

In revising this chapter, first written in 1943, it was necessary to include men whose careers did not come to full bloom until after, long after in some cases, the Rector was dead, so that the chapter leaps ahead of its proper chronological place in the story. It is fascinating to note how their achievements kept piling up, as they will continue to do for many years to come. The record is by no means complete. But even as it stands, it is difficult to make the catalogue a satisfactory one, and the author is painfully aware of omissions which might seem unjustified, even on the ground that the chapter had to be kept to reasonable length.

The most popular career with Grotonians was business, an obviously widely embracing term, covering everything from stockbroking to running a bank or a factory. Frequently it involved the public welfare, often it led to fascinating fields of concern, but it is not ordinarily productive either of broad fame or publicity. The mere listing of graduates who held executive positions in the business world, national and international, would fill several pages.

So with medicine and law: both are great callings, but it is a rare doctor or lawyer, as such, who has much of what is called "news value." The Rector took comfort in the fact that when he retired eighty-eight alumni were lawyers and forty doctors.

In education performance was easier to identify. R. S. Rose, and G. W. Pierson were distinguished professors at Yale, as was Daniel Merriman, who succeeded H. Emerson Tuttle as Master of Davenport College. Arnold Whitridge, author and scholar, was Master of Calhoun College, and George deF. Lord Master of Trumbull. There were numerous Professors who were authorities in their fields (J. C. Hoppin; S. K. Lothrop; Henry A. Murray; Thayer Addison; Ward H. Goodenough; Woodbridge Bingham; John Adams Abbott, and George W. Pierson—to mention only a few). W. Bayard Cutting was an economist of great promise who died before his time. Oliver LaFarge was a noted archeologist, who did much for the American Indian. Ashbel G. Gulliver, a noted teacher of law, was Dean of the Yale Law School for six years. Henry Chauncey, after important work in the Harvard Dean's Office and as executive head of the College Entrance Examination Board, became the founder and distinguished head of the Educational Testing Service. Both Francis Keppel and McGeorge Bundy have made outstanding educational contributions (see below). In the schools F. B. Riggs at Indian Mountain; Edric Weld at Holderness; John Crocker at Groton; Lawrence Terry at Middlesex; Frank Ashburn at Brooks; and Arthur Milliken at Westminster were heads of these schools for many years. Blake Field at Palm Valley; D. R. Williams at St. Bernard's in New Jersey; Roger B. Merriman, Jr. at Arnold; John Chandler at Grosse Pointe; and Shaun Kelly at

318

Woodberry Forest also were headmasters, but for a shorter period of time than the afore-mentioned. Ashburn served terms as Chairman of the College Entrance Examination Board and of the Yale University Council. Louis C. Zahner's work in English at Groton and his influence on teaching everywhere should be noted. At least three schools, Baguio (now Brent), Indian Mountain, and Brooks had deep roots in Groton, and Edward Pulling left the Groton faculty to found Millbrook. If former Masters are included, the list of those in education becomes even more impressive. Remsen B. Ogilby, first head of Baguio, later became the beloved President of Trinity College in Hartford. Julian Coolidge, an outstanding mathematician, was also Master of Lowell House at Harvard. Emerson Tuttle, as mentioned above, was Master of Davenport College at Yale. W. G. Thayer at St. Mark's; Mather Abbott at Lawrenceville; J. P. Williams at St. Christopher's, and Ronald S. Beasley at the Mary Institute in St. Louis were all headmasters who had formerly taught at Groton.

In the Church J. Thayer Addison, John Crocker and Edric Weld have already been mentioned. Addison was Vice-President of the Executive Council of the Protestant Episcopal Church. Malcolm Peabody was Bishop of Central New York, and a member of the Executive Council for ten years. Alexander Zabriskie was Dean of the Theological School in Alexandria, and John Suter, Sr. was Dean of the National Cathedral in Washington. Few things gave the Rector more satisfaction than the work of his successor at Groton, John Crocker, who not only "carried on" magnificently the Groton tradition, but added new dimensions to it, and after more than two decades of leadership in the Church as well as in education, handed over the school to his successor, Bertrand N. Honea, Jr. in 1965.

In the field of literature Arnold Whitridge, Horace Green, Theodore and Kermit Roosevelt, Daniel Sargent, Lincoln, Rogers and Charlton McVeagh, Christopher and Oliver LaFarge, L. and G. E. Brewer wrote biographies, novels, and poetry. Oliver LaFarge's first novel, *Laughing Boy*, won the Pulitzer Prize in 1930. D. Burden, huntsman, naturalist, and adventurer, has written of his experiences. Later on Rutherfurd Platt, J. H. G. Pierson, Christopher Rand, Walter Sullivan, Dean Acheson, McGeorge Bundy, and James Cross were recognized authorities in various fields. C. P. Curtis is hard to classify, but his anthologies and writings are treasured by many. Louis

319

Auchincloss established his place as a leading novelist.* Ellery Sedgwick first edited *Leslie's Magazine,* then *McClure's,* and finally the *Atlantic Monthly.* B. M. Cutting was one of the prominent newspaper men in the southwest. R. R. McCormick owned and published the Chicago *Tribune;* J. M. Patterson the New York *Daily News;* and in the 1960's J. H. Whitney the New York *Herald Tribune.* F. L. Allen, in addition to being a successful author, was managing editor of *Harper's.* Lincoln McVeagh founded and was president of the Dial Press; C. Canfield was president of Harper Bros. & Co.; T. R. Coward was president of Coward-McCann; M. E. Stone of the Gosden Head Press. R. Littell was an associate editor of the *Reader's Digest;* H. I. Stokes was an editor of the *New York Times;* A. M. Bingham founded and edited *Common Sense.* The Alsop brothers were nationally recognized commentators; A. C. Sedgwick's dispatches appeared regularly in the *New York Times.*

In painting the outstanding name is undoubtedly George Biddle, who has not been disposed to credit the school with his artistic success. Some would give Ives Eammell top rank. Howard Cushing was an artist of promise who died young. J. C. E. Taylor has for many years been a professor of Art at Trinity College; F. C. Watkins, R. D. Tucker, G. L. K. Morris, T. B. Adams and P. T. Mitchell are all recognized in their fields. Cushing, Watkins and Morris (who is also a sculptor) all won the Pennsylvania Academy's Gold Medal. F. M. Sedgwick, painter and sculptor, is best known to Grotonians for his busts of the Rector, one at Groton, the other at Brooks. Incidentally, it is rather striking to discover how many graduates have taken to painting as an avocation.

Musical contributions have been small, so far as the writer's knowledge goes. The most promising musician, Blair Fairchild, died with his work unfinished.

* No book about Groton or by a Grotonian occasioned as much discussion as Auchincloss's *The Rector of Justin,* which, in spite of the author's disclaimers, was generally considered to be a portrait of Endicott Peabody and Groton School. The Rector of Justin only remotely resembled the Rector of Groton, and there was no similarity whatsoever between the Prescott family and the Peabodys. To old Groton hands, however, much of the setting, many of the details, some of the minor characters, and at least one major episode were familiar. The result was confusion and much unhappiness. Many felt it a pity that such an important work of fiction should be popularly considered as an authoritative picture of a man, his school, and his family.

320

At least five Groton architects were nationally known. A. M. Brown, J. W. Cross, E. Cross, G. Howe, and H. R. Shepley. There are others whose greatest work is still to come. There is also a group of individuals who have made striking contributions to the public welfare without being directly involved in what is generally known as public life. Such are Fairfield Osborn, President of the New York Zoological Society; Trubee Davison, President of the American Museum of Natural History; S. S. Colt, a bank president in an earlier incarnation, has been Chairman of the New York Port Authority; Morris Hadley, long a member of the Yale Corporation, was President both of the Board of the Carnegie Corporation and of the New York Public Library; E. R. Harriman has served five terms as Chairman of the American Red Cross; J. J. Schieffelin has been Executive Director of the English Speaking Union; C. A. Coolidge served for a time as Acting President of Harvard and was on the Harvard Corporation for thirty years, retiring as senior member in 1965. J. E. Lawrence is Chairman of the Board of Trustees of the Massachusetts General Hospital; A. A. Bliss is President of the Metropolitan Opera Company. Devereux C. Josephs is President of the Rockefeller Foundation; John L. Saltonstall has been Chairman of the Massachusetts Transportation Commission, the Department of Public Works, and the Executive Committee of the Boston Regional Planning Project. Brooks McCormick is Chairman of the National Safety Council. Bradford Washburn, explorer and mountaineer extraordinary, has been the brilliant head of the Boston Museum of Science. Allen Pifer is President of the Carnegie Foundation. Endicott P. Davidson is President of the National Recreation and Parks Association. The author concludes this listing with the uneasy feeling that many who should be included have been omitted from lack of information.

But the most formidable list is that of Grotonians in the aforementioned public life. The catalogue, even with questionable omissions of some who have been active in local governmental affairs, is so long that a summary of chief offices held must serve. It seems best to deal with individuals in the order of their Groton classes.

George Rublee served the country in important positions for many years, in such varying capacities as Counsel to the American Embassy in Mexico and membership on the staff of the

London Conference on Disarmament. He was first Chairman of the Federal Trade Commission, worked for the League of Nations on arbitration missions to the Hague, Mexico and Colombia. In 1938 he was made Director of the Intergovernmental Committee on Refugees.

Pierre Jay was Chairman of the Board of Directors of the Federal Reserve Bank of New York and a member of the Reparations Commission in connection with the Dawes Plan.

Frank L. Polk was a Civil Service Commissioner in New York and President of the Municipal Service Commission. From 1915 to 1920 he was Counsellor for the Department of State, then Undersecretary of State, and, while President Wilson and Secretary Lansing were in Paris, head of the State Department and virtually the head of the government.

Frederick Hale served two terms (1916–1928) as Senator from Maine. He was Chairman of the Committee on Naval Affairs and the Committee on Appropriations.

Charles B. Curtis was Minister to the Dominican Republic and El Salvador. Joseph Medill McCormick served in the House from 1917 to 1919 and was Senator from Illinois from 1919 to 1925. W. Bayard Cutting held various posts in Europe, among them that of secretary to the American ambassador in London. Stuart Heintzelman rose to be a Major General in the United States Army.

Joseph C. Grew, prior to World War I, was stationed in Egypt, Mexico, Russia, Germany, and Austria-Hungary. He was Secretary of the American Armistice Delegation at Versailles. In 1920 he was Minister to Denmark, in 1921 to Switzerland. In 1923 he was sent by President Harding to negotiate a treaty with Turkey, returning to Washington as Undersecretary of State and Chairman of the Personnel Board of the Foreign Service. He was one of the small group who brought about much needed changes in the Service. In 1924 he was briefly Acting Secretary of State. In 1927 he was Ambassador to Turkey and in 1931 to Japan.

James Jackson was manager of the New England Division of the Red Cross during the first World War. In 1920 he was Treasurer of the Commonwealth of Massachusetts and was subsequently re-elected for two additional terms.

Franklin D. Roosevelt, '00, was a member of the New York Senate from 1910 to 1913. During the first war he was Assistant

Secretary of the Navy. In 1920 he was the Democratic nominee for the vice-presidency, being defeated with most of his ticket. In 1928, after a crippling illness which would have wholly incapacitated most men, he was elected Governor of New York and re-elected in 1930 by the largest majority in the state's history. In 1932, at Chicago, he was chosen on the fourth ballot as Democratic nominee for the presidency of the United States; he was elected President, and subsequently re-elected three times for an unprecedented stay in the White House.

W. Tudor Gardiner was a representative in the main legislature from 1921 to 1925. In the latter year he was elected Speaker of that House. In 1928 he was elected Governor of Maine by the largest plurality ever received and was re-elected in 1930.

B. Sumner Welles was Chargé d'Affaires in Buenos Aires from 1914 to 1917. From 1920 to 1922 he was chief of the Division of Latin-American Affairs in the State Department. In 1922 he was made Minister to the Dominican Republic, and in 1924 was sent to Honduras as the personal representative of President Coolidge. In 1933 he was appointed Assistant Secretary of State, and shortly afterwards Ambassador to Cuba, where he was when the Batista revolution took place. Later he was again Assistant Secretary of State.

Dean G. Acheson was Undersecretary of the Treasury in 1933 and for many weeks head of the Treasury Department, resigning later because of his disagreement with the financial policy of the administration. In 1941 he was appointed first Assistant Secretary of State, then Under Secretary, finally becoming Secretary. In addition to his public services he has found time to do much admired writing and to aid the cause of education in many ways. His classmate, Charles H. Russell, was Secretary to the United States legations at the Hague and Berne, and also held important posts in Latin America.

Laurence Curtis was Congressman from Massachusetts for many years. Allen F. Kingman was a Brigadier General in the Army. G. Howland Shaw was Chief of the Division of Near East Affairs in the State Department and Assistant Secretary of State.

Edwin Corning, Sr. was Chairman of the Democratic State Committee of New York and served as Lieutenant-Governor of the state.

Robert L. Bacon was a prominent member of Congress after

1922. His brother, Gaspar G. Bacon, was a member of the Massachusetts Senate and first national treasurer of the American Legion. In 1928 he was elected President of the State Senate and reelected in 1930. In 1932, almost alone on the Republican ticket, he was elected Lieutenant-Governor. James C. Auchincloss was for many years a United States Congressman from New Jersey. When he retired in 1964 he was the senior Republican member of the House. Warren D. Robbins, Sr. was our first Minister to Canada in 1933.

Francis Biddle was in turn Solicitor General of the United States, Attorney General, and Chairman of the National Labor Relations Board.

Bronson Cutting, having been first Treasurer, then Chairman of the Progressive Central Committee, was appointed Senator from New Mexico to fill an unexpired term. Theodore Roosevelt, Jr. was a member of the New York State Assembly in 1921 and 1922. Thereafter for three years he was Assistant Secretary of the Navy. In 1924 he was defeated for the governorship of New York by Alfred E. Smith. In 1929 he was appointed Governor of Puerto Rico, and in 1931 Governor General of the Philippines. In World War II he became a Brigadier General and was awarded the Medal of Honor.

Augustine H. Gray was a Rear Admiral in the United States Navy.

W. Kingsland Macy was United States Administrator in charge of the Imports and Exports Department in 1917. He later became Republican state chairman in New York. Lincoln McVeagh was successively appointed Minister to Greece, Iceland, and South Africa.

William Averell Harriman, after an impressive business record, was Governor of New York; Assistant Secretary of State; Under Secretary of State; Ambassador to the Court of St. James's; Ambassador to Morocco and Russia; and then given the unusual and important position of Ambassador-at-Large. His distinguished career has kept him at the center of most of the world's diplomatic crises for many years.

J. Pierpont Moffat, a career diplomat, was successively Consul General at Sydney, Chief of the Division of European Affairs, and Minister to Canada.

F. Trubee Davison was in the New York Assembly from 1922

to 1925. He was the first Assistant Secretary of War for Aviation in 1927. In 1932 he resigned to run for lieutenant-governor of New York. He had been a pioneer in Naval Aviation in World War I and was a Brigadier General in the Air Force at the end of World War II.

John Jay Schieffelin was a Rear Admiral in the Naval Reserve. Pierpont M. Hamilton rose to be a Major General in the United States Army and was awarded the Medal of Honor.

Sheffield Cowles, long a member of the Connecticut legislature, served as Speaker of that body.

David McK. Key was Consul General at Barcelona, Ambassador to Burma, delegate to the United Nations, and Assistant Secretary of State for United Nations affairs.

James P. Hendrick was Deputy to the Assistant Secretary of the Treasury. Abbot L. Moffat served in the New York State Assembly and as Chief of the Division of Southeast Asian Affairs. Garrison Norton was Secretary of the Navy for Air, as well as Secretary of the Carnegie Institute of Washington, and trustee of the Institute for Defense Analyses.

A. Newbold Morris was President of the New York City Council; an unsuccessful nominee for mayor of New York; and Park Commissioner of New York City. On several occasions he was Acting Mayor of New York. Samuel Reber, after distinguished diplomatic service in many parts of the world, was sent during World War II to conduct delicate negotiations with Admiral Robert in Martinique, and later had a large part in the treaty with Austria.

G. Stanton Babcock was a Major General in the regular Army. Frederic Dumaine was Chairman of the Massachusetts State Republican Committee. John Hay Whitney, whose quiet philanthropies and contributions to many phases of education have been remarkable over the years, was Ambassador to the Court of St. James's during President Eisenhower's administration.

R. Stewart Kilborne was appointed Commissioner of Conservation in New York State in 1965.

J. Graham Parsons was Minister to Tokyo in the critical period after the Japanese surrender; Ambassador to Laos and Sweden; and Assistant Secretary of State. C. McKim Norton is President of the Regional Plan Association.

James Roosevelt has been a Congressman from California,

Democratic candidate for governor, and United States Ambassador to the Economic and Social Council of the United Nations. His brother, Elliott, was Mayor of Miami Beach.

C. Douglas Dillon was Ambassador to France; Deputy Under Secretary of State; Under Secretary of State for Economic Affairs; and Secretary of the Treasury. J. Hopkins Smith was Director of the International Cooperation Administration; Assistant Secretary of the Navy for Air; and Secretary of the Navy. G. Williams was Special Representative of the International Monetary Fund to the United Nations.

Richard M. Bissell was Executive Secretary of the President's Committee on Foreign Aid; Consultant to the Director of Mutual Security; President of the Institute for Defense Analyses; and a key member of C.I.A. His services there received unusual recognition from President Kennedy. Erastus Corning, II, Permanent Chairman of the New York Democratic State Convention in 1962, had served both in the State Assembly and Senate, and was Mayor of Albany.

E. H. Kellogg was long Consul General in Dusseldorf.

Derick V. Webb was in the Vermont Legislature and Senate and was Republican State Chairman. Clive L. DuVal, II is a member of the Virginia House of Delegates.

Jonathan B. Bingham was United States delegate on the Trusteeship Council of the United Nations and is Congressman from the Bronx. T. D. Woolsey is Deputy Director of the National Center for Health Statistics.

John Alsop was Chairman of the Connecticut Republican Council and in 1962 was nominated for the governorship of that State. Franklin D. Roosevelt, Jr. was Congressman from New York and Under Secretary of Commerce.

Sumner Gerard, Jr. was in the Montana Legislature and Senate and was Minority Leader of the latter. Francis Keppel, after a distinguished record as Dean of the Harvard Graduate School of Education, became the United States Commissioner of Education and Assistant Secretary of Health, Education, and Welfare. Kermit Roosevelt, Jr. was consultant to the State Department on Middle East Affairs.

William McC. Blair has been Ambassador to Denmark and the Philippines. William P. Bundy is Assistant Secretary of State for Far East Affairs. Marshall Green was Consul General in Hongkong with the rank of minister and is now Ambassador to

Indonesia. Stanley R. Resor, after being Under Secretary of the Army, is now Secretary.

McGeorge Bundy went from the Deanship of the Harvard Faculty of Arts and Sciences to be Special Assistant for National Security Affairs to Presidents Kennedy and Johnson. In 1966 he became President of the Ford Foundation, and, more recently, was selected by the President to serve as head of a special study of Middle Eastern Affairs. Archibald Roosevelt, Jr. has been a career diplomat, stationed in Beirut, Istanbul, and Madrid, as well as being Chief of the Near East Section of Voice of America.

Robert A. Fearey has been Director of East Asian Affairs in the State Department. He holds the rank of Minister. Peter O. A. Solbert is Deputy Assistant Secretary of Defense for International Security Affairs.

Edwin Corning was in the New York State Assembly. Endicott Peabody was Governor of Massachusetts in 1963–64 and the Democratic candidate for Senator in 1966. He is now Director of the Office of Emergency Planning.

David C. Acheson was Special Assistant to the Secretary of the Treasury. James Boughton is a career diplomat. G. Allen Dines is serving his fifth term in the Colorado House of Representatives and is Speaker of the House.

James E. Cross is Secretary of the Institute for Defense Analyses, having earlier served as Special Assistant to the Secretary of the Navy and as Acting Director of I.D.A.'s Economic and Political Studies Division.

Peter C. Walker, another career diplomat, was most recently Somali Desk Officer in the State Department.

Francis M. Bator is Deputy Special Assistant to the President for National Security Affairs (Economics).

George C. Lodge was the Republican candidate for Senator from Massachusetts in 1962, and later was Assistant Secretary of Labor for International Affairs.

Summarizing, out of approximately a thousand of the Rector's boys, one had been President of the United States; one Secretary of State (and two more acted as such); one Secretary of the Treasury; one Attorney General; ten Ambassadors and seven Ministers (to Denmark; the Dominican Republic (2); Switzerland; Turkey (2); Japan (2); Greece; Iceland; South Africa; Great Britain (2); Morocco; Russia; Cuba; Canada (2); Burma;

327

Sweden; France; the United Nations; the Philippines; and Indonesia. One had been Secretary of the Army, one of the Navy. Three were Governors, two Governors General. There were three Senators; five Congressmen; six Generals; two Admirals; two Speakers of state legislatures.*

An interesting fact is that the Rector never indulged in flag waving. There was no exhortation to patriotism or fame. There was not even a course in Civics! It was a striking illustration of the view many teachers hold that the most important lessons are not so much taught as caught.

38

THE SYSTEM

FOR many years educators and parents wanted to know how the Groton system worked. This would have been natural at any time, once the success of the school was established; and in a period when the educational world was agog with systems, it was inevitable. Mrs. Montessori's method came to full bloom in E. P.'s time. Froebel died in 1852 and his theories reached their fullest development while Peabody was at Groton. In 1900 John Dewey published *The School and Society* and the whole tremendous progressive movement flared up in America. Curricula underwent drastic changes. College entrance requirements altered. Junior high schools and junior colleges emerged. Hutchins at Chicago and Stringfellow Barr at St. John's devised new old systems. Subjective testing gave way to objective. Everybody had a system. It was inconceivable; it did violence to educational decency to attempt to imagine that a man so successful as Peabody did not have a system, too.

---

* Although Mrs. Marietta Peabody Tree, Delegate to the United Nations, and United States Representative to the Trusteeship Council of the United Nations with rank of Ambassador, was not a Groton graduate, she was the Rector's granddaughter and is entitled to mention in this chapter.

As a matter of fact he didn't. He was not only suspicious of nostrums and the untried; he definitely mistrusted short cuts which emphasized method more than duty. He didn't even advertise. He was well content to have other people experiment. If their experiments worked, he would use what had been proved good; but he wanted the proof first, and he stuck to sound simplicities.

Let Martin speak once more:

Peabody was not trustful, but he was completely reliable. When he was on duty, he was the same—always. He always first appeared before the school at Chapel in the morning, when he wore the usual priest's robes. After Chapel, the boys went at once to the schoolroom in the School House—all the boys . . . and then he would come in. He never hurried. He never sauntered. He always looked the School right in the eye as though he were looking for trouble. The quick cadence of his step was always exactly the same. His black shoes were polished. His blue suit, starched collar, white bow-tie also starched, were always exactly and precisely as expected. . . . Under his eye the School filed out to the first recitation of the day. Four hours later he dismissed the School from the same platform. He did it—no one else. . . . At dinner the School stood at their places while he asked a blessing. The blessing never varied. It was short and impersonal. His next official appearance was at supper. No matter what he had been doing during the afternoon, at supper he was back in the blue suit, white starched tie, and black shoes. He asked the blessing. The boys went from the dining room to the schoolroom and he conducted evening prayers. He stood at the desk and read from the New Testament—always. There he knelt down on his knees and read some familiar prayers. Then, when prayers were concluded, he went out in the hall; and Brooks House filed by, and said "good-night, sir;" and to each he said "good-night, my boy," and shook hands.

That was the system. So far as a casual observer could see that was all there was to it. The experts came and talked about Freud and Jung, and looked for hidden significances; and neurotic parents moaned and chattered; and nothing was ever done to change it.

That was the system. Martin wrote remembering the period prior to 1910, but it would have been true in almost exact detail in 1920 or 1930 or 1940. From 1884 to 1941 is a long time for a man to be head of a school or to be head of anything else. Peabody's "system" endured all those years because it was so simple that it never got mixed up with complicated theory. He believed

329

in character, hard work, discipline, and good manners; in the simplicity that he found in Christ.

39

FULL BLAST

E. P. *aet.* 73-83

IN 1920 people had wondered how soon the Rector would have to retire. While he was obliging with the most brilliant decade of his career they speculated that after 1930 he would be past seventy and would have to retire, and they wondered who would succeed him. In 1930 he seemed less retired than at any time anyone could remember.

For instance in the early thirties he wrote a graduate at Harvard:

I am glad to hear that you have been elected President of the Sophomore class. This is gratifying as an indication of people's caring for one, but that is of little importance compared with the opportunity for service that the position affords. . . . This gives you a chance to do much for the University at a most critical moment when there is need of loyalty and devotion. At Cambridge, as everywhere else, things are in confusion. You can do something to help to straighten them out. It occurs to me that if I were elected to this high place I should want to relate myself closely to three institutions in college.

He went on to suggest the Union, the New Houses, and the Chapel, and urged the recipient of the letter to come see him at Groton that they might talk in more detail the possibilities for good.

By way of contrast he wrote to another graduate in this period:

MY DEAR ———:

You are quite right in thinking that I am responsible for the contents of the telegram and the letter which were sent to you the other day.

The fact is we are doing our best to build up in the minds of our

330

boys a high ideal of marriage. When, therefore, it was suggested that two persons, both of whom have been divorced and lately remarried, should make a visit at the School, it struck me that their coming would confuse the minds of those who would see them at Groton. And so I suggested to Mr. Regan that it would be better to have you postpone your visit. There is no personal unfriendliness on my part. In making this decision, I am affected by what seem to me the best interests of the boys.

In regard to the coming of your boys, there would be no chance of our having a vacancy that we could offer for your stepson; for we are full for many years to come. Your boy, as the son of a graduate, would be preferred in the year for which he is entered. It may be that by that time there will be so many sons of graduates that some element of competition may enter in.

I am sorry to find myself obliged to write this letter but you ought to know the motives which actuated me in the course that I pursued.

Sincerely yours,

ENDICOTT PEABODY

At the request of the editor of the *Quarterly* he wrote in 1932 a summary of the condition of the school, in which he said:

Articles appearing in the Quarterly occasionally take the School to task for errors in teaching or in the management of the School. There can be no difficulty in finding opportunities for the criticism of our policies in the various departments of our life. The reason for discovering in these communications little to assist us in correcting our mistakes is that in many cases they come from men who have not for many years visited the School to learn about conditions here. During the last few years, we have invited to Groton experts in education, generally professors from the University, to sit in with the Classes as they have been carried on, and to talk with teachers in the various departments and with the Faculty concerning subjects and methods of instruction. We have also been inspected by members of the Board of Trustees, not only honorable but also intellectual men, and from them we have received reports which lead us to believe, not that we have attained—we should be sorry to hear that—but that they have noticed the advance in education that is being given here. One visitor of exalted office at the University remarked that he had a grudge against his College and his School (which happened to be this School) because the teaching is so much better at both places than it was in his time. When he was asked if he intended to send his son to Groton, he answered promptly, "Most certainly if the boy can get in." Please do not allow us to be misunderstood. We welcome suggestions and criticisms, but if these are to be of value, we urge that they should be made by persons who are familiar with the School in its different departments after having examined us with some care. The Masters and all others connected with the School are ready to give answers to any questions. Entire freedom to explore all portions of the School is gladly given to those who care to come. We ask simply, for the spirit of cooperation from graduates and boys; and it is generally given to us.

A slip from a daily paper has been placed on my desk which runs —"Dr. Endicott Peabody has been Headmaster of Groton fifty years; and still we suspect he does not know what those boys will think of next." The first portion of that statement is incorrect. The second is perfectly true. We do not know what all the boys will think of next; but we find that some of them at least are thinking in terms of this spirit of cooperation, trying to find ways in which the School can be improved and giving us freely and frankly their views and proposals. We hope and believe that as they understand the times in which we live, as we try to help them and ourselves to understand them, they will offer themselves as intelligent servants of the Nation and as enthusiastic fellow workers with God "whose service," as our motto runs, "leads to power."

It is interesting to compare this with a contemporary survey given by a graduate trustee which will be found in the appendix.*

To an alumnus who had asked a pointed question he replied:

22 October 1932

My dear ——:

I quite understand your feeling in regard to the School: for people are naturally wary of an institution while the personnel is in process of change. At the present time, I seem to be in excellent physical condition in spite of having come off my horse the other day (which, by the way, was due to a turning of the saddle). Just how long I shall be here, I cannot tell, but I hope to "stick it" as long as my powers continue at about the level of the last forty-eight years. Please be sure that the Staff of the School on which the teaching naturally depends is on the whole superior to anything we have known before. We had a good many visitors last year examining us, and they all expressed themselves with much enthusiasm in regard to the teaching and the teachers. And so the good work should go on whoever may be at the head. Incidentally, the Trustees, who are a pretty able lot of men, are likely to find a more than

* See Appendix.

332

worthy successor. My earnest hope is that he may a clergyman of our Church.

This and other matters we can discuss when you are next at Groton.

Affectionately yours,

E. P.

He continued most active physically:

25 November 1933

MY DEAR ———:

That gray Irish hunter is nearly all that you cracked him up to be and something more. The something more is a slightly nervous disposition which comes into play at somewhat uncomfortable times. I was riding him the other day, for instance. He met a motor which, running on cat ice, made an unpleasant noise, and the horse wheeled round and made for the ditch, and the wall. That was nothing very bad. Half an hour afterwards, however, as a perfectly harmless old-time Ford approached us he left the road and this time went down a bank and into swampy land before I could stop him.

This means, as you will readily understand, that it would not be safe for my wife or daughter to ride him and not much fun for me as I ride nowadays. If I had the time for two or three hours a day and occasionally for a run across the country, he would be splendid; but in frosty weather and with only the exercise that a groom gives him in addition to my use, he requires careful watching and prevents the pleasure that I like to take in what is called a hack. I should think that in the summer time with lots of exercise he might be perfect for anybody.

The well-intentioned graduate answered:

November 29, 1933

DEAR MR. PEABODY:—

I am awfully sorry that our horse cut up that way. He never did anything like that before that I know of. Indeed, his specialty is loping around the ring at our local horse shows with his eyes half shut and a general air of dejection which is exceedingly humiliating to the family.

There is no doubt, however, that if he is bent on entering a second childhood, he is not the horse for you and Mrs. Peabody to ride and I am, accordingly writing to the moving van man and asking him to go and get the horse and bring him home.

Both Mr. B. and Mr. G. were poorly. The faculty, which had been so stable so long, seemed in a perpetual state of flux. Between 1927 and 1933 twenty-five new names appeared on the list. Even

333

Peabody's best friends and staunchest admirers were worried. Bishop Lawrence, himself an old man and even such a one as the Rector, felt that Peabody should retire, and considered ways of bringing it about. Even he did not care to suggest it to the Rector openly, so in 1933 he wrote the Board of Trustees:

April 22, 1933

To the Board of Trustees
of Groton School—
MY DEAR SIRS: —

In the year 1883 my young friend, Endicott Peabody, asked my advice and help in planning for a boys' school which he hoped to found. Later a Board of Trustees was created of whom he and I are the only surviving members. Groton School received its charter, and in the Autumn of 1884 opened with Messrs. Peabody, Billings, and Gardner as Masters of twenty-three boys.

Ever since then, now almost half a century, my associations with the school, its Trustees, masters, boys, households, and graduates have been unalloyed joy, friendship and mutual service.

Believing, as I always have, that the younger generation should enter into their full responsibilities, I have for several years felt that I should resign but have been deterred by your kind protests. The time has now come when I should act. I therefore present herewith my resignation from the Board of Trustees to take effect on a date before the first of July most convenient to the Trustees.

Groton School has had a great Founder and Head Master in Endicott Peabody and a history happy for all connected with it.

May the spirit which has encompassed it in the past continue from generation to generation.

I remain
Faithfully yours,
WILLIAM LAWRENCE

Whereupon the Trustees, at the Rector's urging, replied:

Every Trustee recognizes that the resignation of Bishop Lawrence as Chairman of this Board marks an occasion too charged with feeling to be.the subject of formal resolutions. Each one of us realizes that even the most useful of men has the right at some time to withhold his services: and were that not always true, we are too grateful for everything which through forty-nine years Bishop Lawrence has done for the School to question his complete freedom of choice in this instance. We do not need his own letter of resignation to remind us of an official association and a personal relationship of which we know no parallel; but we do feel, each and every one of

334

us, that if the Bishop would consent to defer until the Fiftieth Anniversary of the School the resignation he now presents, this final service to Groton would be received with unmixed gratitude. It is a favor we ask. We do not demand it, but if it were granted, we should all with one heart and mind rejoice.

We further request that no answer be given to this resolution at this time.

CHARLES P. CURTIS, JR.
Secretary

And the Bishop responded:

April 26, 1932

To the Trustees of Groton School

MY DEAR FELLOW TRUSTEES:

Such a message as yours of the 22nd is as irresistible as it is gratifying. It and your friendship are of the most valued tokens in my life and I treasure them.

I bow to your superior wisdom and do as you suggest, in the hope that in the Autumn of 1934 the double team of Peabody and Lawrence may pass under the wire fresh and happy in the memories of Fifty Years of Groton School.

I remain
Your affectionately,
WILLIAM LAWRENCE

Plainly the hint had fallen on barren ground. But before this there had been sad days at Groton.

The first real break came in 1930 with the death of Mr. G. He had been poorly for a long time, but his love for the school never flagged. He saw the end coming and he, who had been so timid and so self-belittling, died quietly in 1930. There was a beautiful service in his crowded Chapel. His boys, young and old, came back. More than anything else that day was a gathering of friends. Much as the Rector loved him, it was only as time went on that the full consciousness of what Mr. G. had meant to him and the school came to him. This realization grew with separation, and the affection of nearly five decades increased with his old friend's departure. Even in death Amory Gardner remained faithful and loyal, as his unusual will showed.

After too short an interval Mr. B. went too. Like Billy Wag he had been failing for some years. The Rector encouraged him to take time off, and he spent most of a year in Florida. But the writing was on the wall, where Sherrard Billings read it with

335

One matter gave him deep satisfaction as well as an unusual privilege. When Franklin Roosevelt took office as President of the United States, he asked the Rector to bless him on his way and the Peabodys went to Washington, where, at inauguration time in March, 1933, the Rector conducted a simple service in St. John's Church opposite the White House and with all his heart prayed that the blessing of God might guide and sustain his friend and former pupil. The prayers were the Chapel prayers, and they were never said with more sincerity. Thereafter on several occasions he came again at the President's invitation. And each Christmas vacation around New Year's Day he would go to Washington to visit with Julius Atwood at the Cosmos Club, where they would hold an informal soiree at which the Rector's old boys and Uncle Bish's "swell friends" would drop in. During the day they could be seen trotting together along the street; the Rector's trot big; the Bishop's trot light.

There remained one sad and painful experience in this period, which grieved the Rector and Mrs. Peabody deeply and their friends even more deeply for them. In 1931 there had been one or two annoying depradations at Groton by unknown perpetrators, not amounting to much. One night, however, the Chapel and Rector's study were broken into, or rather simply entered, since they were never locked. The Chapel was desecrated in a minor, but mean, way and various personal belongings either ruined or taken. For instance, Mr. Gardner's silver "Milestone," given to him on completion of twenty years at Groton and after his death always used by the Rector on his own desk, was stolen. It was a foolish, apparently vindictive, and cruelly petty kind of crime, obviously done by someone who knew the place and the people in it. Investigation disclosed that the guilty ones were three college undergraduates.

The indignation of the alumni knew no bounds. There was an organized movement to prosecute the three boys. This was stopped by the Rector. He and Mrs. Peabody were deeply hurt. The nature of the thing seemed so venomous, so near not only their own hearts but the heart of the school, and so utterly foreign to anything they had ever experienced before that they were cruelly wounded. But he would not consent to answering injury with hatred. He simply asked that none of the three should come to Groton again. And the wave of affection and

336

quiet, unfaltering eyes. He came back to Groton, and ill though he was, continued on his cheerful way, until on May 9, 1933, he went over the river.

Hundreds of friends and graduates came to Groton for the service, which was conducted by the Rector, Dr. Thayer, Bishop Sherrill and Bishop Lawrence. It was estimated that nearly nine hundred were present; the throng was so great that all chairs had to be removed, and from the organ loft one looked down on a solid congregation. The Processional was "Ten Thousand Times Ten Thousand" and the Recessional the School Hymn. Every one sang and the thunder of that singing was perhaps the most impressive the Chapel ever knew. The prefects were pall-bearers, with a nephew of Mr. B., and the funeral procession passed from the path to Brooks House, where Mr. B. had spent forty-nine years, between silent ranks of boys in blue suits who flanked the drive, through the Auchincloss Gate and on to the Groton cemetery where he was buried beside his wife and daughter. The Rector read the Burial Service. Something essential in Groton had gone.

But the reminiscences came. "I never knew a man who was so beloved," wrote one. Another told how, as Mr. B. grew older, the reality of another world grew more vivid to him. "He will like it there," he told the widow of an original Groton boy. When he lost his little child shortly after his wife's death long ago, Mr. B. had said to one sympathizing with him, "Yes, yes, but Eleanor could train the little one so much better than I." Still another recalled how, when Chaplain Billings went to the bedside of a seriously wounded American soldier,* the boy grasped his hand, pulled him down and whispered Mr. B.'s favorite double dative, "Mr. Billings, the American elms are for a glory to Groton." One of the most touching tributes came from the fifty American Legion posts in Middlesex County to their good friend whom they had "loved for his many fine qualities and deeds." And one, too, from a non-Grotonian, "I am sorry he has gone. He was a great gentleman."

This second of two heavy losses was a grief to the Rector. For many, many years Billings had been his co-adjutor, counselor, and friend. It was fortunate for him and the school that he could turn to James D. Regan to fill this place, as friend, counselor, and senior master.

* Captain Archibald Roosevelt.

337

protective anger that swelled up from Groton graduates and friends everywhere must have been a large compensation.* No one ever knew what the explanation was. Some said it had been just an undergraduate or club prank. Some said the boys had been drunk or drugged. No one who knew ever gave a satisfactory explanation. But the incredible thing was that not many months later one of the three boys wrote the Rector asking him to officiate at his wedding! And the Rector did.

One of Mr. B.'s greatest interests in his last years was typical of a new trend of things at Groton. There was, over a period of years, a steady transition from the old cut-and-dried classical curriculum. Mr. B. had instituted a course in oral English, which had the Rector's approval and was popular with the boys. Work done in manual training was astonishingly good. There had been a large increase in interest and performance in art. The press, as time went on, printed all material used at school, including the *Grotonian*, the School Catalogue, and a volume of history of China written by sixth-formers one year. Mr. Lynes had given admirable piano and organ recitals for years, and at various times so-called orchestras rose and fell. But now a real orchestra was formed, with masters, boys, and neighbors. To show their ambition, the evening before Prize Day in 1933, its forty-five players gave a concert which included:

Overture: Egmont . . . . Beethoven
First Symphony, first movement . . . Beethoven
Variations on a French Folksong . . . Bizet
Overture to Zampa . . . . Herold
Andante Cantabile, for strings only . . Tschaikowski
Marche Slave . . . . Tschaikowski

Debating had always been stressed at Groton and was more than ever emphasized in these years. In addition to the compulsory societies within the school there were numerous debates with other schools in which Groton won more than its share of victories.

* At a meeting in February, 1931, the Trustees unanimously adopted the following resolution: "The Trustees here record their high appreciation of the self-restraint, patience, and wisdom of the Rector, and their sympathy with him, in this deplorable incident in the happy history of the school. They also assure him of the admiration, affection, and support of the whole body of alumni, teachers and friends of the school."

Peabody had perfected a defense against criticism and the many critics, friendly and hostile, who perpetually offered advice so generously. This was to invite the skeptic or critic to the school and turn him loose, free to look, listen, and ask questions. Most who came to scoff and demolish went away converted. What they had to say the Rector listened to, weighed, and if he judged it sensible, passed on to the faculty or trustees. He never enjoyed criticism, but he learned to put it to use.

He kept his eye for details. In addition to the big building jobs, he each year added to the external appearance of the place; putting in here a Garth by the Chapel in memory of Mr. Gladwin; a World War Memorial window in the Chapel; new athletic fields and tennis courts; building two handsome memorial gates; planting, landscaping.

While others were so worried, he was winnowing and going ahead with his work. Out of all the faculty changes he built up another permanent faculty worthy of comparison with any before, if not superior in promise, and with a high percentage of younger men who each year gathered experience under him. These newcomers were fortified by the veterans and near veterans: Sturgis, Griswold, Richards, Regan, Andrews, Call, Lynes, Thomas, Zahner, Cushing, Jorgenson, Nash, DeVeau, were, in order of seniority, the rocks on which he built.

And he confounded his critics by a burst of brilliant achievement. Better work was done at the school than ever before; college entrance records soared to new heights; undergraduate performance was outstanding. His building program was completed. His board of trustees was as strong as ever. As he approached the fifty-year mark his school seemed more successful than it had ever been in the past. His early boys were grandfathers now, and grandsons were appearing on school lists.

He himself was vigorous and hearty. Graduates vacationing in Bermuda at Eastertime were delighted to encounter a couple bicycling sturdily along; he perhaps in flannels or knickers, the Madam looking like the turn of the century and yet, astoundingly, smarter than and as pretty as any young thing on the beach, with a goodness and wisdom and dignity in her face that no young girl could ever have. Sometimes in the summer, as of old, they went abroad. He could be seen of a London summer's day coming out of Brown's Hotel, very natty and healthy in his brand new gray fedora, blue shirt, and gray suit. In 1932, crossing on the steamer, a former master asked them where they were going. To Lucerne. Why Lucerne? "Cotty rows," answered Mrs. Peabody simply.

Two letters give his views on Prohibition at this time:

July 19, 1935

MY DEAR MR. ――――:

Many thanks for your letter of the 17th and for your patience with one who may be called a "Doubting Thomas". No one had suggested to me that you had in mind "teaching young people how to drink". I was perfectly certain of your good faith and being interested in this difficult problem I desired to do all I could to help you. That is certainly the case and I want to work with all who are striving for temperance, especially among the young.

As I wrote you, I have not been a teetotaler except during the war and while the Prohibition Amendment was part of the Constitution, and I recognize the fact that people will never give up drinking. My hope has been that we could reduce the drinking of hard liquor by laying stress upon beer and light wines. That was almost the battle cry of the Prohibitionists. I always question their sincerity about this for I realize that hard liquor was the national tipple. Now the liquor dealers and distillers are making almost frantic efforts to increase their sales of whiskey, gin, etc., and I am glad to join with people who are in earnest in their determination to thwart them.

I shall be much interested to know about the progress of your work for which you have my best wishes.

Sincerely yours,
ENDICOTT PEABODY

30 July 1935

MY DEAR MR. ――――:

I am enclosing with this a cheque for $10. being a repetition of my February contribution.

Like you, I was impressed by the inherent weakness of the Moderation Society. I so wrote the secretary and pointed out to him that in my judgment there were names on his Committee that were associated with the breaking of the Prohibition law, and in some instances with excessive drinking. I suggested that temperance was a term which had some driving force.

Before Prohibition, I was a member of the Temperance Society of our Church, to which total abstainers and persons who counted themselves friends of temperance but had not entirely foresworn the use of alcoholic liquor belonged. Personally, I was brought up in England and have been in the habit of taking wine at my father's table and of offering it to others on occasions at my own. I realize the violent efforts of the liquor people to force their products upon society, especially upon young people; and I try to persuade our boys as they graduate to use only beer and light wine. There would be no use in counselling complete abstinence in many cases, although I point out that it is advisable during college days. I emphasize strongly the drinking of cocktails, which has lately become such a general habit, counting this the worst possible way in which to drink. I refuse these mixtures myself; and I am hoping that my words may have some influence among those with whom I am brought into contact.

It may be that my view seems inconsistent with yours. If so, I shall be sorry; for I like to cooperate with all who are making an effort to bring about temperance in this country.

Sincerely yours,
ENDICOTT PEABODY

Often he found himself in disagreement with his old boys, but it was very seldom that differences of opinion meant any break in friendship. A graduate who was editor of a left-wing magazine visited the school somewhat hesitantly with his wife. After the visit he wrote:

You must have realized how touched I was by your warm-hearted welcome of us over last weekend. I have, of course, all sorts of pleasant memories of Groton. . . . I was all the less prepared for any special cordiality, because of the fact that my work and social views have made me critical of private schools, in so far as they cater to a special class in society, and a critical attitude is usually reciprocated. You can see then why I was quite overcome by your kindness. . . . Instead of being merely an occasion for reviving pleasant memories, it was one for learning something new about people's capacity for being generous and affectionate, and for instilling these qualities into a whole institution.

Peabody wrote back:

I like to know about all the brothers.* . . . Personally I should like to have you come to talk to us. My policy has been to have the boys informed of the characteristics of the times both by study and by lecture, but I have been rather careful to have the subjects treated by people—conservatives and radicals—who do not hold what seem to me excessive views, otherwise we might easily be thought to be aiming at impressing youth by means of propaganda.

* Seven of them had gone to Groton.

I think you will understand. Please be sure of my admiration for your unselfish devotion to a great cause even if I may not agree with you in regard to details.

Affectionately,

ENDICOTT PEABODY

In 1936 he answered a graduate who was an artist:

15 January 1936

MY DEAR ———:

I welcome your letter in the new number of the Groton School Quarterly; for it expresses in some ways the kind of thing that I have had in mind for a long time. I am encouraged by it to know that you are interested in beautifying our environment, and I am ready to hope that you will lend a hand in helping to improve it.

As I examine the catalogues and prospectuses of other Schools I find examples of accomplishment of a really remarkable nature in some cases, especially in the progressive schools for children. I want to get you to examine some of these schools—one in Cambridge, the Shady Hill School, and the Beaver Country Day School in Brookline. From them you could get a notion of what is possible where there is enthusiasm and hope. Then you might come to Groton and see what we are doing in our instruction in Art.

Lately there has been given to us the Carnegie Art Collection consisting of a large number of books, photographs, and colored prints covering in a way the whole history of Art. Later we are to receive an equally complete history of Music accompanied by many records and a victrola of the best type. The latter will be placed in a room which has been lately done over as a subsidiary to the Library, where we already have the Art Collection. You might have suggestions as to the best way in which to tow the brethren into this library. Furthermore, you might give us the value of your advice regarding the decoration of the School building. My idea has always been to keep things simple at Groton, but I wanted to have buildings that were excellent in form and specimens of the best Art, such as we have, hung upon the walls of the Schoolhouse.

Andover has, as you point out, a remarkable collection of pictures in a beautiful Art Gallery. This might be a thing for us to aim at. In general, the additions to the buildings at Andover, as well as at the Universities, seem to me dangerously near to the point of luxury. We have a goodly legacy from the Payne Whitney estate. The income of this has been largely appropriated for masters' salaries, and I have purposely refrained from laying out a great deal of money on the plant. This still seems to me the wise policy to pursue, but it is not inconsistent with a certain decoration of the buildings and an attempt to collect furniture which can have the qualities of beauty as well as of simplicity.

I hope that my plea for help may find an echo in your heart; for I feel confident that you can be of great assistance to us in this important addition to our contribution to the lives of your successors.

Affectionately yours,

E. P.

His interests were varied:

13 November 1937

MY DEAR MRS. HAWKRIDGE:

I am glad to have you use my name as that of a State Sponsor of the Birth Control League of Massachusetts. The treatment which the League has received by the Massachusetts authorities seems wholly unjustifiable.

Sincerely yours,

ENDICOTT PEABODY

He wired the Boston *Sunday Advertiser* in 1938: "It is of vital importance that Jews and all Christians should under God work together for righteousness and right in a world which is distraught rather than what you speak of as atheistical." In a similar vein he wired Rabbi Herman Rubenovitz: "Sympathize deeply with you in your effort to persuade the British government to retain their mandate of Palestine. Their withdrawal of this would mean a disaster to the world as well as to the Jewish people."

The publication of a book on a boarding school led him to write Dr. Nash, the headmaster of St. Paul's, on that and other topics:

3 April, 1940

MY DEAR NORMAN:

What a mess the Tribune and the author of *Winter Term* have made between them! One's first impulse is to protest to the Herald-Tribune for their want of insight into things. That might possibly bring about a correspondence which might somehow get before the public and result in a newspaper disputation in which people like the author of Winter Term and those responsible for the Herald-Tribune perhaps delight. The wise thing, therefore, would seem to let the thing go by without paying attention to its foolishness.

Incidentally, the report of the book that reaches me suggests that it is unsound in its presentation of a school or schools. The report here is that it is the outcome of the imagination of a person who was

343

as a boy expelled from St. Mark's School. Whether or not that be true, it seems to be evident that he has some sort of a grudge against private schools, in general and church schools, I fancy, in particular. Poor, unwholesome stuff like that is likely to die an early and dishonored death.

What interests me more at the present moment is the report in the paper of yesterday that the appointment of Earl Russell has been cancelled by the authorities of the College of the City of New York. That brought me a sense of relief until I read further that Russell was to be invited to take some part in teaching at Harvard.

You have probably seen extracts from the books for which he is responsible. In these books, he openly advocates the doing away with morality. An excuse for Russell is made that he is correct in his life. One does not know anything about that. The serious thing is that a man with such unsound views should as a teacher be allowed to be brought into contact with college students.

If this be true, it seems to me to call for action on the part of all who are interested in the welfare of youth, especially the authorities of private schools and even more particularly those of church schools which care first of all for the character of their students. One can hardly imagine a more poisonous influence brought to bear upon the minds of young men than the stuff which is presented by Russell as philosophy.

If it be true, this report of Russell's having an appointment at Harvard, ought we not to take a positive attitude and if necessary action in regard to it?

An affectionate message from my wife and myself to all of you.
Ever sincerely yours,
ENDICOTT PEABODY

When a Groton graduate who had been prominent in life was sent to jail, the Rector took long journeys to visit him and wrote him regularly. When someone expressed wonder that he should do so, Peabody said, "He did wrong, but he has paid the penalty. He needs help and friendship and is entitled to a fresh start."

And to Bishop Atwood he wrote in 1941:

There is really encouragement for us in the positions which many of our boys are holding in public life. There are three Grotonians at the most important places in diplomacy, Japan, Canada and Greece; in the State Department Dean Acheson has already found a place, he is next to Sumner Welles and very near to Franklin. A good many of the political offices are held by our boys, while scholastically, one of our men, Thayer Addison, is vice-president of

344

the Missionary Society; Alexander Zabriskie is Dean of Virginia
Seminary; seven of them are headmasters of schools; and a good
many of them are teaching, just ordinary schoolmasters, who, I may
say, incidentally wield in many cases as much influence as those
who are in charge.

40

E.P. AND F.D.R.

THE rise of Franklin D. Roosevelt was naturally of great
interest to Peabody. The family friendship went far
back. The future president himself had graduated from
Groton, where he had had a satisfactory but not outstanding
career, in 1900. He had kept up his interest in the school, and his
four sons went there, James, the eldest, graduating in 1926 and
John, the youngest in 1934. One of them, Franklin, Jr., had been
senior prefect. Franklin Roosevelt, Sr., had for years given a debating prize.

When it became clear that he was likely to be President of the
United States, his connection with Groton involved the Rector
as his former headmaster. People wanted to know what sort of a
person Roosevelt was; what sort of a boy and father he had
been. Was the Rector going to vote for him? Peabody's position
in 1932 is given clearly in a letter to Ellery Sedgwick:

7 November, 1932

MY DEAR ELLERY:

The situation is not as serious as it has been described. To quote
you from another occasion—"It never is." There is no truth whatever in the remark that our "Faculty is as a unit against Governor
Roosevelt". We never do anything of that kind as a unit. As a matter of fact, most of the Masters will be voting the Republican ticket.
Several are voting for Roosevelt. Just who they are, in either case,
I do not know. We do not all tell each other what ticket we favor
and we certainly never consider the matter as a Faculty.

Personally I am expecting to cast my vote for Hoover on the
ground that he is in my judgment an abler man and that he has put

into action policies which seem to me likely to relieve the economic tension in this country. I do not consider personal relations when I am casting my vote for a Government official. It seems to me immoral to do so, in line with the bad traditions of politicians who are always ready to do personal favors for their friends. Franklin I am very fond of, have been ever since he was a small boy. I have been in close touch with him ever since he left School, married him, and have done what we could for his boys at Groton. Incidentally, his third son, Franklin, is now Senior Prefect and is filling the position with remarkable ability.

Franklin was at Groton yesterday week. After dinner, I spoke to the boys, suggesting to them that on Sunday we put aside all questions of partisanship and on this Sunday welcome Franklin Roosevelt as a distinguished Grotonian. I pointed out that on that day we had outstanding Grotonians, representing the ministry, teaching, School, government, and public life. I reminded the boys that it was our constant effort to persuade our graduates to take an interest in politics with a view to service to the Nation; and I asked Franklin to speak to us on this subject. I also assured him on behalf of the School that if he was elected, as seemed not improbable, he could be quite sure that we should claim a bit of honor for Groton and that we should back him to the limit in loyalty and love. Afterwards, Franklin had Coffee in my study with the Masters with whom he chatted in a friendly fashion and departed apparently understanding the situation as we do.

This was amplified a few weeks later to another graduate:

19 December, 1932
MY DEAR ———:

There has been a good deal written about Franklin Roosevelt when he was a boy at Groton, more than I should have thought justified by the impression that he left at the school. He was a quiet, satisfactory boy of more than ordinary intelligence, taking a good position in his Form but not brilliant. Athletically he was rather too slight for success. We all liked him. So far as I know that is true of the masters and boys alike. I have always been fond of him, following his career with much interest and keeping in close touch with him in connection with his boys, for he is an excellent father and keen for the best things for his sons.

I voted for Hoover, thinking that he was the best man in the country to deal with the economic questions and counting it wise for him to have a chance to carry out the policies which he had inaugurated. Now that Franklin has been elected, we shall of course back him up and hope that with a Congress that is in sympathy with the President more can be accomplished than was possible when Congress was inclined to oppose the head of the Government, as has been the case during these last years. While Roosevelt is not in my judgment a particularly aggressive person, I believe that when he is convinced that a thing should be done he has courage to put it through. This was shown in his dealing with Walker. He did a great thing for the country when he dealt with Walker in such a way that the man felt himself compelled to resign. Looking at it in the large, I am distinctly hoping for progress during the coming Administration.

My kindest regards, please, to your Father and Mother.

Affectionately yours,

ENDICOTT PEABODY

Peabody watched with great interest and growing satisfaction the vast political events of the early thirties, and his understandable pride in having a Groton graduate in the White House changed gradually to admiration for what the President was doing and trying to do. He had been profoundly touched at being asked to hold the service at St. John's Church in Washington just before the President began his first term. He counted it a blessing that he was able to return several times for the same purpose. In 1935 he wrote:

MY DEAR FRANKLIN:

In replying to your letter that was addressed to some of the ministers of the country, I want to assure you of my lasting conviction that you have one supreme purpose in mind, the guidance of this country in such a way that all its citizens who are minded to do honest work shall have a chance to secure a living free from anxiety and with an opportunity for the development of which they are capable.

My knowledge of economic principles is not sufficient to enable me to form an adequate judgment of all the policies of your government, but I am quite prepared to believe that many of them are wise; and I have seen the beneficent result of some of them. I believe in the Social Securities Acts and I find admirable results of the working of the C.C.C. in evidence as I drive through the country. I wish that I were sufficiently equipped to take up your plans seriatim. I refrain from doing so, as I trust you will understand, not from a lack of interest but from an inadequate education in this particular. I do most heartily rejoice that there should be throughout the land a greater emphasis laid upon the duty of the citizen to the community and this even among those who were formerly considering only their own interests.

347

The counterfeit presentment of yourself together with the letter which you were good enough to write me the other day is now hung upon the walls of the Schoolhouse. I rejoice in the possession of it for the School. Every day all present Groton boys will pass it and many of them will be, I am sure, inspired by the thought that a former Groton boy is now at the head of the government of their country.

The memory of the brief and personal Service that we had together at St. John's Church on the day of your inauguration is an abiding pleasure to me. Personally, I rejoiced in joining with you in prayer for strength which you would need in meeting the solemn responsibilities of your office. This Service, unbeknownst to you no doubt, seems to have made a deep impression upon the minds of people all through the country and many were strengthened in their faith by your example. It is a great thing for our country to have before it the leadership of a man who cares primarily for spiritual things. At a time when the minds of men are distraught and their faith unsteady, a spiritual leader at the head of the nation brings fresh power to the individual and to the cause of Christ and His Church.

I venture to think that your going to Church means more to the people throughout the land than almost anything else that you can do. It has an influence first upon the members of your family, who will naturally attend Service when father is there. To us in this School, it is a great thing to be able to point to a Groton graduate, now in the highest position in the country, believing in the Church and devoted to its interests. While to the country at large, both to believers and non-believers, it means a lead which a great company will follow as they would not be inclined to do if you had shown indifference to the greatest thing in the world. Ever since the day on which I was ordained in a year that is now far-off, I have thought that the guiding principle of a man's life should be the motive which Jesus revealed as His fundamental purpose: "For their sakes, I sanctify myself that they also may be sanctified through the truth", and I do most heartily congratulate you that you have such an opportunity to carry out this great purpose in your own life with a view to inspiring a mighty company of your fellow-countrymen.

Always your affectionate friend,

ENDICOTT PEABODY

His approval of the President, however, was not always shared by other Grotonians. For example he received this in 1936:

DEAR MR. PEABODY:

After the indictment of Franklin's Administration which the summing up of the record more clearly shows every day, I feel that I must write you in view of our last conversation. There has been such an accumulation of authenticated evidence which bears out the suspicions which I have for long harbored, that I am convinced that the perpetuation of the Administration in office constitutes a real menace to the country. I feel that I must tell you this for I frankly am much upset over your support of an administration which so lacks in sincerity of purpose. And I hate to think of the confusion of mind of the boys growing up under your influence and guidance in trying to reconcile all the government's insincerity of the past four years with the idealism which they are told to look for back of it all. How can the boys reconcile the shocking and venal methods of Jim Farley with the idealism which they have been taught marches hand in hand with a great cause?

I have known Franklin for more years even than you and I have always felt that his lack of sincerity has been the weak point in his character. It was the reason for my strong opposition to his nomination and election four years ago, and it is evidently this same trait in him which has alienated from him the support of so many of the leaders with integrity of mind of both great parties. For certainly he commanded their support in abundant measure at the start, and the support of all of us who wished him success in his arduous undertaking.

I feel that we must face the facts at this election, perhaps as never before, and that we cannot separate the candidate from the record, for upon the record he must be judged.

With love to you and Mrs. Peabody.

Affectionately yours,

———

To which he responded:

MY DEAR ———:

Thank you for your letter of the 19th of October. Believing as you do, it was a friendly act on your part to give me the warning that you felt that I should have.

This is evidently a situation in which you and I do not see eye to eye. I am not at all convinced of Franklin's insincerity. He was at Groton for four years, and so far as I can remember there was no suspicion of untruthfulness or insincerity during his entire course; nor did I hear of anything against his reputation at the University. I am therefore inclined to give him the benefit of my faith in him at the present time.

349

I do certainly bar the head of the National Democratic Committee. Farley seems to me to have done and to be doing much harm in disregarding the principles of Civil Service reform which we hoped for during many years. I suppose that in 1933 a large majority of the offices were filled by Republicans. That does not excuse the flouting of Civil Service regulations; but I suppose it did supply a challenge to the Democrats. It interested me to learn that Trubee Davison, who is of course a thorough-going Republican, likes Farley. He regards him as a politician, but he counts him an honest man for whom he has a distinctly friendly feeling.

The right course in political life must be very difficult to discover and pursue. You may have read of the censure which was visited upon Theodore Roosevelt because he saw fit to consult with Senator Platt, who was counted one of the worst Republican highwaymen of his time. That does not change my view of Farley. It is simply an indication of the kind of things to which the political world has been accustomed in these years.

At the time Franklin Roosevelt became President, things were in the worst kind of doldrums owing to the inefficiency of Mr. Hoover as President. Change of a drastic nature was called for, and Franklin answered the call. Some of his policies have been mistaken. He prophesied that they would be. Others are of doubtful value. Many have in my judgment contributed to the benefit of the people at large and have saved this country from the serious attacks made upon it by extreme radicals. I venture to attribute to him the economic improvement which is in evidence throughout the country.

It is chiefly in connection with international affairs that I count it important that Franklin should be re-elected. Being a good neighbor, a phrase which has perhaps become hackneyed now, has done much to create a friendly feeling towards the United States; while the Tri-Partite Agreement between France, Great Britain, and this country in regard to money seems to me to promise more than anything that has been done during the late years and to have the hope of possibly averting a war which threatens. In this I agree with Mr. Warburg and with one of the leading business men of Wall Street, who stated that in his opinion the arrangement was the greatest thing that had been achieved for years.

The greatest danger to the world at the present time comes from economic confusion. I am not at all persuaded that Landon would be of service here. He seems to promise great financial saving in the East. At the same time, he assures the farmers in the West that they are going to be dealt with most generously if he becomes President. He may be an honest and good man. I know very little about him except that he has been a worthy citizen and as Governor he balanced the budget of Kansas; but he has had no experience in inter-

350

national matters, and he seems to be just a rather commonplace man who might easily be guided by the people who desire to revert to the good old times. Many of our people are looking forward to something better under the leadership of this President.

For the Constitution, I see no harm in Franklin's counting it important to ask for Amendments in regard to the policies in which he believes. That indeed is what the Republicans themselves are asking in regard to at least two laws in which they believe and which have been found unconstitutional.

The insincerity of which you speak in your letter is abundantly evident in the case of men who now profess a deep respect for the Constitution and who at the time that the Eighteenth Amendment was a part of it did not hesitate to break it ruthlessly or, what was still worse, hire men to do so. I am afraid that among these lawless persons are found many people in public life today. The opinions of such men in regard to the Constitution seem to me negligible.

It would not be worth while for us to enter upon a prolonged discussion of matters political. I have thrown off these few thoughts which have been working in my mind since your letter arrived in order that you may know something of what I am thinking.

With love for ——— and her good husband, I am

Affectionately yours,
ENDICOTT PEABODY

We can trace his continuing relationship with the President in a final series of letters written between 1936 and 1942. To Bishop Atwood:

Groton, January 27th, 1936

I wonder if you heard Smith's broadcast denunciation of the policies of the present Government? I did not care much for his spirit, and there seemed to me not much that was new in his address. I must however confess that the financial policy of the President gives me some concern. It is almost universally condemned by business men and by many economists. Roosevelt's purpose, of giving a chance to all the people of this country to live in decency and fair comfort, appeals to me very strongly, but I am not sure that the method employed is not too short a cut for so great a change. I do wish that Franklin had not denounced big business men as a class. There is a dreadful amount of dishonesty in Wall Street and what resembles it in other cities; but one knows that there is also a large percentage of the men who are honorable and fair in their judgment. Smith was naturally quick to criticise Franklin's characterization of the whole class.

351

The White House

February 10, 1936

DEAR MR. PEABODY:

If you had not sent me a birthday card I should have been really worried. Do you know that I have every one of them that you have sent me since the earliest days after I graduated? My love to you both. I hope you will have a very happy and successful time in Bermuda. I myself hope to get off on a destroyer the end of March for about ten days in the Bahamas.

Affectionately,

FRANKLIN D. ROOSEVELT

The White House
Washington

Warm Springs, Georgia
April 25, 1940

MY DEAR MR. PEABODY—

More than forty years ago you said, in a sermon in the old Chapel, something about not losing boyhood ideals in later life. Those were Groton ideals—taught by you—I try not to forget—and your words are still with me and with hundreds of others of "us boys". My love to you and to Mrs. Peabody

Affectionately yours,

FRANKLIN D. ROOSEVELT

3 May, 1940

MY DEAR FRANKLIN:

A thousand thanks for your generous proposal to contribute again the Prizes for the Debating Societies. The books are on their way Grotonward. When they arrive, we shall send them on to you for your much valued autograph.

I am enclosing with this a copy of a letter which I sent to our representatives in Washington; for I want to assure you that we, Mrs. Peabody and I and other members of the Faculty, are wholly behind you in the policy which you advocate touching our relations to Japan.

Affectionately yours,

ENDICOTT PEABODY

7 June, 1940

MY DEAR FRANKLIN:

You are certainly a wonderful Being! Here are the Debating Prizes returned to us with your autograph in each of them and that in a shorter time than we could have hoped for even from a gentle-

352

man of leisure. Indeed, we are most grateful for your attention and your generosity. The boys will treasure the volumes all their lives.

Please be sure of my constant sympathy and Mrs. Peabody's in the almost numberless grave problems which come to you day by day and which you are endeavoring to solve with high wisdom and magnificent courage.

Our love and prayers are always with you.

Affectionately yours,

ENDICOTT PEABODY

June 3, 1940

MY DEAR MR. PEABODY:

I have received your letter of May 23, 1940, with regard to suggested measures which you and other members of the Groton School Community believe should be adopted by the United States in the face of the present crisis.

I need not, of course, assure you that any suggestions or expressions of opinion coming from you and from your associates at Groton will always receive the utmost consideration from me.

I am deeply conscious of the great responsibilities resting on this country in the present dark hour of the world's history. I am also convinced that the people of the United States will not fail in upholding, and, if necessary in defending, the ideals which have made their nation great.

Affectionately yours,

FRANKLIN D. ROOSEVELT

Arizona Inn
Tucson, Arizona
January 4, 1941

MY DEAR FRANKLIN:

I did so hate to give up the thought of being with you at the service on the 20th. I have greatly enjoyed the privilege of helping you to start each term with fresh dedication. You may be sure that I shall be with you in spirit on that day and shall ask that you may be given wisdom and strength to carry on the great service for the country and for the world which rests upon your shoulders.

I am thankful that I was allowed to have some part in your life in the early years and that I have had the privilege of journeying along with you in friendship rejoicing that you have tried faithfully to carry out the high ideals that God has set before you.

We have come back to Tucson with a view to getting rid of a certain stiffness of the back which has bothered us. I can rejoice that we may settle in our new house at Groton prepared to do some

worthwhile work, that we may indeed turn "sunset into sunrise" as some one said the other day.
Our dear love to Eleanor and her husband.
God bless you both.

Affectionately your friend,
ENDICOTT PEABODY

Hyde Park, New York
January 11, 1941
DEAR MR. PEABODY:

Many thanks for your letter of January fourth. I, too, am greatly disappointed that you had to give up the thought of being with us at the service on the twentieth. But I shall be recompensed in part if you and Mrs. Peabody derive benefit from your stay in Tucson.

Let us hope you will both return to Groton with real zest for life in your new home there. Wherever your lot is cast I am certain you will both find worthwhile things to do.

I am deeply touched by your reference to the old days at Groton. I count it among the blessings of my life that it was given to me in formative years to have the privilege of your guiding hand and the benefit of your inspiring example. Nor am I unmindful of all that your counsel and friendship have meant as we have journeyed along together through so many years. For all that you have been and are to me I owe a debt of gratitude which I love to acknowledge. Eleanor joins me in fondest love to you and Mrs. Peabody.

Ever affectionately yours,
FRANKLIN D. ROOSEVELT

The University Club
1 West 54th Street
December 11, 1941
MY DEAR FRANKLIN:

I was in Washington on Tuesday and wanted to tell you in person how I rejoiced in the message that you gave to our American people at that time.

It was magnificent—and will do more than anything else could have done to steady us all and give us confidence in final victory.

I am thankful that you have been given the power to lead us at this time.

With love in which Mrs. Peabody joins me and with a blessing for you and for the superb service you are carrying on for the Nation and for the World
I am,

Affectionately your friend,
ENDICOTT PEABODY

December 12, 1941

DEAR MR. PEABODY: —

Your letter helps. Things are rather hectic but I think we shall settle down into the stride of a long war.

My love to you both,

Affectionately,

FRANKLIN D. ROOSEVELT

Seminole Hotel
Winter Park
Florida
March 20, 1942

MY DEAR FRANKLIN:

It was a joy to take part in the anniversary service and to lunch with you on the fourth of March.

Continuing our journey we arrived in Winter Park where we have been comfortably established ever since. Last week we saw the Review "You can defend America" acted at the Municipal Auditorium in Orlando.

The Play was admirably performed by a large company of amateurs who are giving themselves to what seems to me to be a power for good at this time. Their enthusiasm and earnestness appealed strongly to the great audience which thronged the auditorium and elicited a hearty response from the representatives of all the classes that were there.

I was especially pleased to find that the play stands for the unity of the nation and for the development of the moral and spiritual ideals for which you have so consistently aimed during these last nine years.

I feel sure that it will be an encouragement to you to know of the progress of this service which is being recognized throughout the country and is proving a strong influence in cooperation with your life work.

With love for you and Eleanor in which Mrs. Peabody joins me, I am,

Affectionately yours,

ENDICOTT PEABODY

March 25, 1942

DEAR MR. PEABODY:

I was delighted, as always, to have your fine letter and hope you and Mrs. Peabody are having a restful stay in Florida. I was particularly happy that your plans permitted your participation in the anniversary service again this year.

What you write about the revue "You Can Defend America",

which you saw in Orlando, interested me very much. We need more things like that to maintain and strengthen the national morale. I am informed that this revue has been organized by a group of volunteer actors on a non-commercial basis. This organization, as I understand it, goes from one community to another as arrangements are made for their appearance by some group active in national defense. From all accounts they are making a splendid contribution to patriotism and I hope a large number of communities will have the benefit of witnessing a performance.

If Eleanor were here she would join me in love to you and Mrs. Peabody.

Affectionately yours,
FRANKLIN D. ROOSEVELT

[Post Card]
Groton School, Groton, Massachusetts
Jan. 27–42

MY DEAR FRANKLIN:

A hearty greeting for the 30th. Best good wishes for your new year. In the midst of all the turmoil it is grand to know that you are at the helm and, with God's help, will guide us to the haven where we would be.

Affectionately yours,
ENDICOTT PEABODY

February 9, 1942

DEAR MR. PEABODY:

One of these days you must bring me your very own self for one of my birthday parties instead of sending a card. You know, however, how much I appreciate—and all of us do—the birthday postal card.

Give my love to Mrs. Peabody and tell her I want to see the new house just as soon as I possibly can.

Affectionately yours,
FRANKLIN D. ROOSEVELT

41
FIFTY YEARS ON

E. P. *aet.* 78

OF COURSE plans were afoot for the Fiftieth Anniversary in the spring of 1934. Invitations were sent to all the graduates and many friends. The great occasion was to begin on Prize Day and run to Sunday afternoon. A volume, *Fifty Years On*, telling briefly the story of the school had been prepared amidst considerable doubt by the Rector and Bishop Lawrence as to its nature.

Congratulatory messages poured in from other schools: St. Mark's; St. Paul's; the Boston public schools, especially the public Latin and English High Schools, old and friendly athletic rivals; Lawrence Academy. He also received a signal formal honor when the Board of Regents of the University of the State of New York conferred upon him the honorary degree of doctor of humane letters (L.H.D.) at the annual university Convocation held on October 17, 1935. He was the first independent school man to receive this carefully guarded and sparingly awarded recognition.

The *Quarterly* published the following autumn a full account of the proceedings:

Morning school was carried on as usual until 10, at which time it was dismissed that it might witness the arrival of the President, due at the Bacon Gate at 10:30. He was unavoidably detained . . . when he had found his place in the Chapel the School Hymn was sung and the Service unfolded as arranged. The auditorium (called thus on State occasions only; it is ordinarily the Hall) has never been so full as it was for the exercises of graduation. . . . The Rector opened the meeting, and after greeting the guests he reviewed briefly the school year and the records of graduates now in college. Some of the items concerning the growth of boys amused the multitude. . . . "Assuming the average height and weight to be typical . . . then the average I former will leave the School at the end of his VI form year . . . with a gain of 8.4 inches in height and 52.5 pounds of weight . . . some 3.5 inches taller and from 12 to 15 pounds heavier than the average American. Tests have been taken that show nearly

357

all the increase in weight takes place during the school terms and that many boys lose weight during the Christmas and Easter vacations . . . a VI former, making a gain of four pounds during the School year, loses five pounds in the short vacations" . . . then the Rector introduced the speaker of the day, Abbott Lawrence Lowell, President Emeritus of Harvard. His theme was the need of maximum men to-day. It was a most thoughtful address, spoken with calm conviction, and couched in English that many men aim at and few achieve. Bishop Lawrence followed Mr. Lowell, and his remarks added that personal and very human touch that makes Groton a family rather than an institution. Then came the awarding of prizes, graciously presented by Mrs. Peabody to the various winners. . . . At this point the visitors were bidden to luncheon in the dining room, and the undergraduates disappeared completely . . . for the next two days they were difficult to uncover . . . their meals were taken in the baseball cage, they slept on army cots in the vast gymnasium, they played when and where they could, and they most assuredly played the game to the nth. Over the week-end not one single blackmark was given, not one demerit recorded. Literally the School was on its pluperfect behavior. . . . To luncheon, then, went the crowd, after the President had taken his place on the dais in the dining room . . . the Fort Devens Military Band played music for us during that hour and later at the track meet. That afternoon was ostensibly devoted to wandering about without any pre-conceived route in mind, and it amounted to a constant handshaking party for everyone.

In the evening the Graduates held an informal dinner at the Groton Hunt Club. . . . About 230 men were present for the dinner. To the Rector and Mrs. Peabody, as well as to Bishop Lawrence, 50-year milestones were presented by the Trustees, represented by Redmond Cross '92. . . . Between speeches there was singing . . . and it was by no means grim. Led by the School Glee Club (which Gordon Bell [the Toastmaster] confused with the Fife and Drum Corps) the music went with vim . . . we warmed up with the great school song 'Forty Years On'. It was a happy party. . . .

In the still watches of the night some Graduate with a sophomoric sense of humor . . . climbed laboriously up the great stairs in the Schoolhouse, swarmed up the covered ladder to the tower where hangs 'the outside' and removed the clapper of the bell. . . . Furthermore, he left behind him his pipe . . . the Rector is eager to return the pipe to its owner.

A boiling hot day . . . Chapel at 9:30; there's a record for you. . . . During the morning there was a baseball game between two teams of Graduates in which both sides won by a decisive score. Luncheon was at 1:15 and a crowded affair, at which, by common consent,

358

cigarettes were lighted during the serving of demi-tasse. The Rector announced at the close of the meal that photographs of the Graduates would be taken outside the Hundred House and that smoking was permitted—on the steps! . . .

There was much surprise and delight at the number and variety of the exhibits in the Schoolhouse, and Graduates declared that in the old days such things were never thought of. The Physics laboratory produced amazement with its electric eyes, its experiments in thermodynamics and its numberless examples of class work. In the Chemistry laboratory there were varied experiments in constant operation, and in the Biology room were magnificent charts of the labors of the year, an active young zoo (peopled with fish, birds, bugs, and reptiles) and some incredible exhibits of micro-photography. The press had on view examples of its fine work in printing, and the lower hall was inhabited by desks, chairs, and other useful and ornamental furniture, all made by boys in the woodworking classes.

Mrs. Peabody entertained the Graduates and their wives at tea, and there was a goodly company assembled. At 6 o'clock there was an organ recital in the Chapel.

The seating arrangement for the Graduates' Dinner was done to the queen's taste. Tables filled the dining room, ran out into the hall, turned down V form corridor and entered every study available. The first form to graduate from Groton was there 100% strong, and he was seated at the head table with the speakers. The other forms were arranged in chronological order, with 1911 the most youthful in the dining room. The caterer had prepared for 600 guests. . . . We sat down to dinner 598 strong.

After dinner the old dining room was filled to bursting. Chairs were turned round and every corner of space seemed filled. Gordon Bell was again toastmaster, as he had been so many times in the past. One of the younger graduates spoke first, saying in part:

Mr. Toastmaster, Mr. President, Bishop Lawrence and Gentlemen:
You will forgive me if I speak to you with a certain amount of diffidence. There are only two reasons for my saying anything to-night at all; one is that I am young and can perhaps say a few things that the younger generation of Grotonians would like to have said, the other that I am a schoolmaster, and as such can lay at least a sprig of fresh laurel at the feet of one of the finest schoolmasters that has ever lived and his companions in achievement.

I daresay that I first heard of Groton at a greater distance than most of you. I was a sub-first former at Baguio School (at the very least a foster-child of Groton) in the Philippines. There was a master there named Malcolm Peabody. . . . I remember that one day I walked into that master's study and saw two things on his table, the first was an interesting looking magazine called *The Grotonian;* the other was a photograph of a family group taken in front of a brick building at a school in Massachusetts.

It was several years later that I became a part of that family. I got off the Worcester train and into the horse-drawn barges with the rest of the School old and new. We came into Hundred House hall and shook hands for the first time with the Rector and Mrs. Peabody. I thought then that he was just about the finest and most impressive thing I had ever seen and she the loveliest and gentlest. That was one instance, at any rate, in which my boyhood judgment was good.

It would be unfair to say I was not warned of the dangers of Groton. I was warned. Everywhere I kept meeting people who cautioned me about polo ponies and the luxurious life I would lead, the lazy, indolent life of the sons of the idle rich. I was apprehensive, though perplexed that I should be regarded as a suitable financial addition, but after I had washed a few years in the gleaming soapstone sinks with no hot water, and used the beautiful solid tin basins with their quaint colonial simplicity, and enjoyed the spacious vistas in the sybaritic dormitories, and after I had spent my princely twenty cents a week (I always begrudged the dime that I suspected went to Chinamen whose need was far less than mine) after a walk of a mere four miles, and had kept the delicious food in my shoe locker hidden in a rubber, and had enjoyed the invigorating briskness of a cold shower morning after morning in Mr. Crane's dormitory, I realized that my feet had indeed fallen in a fair place, but a place that was, in terms of luxury, only fair. And it did come hard about those polo ponies. The only horses with which I had even a nodding acquaintance during six years at Groton were two of those remarkable concave animals belonging to the Rector. It is a singular fact that I have yet to meet a horse ridden by the Rector that does not speedily become warped in the middle, as befitting one who carries about such a weighty matter.

I soon became aware that I was a member of a place with traditions; I began to understand what it meant to be one of the brethren. Beyond even the football team and the diamond and the river, I began to perceive personalities and I believe that they must rise in your minds, you who knew them, as they do in mine. Some of you never knew some of them. Some of them have passed on to other lives or other works, but in my mind's eye and my heart's eye, they are a goodly company. . . .

Groton has so many things to be thankful for that it is hard to select any for special comment, but there are two must make us pause. School catalogues talk about courses and tuition and prizes, but I wonder if those things really matter much. There are very few of us who could pass fourth form examinations, let alone College Boards, ten years out, and what men such as Sherrard Billings and William Amory Gardner taught was not courses, but rather a way of life.

Mr. B and Mr. G. when you come to think of it, were that rarest and most priceless of all things, thoroughly good and wise men, and for nearly fifty years they emitted goodness and wisdom unceasingly, though, stuffed Indians that we were, we frequently failed to realize it. For me, almost the only ray of sadness that falls across this evening is that those two souls, who wrought so much of this, are not here to let us tell them that we dimly understand.

And as to Mrs. Peabody, where shall one begin? Did you ever stop to think that even our yarns about her, our jokes, are full of affection and admiration? One never hears anything said of her that has a cruel twist to it. She has taught us all much of what we know concerning beauty and loveliness, goodness and humor. Many of us have been through dark days these past years. From personal experience I know of nothing that revive's one's faith in the race, one's belief that mankind can be noble and good more than to come to Groton, look at Mrs. Peabody, talk with Mrs. Peabody, and think about Mrs. Peabody and what she is and stands for. I can speak only for myself when I say that if, when I am as young as she is, I could know that people feel about me as I know they feel about her, I should be proud and happy till the tears came. But for all us younger of her children, and for schoolmasters everywhere, I can say from a full heart and as it were officially "we are *so* grateful."

Now Mrs. Peabody has several achievements to her credit, but none I think more creditable than that remarkable man, the Rector. He is perhaps the most striking of all her evidences of good taste. Bishop Lawrence and you, Mr. President, have known him far longer than I, you also love him, and you are able to assume a familiarity, which, even at my advanced age, comes hard. To the Bishop and the President, I leave him except for a very few remarks.

The first is a matter of character. Remember that the Rector is a person who by nature is, shall we say, positive. Remember that for fifty years he has been in a position of utter and absolute power. I think that one of the most impressive things about him is the fact that fifty years on he is more tolerant, broader than he ever was. That is no mean achievement.

It becomes a very great achievement when it is done without the surrender of any fundamental principles. It is easy enough to be broad if one is lax. But the Rector to-day, so far as I have been able to observe, still stands four-square for whatsoever things are honest, whatsoever things are true, whatsoever things are of good report. There is a vast amount of sentimental nonsense talked nowadays in education and in life. The Rector has believed for fifty years that a good job is better than a mediocre job, that good manners are better than poor manners, that there is no real substitute for plain hard work, that when all the frills and fads have bloomed and withered, there remains standing always, erect and sure, the simplicity that is in Christ. You and I have always, back through the ages had to have our folly and placed our faith in will-o'-the-wisps. It has been good to know that one figure has stood steady. I imagine that many of us have disagreed with the Rector about incidentals, (that is one of the things he has taught us, to think for ourselves,) but I cannot conceive anyone who really knows him having any doubt as to his rightness on the fundamentals. And if you think the job has not been worth doing, look about you. . . .

And what is the conclusion of the whole matter? What is the real function of such a school as Groton? I had to formulate for my own purpose the other day what it seemed to me the fundamentals were, what it was that a school must have faith in. My whole heart went into that formulation, and as I cannot better it, I repeat it, and I try to speak for the founders as well as for first formers. What is it we had faith in? Nothing very tangible, I reckon. We believed in one another. We believed that between us we could build an educational institution where masters and boys could work and play together not as rivals, not as enemies, but as comrades in an adventure that was fun. We believed in loyalty. We believed that it is better to be good than bad, better to be intelligent than stupid, better to be courageous than a coward. We believed that searching for God, we might find Him, and that in so doing we should learn to live to the good cheer of our fellow men, to be useful, to do good for the country, and so, please God, for mankind, learning here to be fine citizens and good husbands and true fathers. We believed those things, we believe them still.

The good Lord was very kind to us. He gave us beauty in the hills and trees. He gave us unusual means to accomplish a dream. He gave us above all two great leaders, a man and his wife, and they gathered round them that happy band of men who have been big enough to share the dream. Don't pity schoolmasters. To-night you must see and feel things that I know Groton masters are feeling and sharing now, things that though we be rich and successful some of us will never have.

The future no one of us can see. But at least the past has been good and it has been worth while. New forms, new generations, new problems are coming. When the next fifty years have rolled

362

by, there will be few of us who are here to-night present, but may those who lift their glasses to Groton at that time be as much in love with the place as we were. May they be stronger and better and wiser than we were, we who were only the pioneers, and may Groton herself continue to serve the family and the country and God, steadily increasing in spiritual stature and in favour with God and man.

Pierre Jay, second senior prefect and long devoted trustee and treasurer, spoke briefly of the founding of a permanent fund for scholarships, to be a present to the school from the graduate body and to be called the Endicott Peabody Scholarship Fund (the capital eventually reached more than $40,000). Bishop Lawrence then spoke graciously of the Rector, Mrs. Peabody, and President Roosevelt. The latter's address "was informal simple, and direct," and his words concerning education and its relation to living were effective. For the Peabodys' sakes even his bitterest opponents welcomed him, and he and Mrs. Roosevelt, for their part, showed the utmost consideration and self-effacement all through the week-end, subordinating themselves in all things to the Rector and the Madam.

George Rublee, '86, the first graduate, read for the assembled company the following letter to Mr. and Mrs. Peabody:

Dear Mr. And Mrs. Peabody:
Year after year during half a century the signers of this letter were your boys. Some of us have gone far on life's journey. Others are just setting out. In age, experience and interests we differ widely, but there is one emotion which we all share in common. It is our feeling for you. Our appreciation of your unfailing devotion to us in our school days and after deepens with the passage of time. On this fiftieth anniversary of the School we want to tell you something of the gratitude we feel for all you have done for us, and to let you know, if only we could, how much we love and admire you.

We owe much to the School for the education of mind and body we got here, but the most precious thing we carried away was an emanation from the spirit which governs your own lives. We saw you, without thought of yourselves, use all your energies of heart and mind in helping us to learn the true values in life, so that when we went out into the world to prove all things, we might choose to hold fast that which is good. We saw you do this naturally and joyously, as if it was the only possible manner of living, and we saw the happiness you found in the way of life you taught us to follow.

363

There could be no finer lesson, and it has inspired and strengthened us always.

We think of you, our Rector, first as our friend and kindly counsellor, interested in our troubles and successes, and ever concerned for our welfare. But you also embody for us certain ideals; honour, gallant conduct, simple, straightforward integrity of character, true Christian faith and works. We ever associate you in our thoughts with whatsoever things are honest, whatsoever things are just, whatsoever things are pure, whatsoever things are lovely, whatsoever things are of good report.

And you, dear Mrs. Peabody, how can we praise you and thank you as you deserve? Without you the School could never have become what it is. You have held us all together, masters, boys and graduates, in a happy companionship which has had its soul and centre in you. You have made us feel that this School is our home. Through all these years, with sweetness, gracious dignity, and loving-kindness, you have blessed our lives. Your presence has been like sunshine in a shady place. We cannot express what is in our hearts. We can only say to you, as Bassanio said to Portia: Madam, you have bereft us of all words. Only our blood speaks to you in our veins.

Our school has won a place in American life of which we are justly proud. So long as the spirit in which you both have worked, and the traditions and standards you have established, are maintained, the School will serve the country well. You have performed your part in fullest measure. It is for us and those who follow us to see that there shall be no lapsing from your ideals. It is in this way that we can best show our appreciation of the benefits we have received from you.

We rejoice that we can celebrate our fiftieth anniversary together, that we find you as we have always known you, and the School as we have always known it. So to us Groton School becomes a symbol of stability in a changing world.

From our hearts we hope that you may long watch over and guide our School.

Affectionately,

Your Boys

This letter was signed by 426 Graduates and bound in red leather for presentation. Then the Rector spoke briefly his appreciation and thanked the assembly for its gifts. He told the story of the pipe found in the Schoolhouse, exhibited the evidence, and offered to return it then and there. He objected to previous references to concave horses. He said that people sometimes asked him when he was going to retire and assured them all, with his hands thrust straight into the pockets of his jacket as of old, that his successor hadn't been born yet. As he closed the gathering his words were full of deeply tender and thankful feeling.

Next day, Sunday, Communion was celebrated at the eleven o'clock service. About seven hundred people crowded into the Chapel. The Rector preached on the text, "For their sakes I sanctify myself." Assisting him in Communion were Bishop Lawrence, Malcolm Peabody, Alexander Zabriskie, John Crocker, and Philemon Sturges, all but the Bishop graduates of the school.

When all had gone home the bread-and-butter letters began to flow in. Many of them were wonderful letters, of the sort that may come to most men or women perhaps once or twice in a lifetime. It may suffice to quote one which speaks for many:

MY DEAR RECTOR AND MADAM—

The Fiftieth Anniversary meant a great deal to me. I was proud to realize that I was part of such a high tradition. And I was proud and happy to have known you both.

What Groton has meant to me cannot be counted by words. It is as much part of me as my name or my ancestry. And what Groton is you are. To my mind you are inseparable.

The speakers told much better than I ever could how much the School meant. On the other hand they spoke with the voice of many, as a hymn is sung. And in the glorious Paean of a hymn the individual voice is inconsequential. But none the less I, however much a part of the mass, would like to add my note to the heart-felt song of Groton.

There is something that all of us from Groton carry with us in our hearts, as the candles of the School were lit at Epiphany. And it was so easy to feel that on the Anniversary. The years that have passed since School vanished and you were friends again because there was the same thing inside each of us. We fell back so naturally into School ways. The same characteristics gestures and expressions showed. Nothing was changed because the fundamentals were there.

I have found it terribly difficult to tell you what Groton has meant to me. It seemed at first it would be easy, too. But the feeling inside me must be too deep to express. If, however, I have succeeded in putting down on paper any part of what is in me I shall be happy.

365

My love for you both, and for the School that you created, must remain too deep for words.

Sincerely,

HARRY GODFREY, JR.

42

THE STRENGTH OF TEN

E. P. *aet.* 80-84

IN THE article, *Preface to a Schoolmaster's Biography*, already referred to and quoted several times, the final sentence ran: "And he just walked back and forth in the cool of the day." This easy phrase connotes a complacent and unenergetic satisfaction on the part of a creator admiring, enjoying, and dominating his own creation in the refreshing satisfaction of declining hours. Let us turn for a moment to trace Peabody's leisurely meanderings in lonely power from a dawn to evening and night.

By great good fortune there has been preserved a detailed account of a day in the Peabodys' life during the period from 1934 to 1941. In addition to being interesting, it is of paramount importance to the understanding of Endicott and Fanny Peabody.

Shortly before the last year of the Rector's headmastership, Bishop Lawrence wrote Mr. Regan that it would be a wise idea for someone to prepare notes on "the Peabodys at Groton" for the benefit of the ultimate biographer. Mr. Regan in turn suggested to Acosta Nichols, Jr. then (1937) a master at the school, that he undertake the task. Nichols, an observant person himself, conferred with the Bishop and many others who knew Groton and the Peabodys well. He assembled a considerable body of notes, most of which are given in the single chapter quoted here. With the coming of war, Nichols entered the Navy and was prevented from finishing the manuscript. Hearing that the present book was being done, he wrote, "I should be only too happy to play a part . . . in memorializing the greatest and noblest man I have known," and sanctioned the free use of his material. What follows in this chapter is entirely his. It should be remembered that this was written in 1937 and after, when the Rector was between eighty and eighty-four years old and Mrs. Peabody two years younger.

All members of the Groton community rise early, but Mr. Peabody is invariably the first person to be up and about. By the time the "outside" bell rouses the boys, and often long before that hour, he is hard at work at his desk, having already prepared himself for the day by a session of vigorous dumbbell exercises. He has always claimed that this period of the day provides his only opportunity for uninterrupted, concentrated work. His energy at this hour has always amazed his colleagues, who are not infrequently awakened from their slumbers by the arrival of a messenger bringing from the Rector a note penned half an hour previously. On one occasion the writer was returning with Mr. Peabody from Worcester, where they had attended a late dinner. As midnight approached, the Rector expressed regret at the few hours of sleep that lay ahead—he had to get up at 4:45 A.M., he explained, in order to accomplish some work before listening to the broadcast of a speech by Hitler, which was scheduled to begin at five-thirty! Another time, a master was called to the telephone at 6:30 A.M. to be informed that a light was burning in the study of a boy who was in the Infirmary. Mr. Peabody had seen the light from his study, had identified the window whence it came, and had realized that the occupant of that room was ill. Why, therefore, was a light burning?

Shortly after seven o'clock, with at least half an hour of work behind him, the Rector holds a brief service of prayers for his family and such few guests as are up. Following which comes breakfast, a meal that is never without a large contingent of guests. One would think that, living at all times in a large community, and having two meals a day with the school, the Peabody family would prefer the quiet and privacy of family breakfast. But such is not the Peabody way! Usually there are several guests who have spent the night in the house—members of the ever-growing Peabody clan, trustees, parents, graduates galore. These are augmented by such boys as may be relatives

367

or neighbors of any of the house guests. If the number is still below the customary large company, there is always the school to draw upon. During the early part of the fall term there is a steady stream of new boys for breakfast, whose sense of homesickness and loneliness is vastly eased by an hour in the family atmosphere of the Peabodys' table. Despite the numbers of guests, these meals are always essentially family parties, with corresponding informality. The English custom of self-service for breakfast is practiced, and English influence is evident, too, in the quantity of hearty food which is offered—and consumed —at these meals.

Mr. Peabody is the first to leave the breakfast table, in order that he may visit all the boys in the Infirmary before morning Chapel. These visits are an invariable part of the Rector's daily routine, and there are few days in which Mrs. Peabody, Miss Betsy, and Miss Margery do not find time to make the rounds as well. It has been remarked that Mr. Peabody's attitude is a curious combination of sympathy for the sufferer, and incredulity that any one should be troubled by weakness of the flesh. Certain it is that, confronted with his magnificently healthy and vigorously active presence, any ailing boy or master feels a vague sense of shame and guilt for his frailty, and immediately resolves to do all in his power to leave the Infirmary forthwith. If there are few inhabitants of the Infirmary, there may be time for a long chat with each victim; if there are more, it is possible only to have a brief inquiry about health, an expression of hope of an immediate recovery, and a cheerful farewell —almost invariably the word *"Speriamo."* On Sunday the Rector has developed the custom of bringing a flower to each ill boy. The presentation is invariably accompanied by a brief lesson in botany: "Do you know what kind of flower this is?" Nine out of ten times the initiate asserts that it is a carnation, and he is usually right!

Mrs. Peabody and Miss Betsy make the rounds in the Infirmary later in the day, and Miss Margery in the evening, immediately after supper. Their visits are deliberately placed well apart during the day, in order to provide the maximum of pleasure for the boys they visit.

After his visit to the Infirmary, the Rector bicycles to the Chapel. He usually has fifteen or twenty minutes there before the start of the service, which he devotes to selection of hymns and prayers for the evening services, reading, and interviews for which complete privacy is more than usually desirable. During this time he has an opportunity to talk with the Chapel attendants, who are often selected largely because they are thought to be boys who might be especially influenced by such intimate daily contact with the Headmaster.

The order of worship is simple—one familiar hymn, a selection from the Psalms or the Responsive Readings, and a few prayers. The general outline varies little, but within the service there are constant changes that tend to avert monotony. Sometimes the reading of the Psalms is divided by verses, sometimes by half-verses; sometimes the verses are read "antiphonally by sides of the Chapel." Of late years Mr. Peabody has made more of an effort than previously to relate the daily service to the seasons and to world conditions. A number of special forms have been devised for such occasions as the School Birthday, the birthdays of the founding master, etc. All this is done in accordance with the fundamental purpose of making the Chapel services an integral and normal part of the life of the school. Special prayers are said frequently for peace and international good will, and the religious lessons to be derived from the troubled condition of the world are repeatedly stated to the boys. Several of the days of the week have their special significance: Tuesday is "our National Day," Wednesday "the day on which we think of Missions," etc. With increasing frequency Mr. Peabody leads special litanies from a kneeling-desk brought out on occasion to a point in the middle of the main aisle, midway between choir and congregation. This is done to increase the feeling that the school is worshiping together as a corporate whole, with all members on an equal footing. Mr. Peabody has always placed great stress on the value each member of a religious congregation draws from his fellows. He believes that by actively participating in all the services one benefits both himself and the other members of a congregation through the mere fact of unity of Christian action. Hence there are occasional rehearsals in the Chapel, where the congregation practices the hymns and the responses.

When the service is completed, Mr. Peabody takes a short cut to the Schoolhouse by bicycling directly across the grass on the Circle. This is a privilege reserved to him, and only exercised at this time of day, as it enables him, after doffing his clerical robes, to arrive at the Schoolhouse with the rear guard of the school. In recent years the custom has developed of the new boys forming a guard of honor on the Schoolhouse porch outside the Headmaster's study as he enters the building. Now he is invariably forced to pass between two lines of them, giving and receiving morning salutations as he goes.

Mr. Peabody's morning routine at the Schoolhouse is a very busy one from the time he opens school at eight-thirty by sending the boys away to their classes till the final dismissal of school at one. In the first place, there are the actual courses which he teaches. At one time or another he has held classes in most of the subjects of the curriculum, and until a few years ago he continued to hold several Latin classes a week, but now he restricts himself to sixth form and first form sacred studies. His main interest is not the subject matter but the opportunity of discussing ethical problems and school problems with boys who are at the beginning and the end of their Groton careers. Every class begins with a written test, usually ten minutes in length, based on the day's assignments. (Correction of these papers, incidentally, is one of the few tasks that Mr. Peabody spares himself, always passing them on to some master.) As soon as this checkup is made, there is a chance to use the class period for instruction in almost anything that may merit discussion. The value of form is emphasized to the new boys by an inspection of their fingernails and an emphasis of the necessity of having all the proper books and notebooks at hand. Exhortations to hard work, insistence upon thoroughness in preparation, admonitions as to conduct (especially if many first-formers have appeared on the penalty list)—these are heard just as much as are remarks strictly upon sacred studies. With the sixth form class, too, probably fifty per cent of the period is devoted to "*prologomena*," which may range in scope from problems of personal hygiene to the spirit shown in the St. Mark's game, from divorce to the arrangements for Washington's Birthday, from stories of the founding of the school to the advisability of wearing proper evening shoes. In class he resorts to educational tricks to stimulate attention and interest in what is happening in class. One of his favorite devices (for the younger boys especially) is to have boys compete for the top seats in the class. "Go up, boy, go up," is an oft-quoted saying in school when one has done something distinguished, while

"Down among the dead men" is the remark which accompanies failure.

During the morning there is a great deal of work to be done. Firstly, there is a vast amount of correspondence to be kept up to date. There are probably few men who carry on so large a private correspondence as Mr. Peabody. The writer remembers once counting two thousand postal cards for the Rector—enough to supply birthday cards for only a little over a year! Then there are the letters to parents regarding their boys' health, academic progress, and social adjustment. Until recently Mr. Peabody used to handle himself the correspondence relating to boys entering the school, but now such matters are in charge of Mr. Beasley.

The remainder of the morning is devoted to interviews with boys, masters, parents, and other visitors. Any boy who wishes to leave the school for any reason must state his case in person before the Headmaster, and obtain the latter's signature upon a "Leave of Absence" blank. In fact, almost any request of any sort which involves a deviation from the usual routine—using a certain room in the cellar of the Schoolhouse for a photographic darkroom, for example—must be brought to the Rector himself. Finally, after every series of marks, Mr. Peabody sees all the boys whose work has been conspicuously good or conspicuously poor, to commend, exhort, or threaten.

Masters probably take up an even larger proportion of the Rector's time than do the boys. Of late years there has been more delegation of authority than used to be the case, and masters refer a smaller proportion of their problems to the Rector. For example, in former times there was during the morning a steady stream of boys sent to the Headmaster from the class-rooms for slight disciplinary offences. Now it is a rare occurrence when a master fails to handle such problems himself, unless the offense is of a sort that makes one doubt a boy's moral or ethical standards. There are innumerable matters, however, on which masters daily wish to consult Mr. Peabody, matters pertaining to boys, to parents, to the school buildings, to athletics, or such extracurricular organizations as the School Camp and the Missionary Society.

Despite the closeness with which Mr. Peabody supervises the running of the school, he comparatively seldom visits classes, and knows little of the details of what each master teaches. If a man is to be considered worthy of teaching at Groton, he should, argues Mr. Peabody, be considered sufficiently responsible to choose his own course and follow his own methods. Consequently, there is almost complete academic freedom. Within the school, each department is free from any dictation by the headmaster: within each department, each individual master is almost equally independent.

One invariable part of Mr. Peabody's daily routine is the session of calisthenic exercises in the middle of the morning. No matter how hot the weather may be in June or how many papers may be lying on his desk, he never fails to be on hand at 10:45 to participate vigorously in the exercises that the boys are performing. One reason for this vigor is undoubtedly the sheer pleasure that Mr. Peabody takes in all forms of physical exertion, but a more important reason is his wish to set an example to the school by participating to the full in all of its activities. It is probably a source of real sorrow to him that some of his colleagues on the faculty are not equally energetic in midmorning.

Mr. Peabody occasionally condemns actions as being incompatible with the spirit of Groton, while admitting that in other places they might be permissible. Thus he is often heard to say: "I am surprised that such a happening could have occurred here. If a boy wants to do that sort of thing, he should go to some other school. There are plenty of schools where that sort of thing is allowed, but we will not have it here." So the preaching note appears even at such a prosaic time as the dismissal of school.

In addition to the announcements he wishes to give out, Mr. Peabody takes this opportunity to see several boys with whom he wishes to speak briefly. The line is apt to be a dozen long, which means that Mr. Peabody must hurry if he is to be in Hundred House without prolonging the fifteen-minute interval that takes place between the end of classes and dinner. Sometimes even hurrying will not avail, and the meal must be delayed a few minutes, for the exact time of the lunches and suppers of the school depends in part on the Peabody family. Just before the senior prefect rings the bell for general assembly before meals, he is supposed to go to the Rector's study to see if the Peabodys and their guests are ready. If they are not, the school waits. It is remarkable, in view of the frequent arrivals

372

of last-minute guests, how seldom such delays occur, and for what short intervals.

Mr. Peabody is always at hand in the Hundred House schoolroom before dinner during the reading of notices pertaining to athletic activities. It had been remarked that his appearance here is the supreme instance of his absolute absorption in the school. It is a time when there is no special duty for the Rector to perform, and no announcements for him to give out. The only notices are routine lists connected with the program of physical education. Yet to miss these would be to lose touch with the details of an important phase of the school life, which would be contrary to all the Rector's beliefs and practices. So, day after day, he sits down with the boys on the fifth form benches and listens intently to every list.

En route from the Hundred House schoolroom to the dining room, Mr. Peabody uses his football training to good effect in clearing a path through the sixth-formers and masters standing in the hallway. Some are pushed out of the way brusquely— "Move along, boy," is one of the best-known school quotations. Others are urgently requested to step to one side. In any case, the rule is that the school must come through without interruption, and whoever interferes with the smooth transit of the boys —masters, guests, or graduates—must get out of the way.

The same impatience to see the whole school safely assembled in the dining room is evident till the last person is at his place. Though he always greets the ladies and guests waiting in the room before the school enters, he proceeds, as quickly as possible, to the dais on which the Head Table stands, in order to direct the stream of boys flowing into the room, and to discipline those who misbehave. As soon as Grace has been said, he again goes to the front of the dais to see that masters and prefects are in their proper places. Only when he is convinced that all is proceeding smoothly does he take his seat at the end of the Head Table.

As has been suggested above, the Peabodys are good trenchermen, keenly interested in the quality and the quantity of the food at the school table. To make sure that the Head Table will enjoy the roast at its best, Mr. Peabody always does the carving himself, though this task merely adds to the complication of a routine which includes serving himself, maintaining a conversation, maintaining such little discipline as is necessary

373

at the Head Table, and keeping general watch over the order in the entire dining room. His fondness for certain dishes, notably for lemon meringue pie, is well known, and school legend has it that any favors may be successfully begged of the Headmaster after this favorite dessert has appeared on the table.

Nowhere in the life of the school is the family atmosphere of Groton more emphasized than in the dining room. It has often been argued by boys and by some masters that each table should be free to leave the room when all its members have finished their meals. Yet Mr. Peabody feels that it is of fundamental importance to preserve as much as possible the family sense by having the school arise as a unit when the meal is over. The Rector never rings the bell which signifies the end of the meal until he has received from Mrs. Peabody a nod to indicate that she is finished. His efforts to catch her eye to obtain this assurance when she is deep in conversation at the other end of the table never fail to amuse those who observe them.

At faculty coffee, following dinner, the ladies and the gentlemen separate. If there are any matters of school business that require discussion by the faculty, Mr. Peabody is apt to bring them up at this time. If not, the time is devoted to casual conversation and reminiscence. Frequently, when the Rector has received letters from alumni or from foreign correspondents which contain more than ordinary interest, he shares them with the faculty, and sometimes he reads a brief article or essay that has caught his fancy.

For the past several years, the Rector has taken a midafternoon rest after coffee, retreating to a small room on the top floor of his house. Yet even here he does not fully withdraw from participation in the affairs of the school. Many a boy and master have been startled during this period of the day by hearing the Rector's voice, seeming to come from the sky, inquiring the identity of some culprit crossing the grass contrary to regulations or calling attention to some boy who is not clad in the proper athletic clothes.

After rest comes exercise, still pursued by the Peabodys in 1940 with as much zest as in the 1880's. Whatever the condition of the weather, Mrs. Peabody and he do some sort of vigorous physical exercise. During mild weather, this usually takes the form of a horseback ride, most frequently through the woods to the river. In winter, a vigorous walk is all that is pos-

374

sible, or, in really inclement weather, a session pulling weights in the gymnasium. After a severe fall from his horse three or four years ago, and again after his abdominal operation in the early spring of 1938, many people questioned whether Mr. Peabody would ride again. Such people simply did not know their Rector!

However busy the sports program may be, it is never allowed to interfere with the tea hour, during which Mrs. Peabody or one of her daughters or a combination of the three entertain friends, masters, and members of the sixth form. One of the features of the Groton timetable is the immediacy with which supper follows tea. Few visitors can accustom themselves to the ease with which sixth-formers can proceed directly from a heavy tea at five-thirty to the dining room for a hearty supper. Yet it is a regime on which the Groton community appears to thrive.

The Rector customarily is at tea for ten or fifteen minutes, but leaves the company early to work, taking with him his special cup, a monstrous "bath tub" (as he calls it), in order that he may have the equivalent of two cups of tea without the danger of having his work interrupted by succumbing to the attractions of conversation. Meanwhile Mrs. Peabody and/or the daughters are holding the fort in the "den."

There is little difference between the practices of Mr. Peabody at supper and at dinner. Almost always the cryptic phrase "Brook House go by now" means that the Rector and Mrs. Peabody are about to undertake one of their most characteristic tasks—shaking the hand of each boy in the school. There is no sight at Groton that more impresses visitors than this nightly view of the boys passing in line past the Headmaster and his lady, saying a personal good night, some of them self-conscious, other natural, some smiling, others serious. To one who has never shaken hands with a long line of people, it may not be realized how difficult it is to connect names with rapidly passing faces. To those who have attempted such a task, the ability of the Peabodys to make such connections is almost miraculous. Occasionally there is a moment's hesitation, when "Good night, boy" is the only salutation used; occasionally a boy is confused by name with an elder brother, father, or uncle who has been at Groton, but usually the name is on the tip of the tongues of both the Rector and Mrs. Peabody. Not only the name! Each

375

of them usually recalls any personal association that should be made with a boy—his recovery from recent illness or his success in athletics during the afternoon, for example. Such associations form the basis for personal words to the boy in question. It may be remarked, too, that the memory and the associative powers of Mrs. Peabody are even keener that those of the Rector, as was proved (according to the boys) by the happenings of the Fiftieth Anniversary. On this occasion, when hundreds of graduates visited the school, some after a lapse of several decades, the Rector was reported to have had difficulty in placing only two individuals. Mrs. Peabody was said to have improved on this record. She missed only one!

After Brooks House has "gone by," there is often reading aloud by the Rector to any boys that care to come in. In the winter these readings usually take place in the study; in the spring they are held outdoors on the front steps of the Peabodys' house, with the boys sprawled informally in all directions about the central figure. Favorite selections are Jerome K. Jerome's *Three Men in a Boat, Happy Thoughts,* and the "Jeeves" novels of P. G. Wodehouse.

After the reading, while the boys study in the evening period, there is a time for quiet work and correspondence, subject, of course, to numerous interruptions in the form of calls by masters, boys, or graduates. During this time the members of the Peabody family are apt to be together as a unit for the only time in the day. It is, however, a short stretch of privacy at best, and, as suggested above, subject to many intrusions. On two evenings a week the main intrusions take the form of an avalanche of boys headed for "Parlor." There bedlam breaks loose! Tables are set throughout the hallways, and the "den" and the "boudoir" are occupied by groups intent on particular games. Miss Betsy and Miss Margery circulate about the halls, joining in the games of cards, checkers, etc., or their more noisy equivalents. Mrs. Peabody customarily remains in the boudoir, either reading aloud or playing a game appropriately entitled "Happy Family." (Another of the most popular games is equally suitably named "Boston.") At 8:28 the bell rings, the games are brought to a close, and all the boys file slowly in line past Mrs. Peabody, saying good night and expressing their thanks for the evening's fun. Then quiet reigns—for approximately five minutes! Then there is an invasion of the older boys, and the ladies are again busy entertaining pleasure-bent guests. It is impossible to estimate the happiness and reassurance that has been brought to shy and bewildered youngsters by the friendly informality of these Tuesday and Friday evenings. It has certainly justified the very great sacrifice of time and energy involved.

At eight-thirty come the prayers in Hundred House schoolroom, invariably attended not only by the Rector but by the ladies as well. As the latter enter the room, the members of the sixth form rise, but the other boys remain seated, according to school custom. When the service is concluded, the Rector and Mrs. Peabody say good night to all the younger boys, as they pass from the schoolroom en route to their respective dormitories. Forty minutes later the older boys have their turn, though this time it is the Rector alone who reviews them. As there is no regular study period in this period of the evening, and consequently no master to ring the bell, it is up to Mr. Peabody to let the older boys know that the time has come to say good night. He has his own bell, which is rung on this occasion only, but apparently he does not consider this sufficient warning, and the boys are summoned from their studies by the cry of "Bedtime, boys," in tones loud enough to be heard throughout Hundred House.

Shaking this final batch of hands ends Mr. Peabody's usual day, as far as his connection with the school is concerned, except for those evenings when there is Faculty Supper. On these occasions five or six members of the sixth form, plus any visiting graduates (almost never a member of the faculty) go into the Peabodys' dining room for a late snack and congenial conversation. The late snack is apt to be more substantial than such a term would indicate, usually including eggs or waffles, cheese, jam, milk, prunes, bread and butter, cold cereal, and similar delicacies. The atmosphere of informality is established by the table cover, a red-checked cloth reminiscent of Munich beer halls. Self-help is the rule, and amateur cooks have a chance to show their talent. Mr. Peabody in particular provides amusement by his insistence on supervising the last stages of cooking and serving the scrambled eggs. He maintains that he is the only one who can make sure that there are sufficient scrambled eggs to go around, when there is only one small frying pan, and perhaps ten hungry guests. The secret of his success is in keeping the eggs in an almost purely liquid state, so that they may serve

377

almost as sauce on toast, rather than as a main course. There is no time when the Rector's fund of reminiscence and of anecdote is more evident than at these faculty suppers.

At 9:50 promptly Mr. Peabody rises, and takes the lead in clearing away the dishes. From practice he has acquired almost a royal facility in letting guests know when it is time to leave. "I am sorry you can't stay," is one of his most frequent remarks of dismissal, this being said, of course, in a joking way. In any event, the last guest has usually departed by ten o'clock, and Mr. and Mrs. Peabody retire upstairs.*

43

THERE BE SOME SO STRONG THEY

REACH FOURSCORE YEARS

E. P. *aet.* 80-84

THE Rector was growing just a little bit older. One hardly noticed it, and it was hard to put one's finger on it. Yet it was almost possible to envisage the time when he would age.

In his eightieth year he and Mrs. Peabody spent the summer in Europe. They still had many friends in England; "Dear old Arthur" was dead and Herbert Ryle, Bishop of Exeter, and Cochin Griffith. But Sir Walter Lawrence still lived and corresponded, and Mrs. Carnegie, the wife of Canon Carnegie, formerly Mrs. Joseph Chamberlain, and before that Mary Endicott, the Peabodys' cousin, was still there with a warm welcome. After a happy time in England they went to Paris, where a reckless taxi driver involved them in a needless crash, sending the Rector to the hospital with two broken ribs and shaking them both up badly. His opinion of things French was not improved when the company involved in the insurance proved insolvent. He shook his head irritably. "Even while at school in

* Contribution of Acosta Nichols, Jr. See pp. 361-362.

378

England," he said, "I formed the opinion that they were an unreliable people."

By the time school opened, however, he was ready with steam up. And in 1937 for his eightieth birthday he received many congratulatory messages, including a handsome scroll signed by all his colleagues on the faculty. When he went to North Andover for the Brooks School Prize Day, to which he always came and where, as president of the board of trustees, he gave out the diplomas, the Brooks faculty and boys presented him with an honorary diploma, accompanied by a Latin ode written by Herbert Howe, all of which pleased him greatly. The ode read:

> *Ulmus ut in campo, quae per labentia lustra*
> *Semper grata viget, sic viridi ingenio*
> *Et magnis animis viguisti, rector amate;*
> *Poscimus ut semper sic validus vigeas.*
> *Discipuli et domini merita te laude salutant,*
> *Qui defensori praesidioque scholae*
> *Semper eras. Quae nos sapientia conciliorum*
> *Continuo adiuvit, clara diu maneat.*
> *Coniunx tuque benigna, Grotonia gloria, salve;*
> *Pares regnatis servitio Domini.**

This was read, clearly and distinctly, by one of the graduating scholars, and therewith came an enticing bit of byplay. It is probable that not more than a handful of the audience understood the Latin except for the Rector and President Ogilby of Trinity, who was the Prize Day speaker. Certainly Mrs. Pea-

---

* The translation of the ode, also rendered, was:

> Like to an elm which groweth with the years,
> Fresher and greener, even so dost thou,
> In wisdom strong, strong in thy spirit's might,
> Grow ever younger, Rector, well beloved.
> We pray that even thus thou still mayst grow.
> Masters and boys alike are joined to praise
> The constant shield and guardian of our school.
> Long may thy wisdom true, in council tried,
> Which from the first has been our sure support,
> Remain to guide us on our upward way.
> Thou, too, his wife, and Groton's light we greet;
> To-gether reign ye, numbered with the blest,
> Serving our God, to serve whom is to reign.

379

body did not, but during the reading she listened attentively, knowing it was nice. Remsen Ogilby sat in his robes on the edge of his chair. When the reader came to the line "*Coniunx tuque benigna*," he turned to her and doffed his mortar board. Mrs. Peabody, without the foggiest notion of what had been said, graciously inclined her head in return and acknowledged the tribute with a dainty and modest smile, knowing that what was nice at that point concerned her. After expressing his thanks the Rector took the opportunity to point out forcibly at some length the evils of divorce to considerable numbers of divorced parents present.

Trinity College, Hartford, always had a warm spot in his heart. In the magnificent new chapel there is a carved pew end showing Peabody on a decidedly concave horse, and in 1939 Trinity gave him a doctor's degree and made much of him.

In 1938, for the first time in his adult life, he was really taken sick. Seized suddenly one winter's day, he was rushed to the hospital in Boston where a very serious major operation was performed. All Groton held its breath, for the awareness grew that whatever he seemed, he was an old man. But shortly afterward his surgeon, in response to anxious enquiries wrote Bishop Lawrence:

Bishop William Lawrence
1 Joy Street
Boston, Mass.

February 18, 1938

DEAR BISHOP LAWRENCE,

Dr. Peabody has made an unusual recovery from his operation. He has responded to surgery about as well as a man twenty-five years younger might. He has been up and around now since the eighth post-operative day, and we are planning for him to go to Bermuda on March second as he arranged prior to his operation.

I am going to allow Dr. Peabody to resume bicycle riding and rowing when he gets to Bermuda. I believe he will come back fully refres!.ed and able to take over his duties, feeling very much better than ne did last fall.

I can see no reason whatever, from a physical standpoint why Dr. Peabody cannot carry on in his important role at Groton for an indefinite number of years. He seems to me to be particularly young as far as his mind is concerned as well as his tissues.

With very best wishes, I am,   Sincerely yours,

ARTHUR W. ALLEN

On which the Bishop jotted:

My dear Cottie—
Fine, very fine. I am sending a copy of this to each Trustee.
Thanks for your letter. Glad that all goes well. You are a great
couple
Cottie and Fannie
Love to you both and a good voyage
Affectionately,
Wm. L.

For they were off to Bermuda for a change just as soon as Peabody could get out of the hospital. On their return to Groton
Mrs. Peabody fell on her way to visit boys in the Infirmary,
breaking her leg. She had a special bicycle built on which she
could pedal and exercise her leg without getting anywhere. Also
built on to it (it was gleaming white, a most tidy and superior
bicycle) was a little stand on which she could place a book to
read while she pedaled, and there one would find her, riding in
his study, and reading *David Copperfield* while he worked at
his desk.

In 1938 Yale gave him an LL.D. Professor William Lyon
Phelps said:

Dr. Peabody was born near the scene of his whole life's work.
Born in Salem on Memorial Day, 1857, he emigrated to England,
taking his bachelor's degree at Cheltenham College and his degree in
law at Trinity College, Cambridge. Turning from the law to the
gospel, he came back to America and studied divinity at the Episcopal Theological School in Cambridge, Massachusetts. In the year
1884 he became headmaster of Groton School and held that position
more than fifty years. He brought that school to such a high level
that within five minutes after the birth of a male child his name is
on the waiting list. Thus not only do the students and alumni of
that famous institution increase its prestige, but they also serve who
only stand and wait.

Few men can look back over the years with more satisfaction and
gratification than Dr. Peabody. He combined a genius for teaching
with extraordinary ability as an executive.

One reason why clichés and hackneyed phrases are irritating is
because it is so difficult to think of a good substitute. The shop-
worn Latin tag from Juvenal, *Mens sana in corpore sano*, still
precisely applies to the ideals of education followed by Dr. Pea-
381

body. And in these turbulent times, the Latin adjective applies only to the educated minority; indeed it signifies special talent.

We should also remember that the Latin noun *mens* signifies not only mind but character; and while the boys at this school have always received good instruction the chief emphasis has been laid on training in character. As the best foundation for character is religious faith, the school has always provided teaching in the Bible and in the principles of the Christian religion.

As Dr. Peabody considers the immense number of his former pupils who are now pulling their weight in the world, and who so well illustrate the words of Juvenal, he may now use four other Latin words spoken by a Roman mother in response to a question from the lady of the decoration.

Dr. Peabody, Yale has every reason to be grateful to you.

And President Seymour told him:

To you has been granted that for which King Solomon prayed above all things: the gift of a discerning heart. From you have come generation after generation of youth whose feet have been set in the path of wisdom by your righteous and inspired guidance. In deep gratitude Yale confers upon you the degree of Doctor of Laws, admitting you to all its rights and privileges.

He had grown more mellow, more understanding, more tolerant with the years without yielding any of his inflexibility on fundamentals. It was a great grief to him when two graduates of whom he had been very proud and fond were sent to prison for embezzlement of funds. He could not help feeling that somehow he had failed or they would not have made such dreadful mistakes. He was past eighty when he first wrote and then went to see one of the graduates in Sing Sing. He visited him not as a man who had done wrong; that was past and was being paid for; but as a friend who was in trouble, who wished to make a fresh start in the world. What people thought didn't come into it. Here was an old boy in trouble. "I was sick and ye visited me." All questions were eventually reducible to New Testament terms, that was all.

Nevertheless, the operation had been a shock to them both. For the first time nature really forced upon their consciousness that, all the evidence of eighty-two years to the contrary, his mortality would sooner or later involve the weakening of even his mighty terrestrial frame. And slowly, but persistently, there came to him the willingness to do for others what he would never have done for himself; resign the headmastership of Groton while he was still hale and hearty.

He felt fine, but his memory was just a little mite tricky and his legs were not quite as tireless or as steady as they had been. For any other man of eighty-two he would have been amazing, but one forgot that, as Dr. Allen had said, he was a man who for years had been twenty-five years younger than himself. And for Fanny he never had been that old in the last forty years and never would be. She, even more than he, resented the way of all flesh and the relentless calmness of calendars.

Yet there was something uneasy in the air. One sensed it, unspoken, at Groton and heard it openly among the graduates. How was the Rector? Was it true that he had made up his mind to hang on until he was ninety? Parents with boys wanted to know what his plans were. The faculty, devoted to him and trying under Regan's guidance to spare him and the Madam in all small things, could not forget that he had actually been to the hospital.

As he thought about it, he realized that he had to make the decision and take the step. *They* loved and respected him too much to ask or hint. All that had been done was his, and he could count on *them* to the bitter end. What clutched the hearts of many was that if he delayed too long the end might be bitter, and they could not bear the thought of anything but a perfect ending to what had been so magnificent.

Finally, in the winter term of 1939, he decided, and notified the Trustees that he planned to resign at the end of the school year in 1940. He, of course, wrote Bishop Atwood about it:

Rt. Rev. J. W. Atwood, D.D.
c/o Stephen B. Ives, Esq.
Atlanta, Ga.

New York, March 1, 1939

My dear Julius:

I sent you a line the other day informing you of the dismal step which it seemed wise for me to take in connection with the institution of which I have been, for some years, the headmaster. I decided upon this not because I felt any particular weakening or because there was any tendency on the part of parents to cease sending their sons to Groton, but simply in realization of the fact that the masters who form a gallant band devoted to the school were naturally wondering who should take up the baton for the next twenty or thirty years during their time of service at the school. My resignation left the trustees free to go out into the world to discover a successor to the present incumbent and this they are on the point of doing. All our friends, the trustees, the masters and the boys have been most sympathetic in understanding something of the regret which we feel in pulling out. There has been, on the part of the papers also, an interest I should have expected, if at all, at the moment of the actual withdrawal from the school in 1940 or at the time of my shuffling off this mortal coil. The notices which I have seen have greatly exaggerated the qualities of your friend and his performance. This is a great deal pleasanter than if they had expressed a severe criticism but there is an unreality in much that they say which gives one a certain amount of uneasiness but which it is hardly possible for him to discuss. My hope is that the trustees will decide to elect one who is a clergyman and a graduate of the school, the first being the more important. It would, in my judgment, be greatly to the advantage of the school to have a man who was thoroughly versed in its traditions, many of which he would undoubtedly change or modify, who would be so in touch with the alumni that they would continue to visit Groton as freely as they have done through all these years.

We are off for Bermuda this afternoon, sailing on the Queen of Bermuda. We had thought of several places in Florida, among others, Winter Park which you speak of in your last note. On the whole it seemed more promising to try Bermuda again, a place which we have loved for many years and where we have friends with whom we like to keep in touch. I hope that your visit to Atlanta will be as profitable as it is pleasant and I beg that you will give my love to your daughter and her good husband.

Very affectionately yours,

E. Peabody

The news spread like wildfire. Prepared as they were for it, as for the eventual end of the world, those who knew him were incredulous and stunned. It was difficult, if one had known him, to get one's bearings. Even with Europe smoldering again, many felt strangely bereaved. One graduate, seeing the news on the front page of a Boston paper, sat down and wrote what was probably in the minds of all:

The Rector Resigns

The news appears quietly in the papers,
"Endicott Peabody resigns, the head of Groton."
Tomorrow will be showery, business slow,

384

The guns were quarrelsome again in China
Yesterday. The admirals protest; the great men
Deliberate again the recurrent crisis.
A woman was murdered in a crime of passion,
A little child was lost; two former lovers
Divorced; the farmers wish the rain would fall
Steadily watering the harvest in.
It would not do to lose the harvest now;
Unless the crops come in, there is no seed,
Unless the seed is scattered, no more grain.

News, news, from every corner of the earth
In the morning paper, news of all the great,
The ambitious, the conquering, the overwhelmed,
The talkers and the writers and the proud,
The headline masters and politicos,
The passionate, the vicious, the successful,
The little girls in Canada, and Galento,
The Dies Committee, Marlene Dietrich's legs.

But my mind turns again to Massachusetts
And a quiet place that sees New Hampshire hills
And a great bell ringing from the schoolhouse tower
Answering bells within the Chapel tower
And the green grass and apple trees and fields.
This was the way we saw it. In the dusk
A barge with jingling bells pulled from the station
Some twenty boys, commingled old and new.
First in the distance the grey Chapel rising,
Then the brick buildings and the waiting lawns.
A step inside the door and there they stood
Endicott Peabody, Fanny Peabody, always together.
How tell of them when the affections cover
All that they are with such a misty light?

They say the two old titles have been voided,
Lady and gentleman, in shallow days.
But I knew a lady, and a gracious lady,
I cannot fully speak her proper praise.
The way she had of smiling and of speaking,
The simple way she lifted up her hand
Is good to remember. One can write
Such words as gracious, beautiful, or charming;
It leaves the light out and the living truth.
O! second mother to a thousand sons

385

O! actual goodness to a host of boys
We praise you and we bless you for the life,
The good and gentle life that perfumed ours.
With quiet hearts we offer what is good
In the tangled, clumsy pattern of our years,
Casting away the shameful and the bad,
Knowing that you will only see the good,
The brightness of the pattern, the strong threads
That life has not worn down. Take all our lives
To walk upon, to shield your feet and bring you
Glad and at peace to your sure warmth of heaven.

He was so big to our inquiring eyes.
Bigness is easy when the eyes are young.
But this was a bigness never evanescent,
A bigness that grew sturdier and vaster
Hard as an oak tree's heart, broad as its shade,
An elemental thing. The body, to our eyes,
Seemed vast and wholesome; the gigantic hands
And chest and shoulders, the straight back and bearing,
Blue eyes, light hair, and voice that surely ruled.
Integer vitae, scelerisque purus
This was the man that Horace had in mind.

What is ambition, that strange, restless thing,
Self's distillation flavoring the world?
Here was ambition, but not the ambition
Of pomp and circumstance and earthly fame.
In him three loves poured into one vast self
To make a rich alembic of his life.
God was the first. God filtered through his life.
God was in his lips and understanding.
God was reality. God was a passionate quest,
And all things worked together for good
To this man who loved God. We see him best
Robed in the pulpit, hear the familiar voice
Roll through the Chapel. "That is it, my boys."
God was it. He made us lean toward God.
God spoke through this strong priest and for his sake
Hearing him speak for God our hearts believed.

The second love he had was for his home,
A wife and family, the best gifts of God.
O! little hearts that make a mock of love
And cast it out and make it passion's slave,

386

Take your poor arsenal and break it here
On the hard rock of unstained, generous lives.
The rarest beauty torn will turn to shreds,
The holiest radiance dim in greasy hands,
And yet a radiant beauty still have been.
If in the littleness of our time's space,
If in the narrowness of circumstance,
If in the horror of our selfishness
We make a mock of God and mock of love,
In decency's remembrance let us turn
To dignity and trust and faith at Groton.

And the third thing he loved was that same Groton.
All the swift, glad, impetuous years of it.
The boys, the faces, voices, all the names,
A life in each. Those feet that endlessly
Follow the Corridors. Who does not understand?
Who can forget the autumn and the apples
The leaves, the leaf-smoke? Who the winter?
And nobody the spring, the New England spring,
The first birds flying through the timid leaves,
The first trout rising along James's Brook.
The smell, the feel, the sense of all things growing.
In all the cities men remember this,
The President in the White House; the worried men
In Wall Street; the Ambassador to Japan
Through a cloud of cherry blossoms faces east
And through the spices, over unending ocean,
Over the mountains, over all the plains,
Sees other blossoms, sees the apple blossoms
And feels again the glory and the joy
Of being young when it is spring in Groton.

Now you who do not know him, all be quiet.
I will speak now in thoughtful, measured words.
I say this is, of all the sounding names,
A great one of our times. I say this man
Who has no vanity save that of manhood
Standing erect, head back to look for God;
Who has no envy save the wish for heaven;
Who loathes all baseness, but adores the brave,
Who, selfless, never stooped to look for fame,
Who incorruptible would not bear corruption,
Was all that we would have American.
He loved the old world, but he chose the new.

He measured ideas, but he chose the fact;
No scholar, but a champion of scholars;
Dreamer with common sense; setter of standards;
Pious, but good. There is no man
Who ever knew him base in any way.
We disagreed, we sometimes failed to follow,
But always when we turned bewildered eyes
He stood there sure; we wavered and returned
Grateful and yearning for abiding strength
To the shadow of a great rock in a weary land.

A man may best be known by epithets
That cling to him. They call him narrow.
So was the Straight Gate. We are not so narrow
You and I; Broadway is very wide by neon signs.
And swing is broad and Picasso is broad;
Nevada's broad and you and I are broad,
Broad as Sahara and its shifting sands.
So Peabody is narrow. He is in a rut.
For fifty years he has been in the rut,
For fifty years a granite block in a river
Of rushing lives all hurrying to the sea,
A never ending stream of human beings
Washing him in the torrent of their youth.
He's narrow without contact in his time,
Though one might mention as his constant friends
Jesus and all the other sons of God.

I think of him in sunshine, strong and doing.
I think of him as brave, bravest of all perhaps
In the news that he has turned while full of power
To leave the fine creation of his soul
For the sake of others. But he still goes on
As I think of him now, treading the thickets down,
Scorning the weeds and mud, facing the sun.
And an anger fierce as a springing beast
Tears at my heart at the shame of a sightless world
That lies and destroys and smears blind hands
On the beauty of life and utters blasphemous cries
And spews its unspeakable filth
Till the cities' streets run as sewers
And the mind and emotions are bogs
Lit with miasmic lights of shrieking will-o'-the-wisps.
The good lives fade in the night. They are stabbed in the dark.
There is nothing left but despair in a mad and hysterical world.

But when my anger is most hotly impotent
A figure walks across familiar places
And I hear the calls of boys in the evening
Hurrying in from the day. The lights come out,
The night wind breathes from New Hampshire hills
With just a scent of the sea touching new world shores.
A door opens wide and I see them stand
Again in a radiant glow and the world again
Puts on a vigorous splendor and those who are good
Seem good and those who are false seem false
And I say to myself and I say to the sons of my friends
"I am glad to have known these people and glad
To have felt the touch of their lives and my thanks
Go from an o'erflowing heart. We were friends
At Groton. We trusted the Good. *Nunc dimittis
Domine, servos Tuos.*" Because there may yet be a time
When hatred has withered the world, and vengeance has gutted
The dry reservoirs of faith, and dignity lies
Stripped in a blasted world and even cheapness is cheap,
We shall need to turn in our anguish
To the good and the strong and the loving,
To the disciplined, difficult thing,
Free as the bond are free, living as those who have lost
Their lives in the lives of others, and turning our eyes
See them still as they stand, pure and courageous
And faithful, loving and being loved
In a place where the grass is green and the voices
Forever are young and the chimes make mellow the afternoon.

The Rector and Mrs. Peabody went ahead with their plans
for Bermuda. He wanted to be in first-rate shape for the spring
term.

In 1939 Harvard also made him a doctor of laws. The official
citation with the degree read: "Endicott Peabody, the builder
of a famous school, a master honored and revered by generations
of devoted pupils."

44
RESIGNATION WITH RELUCTANCE

E. P. *aet.* 83-84

NOW his task was almost done. A successor still had to be chosen, but his views were on record in that connection and he had given the trustees clear sailing and plenty of time. When the Rev. John Crocker was elected, the Rector was confident that the school would be in good hands. Crocker was a Groton graduate of 1918, football captain and Brooks House prefect, with an honorable record at Harvard, teaching experience at Andover, graduate study at Oxford and Yale, and much experience with college undergraduates at Princeton, where he had won a most enviable reputation as one of the most promising younger men in the church. And, of the utmost importance, he had a charming and fine wife.

When Crocker had been chosen and had signified his readiness to accept, the Rector officially handed in his resignation, as follows:

17 February 1940

The time has arrived when it is fitting that I should hand in my resignation from the Board of Trustees. I do this with reluctance so far as feeling is concerned, but it seems to be for the interest of the School, which is the one thing to be considered.

During all these years, it has been my happy lot as a Trustee to work with the Board in all the experiences of our School life, as well as to receive from them as Headmaster their unfailing backing and sympathy.

It is with a consciousness of profound gratitude for the past and of confidence in the future that I take this action.

I ask that my resignation may take place in the end of June.

ENDICOTT PEABODY

Whereupon the Trustees voted to accept Mr. Peabody's resignation with regret and also those of Ellery Sedgwick, who had been on the board since 1909, and of Bishop Lawrence, who had been on it since 1884. The Bishop's letter and the resolution adopted in accepting his departure are here given:

1383 Brush Hill Road,
Milton, Massachusetts.
October 21, 1939

To the Corporation and Trustees of Groton School:

MY DEAR FRIENDS

When I presented my resignation from your Board some years ago, you kindly asked me to withhold it until a successor to Dr. Peabody had been elected. This has now been happily consummated and Mr. Crocker has accepted.

I therefore present my resignation to take effect at the end of this academic year of 1939-40.

I have been a Trustee from the Founding of the School. With the Headmaster, the Trustees, Teachers, boys and graduates my associations have been ever happy.

With a grateful heart I shall stand aside and watch with sympathy and confidence the life of the School and its second half century.

Yours faithfully,
WILLIAM LAWRENCE.

It was:

VOTED to accept Bishop Lawrence's resignation with regret and the following minute was adopted, a copy of which the Secretary was instructed to send to Bishop Lawrence:

Fifty-five years ago Bishop Lawrence became one of the original Trustees of Groton School. For nearly ten years he served as Secretary of this Board, and on the death of Bishop Brooks he became its Chairman. In both positions he has been wise in counsel, warm in friendship, and zealous in service. Groton School has received much from a bountiful providence, and Bishop Lawrence has been one of its goodliest blessings. The Trustees wish to record their profound thanks to him for his long and devoted association with the School and they rejoice to think that, despite his ninety summers, he is still young and vigorous. During the years to come his example will be a continual guide and inspiration to Groton School, which he has served so well.

The Bishop was a doubtful example of repose to a man retiring, since he was then in the thick of plans for raising money for a chapel for the Massachusetts General Hospital, the need for which had been suggested by Mrs. Peabody. He hoped to complete it in time to present it as a token on his ninetieth birthday, which he subsequently did.

The Rector had certain plans very much in mind. The new headmaster must have a free hand, and both the Peabodys were determined to put a long distance between him and them. After a year's absence they hoped to be allowed to return to make their home at Groton, near the place they loved so much, where Betsy could continue her valuable work in the school and Margery her nursing. The delicate question was, of course, whether having them in such close proximity would embarrass the Crockers, but this point was settled by the Crockers themselves urging that they come.

On June 6, 1940, he received the following letter:

June 6, 1940

DEAR MR. PEABODY:—

At the meeting of the Trustees of Groton School on October 21, 1939, the following action was taken relating to the house for you and Mrs. Peabody:—

VOTED that the committee is authorized to spend up to $40,000. if necessary on the proposed house for Mr. and Mrs. Peabody in which they shall be entitled to reside as long as they or the survivor desires; the said house may be situated on land lent for the purpose by Mrs. Barbara D. Danielson of Groton. In accordance with this loan, the house may be required to be removed from the land when it is no longer occupied either by Mr. or Mrs. Peabody and shall be of such size that it can be properly moved to land belonging to the School and used thereafter as a married master's house. Mr. and Mrs. Peabody will pay the taxes and upkeep of the property and shall be charged a rent not to exceed $2000 a year.

VOTED that Mr. and Mrs. Peabody or the survivor shall receive a pension from the school of $12,000. in lieu of the $10,000. that was voted at the spring meeting.

VOTED that Messrs. Washburn and Gardiner be appointed a Committee of two with full powers to make all necessary arrangements in regard to the new residence of Mr. and Mrs. Peabody within the terms of the previous votes. The location of the house shall not be limited to the Danielson land.

As the Committee appointed under the foregoing votes, we wish to report progress to the next meeting of the Trustees on June 14th, and in doing so, we want to be sure that our understanding is satisfactory to you and Mrs. Peabody, and we are, therefore, writing it out for your consideration:—

RHG

Rev. E. P.

First: The plan of erecting the house on Mrs. Danielson's land has been abandoned, and it is now planned to erect the house on land owned by the School on the south side of Joy Lane between Farmers Row and the Ayer Road.

Second: Mr. Daland Chandler has prepared sketches which he is now having made into working scale drawings of a house substantially 45 ft. by 47 ft., with a small one-story ell, which we understand you and your family like, and which it is hoped can be built at a cost of not much over $40,000.

Third: We consider that the house as planned can be considered within the scope of the Trustees' vote as to size, though clearly near the upper limit. You will undoubtedly agree with us that experience has proved that the final cost of such a house and incidentals connected therewith usually exceeds the original estimate. We understand that you are willing to pay yourself such part of the entire cost as exceeds the $40,000.

Fourth: We understand that it is your wish that the building contract and other necessary contracts be made by the School, with the approval of the architect and that payments thereon be made, in the first instance, by the School. We see no reason why this cannot be done, but naturally we will want your approval of any items running the cost over $40,000. because you will pay the excess.

Fifth: The Trustee's vote contemplated leasing the property to you and Mrs. Peabody for a term presumably to commence when you are prepared to occupy the house after its completion and to run throughout the life of both of you and the survivor provided that it may be surrendered to the School at the option of the occupants. The vote provided that the occupants would pay the taxes and upkeep of the property "and shall be charged a rent not to exceed $2,000. a year." During the occupancy of yourself and Mrs. Peabody, the property will be subject to local taxes, and there is no way of estimating with any accuracy what those taxes will amount to. We suggest taking the matter up with the Trustees at the next meeting with the suggestion that a flat rent be fixed, the School to pay the annual taxes and the occupants to pay for ordinary upkeep of the property.

May I hear from you that the foregoing statement of our understanding is correct? As we shall be spending school funds on the building contract and as our limit is $40,000. to be charged to the School, I think we ought to have for our records a letter from you

393

saying that if we will pay the initial cost of the house from School funds, you will reimburse the School for excess above $40,000.

Yours sincerely,

R. H. GARDINER

REGINALD WASHBURN

This was a most happy outcome. Immediately they set about plans with Daland Chandler, the architect who had done much of the recent work at the school. Mrs. Peabody had a task before her in the Headmaster's House (the Peabodys' House for so long). A great deal can accumulate in an attic in fifty years, let alone all the rest of a big house with its cupboards, drawers, and trunks. But they had to get it done; first that the Crockers might move in, and secondly because they had plans. He had always wanted an opportunity to study, so he decided to enroll in the University of Arizona.

45

THE LAST BOW

E. P. *aet.* 84

1941

THE trustees and graduates had been at work on plans for the Prize Day which would be the Rector's last bow. On May 5 after long preparation representatives of fifty-three of the school's fifty-five graduated forms came to Groton to express the accumulated gratitude and affection of the brethren. They gathered on a Sunday and the Rector preached at the morning Communion service. At dinner the senior prefect presented him with a check from the school, and George Rublee, '86, presented him with a check for $40,000 from the graduates to be used for any purpose he saw fit. He at once turned it with deep gratefulness over to the Trustees to be added to the Endicott Peabody Scholarship Fund. In addition the representatives gave him four richly bound enormous volumes containing snapshots and letters from every graduate who could be reached. One has to read through these volumes to appreciate their unique quality. One wonders if any man ever received such a tribute before. Many of the writers were old men, now, many famous; others were young, with life ahead; but all the letters bore the same message, of love and admiration and remembrance. George Rublee's letter, read for all, spoke for most:

MR. AND MRS. PEABODY:

Your retirement this year from active service to the school is a momentous event for all Groton graduates, masters and others interested in the School. We desire by this visit to bear witness to the affection and devotion which we graduates all feel for you both and to our admiration for the work you have done here through all these years. There is present a representative of every form that has graduated since the School began. So you have before you a kind of microcosm exhibiting in person from the oldest to the youngest the product of your labors over a period of fifty-four years. We are here to tell you how proud we are of what you have done for the School, how grateful for what you have done for us. When you, with Mr. Billings and Mr. Gardiner, started the School nearly fifty-six years ago, you were all very young and had not had much experience, but you did have a pefectly clear and definite ideal. You meant to give your boys sound scholarship, but even more you wanted, I believe, to develop in them elevation and simplicity of character so that when they left you they would not be content with ambition to get on in the world, but would care to be of use to their fellow men and their country. It is all implicit in our School motto "Cui servire est regnare."

Mr. Peabody, we believe that very seldom has it been the fortune of any man to fulfil so completely an ideal as you have fulfilled yours. You have founded and built up a famous school that has had a wide-spreading influence on education in other schools. The fine tradition you have inspired is now so deeply rooted that we are confident it will live on through successive generations of masters and boys. Your graduates in their lives may not have done all that you would have wished, but I think it may be truly said that they have done many things of good report. In public life, in the professions, in education and in business the record of their achievements is worthy of respect.

We are deeply grateful to you for your influence on our lives. We rejoice that you are going to live in Groton where we shall have the joy of finding you when we come back. Let me say, too, that this is no occasion for sadness, but rather for thankfulness for the past and confidence in the future.

As we thought of the coming change we decided to mark it in several ways that would express our admiration and affection for you and that we hoped you would like.

We have made up three great books which we hope will hold a long hand letter to the Rector from nearly every graduate, together with a recently taken photograph of himself. All the graduates will thus be able to express directly the feeling which today I have been trying to express on their behalf. The book is here, largely but not yet fully completed, and I now present it on behalf of the graduates, masters and ex-masters to you, Mr. and Mrs. Peabody.

It will be no surprise to you to learn that the graduates and masters have a very warm feeling for Betsy and Margery who have been so unfailing in their kindness and thoughtfulness towards us and who have done so much to brighten life at the School. So, as tokens of this feeling, I present to each on behalf of the graduates, masters and ex-masters a cigarette box in the form, as nearly as may be, of the paper weight milestones that are presented to masters who have served for twenty-five years.

We have also raised a fund for the School, the particular application of which we want to leave as fully as possible to the Rector. Let me assure him that we have made no "drive." We have exerted no pressure whatever. We have only given the graduates, masters and ex-masters an opportunity to subscribe, so that the contributions represent the spontaneous expression of their feeling for the School and the Rector. This fund amounting to $35,000 is now on deposit in the Fiduciary Trust Company in Boston to the order of Groton School Special Account and it is presented to the School to be dedicated to some object of the Rector's choosing, subject only to the customary right of the new Headmaster and the Trustees to approve the purposes for which the fund is to be used.

And now I have almost done. Mr. and Mrs. Peabody, may I say to you that from our hearts we wish for you every good wish. There can be no break in our relations with you. We count on many more happy meetings at Groton which for *your* old boys could hardly be Groton without you.*

To this the Rector replied in the next issue of the *Quarterly:*

DEAR ALUMNI:
This is the last *Quarterly* letter that I shall have the privilege of

---

* The discrepancies between this letter and the opening paragraph of the chapter are explained by the letter having been written before and the paragraph after all returns were in. The $40,000 figure includes the special gift of $35,000 and $5,000 for the Endicott Peabody Scholarship Fund.

writing as one having authority. That ceases with the boys on the 19th when they disperse to their respective homes. It has never been conspicuous in my dealing with the alumni. There have been instances of exercising authority even with them. On one occasion that I recall, I requested a graduate to do a certain thing. Perhaps I spoke somewhat abruptly. "No," said my friend, "I was obliged when I was at Groton to carry out your orders and now I won't do it." "That's all right," was my reply; "we have two of your sons at Groton." "I surrender" was the quick rejoinder. "What is it you want me to do?" And he did it. Most of my dealings with the older brethren, however, have been on the basis of sweet reasonableness.

It is more than that in the note that I would strike first today. My heart is filled with gratitude for the acts of kindness and generosity with which the alumni have dealt with me in these last weeks. In addition to the gift of William Woodward to which I have referred in my last letter, there has come to me personally the sum of no less than $35,000 contributed by the alumni. This has been transferred to the Scholarship Fund for scholars and students needing aid. For the same purpose there has been given by the alumni towards the Endicott Peabody Scholarship Fund the sum of $5000 which, as it has been coming in lately at this rate, might be used each year for scholarships. This additional increase to our income would be welcome for it would indeed enable us to offer greater assistance than we can offer now to brilliant scholars and to retain at the School the sons of parents whose incomes may be affected by the serious conditions of the times.

Nothing could have been conceived that would give me deeper and more lasting pleasure than the collection of autographs and pictures of the graduates which was presented at our gathering of representatives from the classes of the years 1886-1939. These will be a continual joy during the years that lie ahead. They contain expressions of friendship which I prize above all else and of appreciation exaggerated but valued for the kindly spirit in which they are written. Some of them come from those who were almost more positive in their opposite views in their boyhood time. I am reminded of one boy whose request was not granted and who declared that he would get even with the headmaster if it took a lifetime. At the present moment, he is represented by a son in the Upper School, and there is no trace of the promised retaliation in the attitude of the boy.

The reports from the colleges were duly presented in the *Quarterly* for March. Nothing of surpassing interest has taken place since then. We note with satisfaction that the Class Orator at Harvard is Tudor Gardiner; while at Yale the similar office is filled by MacGeorge Bundy, both of the Sixth Form of 1936.

In the School itself, the members of the Sixth Form have an unusual if not an unprecedented role of honor. Of the twenty-seven boys graduating, ten have satisfied requirements for the diploma; those graduating cum laude are nine in number; while eight are classed Magna cum laude.

In the beginning of our enterprise at Groton, there was published a statement to the effect that "Every endeavor will be made to cultivate manly, Christian character, having regard to moral and physical as well as intellectual development." Through the combined efforts of masters, boys, graduates, and parents this endeavor has been in some measure attained but, as we well know, only in part. Of this we are sure, a sound foundation has been laid for it in Jesus Christ. On it there will be erected gradually a building which we have confidence will become a power for good through the influence of Him whose service is perfect freedom. As the year draws to an end, I find my greatest happiness in the thought that we are in reality carrying out His commandment that we "love one another."

Affectionately yours,

ENDICOTT PEABODY

To these formal acknowledgments and salutations should be added samples of the great mass of personal letters of thanks and praise. One is overwhelmed by the quantity and quality of these. Selections from so many tributes is difficult, and yet only a minute portion can be included. There was always a steady flow, which increased in volume with the years and after the Fiftieth Anniversary and after the Rector's resignation became a torrent. What follows is a random choice from letters written between 1925 and 1941:

We face to Groton when trouble and sorrow come to us and you pour out your affection upon us and we are all so grateful. . . .

There is nothing that I know of that makes a person feel better in every way than going back to Groton. I only hope you realize that and get compensation from it for the amount of imposing that we all do. . . .

We feel that what he was was due to Groton . . . each year he came back to us a finer boy than the year before—I mean morally speaking. You gave him the blessing of faith and you taught by the example of your life all that went to make up his character. Groton will always remain associated in our minds and hearts with the boy who is gone forever. . . .

If you only knew the sense of deep affection that not only———, but both Mrs.———and I have for you dear people at Groton, I

398

think it might please you. It keeps constantly going through my mind as to what a privilege and blessing it has been for our boy to have been with you these several years. . . .

Do you realize, I wonder, just how moving your sermon was this morning. . . . how exalted and yet how humble a man feels after understanding the simplicity of great faith? For that is what I have found in your sermon. . . .

I want to thank you for your sermon this morning; such effect as it had on me (and I doubt not on others) needs some sort of expression of gratitude to you in order to clinch it in my mind. One loses a feeling of arrogance and an absurd presumption, and an honester attitude of mind takes its place. . . .

Yesterday I received the little book of prayers which you so kindly sent me. I wish to thank you from the bottom of my heart. . . . Also please allow me at this time to tell you that having known you is forever one of the very greatest privileges of my life. I have wanted to say this for a long time. . . .

As the years move forward, carrying me with them, and as I have more and more experience running three institutions . . . I realize more keenly my debt to you. . . . My training under you has been invaluable in meeting the variety of situations which have presented themselves during the last few years. . . . So often in my Groton days I did not have the wisdom to understand why you did things in certain ways. Now that I am obliged to control more or less the destinies of an organization and also to meet the variety of temperaments working in that organization, I can more easily understand your just and generous administration of Groton. . . .

[From the father of an English boy] I talked to him about Eton and he said "Oh well, you couldn't expect quite that at so big a school and besides they haven't the Rector" and then he went on to say things about you and Mrs. Peabody which if I wrote them would sound fulsome. . . .

Like nearly all Grotonians I look back at my years at school as not only the happiest, but the most valuable of my life. . . .

. . . the integrity of your high purpose reflected in the grounds, the buildings, the scheme of education and behavior. . . . No sacrifice, no devotion could have been too great for this achievement. In your heart you must know that it is Good. . . .

You will remember that when you occasionally lunch with me at the Downtown Club our progress to the lunch table is slow because so many graduates and parents want to greet you in the lobby and on the stairs. Equally my progress has been slow this last week due to the many who stop me and want to know about your operation and how you are getting along. When I tell them that you are already eating chicken pie you should see the relieved look that comes into their eyes as they realize that the warhorse has lost none of his fight. . . .

[To Mrs. Peabody] You know without my saying anything what my feelings for your most dear husband are. . . . Dr. Peabody is to my mind one of the very noblest of men, as generous-handed as he is generous-hearted. . . .

This short selection may well close with the following from Bishop Lawrence to the Rector just after the latter decided to resign:

Since Wednesday afternoon I have found it difficult to get the subject off my mind. While I am sure that you are wise and right in taking the action, it involves the closing of an era. Your life work in founding and leading the school these fifty-five years, our close friendship all that time, the influence of your character going with the Alumni throughout the world, all these and other thoughts are with me every hour of the day, and I thank God that as our birthday, May 30, is the same, so we have been united, even though in years you will never catch up with me.

Your old friend,
WILLIAM LAWRENCE

On Memorial Day, as he turned eighty-four, he rode as usual at the head of the parade in the village as marshal. His eye did not seem dimmed nor his natural force abated.

There was considerable concern over Prize Day. Of course there would be a huge crowd with the danger of trying tension and harrowing emotion. Those who worried about this reckoned without the Rector. He and Mrs. Peabody appeared on the platform as calmly as if it were an ordinary Prize Day. He was in great form, jovial and amusing, with his unfailing light touch for such occasions prefacing deep seriousness which he did not allow to get out of control. The early part of his speech, much of which was impromptu and lost, was broken by repeated applause and laughter. He had his last Prize Day audience with him. They had come to mourn and he made them enjoy themselves. He said (with unrecorded additions):

LADIES AND GENTLEMEN—FRIENDS OF GROTON SCHOOL:

On behalf of the trustees and the masters and the boys I bid you a hearty welcome and thank you for coming to see us today. This is the last opportunity I shall have to do anything of that kind. Next year I expect to receive a glorious greeting from one who will be in my place and I shall be grateful to him for it.

I am reminded of the situation of a friend of mine who was in almost a similar position to mine, and he harked back and was in the habit of saying,

"If I was only the person I have been!"

But he finally heard of some one in New Hampshire, who used to make a similar remark, "If I was only what I have been!"—until one of his friends said to him:

"Go on! Shut your mouth! You never was the man you have been!"

We had a notable meeting at Groton School on the 5th of May. There came together at that time representatives of all the classes since 1886 save one, whose delegate, after his usual manner, missed the train. Mrs. Peabody and I were deeply touched. We could hardly say so at the time, it is impossible to say now, the depth of our feelings. At that time we received generous gifts—they might be called donations, I suppose—generous gifts from the graduates to the sum of $35,000, which amount has been placed to the credit of the Scholarship Fund,—and from the boys, these boys in front of me now, $350. We did not quite know what to do with that. As I said to them, the first thing that popped into my head was "A horse!" But Mrs. Peabody and I could not ride one at the same time, so I gave that up.

Then I thought of some ornament which could be handed down from generation to generation, but I have six children and it might cause some dispute who should have it. And so we decided upon a section of the wall which surrounds the grounds. It is now pretty well under way and will soon be finished. That one segment of wall will represent that handsome gift of the boys. The inscription we have not quite decided upon. It might be: "In honor of the Headmaster in token of forgiveness on the part of the boys, and to his wife, to compensate her for the Headmaster's mistakes."

There were given us at that time three books * filled with photographs and letters from graduates. It is a remarkable instance, superficially, of organization. The president of the Alumni Committee with the help of friends collected those letters and photographs in two months, and there were mementoes from 800 boys.

At a time like this, one is conscious of gratitude not only for specific things and activities, but still more for the spirit of co-operation which has, we may believe, been developed through the help of friends who have been staunch supporters through all the years of the life of the School.

To the Trustees. I find some satisfaction, not to say pride, in the fact that in 1883 I appointed the members of the Board. At our first

* A fourth volume was subsequently added.

401

meeting, there was a question as to the selection of a Headmaster. For a few minutes there was silence, which was broken only by the loud beating of the heart of one of us; and then they made the appointment that had been hoped for; and they have been good enough, I will not say wise enough, to renew that appointment each year. Through all these years, in troublous times as well as prosperous, they have carried on the finances of the School, and stood by in all the changes and chances of the life of the School.

Gratitude to the masters. It is sometimes thought that the headmaster is the only one who does the work. He himself sometimes has that notion, but others are wiser. One wrote to me some years ago saying that he wished that I would get for him a headmastership. "I realize that I do not know enough to be a teacher," he said, "but I think I could be a headmaster." I may say that he never got an opportunity to prove it.

It is the masters individually and collectively who bear the burden and heat of the day, to whom the excellent work of the School—and I believe we are justified in calling the work excellent—is chiefly due. There, also, I arrogate to myself some credit in recognizing a good man when I see him. The result in the present body of masters is justified. This pride stretches back to the first year of the School when two of the very best that we have had accepted the call.

Gratitude to the graduates and the boys whom we have already commended.

Gratitude to the parents from whom we have received the utmost consideration and friendliness and I may say to an astonishing extent willingness to forgive what may have seemed to them our errors. On one occasion at Commencement at Harvard when Bishop Lawrence assured President Eliot that the graduates greatly appreciated his steady development in kindliness and character, he replied that the Bishop was accurate in his observations. He believed that he had improved. "The fact is," he said, "one cannot associate with parents for thirty years without being a better man." I trust that my experience may have had a similar tendency.

There is one department in which we need to go forward. This is in the relation between school and home in the growth of our religious life. This is a Church School. That means that it depends first of all upon worship and as a result of worship power and enthusiasm in establishing the Christian standards of life. The effect has not been that which we have aimed at and desired. There have been, there may be now in our number some who have not been affected as deeply as we could hope. It may be, however, that there has been developed what one may count a spiritual atmosphere which we all breathe and are consciously or unconsciously affected by. That is the kind of verdict which has been sent back to me by many of our boys fom the midst of their active lives. There is need for closer co-operation between the School and the home in this vital side of our life. In the prayer which we often use in our marriage Service we ask "that these Thy servants may love, honor, and cherish each other and so live together in faithfulness and patience, in wisdom and true godliness that their home may be a haven of blessing and of peace." There are such homes. Some time ago a boy returning to the School after sharing with his people in a sad tragedy told me that he would not have believed that religion could have done so much for anyone as it had done for his father and mother at that time.

There are homes above the entrance to which are engraved in words invisible but learned by the children in their early years: "Whatsoever things are true, whatsoever things are honest, whatsoever things are just, whatsoever things are pure, whatsoever things are lovely, whatsoever things are of good report, if there be any virtue, and if there be any praise, think on these things." It has been well said and the saying is even more impressive, "Most of us are Christians, not because we picked our precarious way to Christ, but because we saw the thing lived out in our father's strong, clear character or in our mother's beauty of unselfishness." Brought up in such a home as we have pictured to ourselves and with such parents, we, parents and teachers, can hope to have a vital part in the development of the men and women needed for a time like this. There never was a time wholly like this. In the history of the world, there have been even worse. It is a time when freedom is threatened by tyranny, Christianity by paganism. There can be no doubt in the minds of those who believe in Christ as to the final outcome. At last, far off it may be, but at last He will prevail; for God is King. Therefore we can believe

"That nothing walks with aimless feet
That not one life shall be destroyed,
Or cast as rubbish to the void
When God shall make the pile complete."

It is our privilege today to serve heartily, sincerely, if need be sacrificially Him whose service is perfect freedom. There must be in home, School, the parents, the teachers, and so in the boys if they will accept it, the supreme purpose of the living Christ; "for their sakes I sanctify myself that they also may be sanctified through the truth; and everyone that has this hope purifieth himself even as he is pure."

There are two things that create our greatest happiness today. The first is that John Crocker is to have charge of this school next year and for many years, we hope, so the future of the school is

403

safe and there will be growth; there will be the right kind of development.

The second is that for our speaker we have one whom I most desired and hardly dared to hope for—the presiding Bishop of the Church,—a leader, a great leader, who in his kindness has been willing to devote so large a portion of his valuable time to speak to us today.

After Bishop Tucker had spoken, Mrs. Peabody stepped forward to give out the prizes. As she came to the front of the platform the entire audience spontaneously rose to its feet and burst into a roar of applause. A great many of them were in tears, happy tears; there was nothing unhappy about it, as she stood there quietly, smiling at them. The applause went on it seemed for minutes. When it ended she blew them all a kiss and when they had sat down said a few simple words of thanks.

After the prizes, Bishop Lawrence, who also received a fine ovation said:

Not one word about the Rector, for I cannot speak much about him. For fifty-six years we have been together as trustees, more years than that as friends, and in those earlier years he told me of his expectation of founding the school. And now for fifty-six years we have been together and I shall say nothing about him more than this —that of all the fifty-six Prize Day speeches he has made, that of this year was lighter and more humorous than the one before, and the one before was more humorous than the preceding one. In other words, as the years have gone on the Rector has mellowed. There were Prize Days only a few years ago when parents rather shrank from coming to the exercises, because the Rector felt, as he told me himself, "It is the only time I can get hold of the parents, and I give it to them!" But with the kindness of Mrs. Peabody and the warnings of some of his friends there grew into his soul a richness of temper and a vein of humor which have made him what he is, and if he went on improving the time would come when there would really be nothing strong or rigid left in him.

Having said this much—and I cannot say more—I am going to read you a paper. Three or four weeks ago, when those books were presented in May, the trustees asked me to write a letter to the Rector. I was about to write a personal letter, and they asked me to write such a letter but at the same time to attach their names to it, feeling that what I would write might represent, as it has represented, their own sentiments about the Rector. Hence this paper which I am going to read has an informality and a friendliness to it which is personal, which belongs to the relations of the trustees and the Rector.

And may I say, this is the last word of the fifty-sixth Prize Day, except that at its close I shall ask the Rector to give us his blessing. The letter is a little long, but you will not get tired. We will ask the Rector to sit.

The following letter was thereupon read by Bishop Lawrence, the entire company except the Rector standing until its close.

To the Reverend Endicott Peabody.

MY DEAR COTTIE:

Now that you are laying down your work as Founder and Headmaster of Groton School, the present Trustees have asked me, your lifelong friend and sole survivor with you of the original Board of Trustees, to write a letter of reminiscence and record in which they may join.

First, may I sketch a contrast.

When in the spring of 1883 you confided in me your idea of founding a boys' school there was no Groton School except as it was embodied in you, and in your hopes and ideals. Today, Groton School—its boys, teachers, graduates, trustees, buildings, endowments, its influence throughout the Nation—is what it is; and this has come about through your character, personality and leadership. We who have worked with you pay you affectionate homage.

May I now amplify this thought by a few illustrations of the consistency with which you have carried your ideals into effect.

Your conscious consecration of yourself, in your early twenties, to the service of God and of your fellow men led you to consider some definite line of action. Your experience as a boy in an English school prompted you to think that by the founding of a boys' school here you could make some helpful contribution to American boyhood and manhood. While you fully appreciated high scholarship, your chief interest was in the development of the whole boy, physical, mental and spiritual; in character which at the base depends upon vital religious faith. Wisely, you determined to restrict your school to such numbers that you yourself could know each boy intimately, and make him your personal friend. You also determined that a consistent development of boy life and character was a matter of years, and that each boy should be with you five or six years. Your method of administration placed responsibility upon the older boys. In your selection of masters you have had in mind the gathering of men of ideals kindred with your own, that there might be unity of purpose and action. The photograph of the first Faculty, yourself, Billings, and Amory Gardner, 27, 27, and 21 years of age, with a total of one year's experience in teaching marks a venture of faith. The present Faculty numbers thirty-five, and the

405

record of their results in college scholarship and in the lives of many graduates devoted to public service demonstrates the worth of faith under wise leadership.

Fifty-six years ago Groton School's plant was a single building on a farm lying on a beautiful slope to the Nashua River, with Wachusett and Monadnock across the valley, a scene now bound up in the affection of graduates scattered all over the world. Today the School has the same beautiful outlook: a Chapel whose chimes rung by the boys sound across the valley; many buildings; and a most generous endowment. These all betoken confidence in you; for you, your character and your leadership have gathered this foundation. They reveal your ambition to give teachers such support that they may be able to do their best work, and to uphold the dignity and attractiveness of their calling. Indeed I believe that the exaltation of the office of teacher of boys which has developed throughout the Country in the last century owes much to your leadership.

As your colleagues on the Board of Trustees, may we say that throughout these fifty-six years we have worked with you in complete sympathy and unity. In this opportunity of continuing our friendship with you, and in the pleasure of service under your leadership we have gained far more than we have given. In the early years our meetings were occasionally ruffled by your difficulty in educating your father, the treasurer, to the thought that money, ever more and more money, was needed for teachers' salaries: an education to which he responded magnificently. He is to many of us the ancient hero of the School.

Of Mrs. Peabody, who throughout your service has been the center of charm, happiness and affection to boys, graduates, teachers and trustees, we think with love which reaches a deep and abiding reverence.

Affectionately,
WILLIAM LAWRENCE AND THE MEMBERS
OF THE BOARD OF TRUSTEES.

Bishop Lawrence: "Now I will ask the Rector to give us his blessing."

Mr. Peabody: "The peace of God, which passeth all understanding, keep your hearts and minds in the knowledge and love of God, and of his Son Jesus Christ our Lord. And the Blessing of God Almighty, the Father, the Son, and the Holy Ghost, be amongst you, and remain with you always. Amen."

46

RETIREMENT

HIS plans for leisure and study did not materialize. Arizona did them both good, but he was in constant demand to preach and speak. He had to forego once more his desire for quiet study and reading. There were friends to see, there was correspondence to attend to. It was pleasant, too, to be able to visit children and grandchildren, of whom there were many. He was one of the least retired gentlemen extant.

They returned to Groton in the summer of 1941 and were delighted with the new house. It was not right on the school grounds, but very near to them. It was only a few minutes walk to the Chapel, whose tower they could see, and the striking of the hours on the Schoolhouse bell was very clear. To the south the view stretched far away over valleys to hills beyond. It was a delightful house. He had a study and she a "boudoir" as of old, and there was a large sitting room with space for familiar pictures and things.

Now that he had opportunity to reflect, he could feel that it had been a good time to resign. In spite of the new and more terrible war, already drawing his family and boys into it, there was much to be thankful for. Things were well with his family. Save for the loss of one beloved grandson they were all safe and thriving. Malcolm was bishop of Western New York and a real power in the church. His wife was all a father or husband could wish. Endicott II was on the Harvard football team and about to be an overwhelming choice for All-American guard. Helen was happily married and Minturn Sedgwick, although he had left teaching to return to business and had disappointed the Rector by not entering the ministry, was a trustee, and a most welcome member of the family group. Rose and her husband were happily settled in New York, full of professional success and good works, with another fine family. Betsy and Margery were with their parents in Groton and the former an important factor in the life of the School. Dorothy and her husband, Trubee Davi-

407

son, were also admired and respected for what they were and did, and the whole family had been drawn closer together by the loss of one of their three boys while he was still at Groton.

Within a short time all these were to be widely scattered. Trubee Davison went back to Washington as a colonel in the Air Corps. Barclay Parsons went to Australia with his hospital unit, and Margery also went to Australia as an Army nurse. Rose was one of the mainsprings of the Red Cross in New York City. Minturn Sedgwick went to England as a major in the Air Corps. Betsy combined her school work with other work at Fort Devens. Young Endicott Peabody was in a submarine; Bill Parsons, who had played varsity football and baseball at Harvard, a lieutenant in Naval Air Force; Cotty Davison who had played against them both for Yale, an air cadet.

As in the last war, Groton as a whole was heavily involved. Word came from old boys from every corner of the earth and all too soon sad tidings, too, with the death of Major Richard Scott in a bomber in Tunisia and Lieutenant Frederick Crocker on a destroyer in the Pacific. Colonel P. M. Hamilton was awarded the Congressional Medal of Honor for heroic conduct in Africa.

At Groton he had left a strong crew. Regan stayed on for one year to help Crocker and was then succeeded as senior master by Paul Wright. one of the new generation. A strong co-adjutor in the Chapel had been found in Malcolm Strachan. The old guard had left or were leaving; Andrews, Call, Richards, Sturgis. Herr Griswold and Twining Lynes were dead, but they had able successors. On the administrative side there were, faithful and wise, Fred Torrey in the office and Miss Ames and Miss McConnell, whose faces brightened and softened when they saw or spoke of him.

---

* R. Minturn Sedgwick recalls the following incident which occurred toward the close of the Rector's headmastership. "It was before there was any widespread demand or controversy about Negro education. Mr. Peabody remarked casually to me that, if a Negro boy applied to the school and passed the necessary examination, he would be accepted. He then added he would be accepted even though it should prove that he was the *only* boy who turned up in the autumn at the opening of school. It was evident to me that the Rector was not anxious to be faced with the decision of taking a Negro, but he was absolutely clear in his own mind that no one should be denied admission to Groton because of race, regardless of the consequence to the school."

In the church there were fewer than he would have liked, but they were in important and influential places. Thayer Addison was teaching at the seminary in Cambridge; Alexander Zabriskie was dean of the seminary in Alexandria, Va. Others were doing essential work in parishes and schools.

In business, Boston, New York, Philadelphia, and many other cities were studded with names of his old boys.

And in Washington or other capitals there were so many of them that there was even talk of a conspiracy. He was still asked to the White House by the President to hold the special services for him at St. John's each year and at the beginning of each presidential term. Sumner Welles was next in rank in the State Department to Secretary Hull. Joseph Grew was ambassador to Japan on the day of Pearl Harbor. Pierrepont Moffat was minister to Canada and Luxembourg. Francis Biddle was Attorney General. Dean Acheson was first Undersecretary of the Treasury, then Assistant Secretary of State. Samuel Reber was the American official who carried on negotiations with Admiral Robert in Martinique. Averill Harriman was American minister in London * and chief figure in many important missions. Howland Shaw was also Assistant Secretary of State. In Albany, Abbott Moffat was recognized as the leading financial authority in the state and a force in the state Republican party. In New York city Newbold Morris was president of the council and on several occasions acting mayor of New York. Harper Sibley, president of the United States Chamber of Commerce, also was first chairman of the U.S.O.

In the newspaper field, in addition to Robert McCormick and the Chicago *Tribune* (in which the Rector took no comfort) and Joseph Patterson's *Daily News*, Joseph Alsop was writing a prominent Washington column and Alexander Sedgwick was writing signed articles for the *New York Times* from the Balkans and Africa.

With the coming of war he could not remain idle himself. Ever since his return from the west he and Mrs. Peabody had been traveling a great deal, so much so that she was worried about him. Now he saw and welcomed an opportunity to serve not only the country, but another cause he loved, religion, and he threw himself into the raising of funds for chapels, chaplains,

* Later ambassador to Russia. Shortly afterward Lincoln MacVeagh was appointed minister to South Africa.

and the whole spiritual welfare of all fighting men.*

There was a good deal of quiet wonder and some criticism that the Rector, even after a year's absence, should decide to take up his residence at Groton. Many felt such proximity would be hard both for him and his successor. Questioned point blank on the matter, John Crocker wrote in December, 1943:

The Rector and Mrs. Peabody's presence here has been, in my opinion, an unqualified blessing. I had apprehensions about it at first and I was very glad that they were good enough not to live as close as Mr. G's house, but as they do now, a quarter of a mile from the school circle. My concern was not that the Rector would interfere, but that with the reverence all of us feel I would not be fully myself. These fears have proved groundless, thanks to the Peabodys' understanding and magnificence. The first year they went to Tucson and since then the Rector has given me a complete sense of freedom. Much as we see of each other, we rarely talk about school policies, but rather of things that have happened in the past, though on one or two occasions I have consulted him about decisions that had to be made in regard to boys.

In view of the fact that the Rector was Czar of the School for so many years, it is inevitable that certain changes must have seemed of doubtful benefit to him. I know indirectly, for instance, that the substitution of voluntary evening Chapel for evening prayers in the House schoolrooms troubled him pretty deeply. But he never mentioned it to me or departed from the principle of letting me work out my own salvation. . . .

He and Mrs. Peabody are in close touch with the School. The Rector teaches I form Sacred Studies; he and Mrs. Peabody lunch with us several times a week; he frequently reads letters to the faculty from graduates or friends; on occasion he preaches in Chapel; every Christmas since his retirement (except for the year in Tucson) he has read the *Christmas Carol*, and every year he seems to do it more perfectly. Above all the Peabody house is a haven of hospitality to boys, masters, and graduates. It would be hard to exaggerate the strength to the School of having graduates able to see him when they return.

It's worth mentioning that on Wednesdays he drives to the town to attend the Rotary Club luncheon. His staunch support has done much to make the Club, recently started, a success and through it we have become more intimate with many fine people of the town.*

* In early 1944 two Grotonians were brigadier generals and one was a commodore.

410

Meanwhile he was lionized wherever he went. For instance, the Headmasters' Association, of which he was the only surviving charter member and of which he had been president in 1899, made much of him and asked him to conduct a short service for them all at each session. He brought his robes and led them in the old familiar prayers. In 1943 it was a long trek on a bitter winter day from Groton to Rye, but he had said he would come and he came, in spite of Mrs. Peabody's misgivings. She sent a wire to Frank Boyden † to have an eye out for him. It was a hard trip, with changes and no porters for heavy luggage. He went on by himself, but slipped and cut his hand, which he wrapped up clumsily. A stranger helped him with his bags and he was struck, as he had been sixty years before, by the uncommon friendliness of people. "It makes one realize," he said, "that in America people are just folks." He arrived just as the headmasters were finishing dinner; looming in the doorway, pale and battered, but keeping his appointment. As he entered, all the brethren rose spontaneously (it was a common thing these days) and applauded. He was full of jokes about his travels and ate an uncommon hearty dinner.

Next morning he began the day for them with his service. His mind went back to the first meeting in '93 and he spoke of how different things had been: at that time peace and prosperity; today distressed nations, men's hearts failing them for fear. Should we schoolmasters not begin with gratitude that we have so great an opportunity for the development of the character of youth, on which depends the salvation of mankind? He quoted a letter he had received from William Lawrence, just before the latter died at ninety-two:

I see no other course than to quietly, firmly, grimly if necessary, prepare for war, its sacrifices, taxes, loss of friends and family if need be, its ghastly, horrible, insane destruction of almost everything that has made our civilization and our happiness. Every man, woman, boy or girl in this democracy is subject to call by the nation for service, for any kind of service, and for any length of time. We are bought with a price. It is the price of liberty.

He urged fortitude under all conditions. The fundamental nature of man is such that he can be finally satisfied with nothing

* He was reported to be particularly effective in his manner of joining into the choruses of the Rotary songs.
† Headmaster of Deerfield Academy.

411

short of justice and freedom and personal equality, and will fight for them with courage to the end. But, he said, in our struggle for liberty and conviction of final victory we must, with God's help, put aside hatred of our enemies. They are so imbued with these things that are abhorrent to us that we must use force to the utmost, but we must also try to cling to the faith that they are also God's children. "Blessed are the peace makers, for they are the Children of God." The other danger which threatens us from within is the destruction of our homes. We must work devotedly to restore and maintain the integrity of family life. He quoted his favorite description of the ideal schoolmaster:

> Of all the intellectual and moral elements which go to make a master—the originality which does not despise method; the flexibility of mind and sternness of character; the sympathy with learners, and attitude of ever learning; the instinctive appreciation of small traits of character; the love of human souls that will count no pains too great to save a boy, that never despairs of a lad; the sense of duty that sustains in wearisome routine; the deep understanding of character that makes the whole life a conscious, though often a secret service of God, the last is, as any wide experience will show, the most precious of all.

And then he launched into the prayers, beginning, "Almighty God, our Heavenly Father, who art the only source of light and life, send down upon our Schools the rich gifts of Thy Good Spirit, that Thy truth may be sincerely sought, faithfully received, and obediently followed." It was William Lawrence's prayer from long ago.

He seemed a symbol standing there. Many of the men disagreed with his theories; many instinctively felt that Groton's way was not their way, but integrity is timeless and character outleaps differences of opinion. The Old Masters, so many of them, had departed. Even Horace Taft, with his wit and tolerance, was gone. Peabody stood alone, as was his wont, a symbol to younger men of both public and independent schools. He was the past, and the living, indomitable present, and what he had been and was seemed the only way if there was to be a future. Looking and listening, one knew that in teaching, as in life, when all the theories and little things are husked off there is seen the one thing that counts; the living personality composing the man who loves God with all his heart and soul and mind, and his neighbor as himself.

In the summer of 1942 he and she went to Squam Lake for a change. Walter Hinchman saw them. He wrote:

"We decrepit sexagenarians arrived in a motor boat, but, soon after, a row-boat came around the point. . . . Fannie in the stern, brave and cool with ribbons and a parasol; Cotty in the bow, very natty with the Groton hat-band on his straw hat and a blazer—still rowing. What Graduate or Master would not have loved that picnic, with "seniores priores", "te duce sequar", "change what you please to call your mind and have another sandwich, old man", all the little familiar language in good flow? May the Rector row many miles yet, with Mrs. Peabody serene and beautiful in the stern.*

* This motif persisted through the years. In January 1944, Dr. Edward B. Krumbhaar, a graduate, wrote: "During a fortnight at Northeast last summer [1943] we were fortunate enough to see a good deal of the Rector and Mrs. Peabody. One day after a heavy storm, he asked me to help him turn out the water from his rowboat on the Yacht Club float ('I don't like to lift too much any more') and the two of us just about managed it. We put it in the water, in stepped Mr. and Mrs. Peabody and they started off, each with double sculls, to row around to their place on Soames Sound, a good part of a mile out and practically ocean all the way. The Rector's back was as straight as it was in his college boat. . . . I wondered how often octogenarian couples indulged in such recreation. Their combined age must have topped that of an average Groton 8-oar! Incidentally, never has he been more entertaining, or in better conversational form, with Mrs. Peabody—God bless her—her own perfect self and imperceptibly guiding the show." Numerous others have spoken of similar episodes.

47

RETROSPECT

A GROUP was sitting talking about him. They were trying to formulate what he had been and how and why. It was difficult, because so few of the ordinary measuring rods were applicable. Numerically, his work had been of the slightest. There were many schools that had in three or four years as many students as he had had in a lifetime; the enrollment of many colleges in a single year exceeded his total. The principle of continuity was also hard to allow for. We had to compare the few years allowed most men to realize a dream with the fifty-six he had had. There were the obvious advantages that came to him by birth and inheritance for which he deserved no credit. But then there was the counter-fact that he had used these advantages to the utmost, which seemed the main point, so far as he was concerned.

One man insisted that to the end he remained a professional amateur. This was a minority view, yet it had force. As a churchman he made no theological contribution; he had neither advanced nor retarded the mainstream of Christian thought; he had held no high office in the Church; he had only fragmentary experience in the ordinary work of a parish priest. As an educator he had had singularly little to do with the dynamic trends and investigations of his time in a pedagogical sense. He never seemed to enter wholeheartedly into the field of theory, as he always fought the idea that teaching can or should be limited to the mind alone. He was primarily a personality, interested in persons, each of whom he saw most importantly as a child of God.

All his life he had been in the minority. When he returned from England he brought with him a conception of the gentleman's place, nature, and function in society which differed from the prevalent American conception. He thought his idea was sound, workable, and he stuck to it. The results he let speak for themselves. His way of life was a gentleman's way. Someone said that while he would have been content had his children married, so to speak, the Joneses, and would not have allowed them to drift away, he was very happy when, in point of fact, they married Parkmans, Parsons', Davisons, and Sedgwicks. His knowledge of America was a minority knowledge; for all his travels, his time was spent and his friends were found among "nice" people. He did not like or choose to work or play among any other kind. Even among this broad minority group he was often an inner minority. Again and again he opposed the mores of his kind. When the prevalent American doctrine was that power and standards came from a great majority, the people, he held steadfastly that power and standards came first from a multitude of tiny minority groups, the homes. When statesmen and authors wrote about the importance of citizenship, he hammered at the moral responsibility of the individual. When they grew excited about rights and privileges, he insisted on the essential nature of duty and standards.

It could not have been done without a hard, indestructible core of inner strength, without a quality of stern inflexibility and dogmatism and ruthlessness.. This core was simple, welded of simplicities. Of course it was enormously helped and made attractive by a rare charm of person and a resilience of temperament. But it was composed of simplicities. Utter honesty; complete outspokenness; a phenomenal capacity for hard work and then complete relaxation; a trust in character rather than in possessions; a conviction of individual responsibility; a sense of obligation to the larger group and larger welfare in the long run; a determination to hold fast to the things which had been proved good; singleness of purpose undistracted by petty or personal considerations; and, above all, perhaps, the faith that he was working not his own work but the eternal work of an eternal God. He conducted himself as though he felt that

> Life, like a dome of many colored glass
> Stains the white radiance of eternity.

Feeling so, he swung in his feelings and his desires not to the things temporal but to things which were forever true. When he preached, he preached simplicities; character, duty, responsibility, love, and behavior.

And yet this central core was still further hardened by a protective and penetrating plating of common sense. He had as keen an awareness of the celestial city as ever Bunyan or Arnold had, but he agreed with Thring about "the almighty wall" and with Butler that one purpose of a school is to produce scholars. He would have heartily disapproved of an estimate of Groton based on its lifeless possessions, but he accomplished the fact that enabled Pierre Jay to write in 1926:

Groton has received in gifts something over $2,500,000; of this about $1,600,000 is in investments and about $900,000 in land and buildings. Assuming 185 pupils, this means an endowment of $13,500 per pupil and assuming a 5% return, an annual income of $675 per pupil. It is safe to say that hardly any, if indeed any other school in this country has an endowment which approaches ours.

And in 1939, just before the Rector retired, the total endowment funds amounted to $3,629,076.50 and the value of the plant was set at $1,762,666.51.

The inflexibility of the central core of his being meant hardship for individuals. One suspects this may account for the rather general characteristic of independence of thought among a surprising number of Groton graduates. The individual who was different at school was different in the face of odds. It was a kind of survival of the fitter. The mildly different were overwhelmed or discarded. The real independents were polished by the grindstone and as a mere matter of survival developed their independence to the point of great endurance. This probably explains, too, why, despite the common impressions that all Grotonians are typical, they are actually, under a thin veneer of custom, about as atypical a group as one could find. The nonconformists lived only at the expense of constant friction. This tempered them and perhaps made their nonconformity less wild-eyed than that of some of their friends, but no less effective.

All agreed that the part Mrs. Peabody played was crucial. He could not have been what he was without her. She was to him as the atmosphere to the earth. Often one is not aware of it, but it enfolds all and is breathed by all, and in or through it are reflected all colors and beauty. Beyond, all is darkness and emptiness to the very gates of heaven; close to the earth the lightning flashes and the thunder rolls, but above and around this area of storms is wrapped the calm, pellucid, and unearthly protection of the upper air. Such was the Madam. She was as patrician as he, perhaps more so. She was innocent, in the true meaning of the word. She was simple, caring nothing for society and its way, but everything for gentility. She might have said, paraphrasing John Adams' words: "No mind but one can see through the immeasurable system. It would be presumption and impiety in me to dogmatize on such subjects. My duties in my little infinitesimal circle I can understand and feel. The duties of a daughter, a sister, a mother, a neighbor, a citizen, I can see and feel, but I trust the ruler with his skies." There was no household near Groton School which did not know her thought and ministry; no boy or family who did not feel her presence. She was as dutiful as he and more unselfish, it may be, because she made it her duty to serve and protect him. Like him she believed by nature. Logic was less potent than instinct; what Whittier called "the reason of unreason." No need to dogmatize. Be transparently what you are and "trust the ruler with his skies."

The analysis did not seem to have got very far. It was a little like attempting to express the Gettysburg Address in terms of grammar, or to describe the Sistine Madonna by a chemical formula, or Chartres Cathedral by blueprints. The thing was there, it was like a great many other things, and it was unique. Someone said, "For their sakes we would all like to have sanctified ourselves."

That was it, possibly. That, and that the work was still unfolding and would unfold until the last of his graduates was dust. And then, still, it would go on into time.

Or reduced to simplest terms, he was big, he was strong, he was single-hearted; he was fortunate, he was lovable, and he was good.

48

I HAVE BEEN A MOST
FORTUNATE MAN

E. P. *aet.* 86

I WENT up to see them in the spring of '43. They had just returned the night before from a trip to Washington, arriving in Ayer at 2:30 A.M. unmet, because the Rector had made a little slip as to the date in his telegram, which vexed them both. But people had, as always, been very kind.

Before supper I sat with him in his study and we reminisced. They were after him again to write an autobiography, but he would have none of it. He couldn't write and there was nothing interesting to write about. A dull book of fifty pages was better not done at all. At supper they wanted to know about each member of my family. After supper we sat around the fire in the big room, the Madam and Betsy and Helen knitting; he smoking a denicotinized cigar and wearing a Groton blazer. They remembered Salem, and she how good looking he had been in his flannels and college colors. We talked of the projected story of his life. When a copy of the first draft was sent him he was too busy to read it for five weeks.

Breakfast was at eight and Mrs. Peabody a trifle severe because he had not told her promptly it was ready. Immediately after breakfast we went into the big room for family prayers, to which the servants also came. We sat as he read the Gospel for the day, and then knelt on the carpet by our chairs for the Lord's Prayer and collects. It was difficult for them to rise and chairs came handy in getting up. His legs were bothering him a bit.

We talked again. I ventured a few words of admiration for what he had accomplished. He waved it aside, simply and decisively. "I have been a most fortunate man," he said. "The things for which people are kind enough to give me credit were largely not my doing and they were very little and for them I have to thank my wife, my friends, the trustees, the masters, and the boys. They forget the failures and the mistakes. But it has been fun and most interesting. I have been a most fortunate man."

Afterward I thought about it. It was true, of course. He had been a most fortunate man; the most fortunate I have ever known, incredibly fortunate. Astounding health, never in a hospital until he was over sixty and never really ill until he was past eighty; a wife in a million, spared and blessed even as he had been, always beside him; six children all of whom were alive, well, and useful; always more than enough money; opportunity taken; a job he loved and could do well; friends who were not only rich and understanding, but generous; opportunity to travel widely and experience much; uninterrupted time to carry out his plans in a tenure of office and virtually absolute power for fifty-six years, a reign, so far as I could remember, unparalleled in history; long, long life and the privilege of living to see his work proved and acclaimed; honor as the world gives it in abundance; all those years untroubled by fear or doubt. Yes, a most fortunate man indeed. And perhaps the final good fortune, the fact that he knew it.

I walked past the School before I left. It looked as if it had been there forever. Boys were coming and going as they always had. The chimes sounded. I knew, that this life which had touched mine so closely was unique; that though the world was at war, it had to be told, however inadequately. I remembered him in the pulpit, as I had seen him so often, pawing with his right hand as though he were digging into us. "That's it, that's it, my boys." The lines from *Rugby Chapel* came into my mind:

What is the course of the life
Of mortal men on the earth?—
Most men eddy about
Here and there—eat and drink,
Chatter and love and hate,
Gather and squander, are raised
Aloft, are hurl'd in the dust,
Striving blindly, achieving
Nothing, and then they die—
Perish; and no one asks
Who or what they have been, . . .

And there are some, whom a thirst
Ardent, unquenchable, fires,

419

Not with the crowd to be spent,
Not without aim to go round
In an eddy of purposeless dust
Effort unmeaning and vain. . . .

But thou wouldst not *alone*
Be saved, my father! *alone*
Conquer and come to thy goal, . . .

Such was the great and good man whom I have tried to portray. I turned and set my face up the road.

POSTSCRIPT

On November 17, 1944, Mrs. Peregrine Acland, wife of a former master, had lunch with the Rector and Mrs. Peabody. Early in the afternoon Mr. Peabody offered to drive Mrs. Acland to the station in Ayer. She noticed he had a little trouble with the foot pedals of the car and he made some pleasantry about it. As they drove, Mr. Peabody remarked "Franklin Roosevelt is a very religious man." These proved to be his last words. A few hundred yards later, just after they had descended the hill, one-quarter of a mile beyond the old golf course now disused, Mr. Peabody slowed the car, drove to the side of the road and turned off the ignition. He slumped in his seat, Mrs. Acland looked at him and to her amazement saw that he had certainly fainted and appeared dead. She went immediately to the house owned by Mr. Arthur Havemeyer, less than one hundred yards away, and sought help.

Mr. Peabody was dead. To those who knew him the manner of his death seemed symbolic; a mercifully swift departure accompanied by a massive final act of will for the sake of another, an act accomplished at the very instant of death.

The Chapel Service was unforgettable. Graduates, parents, trustees, friends, neighbors, fellow headmasters, and many who had not known, but admired, him came from near and far; New Yorkers by a special train. It seemed a triumphant occasion, with sorrow tempered by pride and affectionate gratitude.

Mrs. Peabody died peacefully in 1946. She rests by his side in the lovely cemetery in the town of Groton.

AUTHOR'S POSTSCRIPT AND
ACKNOWLEDGMENTS

Several things should be said about *Peabody of Groton*. It was written at the joint request of Thomas R. Coward and several of the Groton trustees. It was also undertaken with a definite sense of personal obligation as a labor of affection. Originally, the Reverend Alexander C. Zabriskie had expected to do it, but having other work in hand he could not anticipate finishing the task for several years, and with typical generosity he turned over the opportunity and material which he had already collected to me.

From the beginning the task seemed both simple and complex. There was unusual unity of place and action. But this very unity offered difficulties. A chronological account of fifty-six years of daily life in a boy's school is a stiff bill of fare for most laymen. Such a life is inevitably repetitious to an unusual degree. Faces and names change, but the problems of 1890 were singularly like those of 1940. This is especially true in a small school. Endicott Peabody further presented difficulties of his own as a subject for a biographer. He wrote very little that was published; he did not deal in educational theory or in theology in the large sense. He was not an active participant in any of the great political questions of his long day. He taught boys and ran a school and was what he was. In other words his significance was that of personality, of character, and that significance was very great.

Once that fundamental premise was accepted the other things fell into perspective. The next problem was that of presentation. An ordinary biography was the simplest solution, but not a wholly satisfactory one. Mr. Reginald Washburn wanted a *Tom Brown*. Now *Tom Brown* certainly did for Arnold's fame more than Stanley's biography, but one cannot produce a *Tom Brown* on demand. Further, for all its fineness, *Tom Brown* is not all of Arnold by any means, any more than Stanley was. Actually, this book was written first in a compromise form. The story was told through the members of three generations of an imaginary Groton family. The device had a great deal to commend it, but after much thought and on the advice of friends whose counsel I valued, it was abandoned and the present form adopted instead.

422

The question arose, of course, as to the advisability of writing the life of a man while he is still alive. This was an important matter which had to be disposed of before the work began. The advantages were clear; the opportunity for checking facts, the chance to discuss actions and theories, the desirability of personal recollections, the illumination of incidents by the subject's own interpretation; all these had to be weighed against the dangers of hurting where one loved by publishing material necessary to a true portrait, but perhaps painful to the one portrayed; the summoning of old and painful memories from time long past; the rubbing off of scars; the danger of telling less than the truth for fear of hurting. What could be called a living biography should not be attempted without considering all these things. In this case, once the determination to proceed was taken I went to Endicott Peabody and told him that as far as I could I was going to give a true picture of him; that it might be necessary to include material which he or Mrs. Peabody would prefer be left out; that my hope was he would let me send him the manuscript and that he would criticize it freely, indicating any omissions, additions, or emendations that occurred to him, but stipulating that since I had to take final responsibility for the book I was to be in no way bound by his suggestions. To this he agreed.

A typical and amusing thing resulted. When I sent him the original manuscript, which was, after all, his first biography, he was so occupied with other business (being retired and eighty-six years old) that he had no time for about five weeks to finish reading about himself! He then went through the manuscript with great interest and a mass of reservations. He would have reduced the material finally included by at least a third. He felt he was grossly overestimated. One thing particularly distressed him, that in a time (1943) when he felt the paramount need in the world and the churches was for unity, I included several old letters and episodes which might lead to hurt feelings and disunity. They were included because, while they may not have represented his feelings at the time this book was written, they did represent his feelings, as recorded by himself, at the time they were written. Since he read through the first manuscript a great many changes have been made, and the entire book recast. Neither he nor any member of the Peabody family had read it in its final form prior to publication.

Boswell gave me my instructions:* "You, my dear Sir, studied

* Mr. E. F. Benson's dictum has also been much in mind:
"The ideal Biography . . . should, though strictly founded on fact, read like a work of fiction. Selection, arrangement, development, the intertwining of its various threads to form a tapestry, are characteristics of its technique." Quoted by Sir Henry Newbolt in the Preface to *My World As In My Time*, Faber and Faber, London, 1932.

him, and knew him well; you venerated and admired him. Yet luminous as he was upon the whole, you perceived all the shades which mingled in the grand composition; all the little peculiarities and slight blemishes which marked . . . the Colossus." This, I have at least tried to do. And I should add that in a conversation with Peabody when he was most vehement about certain matters he concluded by saying, "But of course you must do just as you wish."

It has been said that a tree can best be measured when it's down, and that is true enough if the object is primarily measurement. If the object is appreciation, is being able to view and sense the living thing, that is another matter. A picture is best painted while the tree is up. No autopsy in the world can be the same as a portrait done from life. This book is not the history of an epoch nor of an organized philosophy nor of a sect nor of a school of education; it is the portrait of a man, and therefore of an individual attitude towards life; a painting of values both mundane and eternal as they existed in a man I knew.

One of the most difficult problems was to avoid making selections or interpretations in terms of my own schoolmastering and other prejudices and attributing the result to Endicott Peabody. This has been much in my mind as a danger at all times. I can say only that as far as lay in my power and discretion it was avoided. Wherever possible I have made him speak for himself, and a very considerable part of the book is actually in his own words.

The main sources of material used were these:

1. About sixty volumes of files containing letters to and from the Rector, now in the possession of Groton School. This accumulation contains letters of many kinds from about 1890 to 1941, but there are certain gaps of years. At first it seemed a serious thing that almost all the early letters saved were to him and not from him, since for numerous years he did all his correspondence long hand and kept few copies. Reflection showed, however, that often what was written to or about him was as revealing as what he wrote himself. Mr. Fred Torrey, Miss Ames, and Miss McConnell of Groton helped me gather this material.

2. The Atwood letters. These run from 1881 to 1943. Bishop Atwood kept everything the Rector ever wrote him, and the collection was an unexpected treasure trove, not merely in serving as an invaluable chronological check, but in that they were all personal letters, written in the intimacy and relaxation of friendship, with no idea that they would ever be seen by anyone save Atwood. They clearly constitute most important evidence. The whole collection (of which only a small part has been used) is now in the possession of Groton School. Material contained in the letters themselves was

reinforced by numerous long conversations with the Bishop over a period of years. My debt to Bishop Atwood is very plain.

3. Files of the *Grotonian* and the *Groton School Quarterly*.

4. Miscellaneous documents, articles, and letters in many places and from widely varied sources to which my attention was called. I trust all who helped me in this manner will permit me to thank them here. In this connection I am especially indebted to Lieutenant (j.g.) Acosta Nichols, Jr., U.S.N.R.; to Mr. Gordon Knox Bell, Sr.; to Mr. Charles P. Curtis, Jr.; to Mr. S. Warren Sturgis; and to Dr. Harry A. Murray for valuable material. It was more than kind of President Roosevelt, with all his burdens, to send me numerous letters.

5. *Groton Myths and Memories* by William Amory Gardner (privately printed at the Rumford Press, Concord, N.H., in 1928).

6. *Fifty Years On; A Short History of Groton School* (Gosden Head Press, 1935). Since I wrote this volume myself for the fiftieth anniversary of the school; since its circulation was restricted almost entirely to the Groton family, and since it embodied a considerable amount of research handled "as well as I could attain unto," I felt free to use it liberally without benefit of quotation marks.

7. Particular papers dealing with Endicott Peabody for which I asked. Such are incorporated in the text. I am much in the debt of Mr. George W. Martin and the editors of *Harper's Magazine* for allowing me to help myself to material in Mr. Martin's article *Preface to the Biography of a Headmaster* appearing in *Harper's* in January, 1944. For descriptions of Mr. Gardner I am indebted to Mr. Richard E. Danielson, Mr. Morris Hadley, and the late Mr. Rogers MacVeagh.

Other acknowledgments to and of sources used are given in the text.

A word should be said as to the choice of selections. Because of Peabody's complete identification with Groton it was necessary to take precautions lest the portrait turn into a history of Groton School. If it is, indeed, partly that, the responsibility may justly be laid to his door. Yet an earnest effort has been made to keep it his story and not that of the place. In choosing letters and other quotations, therefore, the following general rules were adopted:

1. Where a letter to or from him or a communication about him served to illustrate some facet of his character it was included, but not more than one such letter was ordinarily allowed for any one facet in any single period.

2. Where a letter or other excerpt contained important chronological or other facts it was used.

3. Where a letter or other document threw light on Peabody's educational or spiritual practice or belief it was used.

425

4. Where direct quotations added to the pleasantness of the story and at the same time were reasonably pertinent they were used.

5. Where quotations, sometimes at length, illustrated a major contribution of his to American education they were included for the sake of the record; as in the case of his position in regard to faculty salaries.

All quotations, wherever possible, have been checked with the originals and in most cases were copied directly from them.

A further word is in order as to the punctuation, spelling, and abbreviations used in the book. It should be remembered that many of the letters quoted (and some of the longer papers) were written by Peabody hastily in longhand with no idea or intention that they would be subjected to public scrutiny. In all cases his own words are given as he wrote them or as they were originally printed. This will account for the divergent usages which will be found. There has been no editing (except for excisions) of direct quotations from him or anyone else in the book. Excision was necessary to keep the volume within publishable limits. Material was available to make a series of volumes comparable in length to Lockhart's *Life of Sir Walter Scott;* it is my belief that while much additional material may be found as time goes on, it is not likely that any new facts or trends will be discovered which will materially alter the portrait here given.

Lastly, it would be extremely ungracious and thankless were I to omit a few specific acknowledgments: To the Rector and Mrs. Peabody for giving me complete access to any material I needed and for furnishing a good deal I did not know about; to my sister-in-law, Miss Marian Batcheller, and my daughters for helping me with much copying; to the Rev. J. Thayer Addison for reading certain chapters and offering good suggestions and criticisms in connection with those parts dealing with the Rector's religious life; to Mr. Walter S. Hinchman and Mr. H. Emerson Tuttle, my former teachers to whom I owe so much, for the candid criticism I knew they would give when I troubled them to read the original manuscript; to Mr. James D. Regan for unfailing help, encouragement, and counsel; and to Lieutenant and Mrs. Fessenden Wilder for much kindness and support; to her for typing the manuscript, to him for criticism and suggestion. To Mr. Richard S. Russell I am indebted for working out a detailed genealogy of the Peabody family and for allowing me to use the abbreviated form of this printed at the end of the first chapter.

My wife copied page after page of original letters and papers for me and was endlessly patient during periods of intensive work. As always she was unsparing in criticism which she thought would help and did help. But I long since despaired of catching up in thanks

with her whose constant care during happy years has made my
gratitude seem so poor.

F. D. A.

North Andover,
April 20, 1944.

APPENDIX

Letter and Report of a Graduate Trustee
on Conditions at Groton in 1931,
with Peabody's Reply

The letter and report: November 9, 1931
DEAR MR. PEABODY:—
Let me repeat my thanks and gratitude for the opportunity of
coming to Groton.

I think that the School is at once the same School I went to in
1905-10 and a very much better one. I should say that the instruction is far better, more free, more alive, and more eager, as well as
more intellectual. Your newer and younger Masters I liked immensely. Without prejudice to or comparison with the others, but
because I thought that he was not one to push himself forward, I
should like to express my admiration for Mr. ———'s teaching. I
thought he was teaching history to the Third Form with an intellectual candor and freedom from dogmatic authority which is rare
and for which most students have to wait until college. I regret that
this was all that I saw of him.

I am enclosing a few memoranda on various phases that struck me
most. On a few small points I am a bit diffident owing to the fact
that I can not help judging from six years' experience twenty odd
years ago as well as from my recent experience of only two days.
On the other points, on the other hand, I am very confident. I wish
I could be present at a Faculty Meeting and hear my remarks and
suggestions discussed.

I also enclose a copy of a letter I have written to Roger Moore.

Yours most sincerely,

CHARLES P. CURTIS, JR.

427

I think the social divisions between the forms are too many and too impermeable. In a community of 180 an individual should be on familiar and equal terms with as many as possible. To put it another way, only for special reasons, such as keeping the new boys apart until they have learned to belong to the School, or such as keeping the third form (and the fourth?) at a respectable distance from the first and second, is segregation justified. Yet our present arrangement tends to restrict a boy's friendships to boys who were born in the same year that he was, with the result that he passes six years in a community of 180 and associates on familiar and equal terms with scarcely more than a score. It seems to me that this is neither good for him nor fair to him.

So I suggest:

1. Abolish all form officers, the secretary and the two councillors, which make for "form spirit", in which I see no good and much narrowness of spirit. Certainly the lower school should have no officers. Perhaps they are useful in the Fifth Form as training for prefects.

2. Throw open all competitions, for the Grot, for the mangerships, for everything else, to all, irrespective of form; for I see nothing but constriction in any limitation. Maturity will balance talent, and keep a decent order, just as it does in athletics.

3. Mix the Fourth and Fifth Forms indiscriminately in the dormitories. They are old enough to stand it, and it will help the Fourth to mature more quickly.

4. Mix up the Third, Fourth, and Fifth Forms at table. The Sixth is already distributed. The First have not yet become a part of the school. The Second are too young. I understand that the order of seating still remains fixed throughout the term, rotating round the table and past the Masters at the ends. Why shouldn't the order be changed, as often as once a week, at least once a month? Perhaps by drawing numbers out of a box. Mealtime should not be allowed to run any risk of becoming a boredom, and to sit beside one who is not your own choice for weeks on end definitely raises that danger.

I do not like the autumn afternoon situation, and that means football. Leave out the first squad, and take football for all the boys who are not on the A, B, and C, teams. From my inquiries I am sure that a very large proportion of these boys are playing football as a grind and not as a game. I believe that this is true of as many as half. I got four direct estimates,—20%, 30%, 60%, and 75%; and all these came from boys, not from masters.

Unless the boys enjoy football, it is simply not the invigorating and exhilarating sport which we are fooling ourselves into thinking or saying it is. Unless they enjoy playing it, I do not believe they

428

should have to. And, as a matter of fact, now they do have to. For two reasons: first, because nothing else is offered them; second, because they are expected to. Mr. Jacomb gave me a list of all the boys not playing football this term, with the reasons why they are not. Below the Fifth Form, there was only one who was not physically incapable; that is, everyone else who is not playing couldn't play anyhow. Now it is nonsense to think that there is only one boy out of a hundred who does not want to play football. The fact is that there are a great many who do it because they have to, and they have to partly because we offer them no alternative, beyond idling round or going to the village, and partly because we expect them to.

I do not deny that football has advantages. For one thing, its roughness is good, and worth a high price in injuries. Miss McLeod gave me the list of football injuries to date this season and also last year. They are as follows:

1930

Head blow—confused memory	9
Cuts requiring stitches	2
Bruises—nose and face	10
Chest and abd. bruised	4
Shoulder and arm wrenched	3
Back wrenched	6
Wrists sprained	8
Fingers sprained, etc.	7
Elbow dislocated	1
Thigh muscles bruised	6
Elbow bruised	3
Knees	15
Ankles sprained	6
Groin	2
Testicle	1
	83

1931—to November 2nd

Heads—confused memory	6
Knees	13
Shin bruised	4
Thigh muscles	7
Ankles	7
Shoulders bruised	3
Clavicle broken	1
Neck badly injured	2
Groin muscles	4
Muscle side torn	1
Chest bruised	2
	50

What concerns me is why we practically make everybody (but one) play football, as we do. As a sport it has the great drawback of requiring a vast amount of tedious practice. It can't be properly learned simply by playing it, as almost any other game I can think of is learned. Indeed, it would be dangerous to try. A football scrimmage is not a thing to be entered into lightly. The result is that the boys really *play* football only twice a week. The rest of the time they drill, which is poor sport, lacking all the elements we admire in sport, if, indeed, it be sport at all. Some find adequate compensation in the short time they play the game itself.

Why not provide an alternative, a rival game, such as soccer, which provides almost as much of the vigorous roughness we all like in football (with a lower cost in injuries?), and which can be played without much previous drill, or at least in which the play itself provides the drilling? Or touch football, too, which is being played a great deal at Harvard and which is such a success at Milton that there are two touch-football clubs, the Orange and the Blue. Or rugger, which is also played at Milton.

We have allowed football to become a monopoly. I should like to see it stand on its merits in competition with other games. As soon as the football season is over, I understand the boys play soccer. Why not organize soccer teams for them at the beginning of the term? Why not offer them touch-football too? Or rugger, if we have anyone to show them how? And let them choose. Then, if I am right in my belief that a half of them don't get any recreation out of the game we now offer them, they will not be demoralized by the half-heartedness and apathy which is inevitably present in the spirit of those who are made to do something which is an end in itself, as all sports should be, without enjoying it. Drudgery toward further achievement is good for the morale, but drudgery for its own sake, as a sport, is flat demoralizing. And, if I am wrong, no great harm will be done and those who desert football for soccer or for touch-football or for anything else that can be offered will return to football with a better enthusiasm because it will be their own.

The injuries are another thing. The only ones that worry me are those which leave more or less permanent effects, and those which are preventable. Nine concussions in 1930 and six so far this season, fifteen knees last year and thirteen so far this year, six wrenched backs in 1930 and two badly injured necks in 1931, they worry me, for they may well become permanent weaknesses or disabilities, and cut the boy off from some or much athletics and sport in the future; and that is obviously too high a price for him to pay for football at Groton.

I had lunch with Dr. Lanman, who is the surgeon in charge of football at Milton. He pointed out to me that the younger boys, under sixteen, are more likely to be hurt, and seriously hurt, than the older. I do not know the distribution of our injuries over the ages. It would be interesting to find out from Miss McLeod. He told me of his care not to let the overgrown or the underweight boys play football at all, and the promptness with which he takes players out of a scrimmage or out of a game as soon as he sees any signs of fatigue, *before* they are injured. For, he said, particularly among the younger boys, the most and the worst injuries come when they are not fully equal to the game and when they are tired. I don't know enough about the problem to make any suggestions, except to say that I am sure there is a problem, and a grave one. Couldn't you get Dr. Lanman up to give us the benefit of his experience?

I do not see that the Masters are overworked, but I wonder whether they are not overoccupied. Is there any administrative or routine work, such as evening school, the afternoon period, disciplinary records, which could be shifted to the prefects, or better, dispensed with entirely? Certainly every item of such work is done at the cost of a Master's energy, attention, and leisure.

Another thing, however, impressed me very forcibly. Anyone who is fit to be a Master at Groton needs a certain amount of what for lack of a better word I may call solitude; and by that I mean something more than leisure, and something more than merely being alone; I mean being securely alone, free not only from interruptions, but from the fear of interruptions. That is a difficult thing to get anywhere these days, and it may be impossible in a boys' school. But it strikes me as so exceedingly important that I believe every effort should be made toward it. Our Masters get it in vacation time, but they are too long and come too seldom to satisfy the need I have in mind. They are like giving the patient the whole bottle at once, instead of by tablespoonful. Somehow and somewhere can not they be provided with some time at School when they can be securely and freely alone? Only a little such time would, I submit, make life easier and happier toward the end of each term. More, of course, would be required to give us the right to expect any scholarly work from them. However, what I had chiefly in mind was the spiritual necessity of some solitude to men of the kind we want as Masters.

I wonder also whether the boys are not overworked. They have about 26 periods of three quarters of an hour each per week. That is more than 19 hours. Allow as much again for preparation, and you get 38 hours a week, or over six hours a day. There are not many men who can profitably apply their attention to mental labor for so long as that, day in day out. Are you sure that they are not losing in intensity what they gain in time? If the subjects to which are now given four periods a week were reduced to three periods, would the total of achievement increase?

The Rector's reply:

November 14, 1931

MY DEAR CHARLIE:

A thousand thanks for your letter to me of the 9th of November, for a copy of letter to Roger Moore, and for the memoranda concerning the dividing of Forms, football, and Masters' time. To touch on these briefly:

1. I agree with you that the social divisions between the Forms are too numerous and too firmly fixed, and I shall make a great effort to bring them together. As a matter of fact, I have protested against this segregation of Forms but have not seen the way to establish greater unity. It is well worth trying for.

2. Only yesterday I wrote to Francis Parkman suggesting that we should take active steps towards substituting something for American foot-ball. That has become a training and has ceased to be a game. It has lost all element of fun and owing to its close organization, where two or three men attack one, it has become dangerous. There is some element of danger in all foot-ball, but with us today the chances of having sinews pulled, ankles and knee joints and arms hurt are such that the effects are likely to be carried through life. As a coincidence, I received yesterday from Francis Parkman a note asking if we would play an informal game of Soccer with them in Thanksgiving Week; and I have gladly consented to do this. It is encouraging that one should find his mind working with our minds. My preference would on the whole be for Rugger, largely perhaps because I was brought up on it; but I should be quite willing to concede to Soccer if the majority voted for it. Miss MacLeod will give me a full list of injuries after the St. Paul's game which comes next Wednesday. When we have got a little further away, I have in mind to consult parents, masters, boys, and undergraduates at the University, and the Trustees of Schools. Armed with their opinions, I contemplate calling into conference the Headmasters who are willing to consider in a general way the changes which may be proposed.

3. It may be that the Masters have a little more time to themselves than you have gathered. For the married men, there is abundant opportunity for solitude in part of the afternoon and almost every evening. The dormitory Masters are more occupied with details and have less time at their disposal. Nearly every dormitory Master, however, has one free day and very little to do on Sunday. Mr. Billings and I, the organist, and the two Masters who teach in our

432

missions are the only people who are regularly busy on Sunday. I doubt if it would be well to give Prefects charge of schoolrooms more than they already have; for it might interfere pretty seriously with their work. It is only a comparatively small number of Sixth Formers who could look after a schoolroom and at the same time accomplish anything in their own studies.

4. Touching the question of the boys' schedules, my impression gathered from experience is that the boys are not overworked. So far as I know, we have not suffered from illness caused by this. They are free, as far as work is concerned, if not detained for inadequate preparation, from one o'clock to five, except on Wednesday and Saturday, when they are dismissed at twelve-thirty, and have no school until 7 P.M. when evening work begins.

Affectionately yours,

ENDICOTT PEABODY

Excerpt from a Letter Written in 1919, Showing
Endicott Peabody's Handwriting

INDEX

Abbott, Grafton, 43, 49
Abbott, John Adams, 318
Abbott, Mather, 136, 137 n., 142 f., 149 ff., 264
Aberdeen, Lord, 18 n.
Abraham, 259, 271
Acheson, David C., 327
Acheson, Dean G., 319, 344, 409
Acland, Mrs. Peregrine, 421
Adams family, 219
Adams, Henry, xii
Adams, John, 417
Adams, T. B., 320
Addison, J. Thayer, 177, 179 n., 190, 319, 344, 409, 425
Allen, Arthur W., 380, 383
Allen, A. V. G., 35 n., 41 f.
Allen, Frederick L., 279
Alsop, John, 129, 326
Alsop, Joseph, 409
Amen, Harlan P., 210
American Legion, Middlesex Co., 336
Ames, Miss, 252, 408, 424
Andrews, Lawrence, 125, 136, 291, 339, 408
Andrews, Roy Chapman, 255
Arnold, Matthew, vii, 24, 25, 26, 32, 110, 419 f.
Arnold, Thomas, 17, 22–30, 70, 75, 106, 107, 192, 256, 415, 422
Arthur, Pellew, 31, 33, 39, 132, 198, 205, 206, 282 f., 312, 378
Ashburn, Frank D., 315 n.
Ashburn, Mrs. Frank D., 426
Ashburn, P. B., vii
Associations to which E. P. belonged, 191, 212 n., 411
Atwood, Julius Walter: 38, 43, 44, 88, 97, 151, 153, 189, 190 n., 293, 337; E. P.'s letters to him, 50–59, 60–64, 104–117, 128–135, 202–217, 223–228, 232 f., 235 ff., 345, 351, 383 f., 424–425
Auchincloss, Hugh, 286
Auchincloss, James C., 324
Auchincloss, Louis S., 250
Auchincloss, Louis, 320
Auchincloss, R., 127
Avon Old Farms School, 311
Ayrault, Guy, 82, 96 n., 101, 111, 136, 244, 264

Babcock, G. Stanton, 325
Bacon, 203
Bacon, Robert, 213

Baguio School, 216, 222, 359
Baker, 60
Baker, R. W., 127
Balch Camp, 102
Balfour, Gerald, 208
Balfour, Lady, 208
Barnewell, Alex, 107
Barr, Stringfellow, 328
Batcheller, Marian, 425
Bator, Francis M., 327
Beasley, Ronald, 137 n., 319, 371
Beaver Country Day School, 342
Beecher, Henry Ward, 58
Beethoven, 160, 338
Bell, Gordon Knox, 79 ff., 358, 359, 425
Belmont School, 130
Benson, 212
Benson, E. F., 423 n.
Bible, 102, 113, 116, 130, 177, 182, 183, 196, 197, 244, 251, 258, 259, 260, 262, 263, 266, 271, 284, 382, 412
Biddle, Francis, 279, 324, 409
Biddle, George, 250 n.
Billings, Eleanor Stockton, 153, 210, 283, 336
Billings, Sherrard, 15, 38, 66, 68, 69, 78, 80, 82, 88, 90, 94, 95 f., 98, 111, 113, 116, 130, 135, 136, 151–155, 161, 166, 176, 190, 206 f., 208, 209, 210, 219, 227, 234, 252, 266, 270, 283 f., 293, 303, 304, 310, 313, 333, 334, 335, 338, 361, 395, 405, 432
Bingham, Alfred M., 314, 320
Bingham, Jonathan B., 326
Bingham, Woodbridge, 318
Bissell, Richard M., 326
Bizet, 338
Blaine, 212
Blair, William, 286
Blair, William McC., 326
Bliss, A. A., 321
Boissier, Gaston, 130
Boston English School, 357
Boston Latin School, 110, 357
Boston University, 136
Boswell, James, 423
Boughton, James, 327
Boyden, Frank, 411
Bradfield (school), 17
Brent, Bishop, 271
Brewer, G. E., 319
Brewer, L., 319
Brewer, Laddie, 270 f.
Briggs, Dean, 229

437

438

439

441

Regan, James D., 136, 163, 331, 336, 339, 366, 408, 426
Reid, Mrs. Whitelaw, 212
Reid, Whitelaw, 212
Resor, Stanley R., 327
Richards, Henry, 136, 235, 250, 339, 408
Riggs, F. B., 318
Riis, Jacob, 115
Robert, Admiral, 409
Roberts, Frederick Sleigh, 134
Robertson, Frederick W., 55, 130, 131, 132, 179–181
Robins, Davis, 95 n.
Robins, Thomas, Jr., 95 n.
Robinson, Dean, 213
Robinson, William, 4
Rockne, Knute, 101
Rogers, 318
Rogers, H. L., 127
Rogers, Jacob, 13, 32
Roosevelt, Archibald, 176, 331
Roosevelt, Archibald, Jr., 327
Roosevelt, Eleanor, 354, 355, 356, 363
Roosevelt, Elliott, 326
Roosevelt, Franklin D., 121, 281, 295, 296, 337, 344, 345–356, 357, 358, 363, 409, 421, 425
Roosevelt, Franklin, Jr., 326, 345, 346
Roosevelt, G. H., 127
Roosevelt, James, 325, 345
Roosevelt, John, 345
Roosevelt, Kermit, 319
Roosevelt, Kermit, Jr., 326
Roosevelt, Theodore, 66, 104, 174–177, 183, 203, 208, 209, 210, 220, 226, 235 f., 243, 244, 303, 327, 350
Rose, John, 12
Rossall (school), 17
Rotary Club, Groton, 212n., 411
Rousmaniere, Dean, 188
Roxbury Latin School, 110
Rubenovitz, Herman, 343
Rublee, George, 78, 79, 101 n., 137 n., 224, 286, 359, 363, 394, 395 f.
Rugby (school), 17, 18, 23–30, 75, 256, 429
Rumford Press, 425
Ruskin, John, 255
Russell, Bertrand, 343
Russell, Charles H., 323
Russell, Richard S., 307–311, 426
Ryle, Herbert, 31, 378

St. Andrews Church (Ayer), 191
St. Augustine, 16
St. Benedict, xiv
St. George's School, 200
St. James School, 70
St. John's Church (Groton), 191
St. John's Church, Washington, 337, 348
St. John the Apostle, 262
St. Luke's Society, 211
St. Mark's School, 38, 63, 65, 70, 82, 94, 101, 107, 112, 130, 135, 136, 152, 162, 171, 226 f., 252 n., 269, 297, 300, 343, 357
St. Paul's Church (Boston), 153, 208, 209
St. Paul's School, 42, 65, 70, 114, 230 f., 256, 269, 270, 343, 357
St. Paul's (school), 17
St. Paul's (school), York, 16
St. Paul's Society, 118, 120, 427
"St. Peter," 252
Salem, Mass., 1–11, 21, 30 f.
Saltonstall, John L., 321
Sargent, John Singer, 176, 202, 208
Schieffelin, Ed, 45
Schieffelin, John Jay, 321, 325
Schieffelin, W. J., Jr., 127
Scott, Anna Dickinson, 285
Scott, Richard, 408
Scott, Walter, 194
Sears, Clara Endicott, 34, 36
Secondary Education Board, 207
Sedgwick, A. C., 320
Sedgwick, Alexander, 409
Sedgwick, Ellery, 136, 137 n., 286, 390
Sedgwick, F. M., 320
Sedgwick, Helen Peabody, daughter of E. P., 7, 233, 234, 241, 264, 265, 283, 407, 418
Sedgwick, R. Minturn, 7, 264, 283, 286, 303, 407 f.
Seymour, Charles, 382
Shady Hill School, 342
Shakespeare, 140, 194 n., 196, 197, 259, 271, 364
Shaler, 134
Shattuck, Dr., 228
Shaw, G. Holland, 323
Shaw, Howland, 409
Shelley, 251, 415
Sherborne (school), 17
Sherrill, Bishop, 336
Shrewsbury (school), 17, 22 n.

444

445

446

PORTRAIT GALLERY

Fredrick Peabody

*Characteristic Pose of the Rector
in Later Years*

The Rector Shortly before Retirement

Mrs. Samuel Endicott Peabody

Samuel Endicott Peabody

Kernwood, Salem

The Lindens. The house was subsequently dismantled and moved to Washington, D. C.

Fanny Peabody about 1873

Endicott Peabody in 1872

Cotty Peabody in 1876

Cotty Peabody in His Freshman Year at Trinity

*Cheltenham Group. Peabody is seated at the right and Walter Lawrence,
later Sir Walter, stands behind in the middle.*

Trinity College, Cambridge. C. E. Griffith (Cochin), "my most intimate friend," is seated on the left. Peabody standing in the middle.

"My Cousin and I" as John and Priscilla Alden in a Pageant in 1881

Tombstone, Arizona in 1881

Tombstone. This was the church, the first Protestant one in Arizona, for which Peabody raised the funds and of which he was the first minister, although not yet ordained.

Fanny Peabody, "My Little Cousin," about 1880

Bishop Lawrence

The Reverend Julius Walter Atwood

Brooks House, 1884. The original building of Groton School

Brooks House in Later Years

*The Triumvirate, 1884. William Amory Gardner, Endicott Peabody,
and Sherrard Billings*

Endicott and Fanny Peabody on Their Honeymoon

Hundred House. This shows the facade of the original building. The Peabodys' house is at the right with three dormers and kitchen wing.

The Groton Chapel as seen from the Campus

Interior of the Chapel

The Schoolhouse. The Rector's office was just to the left of the left-hand portico. The big windows are all in the main schoolroom. On the walls are carved the names of all the graduates.

The Reverend Sherrard Billings about 1900

Billy Wag

Family Group, 1906. Left to right: Margery, Helen, Rose, Malcolm, the Rector, Betsy, Mrs. Peabody. Dorothy sits at her mother's feet.

Endicott Peabody. Oil Painting by John Singer Sargent

Endicott Peabody about 1905

"Six Blackmarks." Charcoal sketch by Sargent, 1924

The Triumvirate, 1924

The Clergy

The Rector and Mrs. Peabody about 1935

Mrs. Peabody. Oil portrait by Ellen Emmet Rand, 1936

Three Generations. Peabodys, Parsons', Davisons, and Sedgwicks gathered at Groton for the Golden Wedding Celebration